This Sacred Life

Transforming Our World through Birth

ISBN

978-0-6151-4508-2

Dearest Reader,

In this book, I have used quotations from many sources. They may be along the same or similar lines, as what I am trying to convey. I want to share here many different views on the subjects presented. I also use the term Creator quite a bit. Each individual has his, or her, own concept of who our Creator is, and I am not dismissing any person's view of what that may be. I use this word Creator to sum up all the many different belief systems of spiritual and religious people into one word.

I alternate between he and she when referring to the baby in question. I prefer this to using "It," and sometimes I may use just baby, but I felt it was good to use more respectful terminology.

I have researched these subjects for many years in order to present facts as best I can with each topic. However, some of the "facts" may be perceived as "opinion," or "hear say."

It is up to you, the reader, to identify with what is presented in your own unique way. Each of us needs to make our own best choice in what to believe and not to take anything said as something for everyone, but to discern what truth is for our self as an individual.

With that said, have a joyous experience in reading!

This is a Guide for Parents, Birth workers, Teachers and Students of Unity, Peaceful Beginnings, Living in balance & Gentle birth….

Foreword

Zuki, My Dear One…these are the waves of expression as given to me after the first review of your book. Thank you for allowing me this privilege.

[1] Currently as I sit beneath the dome, here on the Life Skills campus, the Spirit of Rebirth, and the Art of Giving Birth to this paradigm shift in midwifery, is honored.

[2] Midwifery, as presented by Zuki Abbott, represents Mother Earth giving birth. I received the awareness of this reality when I visited with a Taos Pueblo artist in spring of 2003. I was so touched by the spirit of one of the paintings that I offered to purchase it from the artist known as Blue Spruce Standing Deer. He said that his mother is a midwife. This is how I began to feel the actual spirit of "Mother Earth Giving Birth." Birthing and Art has formed its own Spirit for me.

[3] My missions, visions and transformations are all linked to a Loving Process Program implementation. Zuki's dedication to midwifery and birthing completes the journey for families in survival training.

[4] Each chapter of this text takes the reader on the Rights of Passage needed for upgrading women's birthing standards.

[5] Zuki presents much solid factual information that allows for delineation of data about the various levels of midwifery. Both novice and professional are shown how to assist and help families, friends and selves through the process of creative birth choices, through the restoration of midwifery to its sacred place among families.

[6] The review of this manuscript has activated new levels of awareness for me. Zuki's skillful gathering of data gives a gentle and personal touch to the timeworn academic programs. You will find these discussions to serve as both catalyst and to give "direct-action strength" for taking back your power as Human Beings...

[7] Here are some lessons from The Ancestors regarding the text:

* We are in the transition from one age to another.

* The times of the Modern Age as it overlapped with the Victorian Age were discussed by Wise Women and Ancestors of The Dreamtime when Mother Earth began her shift into each new age.

* Zuki's publication aligns with the wisdom of those Ancestors, who serve as guides to mass society as our planet allowed for the needed societal shifts into this new age.

You will find gentle guidance in combination with assertive foundations as you read and integrate this process.

1 The Ancestors are with us as we each review this return to "Her-story." The effects of "History" emerge through Zuki's transformation dialogue and support the return to our birthing rights.

2 These eighteen chapters of psycho-spiritual rebirth are given to us at a time when the Ancient way of birthing returns with the rebirth of Mother Earth.

3 The weaving of the tales in this book serves as a divine tapestry that we can at last hang on our walls as proof of the Rebirth of our natural ways as women.

4 Each journey through Zuki's Life Skills abode has resulted in ongoing levels of rebirth and transformation.

5 Midwifery is thusly returned to our circle of life.

AT THIS LEVEL, I AM DISCUSSING THE INDIVIDUAL WORKS OF ZUKI ABBOTT. MY RESPONSES ARE SUBTLE, YET MY MIND IS ALERT. MY MENTAL BODY ALLOWS THIS WEB OF ACADEMIC STORYTELLING TO REMAIN ALIGNED WITH THE SPIRIT OF THE MOTHER WHO BIRTHS EACH STORY. THE SECTION ON VARIOUS BIRTH STORIES ALLOWS FOR THE MAINTAINING OF EACH MOTHER'S CREATIVE EXPRESSION. THIS IS ART IN THE RAW!

Each woman, in "Her-story," validates for the reader the merits of Zuki's practice as a conscious birth advocate. Their stories demonstrate the self-sustaining spirit of family and of giving birth naturally. The trials and tribulations discussed by each family also show the power of The Universal Law of Choice.

I speak, at this point, of the Sacred Laws of the Universal Spirit that are ingrained within the Midwives' tales. From ancient to modern day, we have served as advocates for life.

When the political authorities demanded the death of all first-born boys in ancient Hebrew society, the midwives' pro-life influence was brought forth in the Exodus of a people from oppressive life conditions. This discussion of families, birthing, choices, conscious rebirth, and natural childbirth all stem from the collective consciousness of our Ancestors for whom we are each carriers of seven generations of prayer, resurrection and ascension.

THE UNIVERSAL LAW OF CHOICE is also interconnected with woman's place in the Light. So you see how blessed we all are to have this emergence of Midwifery. The primordial waters have brought us back from the ancient shores into this mountain where The Spirit of Birth has activated the sacred choice in birth, rebirth and giving birth

As Elder and Star Law Guardian, I send forth many blessing to all who will continue this journey with us. We all are teachers. It is simply time to "Walk Our Talk." Mother Earth is Giving birth. Can you continue to journey with her?

Respectfully submitted,
Deborah Morning Star
31, August 2005

Dedication

This dedication goes out to all the families and babies who birth and are born in consciousness and to the ones who attend them with integrity. It is for all who have given themselves the opportunity to experience childbirth, the way it was meant to be. To all midwives throughout time who supported women and their families.

For all the millions of wise men and women who were murdered for ignorance and greed.

For all who bring these new beings into this world with dignity, love and respect.

Also, to the parents and children who have been mistreated or misguided in their birthing experiences, you are the ones who know first hand how hard and forever lasting those experiences have on our spirit.

Also, thank you, for all your research and dedication: Perinatal Scientists, Medical Doctors, Midwives and Childbirth Educators. You have made it clear that women are capable of giving birth without technological interferences. Because of you, we now have scientific proof that to lower risk of complications in pregnancy and birth, we not only need good food and clean water, but also less interference in natural processes.

In Addition,

It is for the little ones who come into this world whole-heartedly, body and spirit intact, without interference. You are the ones who will create a balance in all the sciences of life, and a balance within nature. It is you, who will preserve this abundant planet we inhabit.

Have a blessed journey into parenthood!

Disclaimer

This book is not intended to diagnosis, treat or provide medical advice.

The Publishers, Editors, and Author of this book are neither endorsing nor prescribing any alternative methods of childbirth. This book is for informational purposes only.

Women and their families need to discern for themselves what is needed during pregnancy and the birthing process.

Health is a personal responsibility.

Doctors, midwives and childbirth educators are not the ones giving birth; it is the mother herself delivering her baby. It is not our job to take on the role of the parent, but to empower the parents to give birth to their own children with the wisdom they already possess. We are only facilitators, who support them to remember the knowledge about pregnancy and birth that they already hold within themselves.

Table of Contents

Beginning the Journey

"How wonderful it is that nobody need wait a single moment before starting to improve the world."
~Anne Frank

Beginning our journey together, we will find some relatively new information, some not so new and some outrageous questions to ponder. This path of realization is full of surprises, obstacles and self-reflection. We will be going on this journey together to learn how we can help each other in this world, how to make it more abundant while we are here and more gentle and loving for our children's future.

In this book, I will sometimes jump into my own experiences and reflect on them, on a personal level, as woman to woman, or woman to man. I have quoted those with whom I have had the honor to work, as well as those who have shared experiences with me. In addition, from them all, I have gained much knowledge and wisdom. I feel that it is important for us to learn with, and from, each other on an intimate level. I will share my feelings as though you are my good friend, and I am "spouting off" (sometimes ranting and raving), what I think and feel about the importance of conscious birthing. It is through my own personal experiences, working with birth, that I can share first-hand information about the different ways in which to utilize all the knowledge presented here. So enjoy and be open to new possibilities!

Regaining Our Wisdom

When choosing conscious conception, pregnancy, childbirth and parenting, we take responsibility for gathering our resources and making our own best choices. We have much abundance in our world today. We have access to, and ability to choose from, educational material that informs us of our birthrights. It is up to us to sort through these resources, and this information, and then choose what feels intuitively right for ourselves.

We are here to make clearer and more educated decisions about conception, birth and parenting. We not only can realize how, and why, conception is the beginning of our parenting, but also make educated choices during pregnancy and childbirth that go way-beyond the action of growing and birthing a baby. These choices encompass all aspects of life.

We are a race that gives birth, as all other species do, but we are unique and have a potential for thought that goes beyond instinct. This potential for thought, this intellect, has become more valued than instinct in our society. As a result, we have set aside our innate wisdom, and we have substituted our natural surroundings for a mechanical and technological world.

During this last century, we human beings have been struggling to re-connect our natural relationship to all living creatures. We are now on this planet, at a time in history, when we can make a difference, and we can decide whether we survive and live up to our fullest potential or continue to struggle within our world.

It is vitally important that we start, one by one, to rediscover ourselves through birth, instead of allowing ourselves to be continually violated by the system that has oppressed us in the past. There are a growing number of people now wanting to re-connect and learn about how they got here. They are learning how to go beyond survival and live to their fullest capacity through utilizing their birthrights

We all have one thing in common, BIRTH, and if we're aware we're a part of all natural events on our planet, then we can use this as an incentive to birth our children consciously and within nature.

We have all been born, have birthed, will birth or have helped our friends through birth. We can learn how to become more aware of birth's impact as a race of compassionate beings, by educating ourselves and taking responsibilities for our own health care. In turn, we will have more and more gentle human beings on our planet, who can make better decisions than the ones before them. It all starts with us!

Our Primal Journey

Pre-conceptual imprinting is the primal period before conception, which is probably one of the biggest things we overlook in our birthing culture today. In most pre-industrialized cultures, we had "consciousness" in our lives. Before conception took place, we had rituals that united man and woman: first there was a marriage ritual, and then there was an emotional and spiritual cleansing period for both parents, and finally a ritual to conceive. They all varied in form, but had the community's blessing and hope for the birth of a new Healer, Hunter or Craftsperson for that Tribe. There was a purpose for this new being before she was even conceived.

Today, the majority of people in our society conceive and give birth, unaware of its greater potential in creating a better world. Yet, we have hope. We can imagine a new society that actually wants every baby who is conceived--conceived in love and planned--consciously or not. If we can fully embrace ourselves, as did our ancestors, and know how to tap into our inner wisdom and our intuition, we will then become the creators of our own realities, birth consciously and be able to live up to our highest potentials.

Through conscious conception, we can create beings of compassion rather than destruction. When we find that we are going to bring a new person into this world, we have the opportunity to rethink our purposes and create a healthier environment for our child to be born into. Our parenting begins at conception.

Every thought and feeling we have is manifesting our child from the start. Our cells are carrying all our thoughts and feelings into that tiny little being inside our wombs; he, or she, is being imprinted or programmed by the parents and the environment. Nourishing the very cells in our beings, with love and good thoughts, creates a completely new world within us before that child is even born.

Stored cells, which create our nervous system, organs, brain and entire physical body, carry memories before conception and birth that affects our whole lives. If these stored memories are negative and hindering one's life in some way, they can be released. Through massage and breathing processes, we can re-enter our primal stage of being, "clearing the slate" and regenerating ourselves into a different level of existence (consciousness or paradigm).

Many of us have heard stories of re-birthing, or we have experienced it ourselves. We remember being born or being in our mother's womb. While we might have these memories in our consciousness, they are more likely stored in our cellular memories. Every cell is storing thought, feeling and energy, which is basically what our cellular memory is, energetic memory or "a feeling" of remembrance. It is a chemical reaction. If we can become aware of how new life begins, and how that life is nurtured from conception, then we can transform our world into a more hospitable place for our children to be born into. Doing this may not be easy at first; however, it can be done with practice while not disturbing the sensitive life before birth.

We exist even before conception. All of us were egg cells inside our grandmothers before our mothers were even born. The human ovum in females is a cell that starts forming inside our mothers' wombs before her birth. The imprinting of our tiny little selves starts a generation before we are even conceived. Ironically during the re-birthing process, some people have recalled their grandmother's feelings of fear, anxiety, joy and other sensations from the time of their grandmother's pregnancy with their mothers. As for fathers, they are also from those tiny little egg cells in their mother's wombs, so they also have cellular memories that affect their conscious lives and their offspring's future imprints.

There are other studies around the world of indigenous tribes that also believe in such imprinting. However, due to the invasion of western birth practices and birth industrialization most of them are becoming very rare.

One such tribe is the Aborigines, who view preconception as an important time for imprinting their unborn citizens. They communicate telepathically with each other and the unborn. They desire to live in peace while remaining connected to the earth, with ease and without struggle. Also, there are hidden tribes in Africa practicing peaceful community with the imprints of pre-conceptual knowledge from thousands and thousands of years of wisdom.

"The tribal woman, in a sense, has a consciousness that lies between that of an animal and that of a modern western woman. Her births are successful for several reasons. She has not yet developed beliefs in fear, shame and guilt, and therefore is free from their devastating consequences. In addition to this, like the cat in the closet, she is generally left alone. This privacy not only allows her body to perform its task easily because it is unhampered by outside intervention, it also allows her psychologically to reconnect with her inner self. The inner self speaks to her--just, as it does to the western woman--through her dreams, impulses, and intuition, the difference is, she listens.

~Laura Shanley, from her book, "Unassisted Childbirth" (1994)

This is not a new concept. The importance, of the primal life before birth, has been known in many cultures since the beginning of time. I heard the term "re-birthing" for the first time when I was about eighteen. Re-birthing can manifest in many ways, and always leads back to transformation of the mind by letting go of any obstacles stored in our body's cells from our pasts.

After going through a few sessions of re-birthing, I let go of some insecurities and anxieties surrounding my prenatal time, birth and the first two months of life. It has been a great tool for opening doors to new possibilities that I would not have otherwise known about if I hadn't recognized the importance of letting go of these feelings through the re-birthing process. Today, I am continually learning how to purge myself of these deeply rooted imprints, which I know will allow more room for new and positive situations in my life.

With this first little look into conscious conception, I would like you to write your thoughts below on your own feelings and memories of your primal life before birth.

If you would like more information on re-birthing, search the Internet or look in your local directory for re-birthers in your area who may guide you.

A few of my own personal thoughts and memories:

"I remember feeling scared inside my biological mother's womb. She was fifteen, unmarried, and had been sent far from her home to give birth so no one would know that she had gotten pregnant out of wedlock. She was frightened about what might happen to her, and to me. My little baby body was in fear and knew that my mother was very sad while carrying me. She knew she could not keep me. When I became more conscious of the situation, I was afraid to be born. I felt my mother's anxieties and her loneliness, and I did not want to come out into such a sad world. I remember my birth mother holding me for a short time, sometime after I was born. I felt her arms shaking around me as she cried; I started to cry as well. I nursed for a moment and then someone came into the room where we were and took me from her arms. I lay in a plastic box under florescent lights for two months. Then, one day I looked up and there were two women looking down at me and smiling, one was also crying. They picked me up and held me. I was happy! From then on I had a mother and a grandmother who loved and cared for me."

Your thoughts and memories:

Cellular Imprinting-What is it?

***By: DeAnna Elliot** (-submitted by author)*

DeAnna Elliot is a researcher, Infant Massage Therapist, and filmmaker. Her film "Cellular Echoes" can be found at foundationofglobalunity.org.

New, compelling research indicates that awareness is present from conception forward, and that this opens additional avenues of understanding about personality formation.

From the moment of conception, the Zygote (joined sperm and egg) is in a stimulus-response process with the surrounding environment as tiny protein receptors begin recording information vital to the growth of the newly forming human being. The type of information recorded, ranges from chemical to emotional. Once it has been obtained, it is evaluated and responded to by the cell. The responses are stored in energetic layers within the body as a database of information for future reference for the rest of one's life.

Soon the Zygote is an active fetus that is in this dynamic stimulus response dance with the mother's body. The mother is in the same interaction with her external environment using her senses as her receptors to gather information. Information is then carried in the neuron-peptides and chemicals in her blood stream to the fetus. If she is in a positive state of mind, she is sending constructive information to the baby and the overall response for the baby is one of optimal growth. Blood supply goes to the forebrain and the hindbrain. The forebrain is about love, compassion, higher reasoning and creativity. The hindbrain is about survival and "my will be done." If the mother is in a state of high tension, she is producing stress hormones, which tell the fetus to grow, but in a state of protection, which then activates the hindbrain where most of the blood supply is being sent. For a woman to have a healthy pregnancy she needs a loving partner, a safe and protective environment and good nutrition.

How many women have a stressful relationship, an insecure lifestyle and poor nutrition? Too many, way too many! These are other relevant factors regarding pregnancy. The sense of hearing is developed at 28 weeks' gestation, and before a baby comes into the world, it is listening to the sounds in its environment. Furthermore, because the liquid is right next to the eardrum, the sound is amplified. So consider what they hear: the mother's heartbeat, breathing and blood circulation. They also hear the voices of the parents. If the parents are making sounds that are soothing and peaceful, it will have positive effects on the growth of the unborn child. If the sounds are stressful like fighting, then they have the opposite affect on the tiny "neonate."

According to Dr. Thomas Verny, author of "Secret Life of the Unborn Child" and "Nurturing the Unborn Child," the little one within knows the mother's entire attitude toward her pregnancy and can feel and respond to all of her emotions. Before the baby arrives in this world, it is already quite intelligent and responds to many things. Don't forget these responses are stored in a database of information that gets referred to over and over throughout one's life.

Then the big event occurs: THE BIRTH--the transition from liquid, gravity free, dark, contained and warm, into light, sound, gravity, air, temperature change and usually chaos. Think of the impact of just those factors alone, not to mention any number of invasive procedures and birth complications. Sound overwhelming? In the very best circumstances, it is still quite a big change for this little person to make. Many babies arrive in this world with lots of trauma that is never recognized. The prevailing attitude is that the baby isn't aware of this trauma, or that it will be forgotten very soon. In light of current scientific understanding, this attitude must change for it is absolutely incorrect.

What does a baby need most when it arrives, besides the breast? Joseph Chilton Pearce, Author of: "The Magical Child" says the baby needs a pair of human eyes to gaze into because it turns on the entire brain, and nothing else will. Upon arrival, the human infant is quite helpless, and the eyes and the heartbeat of the mother or father are critical for orientation. Those infants who do not get these things, go into fight or flight and the templates of perception that get formed carry information that puts the system into a state of protection. When the person comes to "resembling experiences" later in life, they will automatically refer to the original response stored in the body, because it is the known established pathway.

We see through the templates of perception that were formed while we were forming. We are creatures of habit. This process happens through the unconscious and is so fast it is almost impossible to prevent. The way to free oneself of habitual responses, that can also be called imprints, is to choose to respond differently to those stimuli that set off habitual patterns in one's character. That is the right use of will, for trying to change things outside of oneself usually never works, yet most of the world functions in this way.

In the work of infant massage, very new babies or babies who have had traumas during their formation period can often cry with the first massage or so, because those traumas are stored in the tissue, so when the tissue is stroked, out come the emotions that had been stored in the data base of the infant. It doesn't mean the parent is doing anything wrong, it just means the baby is expressing the stress held in the tissue.

Let's take an example of a baby whose cord was wrapped around the torso. When it is time to descend into the birth canal the baby cannot move freely through, and the feeling of this is being trapped in the womb. For the baby, this can translate into panic, and later in life, this person could have issues about being in small places, places that are claustrophobic. The early formation experiences both good and bad are the imprints that reside in the cells in the tissue. Infant massage is a tool for allowing the release of the difficult experience, letting it leave the cellular data base, and positive information replaces it with a massage from the parents hands that relate love from them, telling the baby that yes, you belong here, we love you, and you are whole. These are the most important messages a newborn can receive in the beginnings of life. They can antidote negative experiences and produce a sense of well-being for the baby, through this infant massage.

All humans have imprints from the formation period, which consists of conception, gestation, birth, bonding, and into the early years. Infant massage can make those early imprints the right ones, while releasing the wrong ones. This work is very profound.

This research, done by DeAnna Elliot and other peri-natal and cellular researchers, is incredibly valuable to our various societies today. If we continue ignoring its value, we will surely lose a great opportunity to live to our fullest potential. Being a victim of such pre-conceptual imprinting, I am painfully aware of its impact, and I will mention it repeatedly throughout this book. I am now healing the wounds that held me back from a happy childhood and early adulthood, so it CAN be done. It is my personal journey that I desire to share, so others do not have to endure such grief.

It's our little ones, as DeAnna Elliot is saying here, who will need their parents to imprint a world with positive guidance, so they can come into this life fully aware, and be open to transforming the world into a more self-sustaining and loving place.

"I am come that they might have life, and that they might have it more abundantly!" (John 10:10).

When You are Ready to bring a Child into this World:

Today we are extremely fortunate but also over-loaded with options, social pressure, and the opinions of society and the media. Birth has been depicted as horrifying and dangerous—something needing to be "managed," drug induced and manhandled, but this is not the truth of birth. This subliminal brainwashing needs to be shed and reconstructed with positive images.

It is true, this is not the sanest planet in the universe, that's why we're here: to try and help these new beings come into this world in a healthier environment. We need more positive contributors on this planet to enjoy and share this life's incredible journey. It is important to be around those who give you positive feedback and let any negative energy just wash over you. Stay to yourself for a while and meditate on what you would truly like to have for your pregnancy and birth. Educate yourself and explore your options.

I have been to many incredible home births, helped support parents to do their own births without any "professional" assistance and have studied midwifery for years now. Therefore, I am partial to these choices.

The oldest profession in the world is actually giving birth. As women, we are the birthers and healers of our communities. We bury the dead and help raise each others' children, feeding all who need to be nourished and helping each other do the most natural thing in the world: BIRTH!

Midwives have been under fire for centuries because of the ignorance and injustices of the male-dominated governments and churches. Today, hopefully, we are past that foolishness and can recognize that even over thousands of years of famine, drought and disease, we have still been able to survive and give birth without interference from scientific technologies.

You are the boss of your body, baby, and birth. Please do not think that someone you hire to help educate and support you for your baby's birth will know more than you do about yourself. It is your job to sift through any information you are given, to choose what feels right for you and to use that knowledge to better yourself. Never place anyone, not a doctor nor a midwife, on a pedestal.

Preserving Our Roots

Preserving our roots as a family can be done by birthing our children naturally into our own hands. The imprints made by the mother, father and family are extremely important in preserving the family roots. They will be the ones to love, nourish and raise that child, thereby keeping these family roots, traditions and cultures alive and intact from the beginning. The best-known way of doing this is to have only those present who will maintain a close, life-long connection with the child while keeping outside interference to a minimum. In recent history, the roots of family have been disrupted with the wave of the birth industry taking that child from their roots into drugs, violence and ownership.

Parent-assisted childbirth is the oldest way of giving birth. It was not until later in our developed history that the midwife appears. This was when people moved into more concentrated communities, and women were left to care for one another while the men went out hunting for months at a time. This is when we became more dependant on others in birth.

Long ago, when we did not have "experts" in birth, we--as women and men--were the ones who knew how to listen from within and hear the natural rhythms of our bodies. We knew, because we listened to our intuition.

Parents are raising their babies more consciously today than in recent history. A number of birth-workers I have met, and had the privilege to visit and work with, have instilled the ideas and philosophies of parent-assisted birthrights into my consciousness. I have found these concepts to be true through my own study and practice. Today, women and their families are striving toward this way of birthing for themselves, bringing traditional birthing full circle.

I have seen remarkable results in self-reliant parent care and life-style. Parents are learning together that they can birth their babies in a calm and peaceful atmosphere. This can be done with a little help from a friend, midwife, or doctor, but it must be someone who supports this philosophy. It is through this learning and support that we can regain our innate knowledge. Sometimes, this is something we need to bring forth from within ourselves, before we can get beyond this feeling of needing a "professional" to "manage" the most natural human experience: bringing a new life into this world.

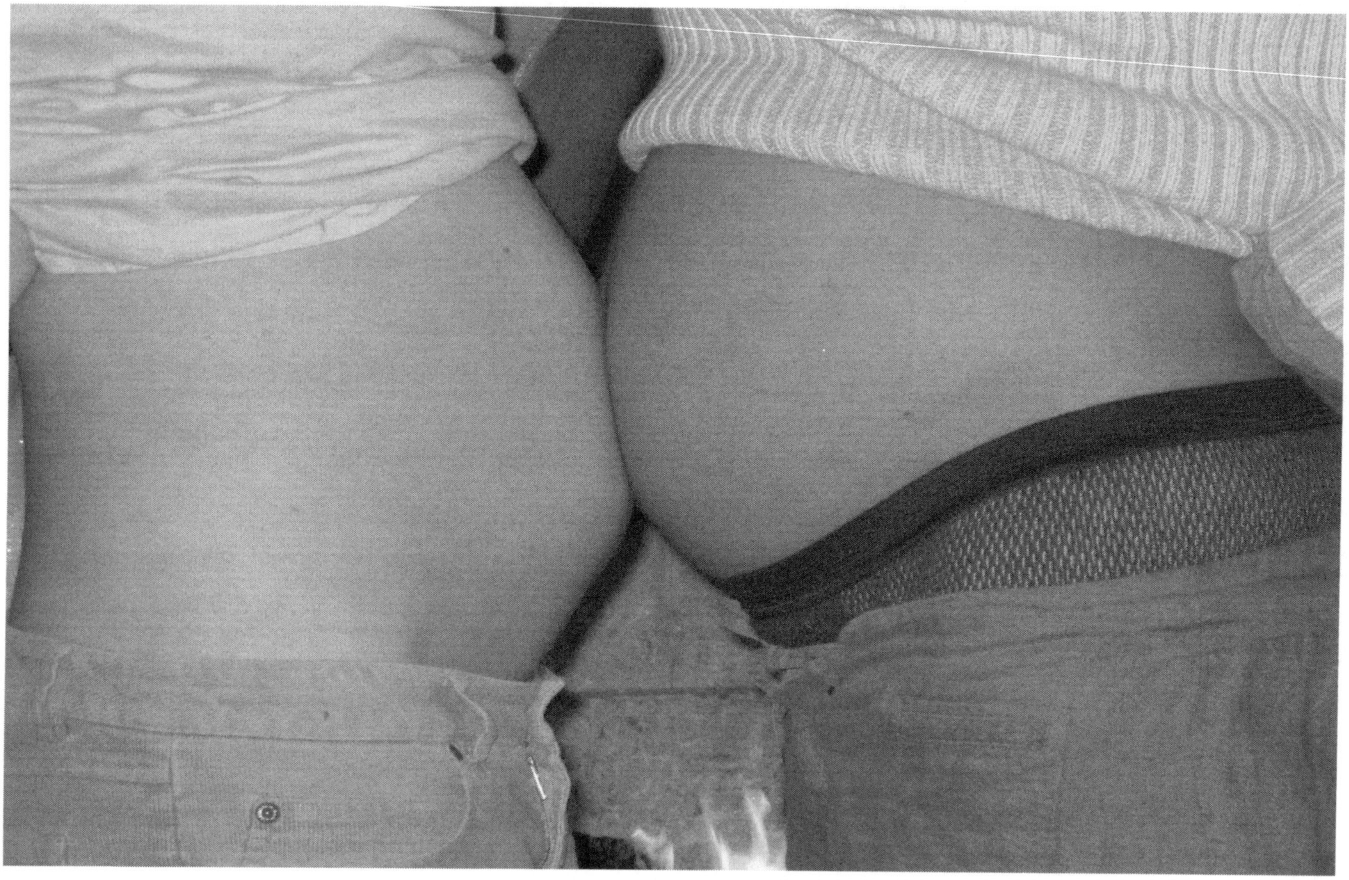

Two new souls meet before they are born...

Higher self

Awaken my Love,

You are Free,

You are One with The All,

You are the Creator,

You are All the Joys and Sorrows,

You are the Reality you see,

You are my Love,

My Life,

My Honor and my Forgiveness,

You are a Part of Me.

Healthy Tips Prior To Conception & in Early Pregnancy

If your diet prior to pregnancy is not the best it can be, add a few supplements and start eating more vegetables, fruit, protein and greens. Good supplements are the ones with no added preservatives; be sure to check labels. I have seen moms who were trying to add healthy things and ended up with a bad reaction to the additives in store-bought generic supplements. Try herbs for supplements; they are more nutritious, less expensive and can possibly be gathered locally. **(See Nutrition and Herbal Medicine)**

These days, the most basic minerals and vitamins are depleted from our food by chemicals and pesticides, so be aware if you want to get the best nutrients from food. Go organic if you can, grow what you need and be sure to get enough calcium, magnesium, folic acid, and vitamins A, E and C on a daily basis from the food you eat. This will help prevent, or minimize, fetal abnormalities as well as pregnancy and birth complications later on. Add herbal supplements if necessary and just be simple about it. Get enough good food in your diet; it really is basic stuff! Think quality not quantity.

Morning sickness is preventable through nutrition and herbal supplements. Approximately half of all women experience nausea and vomiting during the first trimester of pregnancy. This is a combination of the body cleansing itself of toxins, hormonal changes, emotional changes, worries and dietary intake that causes a fluctuating feeling of "ickiness." Taking a pre-conception herbal tea with red raspberry, spearmint and nettles sometimes brings relief. Increasing foods that are high in B vitamins also facilitate an easier transition into the pregnancy. Prenatal B6 helps tremendously. Eat your orange and yellow vegetables: squash, squash, and more squash!

Low blood sugar (Hypoglycemia) is one of the causes of morning sickness. Most moms find that eating frequent, smaller, high protein meals helps keep their blood sugar in balance and reduces nausea and vomiting thereafter.

Excessive vomiting during pregnancy is called *Hyperemesis* and is uncommon. Uncontrollable vomiting is not normal and probably means one of two things: either you need to eat better, healthier foods, and drink more water, or there is an emotional issue that needs attention. I have seen this in women who are in very emotionally taxing or abusive relationships. They have a lot of stress and are not taking care of themselves. There is no medical explanation for this condition.

It is not normal to vomit throughout a pregnancy. Even in the early stages of pregnancy, vomiting is unusual--contrary to what most believe. It is common to have some nausea and maybe to vomit occasionally. However, persistent vomiting can lead to dehydration, headaches, kidney/liver congestion, a malnourished or premature baby and miscarriage, if not dealt with properly.

If vomiting continues, drink plenty of healthy fluids, make some Miso soup with chicken and vegetables or make a drink of seltzer with lemon and honey to take in-between vomiting. This will balance the body metabolically. In addition, eating smaller, but more frequent, meals helps get some nutrition to your baby and into you. Work on affirmations, visualization and relaxation exercises. Seek support from family and friends who you know will be helpful in cases of abusive and emotionally upsetting circumstances. Try alternatives like Acupuncture and Aroma Therapy **(see Alternative Modalities).** Just take care of yourself, do not be afraid to ask for help if you need it, nothing is worse than stress in pregnancy.

In A Doctor's Care:

When you are seeking care from a medical doctor, you need to be even more responsible about taking good care of yourself. The money that doctors are paid is not usually equivalent to the quality of care you may receive.

In a doctor's care, we are seldom educated or told of other available resources or options. The hundreds of dollars you pay a doctor are usually for things you can do at home for almost nothing.

If you choose to have a hospital birth, know that they are more complicated. We have to express our needs and demand our rights, and that is energy we should be using for growing and birthing our baby. This is when a knowledgeable midwife or "Doula" (French: for "mother's helper") comes in handy, if you "need" someone at all. She can be your advocate and work with you from the beginning of your pregnancy helping to find out what your unique needs are. Most Doulas are educated in other areas of birth such as nutrition and massage; some are also apprenticing as midwives and can guide you in that direction if you choose. They will also help with such things as postpartum care, cooking, cleaning and other chores while you concentrate on your labor and rest after the birth. Most of the complications during labor, birth and the post-partum time are caused by "little" things: not getting enough time to rest, not nurturing yourself, feeling overwhelmed about other children who need your attention or household duties. A doula or midwife can help alleviate these worries.

I have worked with doulas over the years, and they are all trained differently. Finding one, who meshes with your divine plan for the home or hospital, is well worth the effort. There are international doula services for prenatal support, labor, birth and postpartum care.

"One of the reasons why some women want to give birth at home is that many hospitals are not good enough. They are not good enough to provide an environment suited for peak experience of one's life, nor for the birth of a family. But more than this, they are sometimes frankly dangerous places in which to have a baby."
~Sheila Kitzinger 1979,

Bringing a baby into the world is not about efficiency, it is not about money and it certainly is not about control or technology. Doctors cannot tell you how or where to birth your babies, nor can I. I am working within a network of women and families who want to support each other through childbirth because we know it has a profound impact on our personal lives, on our children's future and the entire world. If you would like more direction, ask people about their own experiences or ask around for a knowledgeable support person to work with. Either way, finding your own unique path in life is about you and your baby, not about a system that does not respect sacred life events.

Adoption

For those of us, like myself, who have been adopted, or for those who plan to put a child up for adoption, it is vitally important to imprint ourselves with healing and self-forgiveness over the course of our lives. This allows us to have healthy families of our own without the guilt and shame of feeling abandoned, or from abandoning. Through support groups, and by having gentle births, we can share the healing with others who have been in these situations. For those who have given a baby away, or are planning to do so, it is important to get the support and healing you need.

Having a natural birth experience, and experiencing the bonding and grieving process fully, will help tremendously in these situations. This will also allow you to give the child an emotionally healthy start in life. It is also important for adopted women and men, who are having children of their own, to get support and understanding during their children's births, so they too can experience the healing power that birth can have on their own adoption issues.

It is the hardest of paths to be born with no family, with no mother or father. I cannot imagine being without my son, he is the only link I have to any blood relative. I am very maternal and cannot fathom what my biological mother went through emotionally, spiritually or mentally when she was forced to give me away. Years later, I still bear emotional and physical scars from the mere fact that I was not held or breast-fed by my birth mother. I am forever healing those scars. Through birth, I have healed many of those wounds and continue to do so. If anything, we can create a better world for our children's health through conscious adoption and birthing. That is what we have to do to give these babies a good start in life!

There is no reason to separate a birth mother from her newborn baby. It makes the transition much worse and can lead to violent and suicidal behavior for both mother and child even later in life. If we just let the process of saying goodbye work through us naturally, we would have fewer children feeling like their birth mothers did not want them. We would also have more birth mothers knowing and feeling that they did the right thing without as much guilt or shame.

Even when a child is stillborn, similar feelings are experienced. Holding and loving the baby, for the day or so before it is time to say goodbye, facilitates the mourning process. It may be a necessary process for the mother's emotional and hormonal healing.

This allows for a freer and more natural separation than would take place if the mother never saw or held her baby. This also allows the mother to realize that the baby is real and passed from her body, and also allows the family to grieve and then say goodbye.

You now see how important it is to heal ourselves even before giving birth to our babies. It is critical that we become aware of how we imprint on them and of how that affects their future emotional, spiritual and physical well-being. The clearer we are, the more likely our babies will be "born free" of our own emotional issues.

In The Beginning:

Fertility Awareness

During the most fertile time of the month, mucus is one sign that ovulation is about to happen. It is more noticeable in some women than in others, will vary from woman to woman, and can even vary monthly for us depending on what we are going through. Most "regular" women will feel themselves ovulate about two weeks after the first day of their last moon (menstrual cycle.) Women, like myself--who are irregular girls, will feel different sensations about two weeks before we bleed, even if we have 45-day cycles. Ovulation takes place approximately two weeks before a cycle begins in all types of moon phases. Knowing what is going on in our bodies is sometimes tricky to figure out. I have been studying my own body for years, and it is constantly changing. One thing is for sure: I notice my fertile times much more easily now. I have seen my cervix enough times to know it changes with each moon phase. Its nice, pink, plump appearance also lets me know I am in good health. **(See Self-examination to do your own cervical check)**

PMS Scam: Pre-menstrual "syndrome" is not a completely "normal" thing. It does happen though, so we have come to think of it as "normal." However, it is not, and in most other countries of the world, women do not experience such symptoms. With the lack of processed foods, televisions and luxuries, it is rare for a woman to have "PMS," because she is active and only eats what she needs to survive, so there is no hormonal confusion without these "modern" conveniences. In our western, health culture we are usually unaware that we have an inner world, and if it is not in its proper place, well fed or exercised, it becomes stagnant and diseased. That is when we experience pain, headaches, become irritated and "out-of-sorts" during this time of the month called "pre-menstrual."

This does not have to occur, and it can be remedied through simple changes in lifestyle. From my experience, I have gone through different "so-called symptoms" and found that my activity level, nutrition and caffeine intake were the reason for any discomfort I was feeling. After I changed my daily habits, my pre-menstrual discomforts went away, and to this day, I rarely experience any aches or pains. It's great! I was never one to get headaches, or many cramps, but my breasts would be so sore a week or two before my moon that I could not even bear to be touched during that time (and that is half the month!) Not fun. Now, after taking my herbal supplements each day, cutting back on caffeine and walking at least four times a week, my "monthly state of being" has greatly improved, emotionally as well as physically.

Becoming aware of our own fertility, and causes of any "fertility-related" discomforts, is also a way to gain a sense of "birth management." We can use this knowledge in two ways. First, we can keep track of our fertile times and avoid lovemaking if we do not want to conceive a child. Second, we can keep track of when we are most likely fertile, likely to get pregnant, and make lots of love if we want to conceive.

This knowledge is also useful to avoid feeling that we have to pollute our bodies with synthetic, emotionally mind-altering drugs. Artificial birth control makes some of us bloat, have worse pain when bleeding and have fertility problems when going off it. Any type of synthetic birth control product is definitely risky because of the hormones that are used. Using other, non-hormone birth control methods are an alternative to avoiding conception. However, devices such as condoms and diaphragms need a spermicide to work effectively. A spermicide (as a gel or foam) combines with the mucus membranes in the yoni (vagina) making natural fertility awareness difficult because the mucus patterns change while using a spermicide. Therefore, it is best to avoid using it when determining your fertile period naturally, called "natural family planning." Once you know your own mucus patterns over a couple of months, you may find that these "devices" are no longer necessary.

Planning a natural fertility awareness schedule for our birth management may be the best way for us to become conscious of our bodies and to teach our kids about their bodies. Their confidence and self-esteem will increase; they will not be afraid of their bodies and will respect the body boundaries of others. They will be more likely to wait to have kids of their own until they are more mature and responsible. This type of body awareness also teaches our kids fertility awareness as a means of birth management, so they can feel more secure about being the one who has not "done it." This is an alternative to pumping them up with hormonal drugs, which may cause cancer or other ailments that in my mind are worse then having a baby!

We need to start trusting ourselves to teach our children to be healthy people in this world, and we need to encourage and respect them. We need to have faith that we have taught them well. From this perspective of body awareness, they will be able to feel good about themselves in all aspects of their lives.

These children will then have the awareness and ability to bring their babies into the world when they are ready for that responsibility. They will respect and understand how to imprint healthy boundaries and give birth, naturally and gently.

When you are ready to Conceive or already have:

There are a few signs to watch for that may help determine conception early on. If you are a "regular" girl and know your cycles, then it is easy. If you are like me and have 32 to 50 day cycles, this may be a bit more frustrating. Even if you are "irregular" these signs apply, but just a little later than for a "regular" girl.

The most obvious sign of conception is an intuitive feeling that something has taken place, and you are feeling a little different. This feeling can occur the day after conceiving or within the week. You may be more tired than usual and have more food cravings, especially if you were not conscious about what you ate prior to conception, your body may be craving things it has been missing.

Sometimes you can tell just by looking at your body. The area around your nipples might be a little darker or little white nodules might appear around the areolas. Your belly may not seem any different but it feels a little harder to the touch.

Now you have missed a moon cycle and are wondering if you may be pregnant. Some women will want to confirm this as soon as possible. "Do-it-yourself" pregnancy tests are available at most drug stores or super markets. Another way to find out if you are pregnant is simply to wait. Listen to your body; you may experience subtle sensations that let you know you are surely "with child."

Most of us are anxious to know if we have a little one growing inside. We want to run to the store and get a test that will tell us no or yes, immediately. The only issue is that some women will get a "false negative" (pregnant) and others will get a "false positive" (not pregnant). Obviously, this can cause some anxiety either way, and is not how you want to begin a pregnancy.

About two days after conception takes place, Human Chorionic Gonadotropin Hormone (or HCG) begins to be produced by the forming placenta, which is only a cell at this point and excretes HCG through the kidneys. Some pregnancy tests are now available which can detect this hormone very early on after conception takes place; other tests detect this hormone within the first two weeks after conception. The highest levels of HCG are in the urine between the hours of 4am & 7am. That is why it is advisable to perform a pregnancy test first thing in the morning, since the kidneys have not had a chance to get rid of the hormones through urination. However, new pregnancy tests can detect HCG in the urine at any time during the day.

If your "moon" is a little late, and the little bit of blood coming out in your urine is about to turn into blood flow, you may get a positive test result. Red wine can also cause a test to read positive if consumed within twenty-four hours of taking the test. As can any medication or prescription drugs that are being taken. This can be very disappointing, I know from experience.

Getting a blood test soon after conception, or waiting another few days, are your only other options. Nevertheless, if we are aware and patient we may feel a change in our bodies early on, and we will be able to tell if we are truly pregnant.

I have known more then a few women who have also never gotten a positive pregnancy test throughout an entire pregnancy! Some women bleed every month during a pregnancy like a normal moon cycle and have healthy babies, so trusting in your intuition is what this is all about.

Presumptive signs are the cessation of the moon cycle, sore breasts, frequent urination, cravings, and darkening of the areolas. These signs do not always mean you are pregnant; other things such as stress, emotional upsets, yearning for a child, and drastic changes of lifestyle can also bring on these symptoms. Listening to your instincts and to your intuition is the best pregnancy test there is.

If you do get a true positive test early on, congratulations! For us slow testers, be patient. Relax. If it is meant to happen, it will, and without you even needing to know for sure.

Our bodies have their own inner world. If we tap into that world, we may find a great resource center for all of our questions.

Kerri connecting with Talen shortly after birth, December 5, 2006

Parent's Responsibility & Informed Consent

You must be the change you wish to see in the world ...

~Mahatma Gandhi

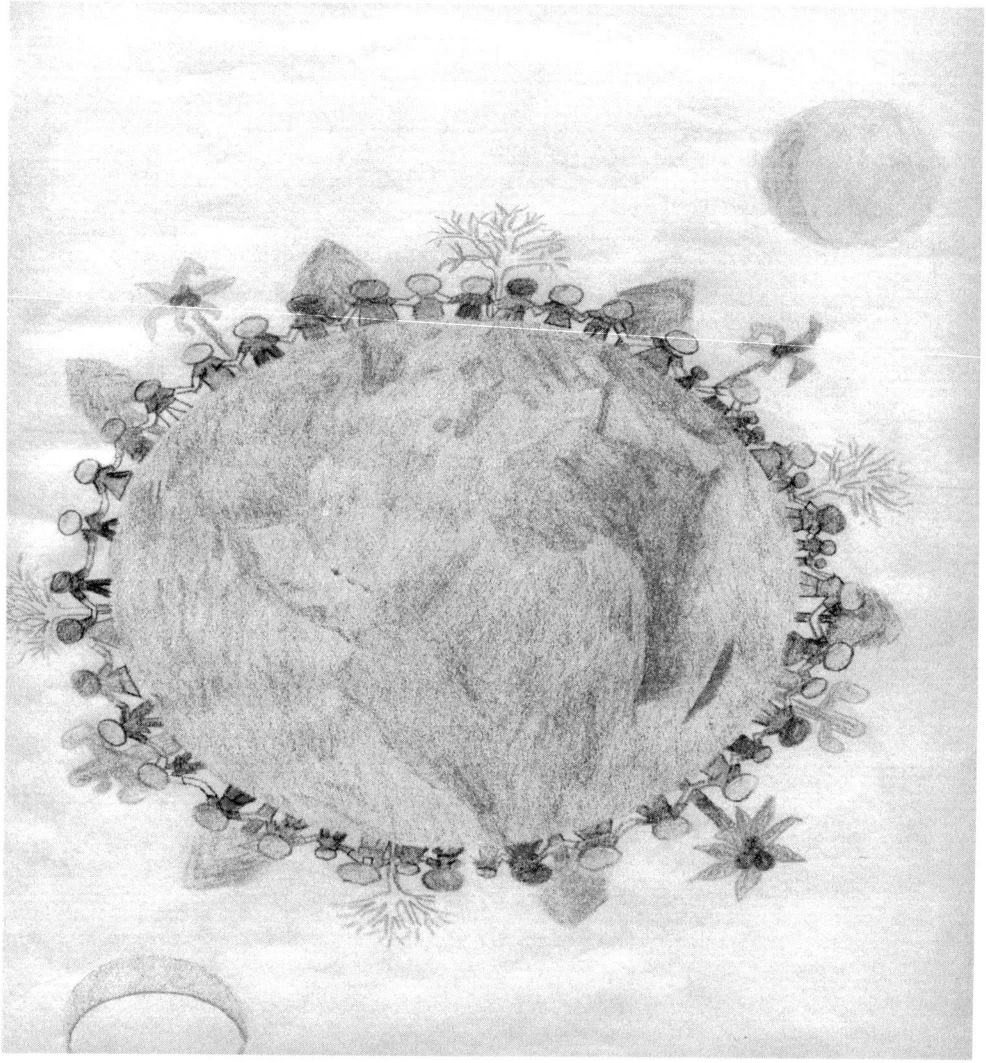

A drawing I made for my son Zack "We are All One" 1989

The Pregnant "Patient's Bill of Rights"

"The Pregnant Patients Bill of Rights" 1986-

The pregnant patient has the right to participate in decisions involving her well-being and that of her unborn child, unless there is a clear-cut medical emergency that prevents her participation. In addition to the "rights" set forth in the American Hospital Association's "Patient's Bill Of Rights," the pregnant patient, because she presents TWO patients rather than one, should be recognized as having the additional rights listed below.

The Pregnant Patient Has The Right:

1. Prior to the administration of any drug or procedure, to be informed of any potential, direct or indirect, effects, risks or hazards to herself of her unborn, or newborn, infant which may result from the use of a drug or procedure prescribed for her, or administered to her, during pregnancy, labor, birth or lactation.

2. Prior to the proposed therapy, to be informed, not only of the benefits, risks and hazards of the proposed therapy, but also of known alternative therapy, such as available childbirth education classes which could help to prepare the pregnant patient physically and mentally to cope with the discomfort or stress of pregnancy and the experience of childbirth, thereby reducing or eliminating her need for drugs and obstetric intervention. She should be offered such information early in her pregnancy, in order that she may make a reasoned decision.

3. Prior to the administration of any drug, to be informed by the health professional who is prescribing or administering the drug to her, that any drug which she receives during pregnancy, labor and birth, may adversely affect her unborn baby. No matter how or when the drug is taken or administered, directly or indirectly, realize that there is **NO** drug or I-V Chemical that has been proven safe for the unborn child.

4. If Cesarean Birth is anticipated, to be informed of this prior to the administration of any drug, and preferably prior to hospitalization. This minimizes the intake for her and her baby of non-essential pre-operative medicine.

5. Prior to the administration of a drug or procedure, to be informed of the areas of uncertainty if there is NO properly controlled follow-up research which has established the safety of the drug or procedure with regard to its direct and/or indirect effects on the physiological, mental and neurological development of the child exposed, via the mother, to the drug or procedure during pregnancy, labor, birth or lactation. (This would apply to virtually all drugs and the vast majority of obstetric procedures).

6. Prior to the administration of any drug, to be informed of the brand name and generic name of the drug, in order that she may advise the health professional of any past adverse reaction to the drug.

7. To determine for herself, without pressure from her attendant, whether she will accept the risks inherent in the proposed therapy, or refuse a drug or procedure.

8. To know the name and qualifications of the individual administering a medication or procedure to her during labor or birth.

9. To be informed, prior to the administration of any procedure, whether the procedure is being administered to her or for her baby's benefit (medically indicated) or as an elective procedure (for convenience, teaching purposes or research).

10. To be accompanied during the stress of labor and birth by someone she cares for, and to whom she looks for emotional comfort and encouragement.

11. After appropriate medical consultation, to choose a position for labor and birth which is the least stressful to her baby and herself.

12. To have her baby cared for at her bedside, if her baby is normal, and to feed her baby according to her baby's needs, rather than according to hospital regimen.

13. To be informed, in writing, of the name of the person who actually delivered her baby, and the professional qualifications of that person. This information should also be on the birth certificate.

14. To be informed if there is any known or indicated aspect of her baby's care or condition which may cause her or her baby later difficulty or problems.

15. To have her, and her baby's, hospital medical records complete, accurate and legible and to have their records, including Nurses' Notes, retained by the hospital until the child reaches at least the age of majority, or, alternatively, to have the records offered to her before they are destroyed.

16. Both during and after her hospital stay, to have access to her complete hospital medical records, including Nurses' Notes, and to receive a copy, upon payment of a reasonable fee and without incurring the expense of retaining an attorney.

It is the obstetric patient and her baby, not the health professional, who must sustain any trauma or injury resulting from the use of a drug or obstetric procedure. The observation of the rights listed above will not only permit the obstetric patient to participate in the decisions involving her and her baby's health care, but will help to protect the health professional and the hospital against litigation arising from the resentment or misunderstanding on the part of the mother.

Parents Responsibilities and Informed Consent

Within the past sixty years or so, childbirth has become one of the biggest money-makers in our country, with no increase in quality of care or safety. Because of this decline in the quality of care we receive, we, as birthing parents, need to utilize our birthrights and begin to birth our babies in a more humane way. If we do this, then most of our medical establishments will need to change to accommodate the desires of its patrons.

As we cultivate the wisdom of our ancestors, this world will be a gentler world and a better place for our children to live their lives.

The impact of "medicalized" childbirth on women, babies and the whole family, has been one of control and of violation. Families have also suffered due to the lack of proper treatment from this type of technological and systematic approach to childbirth. This system suppresses education and informed consent; women and their babies are treated violently and not given options. A system needs to change when it does not recognize the importance of the parents, or for that matter, the importance of these little beings coming into this world.

Today in our American obstetric communities, education and informed consent has withered away. Birthing women need to take responsibility for themselves and to gather information and know their rights within any environment they have chosen to give birth.

Facts

An article, written by Dr. Barbara Starfield, from (JAMA) Journal of the American Medical Association (Volume 284, No. 4, 2000), has given this most recent statistic concerning U.S. health spending and errors. A total of 225,000 unnecessary deaths occur in our country every year, and the breakdown of this figure is as follows:

~Unnecessary Surgery: 12,000

~Medical errors in hospitals: 7,000

~Other errors: 20,000

~Infections in hospitals: 80,000

~Non-Error, negative effects from drugs: 106,000

It is outrageous that 225,000 deaths per year (the ones recorded at least) occur in our one country alone and are the result of mistreatment, misdiagnosis, drug reactions, or just from being in the hospital! In addition to these staggering numbers, we spend another 77 billion extra dollars a year for unnecessary treatments, operations and drugs with no positive results from the money we spend. Sure it is true that there are cases where the medical model of care is needed, and I am not endorsing not "ever" going to seek help when it is necessary, it just makes sense for us to learn when medical attention is truly needed. Prevention is really the answer.

The birth industry alone makes approximately 22 billion dollars a year. Almost one in three women today in our American hospitals ends up with a C-section. It is the most common, major operation performed in our country today. This outrageous percentage has leapt from <5% in the early 20th century to more then 30% today, which is approximately 1 out of every three or four women. In some places in our country, it is much more. In one hospital, in my state, where they take so-called "high risk" patients, it is nearly 90%. Even with that in mind, the percentage should be no more than 5-7% overall. There is no justification for this!

Nearly one in every 33 children in our country will be diagnosed with some form of mental or physical disability due to genetic damage or birth related injuries.

Drugs like vaccines or immunizations, pitocin, epidurals, or antibiotics given during pregnancy, labor and birth are especially harmful as the woman and child are extremely vulnerable and at a higher risks for bad reactions. Often these are in the form of disabilities that are never even diagnosed. Some are minor and are over-looked, but some are obviously severe and need medical attention.

During a Cesarean operation, the baby and mother are subjected to numerous risks. Both mother and baby are 50% more likely to have complications compared to a natural birth, even if the woman is "so called" high risk. The risks of a Cesarean operation include fetal hypoxia (a lack of oxygen) that causes brain damage; accidentally cutting the baby; cutting of the placenta which causes fetal hemorrhage; or fetal injuries from pulling babies out of this incision. For the mother the following complications are associated with this type of operation and the drugs which accompany it: short-term or long-term respiratory distress; postponed breast feeding and bonding with the baby; accidentally cutting of other internal organs; bladder damage; spinal injuries from the drugs given; nerve damage from cutting through nerves; hemorrhage, infection from incision; migraines; back problems; difficulty in caring for her baby and other children; risk of severe postpartum depression; edema in the extremities; allergic reactions to drugs; and, at worst, death. That is not to say that a few percent (a few) would benefit from this life-saving operation. However, in our country it is over-used and abused because of impatience, insurance companies, lack of prenatal education, poor emotional support, and because it makes a lot of people a lot of money!

If we were committing cesarean sections on only those who truly needed them, maybe the "quality" of that operation on mother and baby would be less dysfunctional. Nevertheless, to perform this surgery routinely--as a means of convenience and profit--is careless and lacks integrity.

We need to educate ourselves on what justifies a Caesarian Section and on what can be done to prevent them. We need to know and consider all of our options, and this will help minimize unnecessary operations.

Always get hospital forms for "procedural risks" during the prenatal time before you go into labor. Look over them thoroughly and discuss them with your chosen care provider before entering into a domain when in a vulnerable situation. These forms are attainable through any hospital, and you have the right to have them. Even if you are planning a home birth, it is wise to obtain these forms in case hospitalization becomes necessary. Have them ready, signed or waived. Waiver forms are a very different piece of paper. Ask for them specifically.

Informed consent and education often are overlooked as a part of medical procedures with the excuse that most women do not know what is best for them or their unborn children. The medical establishment takes on the role of an authoritarian parent who makes, and carries out, decisions rather than informing and educating the birthing woman and her family to be empowered and make their own informed choices.

Excerpt from the Book *"Come Gently Sweet Lucina" (1957)* By Patricia Cloyd Carter. The following is a discussion on Grantly Dick Read's book *"Painless, Fearless, Childbirth." (1950.)* Although Patricia respects Reads knowledge as a physician; she is expressing her dislike for the "Need a Doctor" approach. Here is what she says about the conditioning of women to need a doctor.

"Especially in an age in which every girl child knows long before she even knows how to get pregnant that the cardinal sin of pregnancy is disobeying the first commandment thereof, which is "Don't listen to anyone but your Doctor." In an age in which even (the) husband knows that it is impossible for mere wives to know anything about pregnancy, and that even if he's in the mood, and she's in the mood, she must first find out from her doctor whether they can or they can't (have sex). In an age in which our county, state, and even our federal government's work hand in hand with the doctors in disseminating the propaganda that no woman can know anything about pregnancy, and (they) continue year after year to spread (at taxpayers expense) leaflets on pregnancy that are not at all really true."

If we want a better health care system, it is up to everyone, as a society, to become informed and educated on these subjects. With many more options today, we have the knowledge and materials needed for the safest prenatal, labor and birth outcome than ever before in history. All who strive for a better world for our children will choose gentle birth and unhindered birth practices because we know what a great impact it will have on our children's health and emotional well-being. This in turn will create higher and more evolved communities in the future.

"The truth for women living in a modern world is that they must take increasing responsibility for the skills they bring into birth if they want their birth to be natural. Making choices, of where and with whom to birth, is not the same as bringing knowledge and skills into your birth regardless of where and with whom you birth." ***~Common Knowledge Trust***

Consent Form Example: This is for you also to use for doctors and midwives. You also have the right, when hiring, to have your own contract signed!

We, ___(your name/s)___ have chosen to hire:

___(care provider/s names)___ in the capacity of: (List the services provided in your own words) ___(Childbirth educator, doula, midwife, doctor, 'whomever').___

We have also agreed to hire: ___('so and so')___ for the duration of our prenatal, labor, birth, and postpartum period to share with us this blessed event.

We or I: ___(your names)___ will not hold accountable anyone for the choices that we have made.

We only expect ___('so and so')___ to perform at the level of support, care, education, and help, and we hold ourselves responsible ___(your names)___ for any choices we will make during this pregnancy and birth.

We, ___(your names)___ will be able to choose to terminate care at anytime during the prenatal period. If our terms are not met, we will pay ___(name of care provider)___ for all the time spent with us, for educating and supplying us with their services.

We agree to be flexible and communicate any undesired treatments or conflicts in an appropriate way before making any hasty decisions.

Care provider's notes of agreement or boundaries:

____

____

____

____

Care Provider's Signature(s): ______________________________

Date: ____/____/____

signatures:______________________________

Date: ____/____/____

Your Notes and Specific Desires:

____

____

You will word it all differently I'm sure, but that's the gist of a consent form. You can modify it for whomever you work with, and I highly suggest getting it notarized with both signatures. Unfortunately, people are not trustworthy enough to have verbal agreements. Sometimes, in rare situation, it may work out for both parties, but to keep the integrity of the professional relationship, it is wise to have anyone we work with sign a written agreement. Now I have contracts, and it makes each party feel more comfortable and confident, and I have my clients create their own contract for what they want from me. I am opening the door to give them options and choices for the care they want in the moment, and I also want them to feel free to change things along the way as we learn what is needed as the situation unfolds.

No one is bound by anything until the task is over. You always have time to decide with whom, where and how you want your birth to be. This is a very important decision and should not be made in haste. So do not let anyone tell you that you are "stuck" with a care provider with whom you feel uncomfortable. That person will be with you in your most sacred time: pregnancy, labor and birth. Be open to changes and taking risks while listening to your intuition when making choices for your birth; it is your body and your baby's birth—no one else's.

In taking this form with you to your doctor or midwife, it will verify that the care provider is willing and able to provide you with the care you desire. Also, in doing this, you are demonstrating that you take responsibility for the choices you make and for your own education and care. Your decisions are yours, and no one, and I mean, NO ONE, has the right to tell you to subject yourself, or your unborn baby, to any intervention. Plus, you are more likely to get what you want if you demand it and show that you are being fully responsible for your own care choices.

With clients, I usually wait until all the information about choices are given, their needs are clear, and my boundaries are also clear, then they can take time to think about what they want from me and in what capacity they want to utilize my services. We will use a contract to verify all the information we exchange, to "make a deal" and a commitment to work with one another, and then we sign our agreement. Yet, I always make sure there is a clause leaving the door open for change.

Very rarely do I feel uncomfortable with a client. If I do, I usually allow a few weeks to communicate my feelings and listen to theirs. If we still feel uncomfortable, then another care provider may be suggested. It goes the same way if a client feels I am not fulfilling her needs.

Usually when hiring someone to provide a service, we fail to remember that we are the boss in the situation. More often than not, we are conditioned to feel that midwives, doctors and other authority figures are "our bosses." This may be our society's way of keeping us controlled and subservient. We have to build up enough self-esteem to be able to walk into any professional's office and know what we want from them to begin with.

Through research and education, we can know what we want and then be able to remind the care facilitator that we are paying them to do a service for US. We deserve the service to be done well, with proper care, treatment, and co-decision making. Ultimately, the decisions lie with the parents!

We are in this world together to learn and share how to care for one another in a more humane and compassionate way. Doctors, midwives, nurses and doulas are only human and are fallible. We are all doing a job, providing a service for those who want to use our knowledge. This does not mean, however, that anyone should be taken advantage of, pay outrageous fees, not get educated about their own body and options, or be operated on unnecessarily. This is why we need to be "working" together with our health care system instead of being co-dependent on them to do "it" for us. Then we will begin to have better results when we actually, truly need them for something.

Interviewing Prospective Care Providers

One thing I have learned is that, when we make choices, they are never engraved in stone. We do not have to stick to early decision-making efforts. It is wise to be consistent in communicating our needs and weed out the people that will not, or cannot, support our wishes. Researching options, educating ourselves, and compiling names and numbers of health care providers is a good start. Have a list of thoughts, feelings, desires and questions ready when calling each person to make an appointment. Then you will be able to sort out, right from the start, who you might be interested in. This way, you are not wasting a whole lot of energy on someone who does not fit into your idea of what you are looking for in a birth 'partner.'

There are a few things to ask when interviewing any health-care provider. Being clear as to what we are looking for in the beginning of the interview is the first step. If you already know, for instance, that you want a home birth, and possibly a birthing pool, then when you call for an appointment you can start the process of elimination by asking if that is an aspect of their care. Cross out the names and numbers of the people that do not fit your desires. Another priority may be that the person's philosophies (birth, spiritual, religious and lifestyle) are similar to yours. Asking key questions on the phone, before making an appointment, saves you time and energy.

Primary questions such as :

Are you practicing with a non-interference philosophy? How do you go about doing that? Do you always do routine blood tests and internal exams? Are you open to not doing them if I do not want them?"

With these simple questions you will hear a sign in the person's voice on the other end of the phone if, or if not, they are practicing with a non-interference approach.

This is another way of eliminating undesired treatment later in your care. Sometimes, however, health care providers will say anything to get your business, and later, you may find that what was said in the beginning of the relationship changes as time goes on. One example of this is from a former client of mine who had two hospital births before having a home birth. She had expressed to her doctor that she did not want any internal exams during her pregnancy, and the doctor agreed until about halfway through the pregnancy. When she was about six months along, her doctor literally bullied her into having an internal exam and pap smear with the threat that if she did not have one the doctor would not care for her anymore. He said it was "Policy, the Doctors' protocol!" that every mother had to have a pap smear and internal exam before having a baby. Early on, this mom could have asked for a signed form, which stated that she would not have an internal exam unless she so desired one, but, at the time, she did not know that was an option.

Her home birth went great, and we never did do an internal exam. She expressed to me later that it had made all the difference in the world, and that she did not feel inadequate like she had previously. Her birth seemed to go a lot smoother without dragging on. She felt that the last two births were painful and long because she felt invaded and interfered with during the pregnancy and labor. Vaginal exams can place the mother in a psychologically subservient role bringing up issues they may have not been dealt with prior to birth, thus slowing down and making labor very painful.

It is easy to ask for proof that a care provider will stick to their word, and if they do not comply with your early wishes, then it is best to find someone who will and get the respect you deserve, or you can always choose to do your own birth!

Here is a list of questions: Ask these of anyone you interview, even before you meet them, ask them on the phone when calling around to make appointments.

What is your philosophy about pregnancy, labor and birth?

How many moms have birthed with you? In what capacity did you work with them: assistant, primary provider, educator, doula, and postpartum care?

How many had a natural birth? How many at home? Hospital? Birth center?

Do you do routine episiotomies? Do you suture? Do you use glue to repair minor tears?

Are most of the mothers you work with supported to do their birth "their way?"

How many Cesarean Sections have been done in your practice? What were the reasons?

Do you stay with the mother the whole labor or are there other people involved? If so, will I get to know them before I go into labor?

Do you do routine tests, if so, what?

Do I have the option to waive a test or procedure routinely done? (They may say no, but legally you always have the right to waive.)

Do you allow family at the birth?

Can I have my husband catch our baby? Will you support him in doing this?

I want my babies' placenta to remain attached. Are you supportive of this method?

I would like the option to labor and birth alone without assistance. Do you support this idea?

I only use natural medicine; can I bring my own and not have to use yours?

I want to eat and drink during labor because I know labor is smoother when a mom is nourished during this time; is that ok with you?

Do you use a doppler every visit or can you use a fetoscope to lesson ultrasonic exposure to my baby?

Do you require an ultrasound during pregnancy? Would I be able to make my own decisions regarding the use of ultrasound?

How do you deal with "due dates" being to soon or too late? May I choose how to handle those situations if they arise?

How long after the birth do you care for the mother and baby?

Do you take phone calls anytime, day or night, for concerns that may arise?

How would you handle a complication?

Do you transport according to your intuition or state rules?

When you transport, do you come with us?

How would you handle the hospital staff?

If we find that the baby is breech, or we have twins, how would you handle that?

What is your standard fee? Do you do trades? Would I be able to pay visit to visit? How do you deal with late payments? Can I pay half now and half before the birth? Or in segments? Every care provider is different, some will have sliding scales, and some take payments. It's up to you to pay on time and for care rendered, even if you change your mind and switch care providers during the course of care. Always communicate money concerns in the beginning.

All of these questions may be asked to doctors, midwives, or other care providers, and you can modify the questions to suit your needs. However, I highly suggest asking them before you make any decisions, especially about where, and with whom, you will give birth. Remember, you are the boss of your choices in care providers, body, baby and birth!

Do not feel intimidated, this is your life, and your baby's first imprints will be made by the people you choose to "manage" your body and your baby. This will affect the rest of your lives. You need to be secure in your decision-making, and you should be able to get the respect you deserve from health care providers making it more likely that you will get what you want from them. If you do not want intervention; it is your responsibility to become informed of your rights and educate yourself on how this system works. Nevertheless, if you do not want to deal with that system, then educate yourself and do your own prenatal care and birth. It is less expensive and much more rewarding than depending on someone else to take over for you.

I have seen many parents take on this responsibility and do their own prenatal care, birth and postpartum care. I would, sometimes, help by cleaning up afterwards, discussing their needs, and giving support with breast-feeding etc. When parents do their own care and birth, their outlook on life definitely changes, and it seems to be much more open to new possibilities than before. By taking care of themselves and their children with much more consciousness and compassion, they are more empowered than if they had handed over their bodies and babies to science to do it to them, or for them. The impact here is one of empowerment, inner wisdom, joy, and self-reliant satisfaction, which all vibrate out into the world to everyone.

"What Ifs"

Well, "What ifs" are sometimes confused with the "what got interfered with" by others, and they create a scenario that most women are frightened of. It is more common to hear, "We would have died if we weren't in the hospital," than that the poor woman's labor was induced before the baby was ready, and she had an epidural, was strapped to the fetal monitor, and then had a C-Section. She was led to believe that she and the baby might have died without the establishment's interventions. Now, there is a grain of truth in this scenario. She could have possibly died, and her baby also, but she and the hospital put her into this situation to begin with. If she had education, good prenatal care, and a loving support system at home this most likely would not have happened. The need for these kinds of "emergency" treatments is extremely rare.

When doing your own prenatal care and birth, there are things to remember so that you will feel confident, that all is well, and that you are doing the right things to limit the risks of "what ifs." First, trust in your self, your instincts, and your abilities to listen from within. Then get some support to help you through doubtful times.

All throughout this guide book I have listed tools to help you overcome fears and to utilize your innate knowledge by listening to your intuition, using prayer, meditation, and many other modalities to help you move through any obstacles before birth takes place. Complications and "what ifs" are usually the product of other people's scenarios and are induced by societal beliefs, the media and the medical system. Most complications stem from lack of prenatal education, neglecting proper nutrition, not getting enough rest, having a difficult relationship with a partner, and just being afraid.

These things can be neutralized before a birth takes place so there are no obstacles to get in the way of having *"A Clear Road to Birth."* The film, mentioned previously, *by Judy Seaman* is a great example of the concept of healing before a birth takes place. Feeling confident that you "know your body and baby," and believing that you will be able to birth without interference, allows you a freedom to "know" that you will. You can find this inspiring film at *Laura Shanley's website: www.unassistedchildbirth.com.*

This film is one of the first I show to my clients when exploring which path they would like to take. I feel that it helps parents rid themselves of any fear they may have and inspires them with visuals of women doing their own births. This also gives couples the opportunity to assume responsibility for their pregnancies and births, whether I am there or not. No midwife, doctor, or anyone who is hired to care for a women and her pregnancy can birth her baby for her. We cannot hand over our body and baby to people who are not capable of understanding our inner world where we grow and nourish our young

"Is Unassisted Childbirth Safe?"

By: Laura Shanley

"One of the greatest myths perpetuated by the medical system is that hospitals are the safest place to give birth. Stories abound of women dying in childbirth before the advent of modern hospitals. Yet, few people realize that women were not dying due to the fact that childbirth is inherently dangerous, but rather because of the living conditions at that time. Poor women were generally underfed and overworked during pregnancy, while wealthy women were often deprived of fresh air and sunshine because brown skin was considered socially unacceptable. Wealthy girls were corseted from the age of eleven, so that by the time they turned fourteen, their pelvises were literally deformed. These physical factors, combined with various psychological ones (fear, shame, and guilt) led to the problems that these women encountered.

Throughout history, normal, healthy women have rarely died in childbirth. In fact, when birth moved from the home to the hospital in the 1920s, the infant and maternal mortality rates actually rose. A major study done in 1933 showed that hospital births were not as safe as home births. Studies done in the last twenty years prove this is still the case. (Mayer Eisenstein, MD, The Home Court Advantage, 1988.)

When a laboring woman goes into the modern-day hospital, medical personnel and machinery surround her. Often she is told what to eat (generally nothing), what position to be in (generally flat on her back which narrows the pelvic outlet and prevents her from utilizing the natural gravitational force), and when to or when not to push (which interferes with her own instinctive knowledge of birth). Her progress is charted and measured, and she is treated more like a machine than a thinking, feeling, and intelligent adult.

If her labor is not progressing at the speed at which the hospital has arbitrarily decided it should be, she is often given drugs to speed things up. The drugs, however, may make her contractions more painful, which in turn cause her to take more medication to deal with the pain. Not only does this medication prevent her from fully participating in the birthing process, it also crosses the placenta, adversely affecting her unborn baby.

Sometimes a woman's body simply shuts down after all this intervention, and the woman is told she needs a cesarean section in order for her baby to be born safely. Unaware that the intervention she received actually caused the "complications" in the first place, she often consents "for the good of the baby." Nearly one in four babies in this country are now born by cesarean section.

Many women who have given birth in the hospital report dissatisfaction not only with the way they were treated but also with the way their babies were treated. Babies are often taken away from their mothers immediately after birth to be weighed, measured, tested and cleaned. Eye drops are administered "just in case" a mother has a venereal disease, and Vitamin K is administered because babies are supposedly born "deficient."

The same loving consciousness that knew how to grow her baby inside her perfectly knows how to get her baby out safely and easily, if only she will let it. With no one shouting commands at her, a woman is free to relax and naturally birth her baby. After the birth, there is no one there to separate her from her baby. She can hold and nurse him as long as she wishes. Women all over the world are rediscovering the fact that it works best when it is interfered with least."

Food & Herbal Nutrition

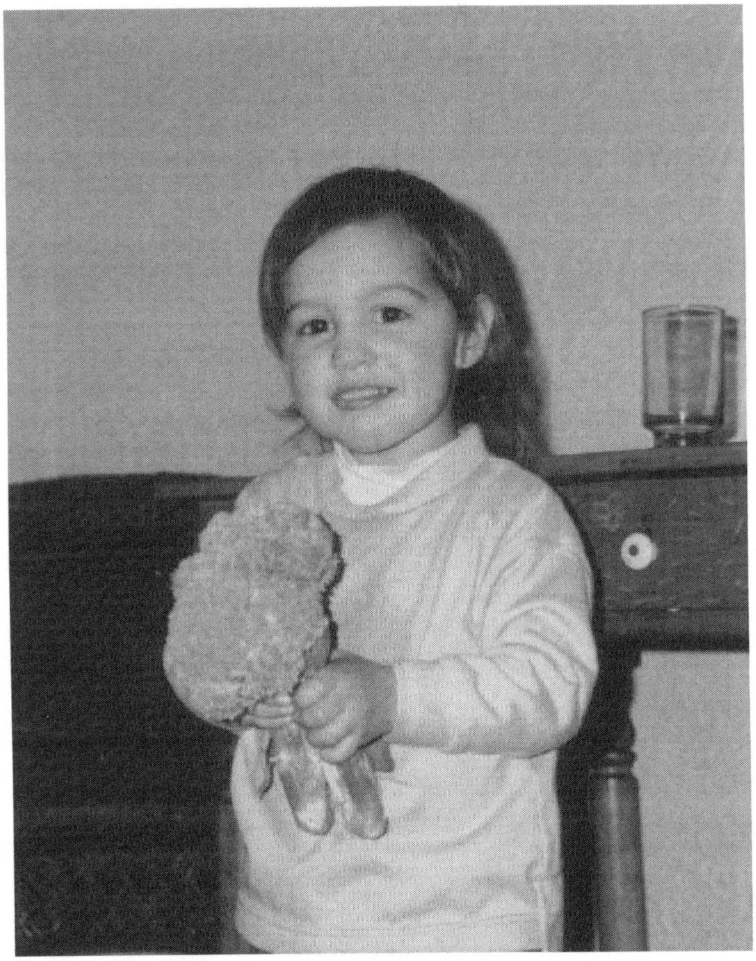

Zack with his favorite broccoli, 1991

Using Food as Medicine

Prevention and Nutrition with the Use of Herbs

YES! You can be a Vegan and Vegetarian during Pregnancy

What Prevention through Nutrition is all about

Herbal Suggestions for Pre-conception, Conception, Pregnancy, Labor and Birth

Getting the Most out of Supplements

Nutrition and the Effects on Pregnancy and Birth

My Own Personal Food Story

Nutrition: Herbs and Food Medicine

"There would be so much less pain and suffering in the world if only we would connect more to nature and all its gifts of medicine, then healing would become a part of everyday life."
~Herbal Healer

Herbs and food are a part of healthy, daily nutrition; the best supplements are in a non-processed form, not in pills unless you make them yourself or find a good source already made. Herbs, if properly used are your best supplements. No vitamins need be bought, or, if bought, at least be aware of the preservatives used to keep them on the shelf. Herbs can be grown inside the house in pots on a windowsill, or outside, in some climates, all year round. This is ideal but not always easy. There are local herb and food growers in most areas; these may be found in the phone book or by asking at the local health food co-op

All herbs and foods are medicine, and are to be used with respect and wisdom. I learned, through listening to my son's desire for certain foods, that food is a supplement in its own right. A basic preventive diet should be a part of our life-style, no matter where we are in life.

For pregnancy and rearing children, some basic facts should apply:

Our bodies need complex and simple foods to maintain health. More than half of your diet should have some form of protein involved. These would be your whole grains, lean meats, fish, nuts, seeds, greens, legumes, sea vegetable (seaweeds), squashes, roots, and sprouts.

GRAINS: Barley, brown rice, buckwheat, bulgur, corn, millet, oats, rye, triticale (high protein wheat), wheat germ, quinoa, amaranth . . . these are all good non-meat protein sources.

LEGUMES: Black beans, fava, kidney, lima, mung, navy, peas and soy.

SEEDS: Sunflower, sesame, pumpkin.

Brewer's nutritional yeast is also a good supplement to use on foods, for B vitamins and minerals.

NUTS: Almond, brazil, coconuts, walnuts, pine nuts, soy nuts, cashews, walnuts. It is easy to get these by making nut butters, and Yummy to eat!

SPROUTS: Mung, alfalfa, fenugreek, quinoa, sunflower, wheat berries, broccoli, and lentils.

Good food combining will create even more protein, and your foods will help digest one another when used appropriately, for instance, using grains with milk, and rice with beans. There are different concepts of food combining, but this is one. Whole grains (50% of your diet), fish and lean meats (20%), vegetables and fruits (25%). The other 5% is for your, once in a while, snacks and fluids. Fruits and sweets should be used sparingly, and of course, water and herbal drinks should be a part of your daily consumption for hydration. Avoid refined processed sugars and flour. Some may be allergic to wheat and dairy, and for those, these products need to be eliminated or used VERY occasionally. This is a preventive, simple diet.

KEY WORDS: LISTEN TO YOUR BODY'S NEEDS

YES! Vegans and vegetarians can stick to their normal diets! However, sometimes we need to eat differently depending on what our bodies are telling us we need. Prior to my pregnancy, I had been a vegetarian for several years, yet I listened to my body's need for meat and dairy during that time. For others, it may be less dairy and more of something else. Overall, it is just a matter of hearing what our body is telling us to eat, though there are some things to think about while on a vegan or vegetarian diet.

Essential fatty acids and oils (EFA's) and Omega-3 fish oils--which contain DEA--are important for fetal brain development. Avocado, flax, whole grains, legumes, nuts, veggies and fruit may be sufficient for a healthy well-rounded daily diet in Vegan or Vegetarian pregnancy.

Always remember if you are "craving" sweets, it is protein you need. If you are craving salt, salt your food to taste, however, use sea salt, do not overuse Iodized table salt, because we can receive essential Iodine from our fresh veggies. Our bodies actually need more salt during pregnancy, but only an extra pinch now and then. Our bodies are made of water (75% or more), salt metabolizes in water and helps digest proteins more efficiently. This actually has been controversial. Most of us think that we will retain water if we eat salt, but it is the opposite. Check out the *"Brewer's Diet,"* which was created to prevent complications from lack of proteins and salt in one's diet during pregnancy. These deficiencies can lead to pre-eclampsia, PIH (pregnancy induced hypertension) and toxemia, which are all inter-related.

Dr. Tom Brewer came up with a simple diet guideline in the forties and fifties for this dilemma. You can find his diet on his website, *http://www.blueribbonbaby.org/*; it is very useful in the prevention of metabolic problems in pregnancy. When we are pregnant, and when not pregnant, we still need salt in our body to be healthy. This does not mean to overdo salt; it is only good if used sparingly. Salt is a mineral that was actually in most foods prior to our taking it out of the earth to make into a product: table salt, which we now add back into our food. It is the same with many other minerals that have been destroyed in our food processing industries. I am not talking about the salt preservatives now in most store bought foods, those are not the "good" salts that we *need*, in fact, those salt preservatives may cause damage to our cell production.

Fluids are stored in our body organs for birth; this is normal water retention and is not harmful. It is actually healthy and helps to maintain balance in our metabolic systems. Unhealthy water can be stored in the extremities (around the knees, face, ankles, wrists, fingers), when we are not getting enough from food. These vital fluids are drawn out of our organs into the body's tissues to protect the organs from the dehydration they are suffering because of a lack of sodium in ones diet.

When there are not enough proteins and sodium in our diet, we become "toxic" and susceptible to pre-eclampsia and toxemia, which can damage the liver in severe cases. These conditions are rarely seen in women who eat and drink properly.

All these nutrients are interdependent of one another. If you have a balanced diet, you will be preventing numerous amounts of complications through eating properly. Eating well maintains your health and supplies your baby with a highly functional brain, circulatory system, nervous system, and in growth. It's worth focusing on your nutrition before you conceive. It will eliminate most problems with conception and early pregnancy, because you do need some minerals and proteins, to begin with, to maintain a pregnancy and lessoning or eliminating morning sickness symptoms. Eating well before pregnancy and during pregnancy is much cheaper than paying numerous hospital bills later, as it is more likely a child will develop poor health if the baby begins life with complications due to nutritional depravation. These complications range in all sorts of areas. It is a matter of risk.

Premature birth, neurological impairments, kidney dysfunctions, digestive disorders, cleft palate, mental (mild too severe) retardation, physical and mental dysfunctions are very common in babies whose mothers have not been properly nourished. You can prevent these risks with a balanced and healthy eating lifestyle. Not ALL of these risks will reflect a mother's nutritional habits, sometimes they can happen regardless. However, it is minimizing the risk through making good nutritional choices. Avoiding hazardous chemicals, pollution and un-clean water as well.

Although some medical care providers will tell you that they do not know why some women become toxic or pre-eclampsic, it is a preventable situation through proper diet, hydration and circulation. Medically, the symptoms, such as high blood pressure, swelling, protein in the urine, and headaches or dizziness are usually treated by inducing labor. However, in all actuality, diet is the simple cure, and inducing a labor/birth may only cause more harm for both mother and child.

Labor and Birth are Affected by Nutrition.

A mother who has not eaten properly and has not been hydrated well during pregnancy is at risk for:

Pre-term labor/Early miscarriage: This leads to hospitalization and medical interference. Risks for the mom are: losing the baby early; having interventions which may lead to future fertility problems; and caring for a sick baby that may have a long-term illness from the effects of poor nutrition. Long term damage to her kidneys, bone structure, teeth included.

For baby: risk of infections from needles and from other sick babies in the NICU (neonatal intensive care unit); respiratory infections; brain injury from prematurely formed skull bones; numerous other internal injuries; and long term, mild to severe, handicaps.

Labor: The mother's labor may be slow and rough, taking longer than if nutrition had been adequate to prepare her system for labor. Longer recuperation time post partum.

Tearing: With the lack of essential nutrients, women are more likely to tear, either from the lack of EFAs, improper hydration, or inadequate protein intake. All of which build strong muscles and tissues that will stretch and recuperate faster after a birth.

Painful Birthing: If muscles and organs are not nourished, they become sluggish and stagnant, which in turn creates more strain and pain.

Hemorrhage: In birth, when nutrition is not adequate to supply enough oxygen to the blood vessels to clot properly (Iron deficiency), it is more likely there will be excessive bleeding, and retained placenta.

NOTE: Also to avoid pregnancy, labor/birth complications and premature birth, be mindful that nutrition plays a huge part in prevention, but another aspect of this prevention is also **AVOIDING** a few key things. These things are something you **CAN** control. Not smoking, not drinking alcohol, keeping away from chemicals, paint, fumes, over the counter drugs and street drugs, drinking water that is contaminate. Sugar (includes pop), Caffeine coffees and teas, are also good to avoid or use very sparingly, to prevent pregnancy or birth complications.

Making green drinks for storing Vitamin K

Sprouted seeds are an excellent source of Vitamin K, which we need in the last few months of pregnancy. It stores in our bodies and facilitates clotting factors in our baby's system and is stored in the baby's "brown fat" for the birth. By eating sprouts, you and your baby will heal better, and NO synthetic vitamin K shots need be injected into baby's body. These routine shots may cause damage to the baby. Drinking sprouted seeds is easier since you can get more nutrition from a concentrated drink then by eating them, but eating them is also good for extra vitamins in salads or as a snack in between meals. Either way, seeds are nutritious and full of living enzymes, which are good for your cell production and digestive system. This was not an issue long ago when people ate simple green diets, which are inexpensive and more nutritious.

Seeds are sprouted by soaking them overnight (softer seeds need only a few hours,) and then straining them. Over a few days, they should be washed and strained once a day until seeds sprout. Hard seeds take a day or so longer then softer seeds. Sprout containers are easy to make. Use a mason jar, or something like it, and a small-holed screen or cheese cloth over the top of jar, held with a rubber band or something secure. After rinsing, set the jar in a shaded location and tilt it, at about a 90-degree angle to drain, then after a few days put the jar in a sunny location where it also can get airflow and continue the rinsing/draining cycle until the sprouts are ready to eat. A hanging basket over your sink works great, especially if your sink is in front of a window. You can easily rinse your sprouts, then leave the jars tilted in the basket to continue draining.

Here are a few combinations of "Green Drinks" and foods to consider.

Green Drink

2C buckwheat lettuce
1C sunflower greens
2C alfalfa sprouts
Juice all. It turns into liquid chlorophyll. . .

Smoothie:

3 T spirulina
1 banana
2C milk (almond, cow, or soy)
2 T Molasses
10 Almonds Raw
Blend together all ingredients and drink within a few minutes, or store in fridge and re-blend later. . .

Simple Smoothie:

2T spirulina
1C apple juice/papaya
1 banana
Blend and Enjoy!

High Protein Smoothie:

1C alfalfa greens, blended
1TBS protein powder

2T agave nectar or honey
1T molasses
1 banana/mango/papaya (one or all)
1 Tsp of flax oil
1 C-fruit (your choice of: strawberries, raspberries, blackberries, blueberries)

From the book "Survival Into the Twenty First Century,"

by: Viktoras H. Kulvinskas, M.S.,

Sweet Comfrey Soup:

15 medium comfrey leaves
1 avocado
1 small chopped zucchini
1 cup carrot juice (freshly juiced)
Blend and serve!

Rejuvenation Nectar:
(Great for storing your vitamin K, and getting enough protein in Vegan diets)

You need a manual grass juicer, or an electric grass juicer will do.

1 cup chopped sunflower greens
4 tbs. Sauerkraut
1 cup chopped buckwheat greens
1 stalk celery
1 cup alfalfa sprouts
1 cup spinach
1 clove garlic
1 cup favorite Weeds
(ex: dandelion etc. optional)

You may add fresh carrot juice to sweeten. Blend together and drink within five to ten minutes.

***My Favorite:* Garlic Green Dressings:** spirulina, agave nectar (optional), tahini, garlic minced, lemon juice, balsamic vinegar, avocado.

Green Salad Dressing: spirulina, avocado, tahini, lemon juice, 1 Tsp flax oil, a smidge of agave or honey to taste, and balsamic vinegar or apple cider vinegar.

Your own variations will be fun to experiment with; I love making my own food medicine, its fun!

A daily healthy diet for the soon to be pregnant mother

Eating small frequent meals is best as you will digest and metabolize quickly and more efficiently.

Morning:

Bread (chose from whole wheat, spelt, rice, non-white yeast, millet or sunflower bread--Ezekiel bread is best for protein,) one bowl of oatmeal or two eggs, a piece of fruit or a small salad with tahini dressing. Try to make your own dressings to avoid preservatives and get extra nutritional values. A glass of water, juice, tea, milk, soy, almond, or rice milk.

Snack:

Whole Wheat or bran muffin, apricots, figs, almonds, apples, cheese, high protein crackers, water, tea, milk or substitute. Just eat something good for you!

Lunch: Lentils, lean meats, vegetable, flax oil or butter on veggies, avocado, nuts, grain cereal, water, juice, tea.

Supper: Large salad (mixed greens) with grated cheese, purple cabbage, beets, carrots, tomatoes. Make your own tahini dressing with lemon juice, flax oil, hemp seeds or almonds, sunflower seeds, greens, omega-3 oils or fish.

Dinner: Lean meats or vegetarian main course, veggies, water, tea, milk or substitute.

Before bed: Cheese and crackers, orange, papaya, water, tea, milk or substitute. Salt to taste!

It seems like a lot, but I put here several ideas for each meal. You do not have to eat from all of the suggestions just choose what is high in protein and less in preservatives. Making your own dressing helps by adding more minerals and vitamins and proteins into each meal. Each meal should have more whole grains and proteins than other foods, but get those greens and essential fatty acids in your diet to help maintain good food assimilation throughout your internal organs and good cell production throughout yours, and your baby's, life!

Vitamins and minerals are also in most of these food categories. It is important to get enough Folic Acid in your diet before conceiving and in the early stages of pregnancy to prevent any damage to the cells that are building the baby. If you are not getting enough of these vitamins and minerals in your daily food and herbal consumption, it can cause premature separation of the placenta and increases the risk of hemorrhaging. Although I have seen moms who had horrible diets have healthy babies, it is again, a matter of risk.

Most foods in a balanced diet have folic acid, although it is always a good idea to take into consideration what you eat and the quality of your food. Vitamin supplements are not going to hurt you if you need the extra nutrition, but the dosage on most bottles are way over what you may need. If you are already getting enough through your diet, and supplementing herbally, you most likely do not need any supplements. Over-consuming pills is not just expensive but can be detrimental to your health. They go to waste in your system and can cause problems with your digestion and renal activity, so eating well may be a better solution. Whole grains, organ meats, nuts, leafy green vegetables, and mushrooms have folic acid in them.

A *Cleft Pallet* (a deformity associated with Folic Acid deficiency) is known to be more prevalent in cultures where these foods are not as commonly eaten, and vitamins are not easily found. This is when the nasal passage and upper mouth cavity (roof of mouth) do not fuse properly in their early development. Folic acid and other good vitamins and minerals are known to prevent this abnormality.

Getting enough calcium and magnesium is also important. About 1200 grams a day of it can prevent circulatory and neurological damage as well as muscle stiffness and soreness. Dairy, almonds, spinach, tofu, tahini, and sesame seeds are some of the foods that have calcium in them. A magnesium/calcium combination is optimal, they work together to be absorbed more efficiently. Taken at night before bed, while you are resting, works best. A glass of papaya juice will help assimilate these nutrients, if taken in pill form. Nettles, raspberry leaves, alfalfa, and oat straw are other ways in which calcium and magnesium and other trace mineral are taken. This can help to alleviate cramps in your legs, varicose veins, muscle and bone aches.

Your diet should contain a significant amount of protein:

About 75-100grms a day prevents numerous pregnancy-related issues, such as morning sickness, sore muscles, headaches, (G.D.) gestational diabetes, (PIH) pregnancy induced hypertension, pre-eclampsia and toxemia. It is well known that eating enough protein, even when vegetarian/vegan, can create healthier babies and better birth outcomes.

Iron is needed to help produce the carrying capacity of oxygen in your red blood cells for both you and your baby; you need 30mg more during pregnancy. It can be found in green foods, almonds, meat, fish, whole grains, leafy greens, and it needs to be taken with vitamin C for better absorption. Therefore, drinking or eating an orange or some papaya one hour before, or after (within a few hours,) eating iron rich foods really helps. Taking a supplement of this is not always a good idea since it can become toxic in the blood if not properly taken. There are over-the-counter herbal iron liquids that are easily assimilated through the kidneys and liver without the accumulation that some iron pills may have. "Herbal Iron" is a good liquid green supplement found in health food stores. There is also a brand called "Floradex" that is very good. Herbs and fruit juice are the ingredients. However, getting your iron in foods and green drinks is an easy solution.

A lack of iron in your blood can cause hemorrhage, fetal distress from lack of oxygen, and postpartum difficulties and exhaustion. Iron deficiency affects the liver, and in turn may also affect waste elimination through the system. We only have one liver in our lifetime, so it is wise to give it the nourishment it needs. Dandelion root, burdock root and yellow dock have been known to support the liver and aid in the absorption of iron.

B-Vitamins are essential for the cell's reproductive organization. If you are lacking in B vitamins, you are more likely to have morning sickness and stress on your organs leading to vascular problems. Lack of B-Vitamins can also lead to birth defects. Folic acid--a B-Vitamin--and B-12 work best together with vitamin C. A product that I personally like, if I feel the need to supplement, is "Emer'gen-C." It comes in many flavors and is easily taken by mixing with water; it is a Vitamin C supplement that comes with Folic Acid, B-Vitamins and trace minerals.

All these vitamins are working together to be absorbed and move through your body to your baby. Getting them from an herbal source or through your food is optimal. If over-used, pills can be taxing on your digestive process. Use common sense in taking any supplements, and eat well so you don't need too.

Summing it all up:

Eat well. Make your own ingredients. Skip pills and get enough protein and greens in your daily diet. Drink clean WATER!

A good recipe for high protein shakes:

1 quart cow or goat's milk, or a milk substitute such as almond, rice, or soy (I personally like almond milk best, and it's easy to make yourself and a lot cheaper than buying it (see recipe below)).

1/3 cup of protein powder (I like spirulina powder, but there are other good ones in health food stores.)

2 raw organic eggs

1 banana

1 tbs. molasses or honey if you are not having blood sugar problems

2 tbs. brewer's yeast or sea greens

A splash of nutmeg, vanilla, cinnamon for taste

Blend smooth and drink daily, Approx: 50 grams of protein.

Make your own protein, vitamin and mineral rich Almond milk:

A 25 lb bag of raw almonds will last about a month when making almond milk. If you have a large family or want to have more quantity than that, buy 50 lb bags at a time, in the long run it will save money.

For a gallon at a time, take 2 cups of raw almonds and soak them for about 24 hrs in eight cups of filtered water in a glass jar. Add water as it gets absorbed into almonds and keep at room temperature. Next day, put a few handfuls of the almonds and some of the soaking water in a blender and blend for a few minutes. You will want to fill up the blender only halfway with equal parts of liquid to almonds, because they will expand when you blend them. Then use cheesecloth in a strainer and strain the liquid into a glass jar. Do the same for the next soaked batch of almonds; add a tsp of vanilla per quart for taste. You can also add other spices as you desire such as cinnamon, nutmeg, cardamom and clove. These are all tasty in almond milk. Children love this milk and it is much better for them than cow's milk or even soymilk.

Summer cooling drink

Brew a large jar of red raspberry leaf and/or peach leaf tea, let cool, then blend with frozen melon, or ice cubes. You can also add some fresh berries: blackberries, strawberries and raspberries, bananas, or apples juice. It is refreshing and has good minerals and vitamins for your summer days in the sun.

Pre-Conception Herbal Suggestions

Once you have decided you are ready to conceive, get yourself on track with a balanced diet, then add herbal supplements that increase fertility.

These are hormonal stabilizers and endocrine balancers:

Angus Cactus is a pituitary regulator. The pituitary glands are responsible for the regulation of hormones for the reproductive cycle.

Vitex, Red clover blossoms, Red raspberry leaf, Black haw, Blessed thistle, Squaw vine, Sarsaparilla, Licorice root, Fenugreek, Siberian ginseng, False unicorn root, Wild yam, and Gotu kola may be taken in equal parts together; a cup a day, for up to two weeks pre-ovulation, will heighten your chance of conceiving.

After two weeks, it's good to take a break and see if you feel any changes. If you feel good about the changes and are feeling like you want to conceive, wait until you have gone through one full cycle while using these herbs. Stop taking them after the first two weeks you tried to conceive.

For moms who have miscarried, you may start taking False unicorn root for a couple of months before conceiving. You can make or buy a tincture, or get the root and make a tea out of it to sip throughout the day with your Red raspberry leaf. This will help to prevent miscarriages if they are due to hormonal imbalances. If the miscarriage was because of abnormalities of the conception, then it will not work. You can safely continue taking False Unicorn throughout your entire first trimester.

Herbs to start once you have conceived:

Raspberry leaf, red clover, oat straw, borage, nettles, and alfalfa are all good together in a daily mix for drinking. Red raspberry is the main ingredient, and then half of all other herbs mixed in. I usually make a jar labeled, "women's herbs," and make a batch that lasts me throughout the month. Each day take a four-finger pinch full of herbs and put them in a quart jar. Cover with boiling water and let steep for an hour. Strain and drink warm or iced throughout the day. I use cotton unbleached tea strainers so it's easier to reuse. Metal strainers bring out too many not-needed metals into the infusions. Cotton, bamboo, glass or wood when soaking, pouring, straining, and stirring are the best tools. This combination of herbs is full of nutrients and minerals. These herbs are also easily put into capsules, if you are one of those people who cannot sit down and take the time to have some tea. Then grinding your herbs into powder and taking them that way may be beneficial. You can buy your herbs, and then put them together in a coffee grinder, blender, or use a mortar and pestle, which is the traditional way, then put the ground herbs into capsules. Veggie-made caps are best for digestion.

Six weeks before an Estimated Due Date "EDD":

Continuing the pregnancy tea throughout these last few weeks. You may want to take days off to do something else, but do not "slack off" on your nutrition, especially at the end when you need to store up your energy for labor and birth.

I usually suggest starting to add a few herbs to your daily tea mix at this time. On top of the usual blend of red Raspberry leaf, add some squaw vine, nettles, and alfalfa leaf. This will help with vitamin K for clotting.

Since it is a fat-soluble vitamin, it needs weeks to get stored in mom and to be stored in baby's system before the birth.

No vitamin K shots are necessary unless your baby develops a severe hematoma of the head (which may rarely cause inter-cranial hemorrhage), this very rarely will happen in a gentle birth; however if it does, then vitamin K, or equivalent herbal supplements, can be taken by mother so the baby gets it through her milk.

Squaw vine herb supports a natural tendency to have "practice" or "warm up" sensations (contractions); re-named to be pleasure sounding, these are also called "Braxton Hicks," named after Dr. Braxton.

I also suggest to moms to start to take some primrose oil before bed, about 500 mg. This supports surges of the hormones called prostaglandins and relaxin that soften and prepare the cervix and membranes to get ready for labor and birth. I have seen amazing things happen in birth with the use of primrose oil.

For first time moms, primrose oil gently increases sensations over a longer period allowing a slower beginning stage of labor. Once in non-stop labor, it rarely becomes long and drawn out with the use of primrose oil. It also can facilitate the softening of muscles, like a lubricant, and this gives baby more room to ease down into the birth opening slowly without struggle. For women in their age of "change" it is also very beneficial for balancing hormones.

Now you are ready to have a healthy-balanced earthy-food and herb adventure!

More Recipes:

I am using vegetarian recipes because I feel that not all people need to eat meat and that meat is easily added to anything.

Dried Tofu Miso Soup

Great for labor to keep your metabolism, blood sugar and energy balanced.

4-5 cups of water

2 cups dried tofu, soaked in warm water and cubed

Add carrots, scallions, or whatever you have a craving for at the time!

1 cup onions, sliced in half moons

1 cup Wakame (sea vegetable) soaked and sliced

Quinoa Salad

2 cups quinoa, black or white grains, cooked on low until water is evaporated

Slice up into small pieces: carrots, zucchini, onions, garlic, sweet potato, broccoli, celery, or other veggies you like.

Sauté these while quinoa is cooking. Mix together, putting quinoa in with rest of veggies, top with goat cheese in individual servings and put some "Bragg's" (amino acids) on top. In addition, I like slicing avocados to top it off. Serve warm or chill for summer days, but try to eat things at room temperature when possible. It's better for your digestion.

Throw in some hemp seeds (which are extremely high in EFA's and proteins), pumpkin seeds, sesame seeds, and a sprinkle of Brewer's yeast, if you like (contains essential B vitamins)

High Protein Bean Salad

Cooked beans: fava, kidney, pinto, black, cannoli, and/or chick peas. Marinate in lemon juice and olive oil for twenty four hours in the refrigerator, then stir in chopped scallions, fresh mint, and add more lemon juice if you so desire. Eat cool or warm.

Facts about Food:

In the early twentieth century, due largely to the automobile, more and more people moved from small working farms to the cities to keep up with the industrial times of mass production. When people moved and left their farms, or sold them out to large grain, tobacco, vegetable and meat companies, we lost our organic farmers to chemical-based corporations, now the primary controllers of our food industries. At the same time, birth also became more industrialized. Everything was concentrated into smaller and smaller spaces, as well as larger systems of production. When birth and food became industrialized, we lost a great freedom. Today, we need to become more aware of how we eat; we need to grow more of our own food and be frugal with what we buy from stores.

GMOs (Genetically Modified Foods) are a huge business. Taking the genetics of food cells, largely through chemical processing, and changing them creates an entity that cannot be reproduced naturally through the seeds. These foods are missing their nutritional value and genetic properties, thus their link with our own bodies' cellular history is lost through this process. Everything is changing: seeds from most store-bought foods cannot be re-planted; they are stunted; cells are manipulated so they no longer reproduce. All this so the food industry can make more money and keep us from growing our own food.

Is this healthy? I don't feel it is! I want to be able to save seeds and grow my own food; if I have to spend extra money to do it, I will. I would rather do that than let my family and friends starve later. Seed banks, another huge business, make money from the other corporations that mess with the genetics of our food. Seeds that do not reproduce leave us at the mercy of these companies because then we have no choice but to buy seeds from them year after year. It is a huge, vicious cycle, but to be able to preserve our future for our children, we need to be made more aware of the food industry's plans to control our lives through food, and the birth industry through birth. They are "one in the same" as far as the basic things in which we would need to survive: food, water, and bearing our children. If we continue to allow such control over our basic needs, eventually, we will not have any control over our lives at all, and our children will be the ones left behind without a chance of a self-sufficient world to live in.

Solutions:

Buy as little as possible from large markets that support processed foods. Buy in bulk: seeds, grains, concentrated soaps, oils, herbs, containers etc…

Support small family businesses; choose a Ma and Pa shop to buy basic bulk foods.

Grow as much as you can at home or from a co-operative center gardening in your neighborhood or larger community. It saves time and money because everyone shares the responsibilities of the planting, growing and harvesting.

~Give birth at home, with good education and support. You will be at the forefront of a healthy trend that will become the norm after a while.

~Become more responsible for your own health care.

~Recycle by reusing plastic, paper, glass

~Limit visits to doctor and hospital for things you can remedy at home.

~Educate yourself about homemade remedies, or get some help from someone already studied in self- care who can teach you more about it.

~Seek a local alternative health care provider; get informed of the independent healers in your area.

~Look at labels on food and try to stay away from things you cannot pronounce.

~Save your seeds from organic fruits and vegetables that are not Genetically Engineered.

All these basic things can change the world drastically. If only each of us does our little part we would have a 180 % turn-around within just a few years; our industrial companies will have to change to accommodate our new needs. They will have to re-invent themselves to maintain their businesses with the quality we demand by taking better care of ourselves.

A tree may be planted at the birth of a child, each year another tree is planted for the child's future abundance, and this becomes the inheritance of the child for his food supply. Fruit trees, nut trees, and berry plants are all essential for the future of that child and his and her family.

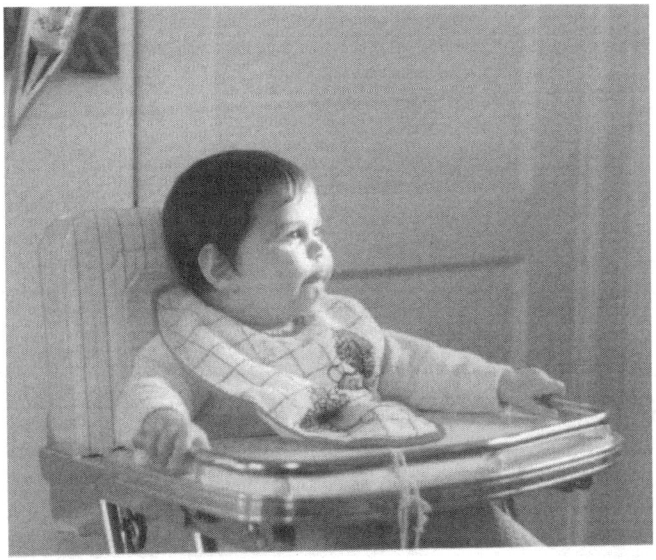

Zuki 1971

My Personal Food Story

I was bottle-fed, forced to eat solids when I was not ready, and slept in my own room, all of which created anxieties that I remedied through eating, later in life. I realized soon into my teens that I could control my body by not eating, becoming anorexic and depleting my life force. I soon had to re-learn that food is medicine.

With the conception of my son Zack, my unhealthy days of starving myself came to an end. I awoke with the deep sense that I was with child within a few days of conceiving him. I had not eaten well for some years and was depleted in protein and minerals. Then, I could not stop eating!

I ate mostly greens and started to eat meat again after 5 years of being a "so called" vegetarian. My body wanted well-cooked lean meats and greens, tuna with jalapenos on wheat bread, and occasionally juices and milk, but mostly I drank water and herbal tea.

My body recuperated fast as I was 18 years old at the time, and my young body made it through the drastic transitions of my years of poor nutrition. I gained 60 pounds, and my midwife was proud of my weight gain. I was not concerned about the weight gain myself since I started out too thin. I enjoyed my growing belly. After the birth of my son, I lost 35 pounds almost immediately. My son weighed in at 8 lbs 2 oz and was 21 inches long, not a very big baby, but a healthy one. The placenta, amniotic fluid and extra protective water weight must have been the rest of that 35 pounds I lost that first day after the birth. As well as the burning of calories in labor, as I only had a four-hour labor and went right into "active" labor from the start.

I also continued to eat well throughout my breast-feeding months minus the meat, which I became less attracted too after the birth. I finally lost all my pregnancy weight during the next year. I gained a sense of good nutrition from my pregnancy and ate well thereafter. I learned the basics of vegetarianism much more wisely after the birth of my son, and we stayed vegetarian for years.

When Zack reached an age, around seven, when he wanted meat, I let him dictate what he needed instead of imposing my own food beliefs on him. I felt, however, that it was a good idea to clue him in on where meat came from, and why it is not so good to eat certain types of meat. I explained the differences between free-range animals and caged animals. How that affected the healthiness of the meat, and the energy that would be in us if we ate an abused animal. I did not eat meat myself, but I allowed him the freedom to make an educated choice and to follow his instincts.

When I finally found out about where meat came from, at around eight years old, I was mortified and quit cold turkey! I could not understand why people would hurt animals in that way. I believe I was more upset with how the animals were being kept and treated than anything else. When my son wanted to start eating meat, I showed him the different ways that animals were kept and treated in stockades, in fields or small farms, free range or cages. He saw the difference on his own and chose to eat certain kinds of local meats and fish that we knew were humanely treated while alive. In addition, the chemicals, hormones and pesticides, which are used in factory farmed meats and fish, were an issue with me. I did not want my son ingesting poisons that would change his natural hormonal balance. I expressed this to him, and he agreed.

Listening to our children's nutritional needs starts in the beginning, just after birth, with breast-feeding, and then by following the child's lead about when they are ready for solid foods. Introduce solid foods slowly into your child's diet, be aware of what it is they need, and don't force foods upon them that seem to irritate their digestive system just because it's something you think is healthy.

Changing our own perceptions about food will also help to create an intuitive system for parent and child surrounding food behavior, and then we will have less undernourished and food-dependent people. These children whose needs have been listened too will be more conscious about food and health in their future.

Not all of us have these resources, and I want you to know you are not alone! Somehow, someway we will be changing our lifestyle to adapt to the ever-changing environment. It is good, at least, to try to lessen the affects on our children's lives by becoming more aware of the quality of our food and water.

Food Prayer

Thank you Mother for this food we eat.

Thank you for the water we drink.

Let this food and water be our blessing.

Let us be nourished by this bounty.

This food is our health.

This water is our substance.

All we eat will bring us closer to the earth and all of its creations.

Amen.

Zack a year old eating his first noodles 1990

Intervention & Complications, Go Hand in Hand

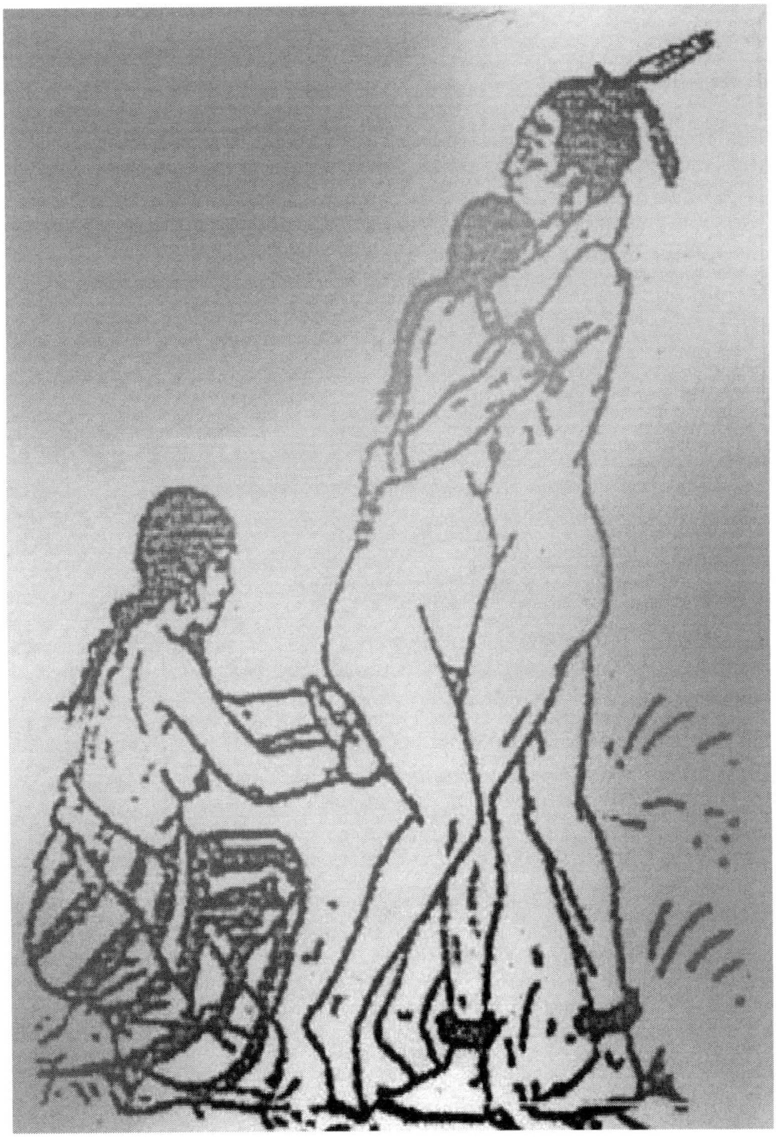

Interference and Complications

Go hand in hand

In our general birth practices today in America, many women are being subjected to unnecessary procedures, which in turn create unnecessary complications. It is strange to intrude upon pregnancy and labor, yet it is now so commonplace that it has become the normal process of birth for our culture. Unfortunately, few women are aware of the risks involved of common interference. Expectant mothers are foretold by friends or family of the array of procedures to expect. However, not many know that the subtle practice of intrusion may actually cause these problems, which most of us are seeking to avoid.

"Every doctor enjoys his intervention. That is what his skill and training are for. Some think that nature is in constant need of improvement and others that nature can't be trusted, but one kind of intervention leads to another and then the doctor is kept busy seeking remedies for his own actions."
(Franklin, quoted in Korte and Scaer 1990:109)

In our country alone, we have an abundance of money invested in birth; we are spending approximately 22 billion dollars a year on birth in this country alone. This includes investments by medical people in equipment, fetal monitoring, drugs, people to administer the drugs, needles, plastic tubing, blood tests, sheets, and the little time spent actually caring for the patient. Medical equipment companies are making a fortune on birth—the most natural process in the world!

From the turn of the twentieth century, medical birth practitioners have placed a $ sign on our lives. For many centuries before that, women gave birth with little or no payment required: maybe a few chickens, some homemade bread, or a quilt would be a fair trade for a midwife's services. Or nothing, since birth was so commonplace, that a lot of women just did it on their own, possibly with grandmothers and other siblings present, but no payment took place.

Once the medical profession placed its hands on our well-tested natural functions; it turned into a nightmare. When a woman today goes into a doctor's office because she is pregnant, it costs her not only money, but also the risk of infection when sitting on a table in a gown owned by the office. This puts her and her baby at risk for difficulties ranging from the common cold, to air-born diseases, emotional stress, and physical complications from just leaving her home to go to a place where many people are sick. She puts herself into the hands of people she does not know, and then she is poked and prodded, emotionally put down and disrespected. I have heard so many women say that their care provider was concerned and wanted to place them on medication for high blood pressure, when, in fact, they were just nervous, dehydrated from the trip or exhausted from having to drive there then wait to be seen to begin with, which caused the high blood pressure. Not to say some women do not have a true blood pressure problem, but this scenario happens too often to always be the case.

"Professionals, in general, receive their benefits and incomes in an amount proportional to the abundance of abnormality, sickness and complications" (Stewart 1997:23)

Once subjecting ourselves to the "authority" of the medical establishment, many women have said they felt un-cared for, that the doctor was in a rush, their questions were not answered, they felt inferior or just not heard. How is this good? Well, this scenario is why there are so many problems. More often than not, when a woman does not educate herself or have support in making educated decisions about her health and her birth, she is more likely to have interferences, which are as common as routine internal exams, tests that she may not need, drugs during labor and birth, fetal monitoring, and of course the unnecessary C-sections.

Ruled over by someone who barely knows us, someone who is trained in intervention and not prevention, the chances are great for complications. If we seek preventive care and educated support, we are likely to receive a growing experience, not only for the mother, but the father and the whole family. No one gets left out of the fun at a home birth, everyone is respected and listened too, questions are answered, and you usually do not even have to leave your home and expose yourself to illness and undesired travel. For instance, most of my clients receive their prenatal classes and care from me--by me going to their home and meeting with the whole family, no one feels left out unless the mother herself does not want someone there. All procedures are done at home. This is possible because they are very simple things to do at home, even mom can do most of them herself, but if further assessment is needed, she can go to a lab or another care provider. However, this is extremely rare, since all women are screened for pathology from the beginning, and many common issues can be resolved in the home through nutritional and herbal care. There is no need for internal exams, and no one has to do anything they do not want to do. Even in the hospital, you do not have to do what they want, if a test is asked for and the patient does not want it all she has to do is be brave enough to say "No."

Waivers are there, they just do not want to tell you about them because they make money off every test and procedure they do. Believe it or not, they are trained to do this type of coercion in medical school; it is a common practice to teach students how to get patients into "routine," expensive testing early on so they feel trapped in continuing with that particular care provider. There is less confusion for the doctor because he has everyone doing the same thing. Like on a conveyer belt, you're in & you're out, you had all your shots and who's next! It is horrible, but true. There are some genuine doctors out there who really do care, but most of them do not have time to see us as an individual. That is why most people all over the world prefer midwives. Women know they are going to be treated like individuals and will be cared for with respect. We all want our newborn babies to be treated with dignity and love and not be tossed around like they are property or some experiment.

These are words not only from myself, but from clients and others I have spoken with over the years, who have had the experience of feeling like they were the property of a hospital, or that they were disregarded as just another patient and not a person, but you already knew that.

"A labor induced by the doctor can end up a Cesarean delivery because a baby that's not ready to be born will naturally show more distress on fetal monitors, distress at being summoned prematurely."

~From "Confessions of a Medical Heretic" (1979:54), by Robert S. Mendelsohn M.D.

To minimize risk of complications during pregnancy and childbirth, seek education, get informed of your options, do your own care and birth, find a midwife if you feel your not ready to take it all on yourself, or Doula, to have good support before entering into the unknown environments of any establishment that is not your own.

The chain reactions of Interventions

(Hospital or clinical environments)

Leaving your home

Being exposed to sick people

Compromising your labor by driving in a car

Entering into a place where there are strangers

Bright lights

Other women's voices in labor

Putting on a gown with the hospitals name on it making you their property

Having internal exams

Possibly not being allowed to eat because supposedly they are concerned about you choking on your own vomit (Lack of nutrition causes a shift in energy resources, and other interventions "play out" because you are tired and hungry.)

Getting poked with needles

Having a fetal monitor strapped to your belly so you cannot move

Having strangers come in and out

Feeling nervous from all the chaos

Your "fight or flight" reaction kicks in

You become instinctually protective, which slows labor down

The doctor decides to put you on Pitocin (a synthetic Oxytocin to increase contractions), because your labor slowed or stopped from the above interventions.

You're in more pain now and want an Epidural (which contains narcotic drugs to numb you and baby)

Now you are numb, cannot feel contractions or when you need to urinate, so a catheter is put into your urethra to drain urine and leave you doubly immobile

Labor is likely to slow down or even stop

Your body is not responding to natural labor because it has become unnatural

The Doctor is worried because the baby's heart rate is going too slow or too fast because the drugs and interventions have caused distress in your baby

Now all they can do is perform a C-section

This is "saving" you and your baby--from the symptoms they caused themselves and that could have been prevented to begin with. If you educate yourself and find the support you need, you will never have to live out this scenario. Look at the fine print about any drugs and procedural risks before you enter into the hospital.

In some cases when a woman is ill, has a disease, uses drugs, alcohol, smokes, or is just not taking good care of herself, the hospital is useful. However, even in some so-called "high risk" women, home tends to be the safer place in which to birth a baby. You, as a "consumer" of a hospital or clinic (this means birth centers too!), need to be open and knowledgeable about all options in health care. Not all situations can be treated the same way because each of us is unique and this should be recognized.

Do not wait until you are in labor to read the consent forms. This is the time they usually get you to sign numerous releases because you are under pressure, in an emotional situation, and may not take the time to read it fully. It is blind faith signing your life, and baby's life, away. On any release form in the hospital, you will read what the drug or procedure do to you and the risks involved for you and baby, short and long-term risks. Lifetime damage is also a risk of any drug or procedure done, especially during birth. Read carefully and do not sign until you can go over it with your care provider to be sure it is what you really want to do.

Intuition: Your Most Powerful Birthing Tool

By: Erika Peterson Bartlog

One of the most common questions women who are planning an unassisted or home birth ask is, "But how will I know if something is wrong?" Our Western mind immediately leaps to the idea that if we just have enough information or training, we will be safe. The real answer is both simpler and deeper: ***Intuition!***

Unfortunately, for most of us, culture has long since separated us from this deeply valuable sense. We have been trained to believe that only doctors, instruments, and tests can decipher what is happening in our bodies. Because we believe that doctors and medicine exist to "help" us, we assume that if they discount our intuition, it is because our intuition is not helpful. However, like most human endeavors, the practice of medicine is complicated by competing agendas. In America today, hospitals exist to make profit. Doctors may be so motivated by the desire to "save" patients and the psychological thrill they get from wielding that power that they see illness where none exists. Lawyers and administrators seek to limit liability; in a medicine-worshipping culture, this means action is always more defensible than inaction. Your intuition will not make anyone money, grant anyone adoration or power, nor assure someone else of your safety. But your intuition can save yourself, your baby, and your family from trauma, interference, injury, and even death.

What is intuition? Intuition is a deep, animal sense that guides the actions of your body. Intuition does not care about propriety, politesse, or decorum. Its commands are quiet, but imperative. It is ignored at peril. Intuition is all about YOU: it tells you what your body and spirit need, heedless of the agendas of others. When you make a decision based on intuition, you feel calm inside. It feels as if the decision has resolved - the tension you are feeling and you can say to yourself confidently, "Yes, this is what I need to do."

It is easy to confuse intuition and fear. Fear also manifests as a "voice," but of a very different kind. Fear yells. Fear increases the chaos in your mind. Fear throws out a hundred options -intuition is what helps you choose that one correct path. If you are actively freaking out then you probably aren't working on intuition. Regardless of what you've seen on

TV, even a true medical "emergency" rarely unfolds in minutes, so if fear has gripped you, stop for 5 or 10 minutes. Sing a song. Relax into your body. Laugh. Your body is not alien to you - your mind has contact with every cell at every moment. Your intuition is the way your brain telegraphs your body's needs to your conscious mind. When it speaks, it will say something simple like "go," or "get out of this chair," or "squat." Unlike intuition, fear is not a body instinct. Fear is an instinct of social animals that protects them from becoming outcasts-- we fear punishment, banishment, and embarrassment. Give these fears no place in your birthing mindset! Birth happens at an even deeper level of our animal consciousness. Birth involves only a female body and her baby. Moving society out of the way lets intuition guide your body to the actions you must take to let the physical event of birth take place.

Getting in touch with your body intuition is about stripping away the layer of logical thought and social expectations and dealing with just your body and your inner self. If this isn't something you're used to doing in your life, start practicing now: every day, sit quietly and listen to, visualize, or feel your body and your baby; ask them questions and listen for the answers; picture your insides and scan for things that don't look right; inhabit your body fully and make an inventory of how each part feels. If something is troubling you, ask yourself first - if you do not know if something is wrong, there is no way anyone else can either. If you are told that something is wrong, ask yourself. "If you don't feel wrong, chances are nothing is wrong." Trust that your mind will never let you ignore illness or danger.

"Does acting only on intuition mean there's no chance you'll transfer?" Of course not, but it means that if you do, you'll be in a better position to control the outcome of your situation and more accepting of the choices you make.

Before my first daughter's birth, I did **all** *the research. "Every time I asked my midwife about a topic, it turned out I already knew more about it than he did!" (yes, he!). However, I ended up birthing in a hospital anyway. Nonetheless, I feel my intuition guided me to the best birth I was capable of having at the time. I fired my midwife at eight months and planned to birth unassisted. Five days before my birth, my water broke. After three days, I went to the hospital but it turned out I'd only had a leak. Though I was contracting every 2-20 minutes for that entire time, I was only 4 cm dilated and they sent me home. My contractions continued apace. Two days later, my water broke again for real. As I watched an ice storm moving in on the Doppler radar, my whole being said, "Go." When I got to the hospital, I ended up accepting Pitocin, IV antibiotics, Demerol, and finally an epidural, but I delivered my posterior daughter vaginally in three easy pushes. Doesn't sound like a triumph of intuition, does it? It certainly wasn't what I had wanted, but, in retrospect, it was what needed to happen. Had I not fired my midwife I would have been sectioned days earlier for "failure to progress." After the fact, I could clearly see that my intuition sent me to the hospital because that was the only way it could figure out to force me to lay down and rest. I was extremely agitated and had read too many things about walking during labor, bouncing on balls, etcetera, and etcetera to "get things going." I had not slept more than 20 minutes straight in five days. Had I been listening to my intuition all along, I might have understood that rest was all I needed. Intuition has nothing to do with following what you "want" or what you "should" - it is all about doing what "must" be done.*

My second pregnancy and birth were entirely unassisted and blissfully intuitive. The morning of the birth, I had an irresistible urge to go grocery shopping. Normally, I'd do this by myself, but I insisted my husband come along. We had two stops to make, and my contractions started while we were at the first store. By the time we were leaving the second store, about two and a half hours later, I knew why I'd brought him along - I needed him to drive home! When I got home, I was ravenous - I ate two bacon, lettuce, and tomato sandwiches, a chocolate donut, and a big glass of milk. Try that in the hospital or even with a midwife! When I threw up an hour and a half later I thought, -Oh, this can't be transition, these contractions just feel like menstrual cramps." (Nothing like Pitocin!) A few minutes later, I took off all my clothes, and half an hour later, I got down on all fours, pushed through two contractions, then got up on my knees to catch my baby as her body came through on the third contraction. I thought nothing of any of these actions. I simply did what felt like the only thing to do. It was simple and easy (though I'm not going to say it didn't hurt!).

It is tempting to think that knowledge will save the day. It is certainly a lot easier to load up on facts, figures, and techniques than to revamp your entire relationship with your body, but birth is not about information. It's about your body, and intuition is how your body communicates with your conscious self. Bone up on it now, and it will serve you not only during your birth, but also in your personal life and as a parent."

A Supportive Home Birth Experience

If you have a midwife, you should call her when labor begins so she can get ready and prepare herself to come when you need her. Midwife attended births may have some restrictions depending on each individual midwife and how she works. Ultimately you are the boss, still, even in a midwife/client relationship.

A Home Birth With a Midwife May Look Like This:

You will receive kind, loving and respectful prenatal care and options regarding your needs and wishes for your birth.

With a midwife, you will have another woman to support you who knows how it feels to give birth (assuming the midwife herself has had a child).

When you feel like sleeping, you can sleep.

When you want to eat, you can eat.

You are free to walk, take a bath, rest, listen to music and dance.

You can be at peace with your baby and birth.

No internal exams are required. It depends on the midwife, but remember, you are always in charge!

No drugs are forced on you, but are there if needed.

Herbs and homeopathy are provided.

Any position you want to be in, you can.

There are no strangers coming in and out.

You control the environment.

Your partner can help you deliver the baby if you desire.

Mom and baby peacefully give birth with love surrounding them.

You can be as loud as you want.

If you want to be totally alone, it is your choice, and no one can tell you otherwise.

Most midwives practice under rules and regulations. However, if you have an intimate relationship with your midwife then you will be able to communicate and discuss anything that may arise instead of being told you have to abide by those rules and regulations. Sometimes she will bend time limits and do whatever she feels is within safe boundaries, to make sure you can still have your desired birth without being another product of rules set by an authority that does not know your situation or you! If there is trust in the midwife/client relationship then all work together to make a healthy outcome for everyone concerned.

Parent Assisted Birth- Also Called *Unassisted Childbirth and Free Birth*

Doing your own pre-natal care and birth is less hassle. No one is there to distract you, no appointments to make, no apprentices to deal with, no one else's schedules to live up too, and no state rules and regulations to tell you what to do. Maybe you can have a friend or family member help with cleaning and food preparations afterwards. Parents can do their own care as they have done throughout history without a "professional" instilling their rules or personal beliefs on you. You can listen to your inner voice more clearly without distractions. It may be the most fulfilling experience of any of your birthing choices.

What a Parent Led pregnancy and birth may look like:

You do your own prenatal care by reading and researching how to do it. Largely through nutrition, affirmations, and individual needs preparation. This is called "Unassisted Pregnancy" or UP.

You do not have to schedule or pay anyone for your care. Thus your child is literally Born Free!

You do your own inner work on yourself to boost your confidence.

You have your own desires and dreams fulfilled.

You can labor in your own time without anyone telling you that you are too slow or that you are not laboring as the books say you should.

You can move through your birth with peace and privacy in your own way.

You do not need to worry about others watching you, or have someone charting, what you are doing.

You can listen to your intuition without being distracted.

You and your partner can make love and enjoy the birth process without intruders.

You do not have to talk to anyone and be interrupted.

You are the boss of your body and your birth!

Doing our own births may be challenging. Society and family may ridicule it and not be supportive, and it can be difficult to find positive feedback from others. Nevertheless, if the birthing parents are taking responsibility for their own health-care and gets education, very rarely will they need outside interference. From those I have supported to do their own births, I have seen great strength gained, inner wisdom and self-esteem, which all are invaluable to becoming positive role models for our children.

Remember, listening to your instincts also means asking someone for support who knows about pregnancy and birth if that is what you feel you need. To me, parent assisted childbirth does not necessarily mean NO HELP! It just means that you are your own caregiver and birth attendant, so do not let your ego get in the way of having a safe journey. If needed, find someone supportive of your choice and willing to be there for you in the shadows. You will then have a back-up plan and not have to run to the emergency room and be interrogated for something you could have done at home with some support and knowledge of what to do. At home, it is important to realize that you are still in charge, even if you have the best midwife in the world; you are still boss and no one else. Trust should be established with midwives before the birth so that when you're in labor you can be free enough to say and ask for anything you need. Even if that means asking her to step out for a while and take a walk!!!

"There is no magic number of hours beyond which labor should not continue ... "

~Dr. Emanuel A. Friedman (developer of the "Friedman Curve")

The *"Friedman Curve"* is a graph of statistical "averages" for the length of labor. This study was probably done in a clinical environment, but Dr. Friedman even admits it is not the complete answer. Only intuition on the part of the patient and her caregiver can determine when a labor needs attention. Unfortunately, women are lied to in the birth industry; they are told that birth is inherently dangerous and that doctors are the only ones allowed, or know how, to deliver babies. In not so many words, our medical system has brain washed women and their families in the past decades into thinking we are not capable of doing what our Creator created us to do.

Through years of propaganda and coercion, women have now become afraid of their bodies and birth, but this will change. Recently, in the last 30 years or so, women have been standing up and demanding what is right for themselves and their families; they have studied and researched what they can do, and are doing it! Now women are realizing that birth is not just an isolated event. We are imprinting onto our children the way we think and feel, and if we have better birth experiences then we can change the world for the future of our children's lives and allow a better way of living, in consciousness and freedom.

If we take responsibility for our education and care, seek better care and demand it, then in future births, we will get it. It is US who need to change, then the system will change with us, so be strong and speak out; this is your body, your baby and your birth, not anyone else's!

Medical establishments think that we are not interested in knowledge concerning our bodily functions, so they assume the responsibility of pregnancy and birth because of their belief that our families, and we do not have any desire to learn or take responsibility for ourselves. We need to learn how to take on our own health care. If we start taking that responsibility then we will get far in changing the quality of care we receive when seeking it from the medical establishment. It is better to know what we are talking about when going in to see a doctor or midwife for care than not knowing, and placing our trust in them to do it for us. Once they see that we are knowledgeable, they will not put us through unnecessary procedures; therefore, we will not be faced with as many interventions as we would when going into the situation without knowledge. It's when we go in and let them take over and make our decisions for us, that we lose our rights and interference becomes much more probable.

Doctors just do what they are taught to do in school, which is to manage the human body and take control over what happens to that body. In birth, it is the same; doctors take authority over birth because we are not taking it ourselves. Until we take care of our own health and births, doctors will manage our system of care without needing our approval.

I have spoken to doctors and midwives who did indeed express their desire for women, and people in general, to start taking better care of themselves and get more education. Then their job would not be as complicated, and there would not be so many demands on them to take over and make choices they know are not the best choices to make.

Preventive measures are essential, and education is needed to do this. It is never too late to begin a healthy outlook. It is better to start earlier rather than later; however, and good prenatal care can affect your child's health for his/her entire life. So begin as soon as you can. Start Now!

If you want to avoid routine procedures that take place in hospitals, then don't go to a hospital. If you want to avoid any complications from other's interference, do not let others interfere in your birth. It all sounds so simple, and it is. Just let nature lead, and you follow, then your outcomes may be remarkably more satisfying than if you submitted to the professionals to expose and impose their great technology on you and your baby. It is a matter of risk. We take for granted the power of our inner wisdom and forget that it is actually doing what it needs to do in whatever situation; out of fear, we feel that we need someone else to manage our births for us. So first, to prevent any complications, re-think reality and create a space where you will prevent yourself from thinking and feeling negatively.

Do your homework! Affirmations, visualizations and alternative modalities are the key in re-programming a better birth experience inwardly and outwardly. This is prevention, and it creates the foundation of a healthy lifestyle. It is SIMPLICITY itself.

VBAC: (Vaginal Birth after Cesarean)

The saying "Once a Cesarean always a Cesarean," has created a multitude of difficulties in subsequent births for mothers who have had a previous C-section. The more C-sections a woman has, the risk of death becomes even greater than before. Not only does the uterus suffer after being cut open, but also the drugs used during this type of operation remains in a woman's body for many years to come. This makes her recovery harder each time she delivers this way.

During a Cesarean delivery not only does the mother herself acquire short and long-term affects from the drugs and incisions, the baby does also.

In America, Cesarean sections are done much too often to be technically necessary. Almost one out of every 3 women is being operated on to deliver their babies. The "repeat" C-section rate is almost 98%. Doctors are telling women that the myth of "Once a Cesarean always a Cesarean" is truth, when studies show that it is not. More then 88% of women with previous C-sections can deliver naturally without any difficulties. Nutrition, exercise and working on past issues that have to do with the previous C-section can undoubtedly prevent many complications during a VBAC delivery. The more C-sections a woman has, the more she and her baby are at risk for operative complications due to scar tissue, drugs used for the operation itself, and also blood clots which are caused by the previous C-section moving into the mother's heart and lungs causing severe damage or death.

The female body is an amazing vehicle. A natural birth is extremely healing for women who choose to have a VBAC. I have witnessed many women birthing at home who were previous C-section victims, the reasons for their C-sections were not valid to them. The excuses given by their doctors were that the woman herself could not give birth to their baby because of Cephalic Pelvic Disproportion(CPD), dates being off, fetal distress that was caused by intervention to begin with, and just not convenient for the doctor, labeling them FTP which means, failure to progress or "Failure to be Patient" in some circles. After experiencing a natural birth, many women report that they finally felt like a whole woman.

The C-section had not only damaged their bodies but also made them feel inadequate as a woman and a mother. Plus, other areas of their lives that they thought had been stable, previous to their operation, had fallen apart. After a VBAC, women have expressed a healing of their minds and bodies, which permeated all aspects of their lives.

My HBAC Water Birth of Gemma Lourdes Nagel

By Patti Caparella Nagel

Born December 22, 2006

8 lbs. 6 oz. 21" long

My quest for a natural birth at home began when I learned I was pregnant with my first baby, Maya, nearly two years before Gemma's birth. I enlisted the help of a well-reputed midwife and naively expected everything to progress perfectly. Because I had a blissful and healthy pregnancy, I expected labor and delivery to be the same. I labored at home for nearly 24 hours and when I got to the point of thinking about giving up as all laboring mothers do, no one really encouraged me to go on, that I could do it and that it probably wouldn't be much longer. I felt there were many other failures and scenarios that could have been handled very differently, with most likely an entirely different, more positive outcome. Later, I realized I was in the midst of transition when we transported to the hospital which resulted in a cesarean section for failure to progress and CPD. I immediately felt robbed and cheated of my birthright as a young, healthy woman and further grieved for the loss of a gentle, natural birth for my baby daughter. Soon after Maya's birth, I began researching VBAC and knew the next time I conceived, we would pursue a vaginal birth.

Early May 2006, I learned I was pregnant for the second time. I was excited and touched that another beautiful soul had chosen me and my husband for her parents. I immediately settled into the pregnancy and started researching options for VBAC. Because of where I live in the rural mountains of Colorado and the lack of an urban trauma hospital with all of its emergent amenities, no hospitals will perform VBACs outside of Denver or Colorado Springs. If I were serious about this, I would have to travel to Colorado Springs or Denver to have my baby. At that time, a home birth VBAC was out of the question. Too risky, I had thought. Since my mother-in-law lives in Colorado Springs, I settled on that location and found an obstetrical practice that I thought would work. I attended four monthly appointments there before I got the distinct impression that should I stay committed to these doctors and midwives, I would end up with another cesarean section. During all this time I had been reading many, many books about VBAC and information online from sources such as ICAN and many other helpful websites. I was quickly learning that a home birth VBAC poses little risk to a healthy mother and her baby. Added to that information, a friend called me to tell me excitedly that her good friend had just had a VBAC home birth with a wonderful midwife named Zuki and said that it was the most wonderful experience of her life. I approached cautiously but was intrigued at the possibility.

Soon after, I called Zuki and we talked on the phone for nearly an hour. It was late August and I knew my EDD was quickly approaching and that I had better make a decision. Over the phone, talking with Zuki, I immediately felt a strong connection with her and we made plans to soon meet. At our first meeting, I was surprised at how connected I felt with her. I wasn't meeting a stranger, someone I had never met before; it was like reuniting with a long, lost friend. Not long after, I, with my husband's blessings and agreement, made the decision to birth at home. I had read so much statistical and factual information that I felt at ease with the potential risk involved – less than one percent of uterine rupture. Plus, all the signs I was receiving from the universe told me to move forward on this path. Most of all, I listened to my heart and the baby growing inside me.

With my knowledge of mind-body connection and with Zuki's many helpful suggestions, I immersed myself in as many positive self-healing and transformational techniques as I could think of. I wrote and read daily affirmations, listened to visualization/meditation CDs, chanted, studied hypnobirthing, saw a counselor to resolve my past birth issues, talked to my mother about my own birth, watched enlightening and empowering birth videos, contacted other VBAC moms, chanted and reaffirmed that this was indeed mine and my baby's path to birth. We would do it at home and have a gentle, peaceful birth free from the drama and trauma of hospital birth.

My very first prenatal appointment at the doctor's office in early June showed an EDD of December 13; however, judging from my last menstrual period it was December 24. The doctors used the earlier due date which never felt right to me. I knew my body better than they did. And I trusted myself more than I trusted them.

For many weeks prior to the birth, I had been having fairly strong Braxton Hicks contractions preparing my uterus. It was hard to judge if they were getting any stronger or more intense because it was all happening so gradually. On the day of December 21st, Zuki had scheduled a prenatal appointment with me and decided she would hang out a few hours to visit. After the check-up, we chatted and had a nice visit together and I remember joking about it being winter solstice and new moon, a powerful time energetically that might send me into labor. She left to start her car and soon came back to the house saying it was dead and she needed a jump. We tried jumping it a few times with no success. And as someone who listens to the answers the universe puts forth I said to Zuki, "Hmmm, maybe this is a sign you should stay."

Although my husband Brian was able to jump start Zuki's car immediately after arriving home, we had already decided she should stay. We all settled in and had a nice dinner together, watched a movie and went to bed early. Little by little, I felt my surges intensifying, becoming a little stronger and a little more frequent. I lay down to rest for the evening and realized that when I couldn't sleep I was actually in labor. It was around midnight and baby and I were on our way. After checking in with

Zuki, she encouraged me to try to sleep and get as much rest as possible. I reluctantly headed upstairs to bed again and two and a half hours managed to pass by but I never actually slept.

Around 2:30 am, I felt my surges intensifying even more greatly. Brian got up with me as I went down to wake Zuki. Within minutes everyone was up and doing chores preparing for labor and birth. I labored on hands and knees and used the birth ball to ease the sensations while Brian and Zuki made preparations for the day. In between their chores they attended to my needs, feeding me, giving me drink, massaging my lower back, squeezing my hips, providing support of all kinds. The first few hours passed rather quickly. I remember it being around 6 am and Brian calling my good friend, Kim to come over and watch Maya. At that point I was laboring in the birth pool which helped tremendously in easing the intensity of the surges: rolling around in the pool from hands and knees to squatting and spiraling to floating on my back, all the while Brian doing light touch massage, caressing my back and squeezing my hips. The pain relief of warm water combined with the loving touch of my husband was magnificent.

Kim's presence at our birth was yet another great sign of being in rhythm with the universe and a great lesson in trust and being in the flow. We were planning on Kim's presence at our birth provided I went into labor before December 21 when she was scheduled to fly home to Illinois for Christmas. But as the universe would have it, a major snowstorm hit Denver and grounded all flights for a few days. Her flight was rescheduled for Sunday, December 24, thus allowing her presence at our birth as originally planned. We couldn't have planned it any better and it was such a blessing to see it unfold the way that it did.

I remember thinking that I was progressing really well towards full dilation. Zuki checked me a few times and each time, my cervix had dilated further and further giving me encouragement especially when I had gotten past the point where I had been delayed in my first labor. It was not long before she said I was nearly fully dilated but there was one last little bit of cervix left. The baby's head was inching downward and getting closer and closer. I don't know how many hours had actually passed from the first time she said that to the last. It seemed like eternity. Throughout the day, I lost track of time and tried to not be cognizant of it. I learned during my first labor that I depended on the clock too much and that made me discouraged contributing to the final outcome. This time I would ignore the clock no matter how long it seemed. I changed positions and rooms frequently. I went to the shower where Zuki and Brian flooded my back with warm water. I leaned on the birth ball. I sat on the toilet. I hung on Brian. I squatted endlessly with Brian supporting my full body weight from behind. He was working just as hard as I was -- almost! I tried pushing and resting in a semi-reclined position, with legs up in the air. From there, moving to a side-lying position while Zuki tried to hold the last bit of cervix open while I pushed the baby downward with each surge. I was spent, sore, swollen and exhausted and a few times expressed concern over how much more I could take. This time, however, everyone supported me. "I'm not giving up on you," Zuki said. "You're doing it. You're having your baby!" Kim said. "We're not going anywhere," Brian said. That is what I needed to hear.

Brian and I went to the bathroom one final time. Once again, I sat on the toilet, squatted during the surges all the while moaning and singing my birth song. Kim came to the bathroom and announced that she and Zuki had changed the scene in the living room a little. Pillows were positioned against the couch for me to lean on. More space was made as furniture was moved out of the way, the lavender candle at my birth altar was lit and the lights were dim as darkness was just setting in on this first day of winter. The only lights I remember were the Christmas tree lights giving a warm, comforting glow to the room. This time, I settled against the couch with Kim behind me and Brian in front of me ready to catch the baby. With each surge, I stood supported in a squat by Kim. Everyone was encouraging me, the baby's head was completely visible and with a mirror I could see it myself. Brian led my hand down to feel the baby's head and I knew we were almost there. Brian and Kim chanted Nam-myoho-renge-kyo loudly and fervently as they had through much of my labor. Kim chanted directly in my ear and that gave me strength to continue as I summoned up great growls, groans and moans pushing the baby downward with each surge.

Around this time, Zuki put me on O2 as the baby's heart tones were slowing. It was not until later that I learned the reason why. Zuki never let on her concerns, thus not alarming me at all. The oxygen was great and allowed me to breathe deep, calm down and rest between surges. Apparently, it was just what my baby needed, too.

As the baby was crowning, we heard Maya's cries coming from upstairs where she was waking from a nap. Kim yelled up to her coaxing her to come downstairs but ended up running upstairs to get her just in time to see her baby sister born.

Tired of squatting, and feeling like my legs were going to give out, I expressed my desire to head for the pool. "Sure, if you can waddle over there, more power to you," Zuki said. With support on each side of me, I waddled to the pool and needed assistance in getting each leg over the side. With the baby crowning and birth imminent, it felt like I was holding a large watermelon between my legs as I tried to maneuver myself into the pool. No easy feat but once I was in there, I knew my baby would be born soon. With each guttural groan, my baby's head moved further down. I could feel her fuzzy, soft hair and her head halfway outside of me. With a couple more pushes, she was born into the water. Before I could reach down and bring her up, Zuki unwrapped the cord from its entanglement around her body – thus the reason the pushing phase took so long. Zuki said my body knew to take it nice and slow. I brought my baby up, all covered in vernix and just starting to pink up. I sucked the mucous out of her nose and mouth and blew a bit of air into her mouth – the kiss of life. She never really cried like many babies born in the hospital. I've learned that is common with gentle birth babies – very calm and very aware. She was absolutely beautiful and so aware, I felt like I was looking into the eyes of a wise, old being. My husband and I wept with joy; we had done it – a natural, vaginal waterbirth at home and so blessed we were to have this beautiful baby now with us. My dream had come true for a safe, gentle, peaceful birth.

Not long after the baby was born, I was helped to move to a nearby chair to wait for the placenta to be born. Over an hour later, with one or two surges I felt it slide out of me. Immediately, Zuki tore off a couple small pieces and had me eat them as it would prevent any potential hemorrhage – the best preventive medicine. After Zuki cleaned me up, I soon settled down to a wonderful night of rest with my new precious baby safely in my arms.

I feel so fortunate and blessed to have met Zuki and to have enlisted her help with a home birth. I am quite certain, had I not followed this path with her, I would have ended up with another unnecessary cesarean. The connection I initially had with Zuki has deepened greatly and has extended from me to my family. Zuki has quickly become a part of our family and is like a sister to me and my husband and an aunt to Maya and Gemma. We are forever grateful and blessed to have her in our lives and I look forward to a lifelong relationship.

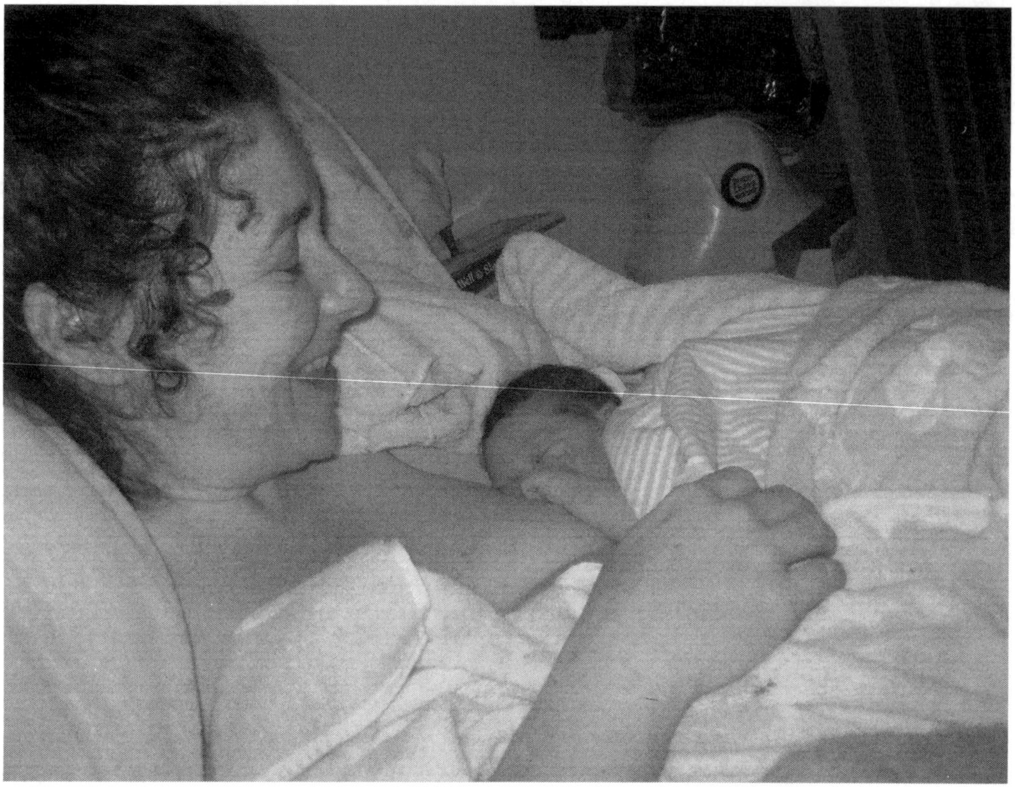

Patti with baby Gemma Lourdes Nagel, born at home in water 2006!

Realization - About Others and Ourselves

Self-realization is not an easy road, however it is fulfilling. When we start to realize that we have been tricked and manipulated into giving our babies and our bodies to science all these years, how is it going to feel? Well, humiliation is one feeling; denial is another. Denial is certainly the easiest, and it is common to hear: "Oh, doctors aren't so bad," or "They only did what they had to do" or "My baby would not have made it" or "I would have died!"

We as women certainly do have a way of making others, and ourselves, feel better in the worst of situations. We genuinely want to trust everyone; we want to believe that everyone does the right things for the right reasons and that no one would ever want to intentionally be of harm to us. Well, some truth is hard to swallow, so all we can do is learn from our mistakes the best we can.

From a mother who had three inductions before her due date...

"The doctors always said I could not give birth vaginally to a baby more than 7 lbs, so they always induced me a few weeks before my due dates. My babies were good size babies (7lbs, 8lbs, 8lbs,3oz before the due date). Then after having three more kids at home (9lbs, 10 lbs, 9 3/4 lbs) with no complications and at term!, I realized I was manipulated into my previous inductions and wanted to help other women by warning them of that sort of thing." ~Mother of six

This mom felt "ripped off." She had been fooled by her doctor, and her right to experience birth naturally had been taken away. She now knows birth is a healthy and normal event and not something that needs to be managed. She learned from her mistake. That is all any of us can and need to do.

If we, as women, realize that it has been too long since we were treated as humans and not some birth "machine," then we will begin to take back our birthrights. Now is the time to do it. Action and education will take us far down the road toward better births in our future.

Women are wonderful; we are such caring, open and loving people, we would not want to think that anyone in the health profession wants to harm us, but sometimes they do. We need to start to open our eyes, listen to our hearts and forgive ourselves for the past, then move forward. Emotionally, we need to heal ourselves. It is a long journey, but well worth every struggle at every turn.

The Misogynist

From Taber's cyclopedia medical dictionary: Misogynist:

"One who hates women"

In psychology class I realized that people who go into a field where they act as an authority figure, in not all of course, but many of the cases, have psychological dependencies. It is an unhealthy relationship wherein they are co-dependant on the people who look up to them for their wisdom and advice. This varies from person to person, and yes, there are a few that are sincere, are really in their heart and want to help people. Nevertheless, just think of it, you would have to be nuts if you really enjoyed cutting someone open, or causing pain in some way by doing procedures. Wouldn't it be something the professional would have to enjoy, on some level?

It is a fact that most health-care people, who have chosen to inject, cut others open, assist in operations or caring for people in the hospital, enjoy their jobs. Sticking catheters in a woman in labor and taking blood, causing unnecessary pain to vulnerable mothers and babies is, unfortunately, what they are taught to do. They feel that they are only doing they're job, but on some level they must enjoy being in control and having authority over someone else's life.

"My impression of gynecologists, as a woman going to one in my teen-age years and early twenties, and later my encounter with them in medical school, is that there were an awful lot of gynecologists who were misogynists, who seemed to have chosen that field as a way to act out their dislike for women. I believe that is true. It's a sweeping generalization, but that was my experience." ~ (quoted in Mitford 1992:103)

Don't go blind from those bright white coats or florescent lights!

When I was doing my internship at a midwifery clinic, I noticed, for the first time, such behavior coming from some midwives; it astonished, scared, shocked and saddened me. I questioned some of them, now-and-then, about things I saw that were, to me, obviously wrong yet were taken for granted by others who just wanted to do their work and get out of there. My mind would not ignore such behavior, so I challenged them. Of course, challenging the head of an intern clinic where I was supposed to be getting training was sort of a risky thing to do. I needed to be true to myself, so I did it anyway. I was reprimanded, but I am glad I did it. Like I said, this road of healing and self-realization is hard, but consciousness is clear.

We are trained, at such a young age, to accept blindly things that are not right that when we become adults we continue to accept these same things even though they do not benefit us. We need to wake up from our conditioning and take back our power of choice.

So far, in all my years of study and practice, nothing pains me more than seeing a woman not trust in herself. You do not have to trust me, or anyone, but trust in yourself. "Know thy self" is the first passage to enlightenment; it is a natural gift from our Creator to utilize our highest potential.

Give yourself a chance to understand and heal, to nourish your goodness and become one with ALL. You are connected to every one and every thing; that is why you exist. You have the understanding of every living being in every cell in your body, and that is because you are the creator, you are made in his/her image, so you are all powerful. You make the decision to change or follow; you are your own leader.

Do not allow any religious and societal myths about childbirth to handicap you or keep you in fear. Supposedly, we sinned from the beginning of time. Eve was put on earth to rob men of their fruit? Now come on, I know as women we have been through it all, but that is just too ridiculous for me to swallow. Who is having the babies? Not men, but they are co-creators of them and thus just as responsible for shaking the tree as we are.

Let the past be in the past and move on into a future of gracefulness. As a society, we are responsible for each other; we are the creators of our own realities. Birth is a healing passage that we all can benefit from and pass onto our children to improve their lives. Our future can be better than any other time before us.

"All is Possible Within You"

We have been programmed with information from our families, media and society. Our fears come from this emotional programming. We only need to recognize this and ask ourselves is it "the truth," or is it someone else's perception? "Is this really my own reality? Or is this media and society creeping into my subconscious mind?" We need to discern our own reality and see it apart from other's influences on us.

Sometimes, coming to terms with what is really happening is not easy. It puts pressure on us to learn from our mistakes and our conditioning and accept our humanness. Then we will be able to change our perceptions and our outlook on life.

Judgments come from our conditioning. They come from other people's perceptions about how someone else looks, dresses, wears their hair and how they "seem" to be. The first sign of growth and independence is when you realize that your perception of reality is being influenced by your family, church, friends, media, school, and all your social imprints.

When this happens, it can be scary. You may feel cheated or lied to, sad, angry, and even a little depressed because you have believed in these false images for so long. To heal, it will take some patience and self-forgiveness on your part. Our "true" selves are somewhere in there, sometimes just below the surface, and other times deeper. As we learn how to open our minds, hearts and spirits, we will be able to recognize our own truth much more easily and be able to discern what "our truth" is verses our subliminal imprinting, conditioning or judgments. We are all able to change our perception of reality and lift it to a higher level. We are created to use this potential.

Re-routing the receptors in our brain can be done, once we realize it is possible. Our bodies feel what we think and respond to our thoughts. The old negative programs will not be able to survive with the movement of positive energy filling the space in our brains cells. This is actually very scientific stuff, but I am not a scientist, so in my own words this is how I see the mind working and ridding itself of old perceptions or patterns, without electric shock treatments, or drugs to suppress emotions.

Creating a new reality is a practice. It takes time, persistence and patience to build this practice. In our daily lives, we tend to get fixed on what we do to merely survive. When we do this inner work, we are not fixed in survivor mode but in a bigger picture mode.

What can I do for the betterment of this planet? When I leave my home, what can I do to benefit myself, my family, and another being?

Everything we do can make a positive impact on everything else in our daily lives. We can give hope with just a smile; we can help others, friend or stranger, by merely listening when they need to talk; we can ask, "What can I do?" when we hear of someone in need. We can change someone's life in an instant with a look, a nod, a hug or a handshake. It all depends on us to realize the greatness we can create. We are coming out of the "ME" generation. And even the "ME" generation (which is my generation) is realizing that their lives have been sugarcoated and superficial. They, too, are beginning to wake up and become more conscious. It is just a matter of time for all of us to be re-awakened, and it will happen, but for it to happen in harmony--and not in conflict--we need to be open to the change.

Preparing ourselves through our birth practices, we become stronger in mind and body. This cultivates in us a true essence of self, which arises from the beginning of all life. Once we re-awaken to our greatest potential, then we will be able to share this abundance of knowledge and wisdom with all others.

Prenatal Care & All Care Concerned

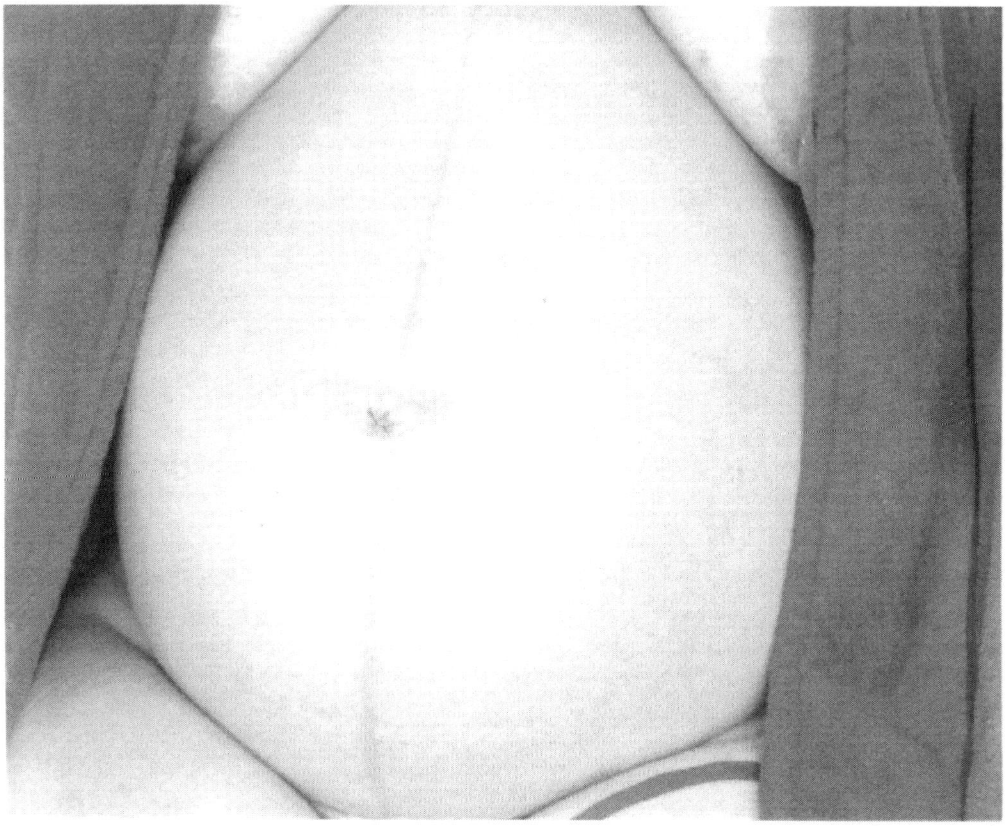

Nina's beautifully full pregnant belly with her twins 2006.

Prenatal Care Charting

Medical Abbreviations and their Meanings

Standard Tests and Alternatives

Rhogam Debate

Ultrasound

"Ultrasound Scans: Cause for Concern," by Dr. Sarah Buckley

Myths about Women over Thirty Having Babies

Today, as the cost of living continues to rise, we need to learn how to take care of each other, to care for ourselves, and to better care for our children so they also may have a future of sustainability.

Birthing our babies within a circle of women, as we have for centuries, we can guide and support others to do the same. We know what our needs are in pregnancy and childbirth, and we know enough to demand good health management. We are the ones who will preserve the dignity of our children's future pregnancies and births.

Prenatal Care

"Experiences have clearly shown that an approach which "de-medicalizes" birth, restores dignity and humanity to the process of childbirth, and returns control to the mother, is also the safest approach ..." ~Michel Odent, M.D.

When you have decided how you are going to handle your pre-natal care--whether hiring someone or doing it yourself--there are some basic guidelines to follow. Above all, listen to your inner wisdom and follow your own instincts.

It is your responsibility to obtain the information and education needed for good preventive care either by finding it yourself, seeking it from a midwife or even asking a physician when indicated.

Not all care providers give education or options for birth. Therefore, it is wise to do your own follow up care if working with a midwife or doctor. This is because not everyone's unique needs are met by others; only you can give yourself the care you deserve. By just being responsible for your own health, regardless of circumstance, you are enabling yourself to be a better teacher and supporter of other women and families when you know the "ins and outs" of what's needed, or not, during prenatal, labor and birth.

Record keeping allows you to keep track of your progression and notice when things seem like they may be getting off track. Possibly keep a journal; it keeps vital information of the patterns of your growth, your baby's growth, and variations in your health in general. Nutrition, cravings, emotional state of being, and any other feelings, thoughts and desires should be noted.

Vital signs for each individual will vary slightly, and you will know what's normal for you after becoming familiar with your unique patterns.

Temperature, Pulse, Blood Pressure are basic vital signs:

Learning how to take your own vitals, and keeping track of your own unique patterns, is easy and important in self-care. It will also help you take care of your family and friends should they need support or help with their health concerns.

Below are the normal "averages" of your vital signs:

Blood Pressure (BP): 90/60 to 140/90

Respirations (Breathes):14-20 a minute

Pulse: 60-100 Beats Per Minute (BPM)

Temperature: 97-99.6 degrees or 36.1-37.6 C.

Everyone is different, but somewhere within these averages is considered "normal."

I have had a few friends resist their diagnosis of high blood pressure, knowing it was not right for some reason or another. Their doctors wanted to put them on blood pressure medicine after checking their BP only twice, and both times in the clinic. After checking one of my friend's BP at my home while relaxing and visiting, her blood pressure was fine. After discussing this situation, she realized that when she went to the doctor's office, she was nervous, dehydrated, fearful, and exhausted from the half-hour drive with her toddler. The next visit, she tried to be more aware of when he took her BP and how she was feeling and thinking. She realized that the doctor instantly went to do her BP. When she asked him to wait, he replied, "Why?" She told him that her BP was high the last few times because she was nervous, and he needed to let her take a break for a minute and then check her BP. After about ten minutes, a glass of water and time for her to catch her breath, the doctor checked her BP and it was normal. She asked, "So, do I have to still take that medication?" The doctor hesitated and shrugged the whole thing off, replying: "Well its fine now, but ... I still think you need medication." The story ended with her going to a midwife and having a great home-birth with no high blood pressure problems--not once.

Nutrition, hydration, emotional well-being, physical complaints and other factors should be documented in your file in order to identify any correlation between different events and findings. In this way, you can determine if there is any real pathology that may need extra attention.

When doing your own birth, prenatal information is of great importance. Keeping records enable you to prevent any complications before they get out of hand.

For example: Your urine has always been normal, one day you check it and it has nitrates in it, maybe mild, but they're there. You then have a little trace protein, and wonder what's happening? You may feel a little irritation when urinating and did not realize yet that you were starting to get an infection of your Urinary Tract (a UTI).

With testing, which you can do at home, you will know something is amiss. Listening to your body's cues and following up with them is essential. With education you will know that this is quite possibly a sign that you are not drinking enough water and that your bladder may have a build up of bacteria as a result. This situation can lead to a Urinary Tract Infection, which can end up as a kidney infection if not prevented. Without testing, you may not notice that anything was going on until the situation was serious and then have to wait a day or two more before getting in to see your health care provider.

Drinking cranberry juice, unsweetened (or Vitamin C), uva ursi tincture or tea (to clean out kidneys and bladder), more water, and walking each day to circulate your system, you may relieve those signs in your urine within a day or two. Then you did not have to wait until it got so bad that your midwife, or doctor, had to put you on antibiotics, which compromises the kidneys even more.

There are reasons why care providers check these things in a prenatal exam. For one, we are not you; we keep records because we only see you a few minutes a month. We do not remember every little sign and symptom you have, that is why it is written down. Your memory may also fade between visits; therefore, keeping your own records will empower you and enable you to share your findings with your care provider, or remedy them on your own before they get out of hand.

Other things to consider when charting yourself:

Write down how you are feeling emotionally each day or every few days. Keep an account of dreams that may have had some meaning to you about your pregnancy and birth. Do affirmations to prevent any emotional or mental obstacles that may arise later during birth. Listen to yourself, your body, and your baby. Pay attention to what is transpiring within yourself. Charting these things can help you access what you need to focus on during your prenatal time to prepare for the big day.

Overall health prior to pregnancy should be recognized and noted. Do not hide any information from yourself or your care provider. Things can get out of hand when, to begin with, you do not recognize problems that can be prevented. For example, I ask my clients about their emotional state of being, then chart: "doing great," "feeling good," "not so good," "sad," "worried," "relaxed," "had a dream about ...," "she wants more homework to do," "may need a vacation," etc. Then I can give them extra attention, if needed, with a special affirmation, and follow up on the next phone conversation or visit. These notes can "forewarn" a potential complication by recognizing certain signs or symptoms instead of waiting to find out later if we "should have, could have or would have" done something to prevent the potential difficulty to begin with!

Also, charting weight gain, weight loss or weight unchanged in a chart can show the steady growth, or lack thereof, for both mother and baby without so much guess work.

I personally do not feel weight gain is a significant sign of anything, unless the mother is unhealthily gaining too much, or too little. This can be checked through discussion with the mother, only she knows if she is gaining enough for herself and baby.

These are things that are all visible if done, at minimum, every two weeks. It is necessary to watch these things because of the rapid growth of babies, as well as the rapid deterioration that can take place in one's health if these signs are not attended too. That is why keeping your own chart is an invaluable tool.

Since most prenatal visits are only once a month, and not for a very long duration, questions and concerns are sometimes overlooked or forgotten as a result of being in a rush to move onto the next patient. So charting is a good way of getting to know yourself better and of preventing any complications. If you do your own birth chart, regardless of whether you have a care provider or not, you are educating yourself to be fully involved, and you become aware of your own strengths, needs and choices without the mystery of what's in that little manila file. And remember, you always have the right to have a copy of your prenatal records, no matter who you have caring for you.

Here is a sample chart with basic things on it to use for your care.

Name:________________________________EDD_______________

Father's Name_____________________________

Other Children's
Names____
____

LMP____________Pre-pregnant Weight_______Blood type_______

Bleeding during pregnancy?____

Disorders____

G___P___SAB___TAB___Date you feel you conceived___________Date of first movement________First heart sounds heard_______

Special notes about your LMP, conception, concerns and thoughts

____
____
____
____
____
____
____
____
____

Date_________________Weeks______________________________________

Fundal height____

Weight____

Baby's movement ____

Baby's position ____

Baby's Heart Rate:
____
____

Notes:____
____

Urine Color

Ph

Proteins

Blood

Ketones

Glucose

Comments:

Vital signs:

Pulse

Blood pressure

Temperature

Any headaches

Nausea /vomiting

Dizziness, aches or pains:

Yoni Exam:

____

____

____

Other signs, or feelings, about this pregnancy and birth:

____

____

____

____

____

____

____

Labor and Birth Chart

Name_______________________________EDD__________

Father's name ______________________________

Other Children(s)
Names_______________________________________

____

Blood type __________Vitals baseline: ____________________
BP________Temp______Pulse__________Dilation________effac._____stat.______

Any Previous complications in pregnancies, Labors and births (Explain)

____

____

____

____

____

____

Date practice Labor began:

____

____

First signs of progression:

____

____

____

Feelings, emotions, physical sensations:

____

____

____

____

Notes: (How you are feeling, how many sensations a minute, hour, day. Is there a bloody show, mucus, fluid, gush, trickle)

Times: (when first felt Labor begin, stop, start again, rest, progress)

Food and fluid intake:

output:

urination________________________________

bowels________________________________

vomit________________________________

This chart is for your personal use. Also in cases of transport, it has your vital information and will help facilitate better outcomes in a hospital environment. Instead of the hospital staff needing to fumble around trying to figure out who you are and what you are doing there, they will have your information to assist them in their care of you. This is the basic prenatal care chart for labor and birth; by charting, you can keep track of the progress of your pregnancy, and you can monitor your well-being and that of your baby.

Abbreviations: Understanding "The Language" for better communication with care providers

EDD: Estimated Due Date: A good resource to have on a chart to follow the growth of your baby, and the consistency of growth in relationship to the time of the EDD. Only 3-7% babies actually arrive on their EDD. It is "normal" and very common to give birth a few weeks before, or after, an EDD.

LMP: Last Menstrual Period. Most of the calculations for ovulation are about 14 days after LMP, but in all actuality, ovulation can take place anytime. So when trying to determine your EDD, you can be a few weeks either way. This also applies to skipped moons, when this happens women can think they got pregnant one month earlier because of the missing moon, but in all actuality it could have been much later. This also affects the EDD.

G: stands for "Gravid." This is how many times you have been pregnant, including miscarriages and abortions. It will help determine certain needs, physically, emotionally and nutritionally.

P: Stands for "Para," and is how many live babies you have birthed.

SAB: Spontaneous Abortion or Miscarriage: before 22weeks. List how many you have had.

TAB: Therapeutic Abortion. How many medical abortions you have had whether surgical or as "an abortion pill" that is taken at home with suppositories.

Fundal height or FH: This is the measurement in centimeters of your uterine growth, and is a measurement from the top of your pubic bone (O cms) to the shelf of your uterus. This is usually within 3cms of your weeks' gestation, but varies widely among women and especially with multi-gravid women (women who have had many pregnancies). It is good to keep records of your baby's growth and your weeks, collaborating on the two.

Effacement or EFF: This is in relation to cervical thickness. It is approximately 1 inch thick in a non-pregnant woman, but varies. During labor, the cervix will lengthen and stretch thinner and thinner until fully effaced. "Effac" is measured by percentage, 30%, 50% etc. Until 100% is completed, this is when there is no thickness left in the cervix. You can be fully effaced and still not dilated, so it does not determine dilation or duration of Labor. You can also be fully dilated and not have full effacement. If effacement is taking place, but dilation is slow, a doctor may say that you're not "ripe" and then induce you artificially with Pitocen. A "ripe" cervix is one that is doing something and preparing for birth. Remember that when confronted with threats of induction. Often no inductions are needed, and the situation should be re-evaluated again in a few days before making any hurried decisions. By then you may be in labor on your own, avoiding possible dangerous side effects from the drugs they use to induce birth.

"Dil"/Dilation: Is the opening of the cervix. This can be determined with internal measurements, one finger being about one centimeter dilated; some fingers are large and may be two centimeters around. This is one way of measuring progression in Labor. A mom can be dilated and not be in Labor. I for one, was four centimeters dilated, 50% effaced, and my baby's head was +1 station for over a month before his birth. Therefore just because you maybe dilated a few centimeters before actual labor begins, you are not necessarily at risk for a premature birth. Babies will hang in there until it is the right time to be born. Another example is a client who was six centimeters for more than six weeks before her birth! Her baby was very low and also in a strange position; it took him six more weeks to get in position for his birth, then he was ready and came on his EDD within ten minutes after the first sensation.

"Stat"/Station: This is the relationship between your Ischial Tuberosities (sitting bones) and the baby's head in the pelvis. Once the baby descends into the pelvis, it is measured by "station" through an internal exam (-2 -1 -0 0+0 +1 +2) to see if the baby's head is in "position" and how low he is in the pelvis, but like these other internal findings it is usually not needed if you are doing your own birth. Even if someone else is doing it with you, it is only for your information that these things are charted. When you are caring for yourself, without a "professional" care provider, it is best to rely on your own intuition, ask for support when needed, listen to your inner wisdom and flow with labor and birth; your body will do the rest!

Standard tests done Prenatally:

Medically Managed Care

Most standard tests during a pregnancy are taken with the intention of ruling out some kind of pathology, to prepare for a difficulty or to remedy a situation that could get out of hand if not dealt with before birth takes place. Most doctors and midwives do these standard tests at the beginning of prenatal care. Some tests are preferred regardless of existent condition.

For example: If you had a pap smear already that year, and it was perfectly normal, the health care provider may try to do another one anyway. If you ask your care provider if your record of the last pap smear would be good enough evidence that you are free and clear of any illness, they may not insist on doing another one. You always have the right to waive (deny) an unnecessary test regardless of the health care provider's protocols. This is your body and your baby, and no one wants to put themselves, or their baby, at risk from unneeded procedures. What's the big deal? Well, some women prefer to "go it" untested for many reasons; one is because it may place themselves, and their unborn, at risk of subtle to major complications. Remember, tests are subjective, they are not 100% accurate at all.

Routine blood, urine, and internal exams are rarely found to be of any help because they do not take into account your ability to remedy a situation, or prevent a complications, through a change of dietary intake or other preventive measures. Most midwives, however, do consider these. I will list the standard tests here and try to explain a few things about each, so you can choose what it is you may want, or avoid.

Blood tests in first trimester:

Hgb, and **HcT**: these are Hemoglobin and Hematocrit, normal levels Hgb 12-16 / HcT 37-47

The hemoglobin test measures the oxygen carrying capacity of our red blood cells. Those who are truly anemic are at risk for pre-term labor, liver dysfunction, smaller babies and hemorrhage. In high altitudes, it is normal to have an HgB of 12 or higher because the red blood cells need to conserve their oxygenated blood for the higher climate that has less oxygen. Therefore, that does not mean you are not at risk for anemia if your HgB is seemingly higher than normal unless you show symptoms of anemia. At sea level, it is more common to find moms who have less Hgb, because there is less of a need to conserve. If a mom is adequately nourished, she is not likely to have this problem. Iron is absorbed well and very quickly. If it turns out to be a situation needing attention, there are herbal remedies and food adjustments that can be made. One great source, out of many, is increasing our intake of green-leafy vegetables. Another way is to add some alfalfa or nettles to our herbal pregnancy teas. Floradex is a product from Europe that is "herb and fruit juiced based" which can work within a few days if taken regularly. This can be found in most health food stores, or ordered by your local food co-op.

A few symptoms of truly anemic moms are lethargy, dizziness, looking pale, feeling weak, bruising easily, heart palpitations and shortness of breath. Poor nutrition accounts for most anemic mothers, and can be remedied with a high whole grain, green vegetable diet, with good caloric intake and hydration.

MCH: Mean Corpuscular Volume, this is the hemoglobin level of each red blood cell.

Normal value 26-34.

Platelet Count: measures clotting factors and acute infections as well as any hematological pathology. Normal range is 150-440.

WBC: White Blood Cell Count, also called Leukocytes, can be found in urine. This looks for infection--viral or bacterial--anemia, and any blood diseases.

VDRL and RPR: this is a test for syphilis.

A "non reactive" is a negative result. Today in the U.S., numerous cases of syphilis have been documented, with about 40 million infected people from all types of backgrounds. You are at risk if: you have had numerous unprotected sexual partners, are an intravenous drug user, traveled to Asia, the Caribbean, have lesions or sores in the genital area, are experiencing recurring illness with fever that may remedy itself. Unless someone is actively carrying the primary syphilis virus, it is non-reactive or negative. Babies born to mothers who have been exposed to this virus are at risk for congenital abnormalities; when born, they will have the degree of the virus the mother has at the time. If treated prior to pregnancy, usually with Penicillin and by improving diet and lifestyle, the risks are minimal. Once the Penicillin is out of the mother's system, she will need to be retested to see what stage of syphilis she is in, if any.

Humans have always had some sort of disease, or virus, that has plagued us since the beginning of time. These worst-case scenarios have not yet diminished the human race.

Rubella antibody titer-test for German measles

An immune "positive" is a negative result. I was laid off from my day care job when I became pregnant because of the fear that German Measles are more prevalent among young children, and the facility did not want to be liable. It is well known that contracting this "toga virus," can change the embryo's cellular makeup and create an abnormality. The worse case scenario is if you are exposed to this virus (in the "primary" stage, which is if you have never been exposed before) early in your pregnancy. Your unborn baby can be affected tremendously. Nevertheless, if you, as 85% of all adults did, have it as a child, the effects are not as great. Moreover, the more pregnant you are when exposed, the less of a chance that the baby will be affected. German Measles is contracted through air born pathogens, or anything that has been contaminated by nasal or mucus membranes with this virus. Therefore, to have a pregnant mom sitting in a waiting room with small sick children, and who knows what else floating around, is absurd. If you didn't have something before going to a clinic to be tested, then you are just exposing yourself to that risk.

RH factor: A, B, O, AB, Blood typing Rh -, Rh +, Du+, Kell +

This test finds out what your blood type is. This can be done at home if you are doing your own care and birth **(more information below)**.

Different combinations, for example, AB+, ABO-, may result in incompatibilities within the couple. If you're trying to conceive and having a hard time, this can be remedied through building immunity with your partner's blood. If incompatibilities are the reason for fertility complications, this blood therapy may help. This is a medically managed procedure and consists of injecting your partner's blood into your system so that you can build immunity to his blood and conceive without your antibodies attacking the baby.

HAV Ab/igM: This test for Hepatitis B or other active "Hep." There are several types of Hepatitis, they all affect the liver and unless proper treatment is found, they can become deadly. "Type B" is the one we test pregnant mothers for because it is the most dangerous if transmitted to baby. This type of hepatitis is contagious through sexual contact with a "positive" person, or by getting tattoos, being an IV drug user or getting blood transfusions. It is also found in contaminated foods, especially in certain parts of the world where the sewer systems and drinking water are not that sanitary.

HIV: Human Immunodeficiency Virus Test, usually optional, but preferred.

A negative result is normal. It is common from time to time, however, to have a false negative or false positive result. It can be acquired through sexual activity with an infected person, blood to blood contact, IV drug use or blood transfusions. It is a danger for health care workers who accidentally get stuck with a needle or gets fluids of an infected person in a sore, or cut, on their body. During pregnancy, the mother and baby's blood system is separate, but HIV can be transferred through the antibodies that develop during gestation and are transferred in the blood that houses the place in the uterine lining into which the placenta will grow. A mother, even with this immune deficiency, can give birth to a baby. There are some midwives and doctors who believe that even if a mother is HIV pos., she can still have a gentle birth. It would actually be more logical for her to birth gently, since any disruption to the baby or placenta can cause blood transference. AZT is usually given to pregnant mothers to lesson the chance of her offspring contracting the virus.

Precautions are taken to protect the health worker from being exposed to bodily fluids. If however, she is far advanced in this situation and has Syphilis (which evidently is more the problem with this immune deficiency than HIV), it can turn rapidly into AIDS. She may not be healthy enough to carry a baby to term and may not be able to have a healthy baby who will live a full life, but some may. Most babies (50%) are found to be HIV positive within nine months of birth. These babies have a harder time with growth, brain development, and usually have enlarged livers and spleens.

These blood tests are done all at once with your first blood draw. One drawback to these tests is that you are exposed to pathogens just from being in a hospital, or clinic, and having a needle poke you. Another drawback is more psychological; any interference with your body creates stress hormones that are transferred to baby. Most women do not feel comfortable being poked, and sometimes being poked more than once for the same test because the intern, or nurse, messed up the first one, but some of us don't mind and are fine with it. It is always your choice. If you feel you're at risk for something, get tested!

After the standard blood tests are done, you also have a urinalysis taken at each visit. You give the practitioner your urine, and then they dip a stick in it that has a chemical reaction to show what, if anything, is happening within your system. You can see many things in urine, and you can become more familiar with your diet and hydration by looking at the color, consistency and noting its odor. It is helpful to keep a glass cup aside, clean and dry, for testing your own urine.

Protein: neg-trace is normal; this will show Albumin/protein in urine.

Glucose: neg-trace is normal; this will show sugar in urine.

Nitrates: neg-trace is normal; if feeling ill, and kidney or bladder infection is present, it will show nitrates in the urine.

Ketones: neg-is normal; this will show if you have been eating well or not.

Bilirubin: neg-is normal; this will show if liver is being compromised in any way.

Leukocytes: neg-is normal; this will show if you have any white blood cells in the urine: infections and blood carry WBCs (white blood cells).

Blood: Neg-is normal; it will show if a bladder or kidney infections is present. During labor, it is normal to have blood in the urine since the capillaries are stretching and breaking as the cervix is opening. Also, after making love, some women may have a little blood from the irritation of the capillaries on the cervix; this is not dangerous but can worry some moms when it is found.

Some urine testers even show more, but this is the standard test strip. If you have a negative to trace result, you are assumed to be fine. It would be necessary to do further testing, if the urine test was positive over a period of time. At home, this test is easily done by purchasing these urine test strips.

If you have, for example, a bladder infection (which can lead to a kidney infection if not treated), your urine would possibly have: protein trace to positive result, blood, nitrates positive result, leukocytes' trace to a positive result. This would be the time to take some uva ursi, drink lots of water and cranberry juice, unsweetened (Vit. C) and then retest in three days; it should be fine if you take care of it with these remedies. Kidney infections can lead to serious pain if not prevented through good hydration and hygiene. There are also many homeopathic remedies that work great with this.

*Do not make love during a **UTI** (Urinary Tract Infection).

Blood tests and other tests later in the second and third trimesters:

Amongst most medical providers and even some midwives, retesting blood is very common throughout a pregnancy and even several times before the birth. This is depending on your particular provider and his or her protocols. Again, you are hiring these people to care for you; you are the boss, and if you do not want any of these tests, you can waive (deny) taking them by signing a form. Some care providers will respect your decision, especially if you have read up on these tests and have a good reason why you do not feel they are needed. Some providers may say, "Well that's not my style, and I cannot work with you if you do not want this test." Then it is up to you to decide if you want to keep this particular person as your care provider, find one who meshes with your style, or go it alone without having to justify your choices to anyone.

Yoni Tests (Vaginal exams):

Usually when you have your first initial exam and they take your blood for those tests I have listed, they also want to do an internal exam of your cervix and palpate your uterus, as well as take a culture from your yoni lining and cervix to test for the below (you may slightly bleed afterwards).

Gonorrhea: May have smelly discharge, can be asymptomatic, which means you have no symptoms. A pap smear is a way to find out.

Chlamydia Discharge: Sometimes there are no symptoms (asymptomatic); a pap smear/blood test is a way to find out if you have this.

Cervical cancer: Cervical Dysplasia (pre-cancer cells), it tests mild to severe.

Herpes infection: One out of four of us have some type of herpes and it can be dormant, if so, unless sores are apparent, no worries. Natural treatments can be applied to suppress them for birth.

Strep Bacteria: This is done through a swabbing either the yoni, anus or the throat, also called GBS testing.

Yeast infections: Normal if there is a white, or sometimes a bit yellow, discharge. This may increase with pregnancy since the yoni is very sensitive and works to keep out bacteria; it is a normal response to protect against infection. It's naturally "cleaning out!"

Trichomonas: A fowl smelling green discharge. Can be serious if not treated.

***Unspecific* Vaginosis:** Itchy, red, sore. There are many natural remedies I will list to help with this.

If any of these tests come out positive, there are natural remedies to take if you have a few months to heal before your birth. In a medical environment, they will most likely put you on antibiotics that can affect the baby's kidneys and immune system as well as cause problems with your immune system and kidneys making it harder for your body to fight future infections. It is a vicious cycle.

If you're found to be positive for any of these yoni infections, you are likely to be told that a Cesarean Section is the only option since the baby would contract these viruses through the birth canal when being born. Antibiotics during labor and after birth are also the common practice of medical care providers, disregarding the side effects on both the mother and baby's organs. This is usually due to "liability paranoia" on their part.

If naturally treated, depending on the severity of these infections, they can be prevented, remedied, or stabilized with herbal or homeopathic remedies before the birth without any nasty side effects. There is the theory that the baby can contract viral infection from fluids picked up from the mother as the baby descends the birth canal. This is unlikely, the baby has its own sterile fluids that are not infected with mother's infections, and they are creating a barrier around the baby and providing blood, which is also sterile.

In addition, amniotic fluids wash the infections out, down and away from the baby. This is a natural mechanism that enabled us to survive all these thousands of years, when tests, antibiotics and cesarean sections did not exist. However, infections have always existed and are a part of our lives still to this day, even with all these medical procedures and "cures." Still, infections should be treated in whatever manner you find fit as soon as you find out you have one. Although, it is not recommended to use over the counter yeast treatments while pregnant because of the high level of mercury and other chemicals used to preserve them.

Sexually transmitted diseases such as Herpes, Chlamydia, or Gonorrhea can be remedied through proper diet, with an acidophilus supplement, garlic intake, garlic suppositories, homeopathic remedies, and increased circulation by not wearing any underwear and walking each day. After a shower, air-dry your yoni so moisture does not irritate the area and create more bacteria; eat lots of greens, proteins, yogurt with live culture enzymes, take vinegar, sea salt baths and refrain from sex. While simultaneously treating the infected partner, even if he has no apparent symptoms.

Colloidal Silver, which is a natural pro-biotic (antibiotic), has been known to help these infections, or at least suppress them for birth. An "Unspecific Vaginosis" is one that cannot be found during an exam or from tests but is apparent to you. Itchy, sore, red vulva and labials are annoying and can be due to the increased amount of oxygen in your lower tissues from the pregnancy. Not wearing underwear so the area can have better circulation, air drying after bathing, getting enough rest, drinking lots of water, and increasing the nutritional value of your food can be sufficient in caring for this type of irritation. Garlic is also good for common yeast infections. Put a raw garlic clove inside the yoni for a few hours each day to fight off localized internal infections. When doing this, your yeast will increase the first day or so, accumulating all the bacteria, but then leaves quickly. So if you find that your mucus is abundant after doing this, do not panic, the next day it could be totally gone.

Herpes Simplex Virus can be treated with the above, also be aware that herpes sores can come forth when you are under stress and lack a proper diet. A good daily meditation and relaxation practice can help as well as getting enough folic acid and B vitamins in one's diet. I have seen genital herpes a few times in pregnant women. We used the above treatment along with a colloidal silver compress, and in a few days the lesions were gone.

* Avoid Colloidal Silver if you are allergic to silver.

Rho-Gam Dilemma

When your Rh is Negative, this may pose concern for your care provider, or it may not, depending on how schooled she is with Rh- moms.

In 10-16% of Rh- mothers with Rh+ babies, they may become "sensitized." This is the mixing of the babies' blood with maternal blood. This is not good, and it usually happens for several reasons. Poor nutrition, prenatal intrusion, Amniocentesis, Chronic villi sampling, Cesarean birth, an unhealthy mother: all these lead to unhealthy placenta and the likelihood of premature separation of placenta and "sensitization."

Today, this NEW prenatal procedure tries to eliminate sensitization prior to birth. Prenatal Rho-Gam is administered at 28 weeks gestation, the theory behind this, which is not currently proven, is to prevent this mixing of blood between mother and baby. This antibody, currently given prenatally, has had no significant results in preventing sensitization at the time of birth. These are very few women, and nine out of twenty-five women with the prenatal injection become sensitized anyway. Unless a mom has an abruption of her placenta during gestation, she does not have to worry about this type of prevention. When this does happen, a direct Coombs test is done to identify antigens in the mother, which are activated if their blood is mixing. Moreover, if positive, she will then need to take some type of therapy so her baby is not brain damaged, or compromised before the birth. If sensitization happens at the time of birth, the baby is at risk for "New Born Jaundice." Depending on how long the baby is sensitized during birth, liver failure can result. There may need to be a blood transfusion, in severe cases, that in itself poses great risks to the newborn. The worst-case scenario can cause death. That is why preventative nutrition, no intervention and having a gentle birth can prevent disruption of the maternal systems and also prevent the abruption of the placenta prenatally, thus making sensitization less likely to happen.

A baby who is Rh+ in an Rh- mother poses little risks, unless a severe situation occurs. The risks of Rho-Gam have been only recently studied since it has only been experimentally used for thirty years or so. When Rho-Gam was first invented, it was given to moms postpartum within 72 hours of birth, which is the standard time to administer the injection. This time frame was originally chosen because this was the standard discharge time in hospitals. This method was adopted to insure against the rare chance of the mother becoming sensitized, leaving her at risk for miscarriages in future pregnancies. The mother's antibodies react to the babies Rh+ antibodies as invaders, causing the mothers system to attack the baby as a virus or disease. Nevertheless, as I said before, it is rare. Mother's blood and baby's blood are two separate systems, and, until birth, if at all, should not mix with a healthy mother.

To prevent Rh sensitization, you need to have a healthy lifestyle. Many women, who become sensitized, are in poor health and have intervention at birth causing ruptures of the placenta prematurely.

A well-nourished Rh- mother with an Rh+ baby who has a gentle birth has less chance of sensitization because the birth is not interfered with; the placenta is not rushed or pulled on and the umbilical cord is not cut immediately. I have heard doctors instill fear in women about this situation, telling them that they will die if they do not receive this drug. And why? It has nothing to do with the pregnancy at hand, but with the possibility that the next pregnancy will be compromised. It is a fallacy that the mother will die if she doesn't receive the injection.

In those rare cases when a mom is in an accident or has complications with her placenta, her baby is at risk, not her; it is the baby who may not be able to survive the mother's antibodies attacking it. But if a mom is well nourished, does not smoke or drink alcohol, doesn't have interventions such as a Cesarean births or drug induced labor, has a gentle birth and no one cuts her baby's cord right away, it will cut the chance of "sensitization" in half.

When Rho-Gam did not exist, Rh- mothers still had babies; if they didn't, we would not have anymore Rh- people on the planet, but obviously we do. When they came up with this Rho-Gam, there was a higher incidence of sensitization, most likely because women were not as healthy in the early days of its experimental use. Women were told, first of all, not to gain much weight, so they were already unhealthy from that, then they were told that smoking was ok during pregnancy because this helped them to minimize weight gain! This compromised their babies' health from the start and made it more likely for their placentas to detach prematurely from lack of nutrition and oxygen. An injection of Rho-Gam was a good idea for those women if they wanted more children in the future.

I have had a few clients who were Rh-, and they did not want the pre-natal or postpartum Rho-Gam because they did not receive it with their other children. Some of these women had many children, some of the children were Rh+, and some were not. If both the father and mother are Rh-, there should not be any concern about getting Rho-Gam because more likely than not, the child will have the father's blood type. In some cases, the baby will have the mothers blood type, and then the baby and mother are both Rh-, and therefore has no "+" antibodies to be concerned about.

A simple prenatal blood typing kit may be used with the father and other children in order to see the blood compatibility pattern in the family. Obviously, if there are other children in the family, they did ok before, and the current pregnancy should not be an issue if mom is taking good care of herself. Postpartum blood tests can be done after the placenta has been born by taking a sample right from the placental sight, from a vein or the umbilical cord blood. At home it can be administered to a blood test card (*an Eldon Card*), which within minutes will tell you what the baby's blood type is without poking the baby or rushing the placenta. Remember, you have a few days to administer the Rho-gam if you so desire.

"These findings, coupled with a greater understanding of birth, indicate that the prevailing practices and beliefs about childbirth are based on false, outmoded, or unverified assumptions"

~Barbara Harper "Gentle Birth Choices, Ch 3"

Adopting routine prenatal Rho-Gam injections has not been proven safe for several reasons. One, the anti-body is made from the anti-D human immune globulin taken from human blood, which can carry other people's blood born pathogens. As well, this immunization contains Thimerosal, which is mercury, as a preservative; this is highly toxic to anyone's blood stream and can cause an array of complications in both the mother and baby. On the website "*Thimerosal Litigation*" (pertaining to the affects of the administered vaccine), there are numerous studies that show that the Rho-Gam vaccine, when given prenatally as well as postpartum, can contribute to: Autism, Alzheimer's, Multiple Sclerosis, Fibromyalgia, Lupus, Chronic fatigue syndrome, Arthritis, Depression, Bipolar disorder, and infertility in people whose mothers had the vaccine prenatally. Vaccines (immunizations) given to our children contain these preservatives and these risks also.

An ***Indirect Coombs Test*** is done postpartum on a mother to find out if she is carrying the sensitized antigens, although some researchers have found that these Coombs tests are not accurate up to 92 days postpartum. So by then, if the mother was sensitized, the damage may have already begun, that is why doctors and some midwives prefer to give Rho-Gam prenatally without really evaluating the situation to see if it's benefits outweigh the risks involved.

However, two products currently on the market from Canada and Europe do not have the Thimerosal and mercury preservatives in them. They would have to be requested by the patient as American physicians do not necessarily have this on hand and may need to purchase them by special order. Because of the lack of education concerning Rho-Gam, and its side affects on mother and baby, not many women know about it, and therefore receive the vaccine without even understanding the risks involved.

Concluding the Rho-Gam issue: become informed of your choices, understand your personal risk, and be aware of the risks associated with vaccines for you and your baby. If your doctor or midwife dismisses your concerns, you can find other support with many well-educated care providers who know that the risks with prenatal and postpartum Rho-Gam are many, and they will help you find alternatives to this choice.

Univax Biologics, Inc, in Rockville, Maryland has the Thimerosal Mercury free anti-D Rho-Gam if your doctor or midwife needs to know where to get it. *Anne Frye, "Holistic Midwifery Vol One" (1995)*

How to Change your Blood Type

Recommended further reading: *"Polly's Birth Book, Obstetrics for the Home" by Polly Block*. This book refers to many great things, including ways to deal with Rh- moms in pregnancy and birth and to even change the Rh status through specific diet. This book has been well used by obstetricians, midwives, and parents for over thirty years. You can find this book online.

*(Author's Note) *Do NOT do this while you are pregnant! Wait until you are in between pregnancies:*

From"Polly's Birth Book" ~by Polly Block,

There are a number of women who had begun their childbearing years RH-. When they had continual problems with pregnancies, they began seriously to build their blood and their general health. In each case physicians, not the mothers, discovered a change in their RH status. They were now RH+. The doctors were astounded and called for additional tests and reports. They could not understand why a mother, who had been RH- for years, was now RH+. These women all shared something in common. In each instance, these women had concentrated on purifying their blood by changing their diets so they had exceptional nutritional intake.

-Eat fruit for one week.
-Eat fresh, raw, homegrown foods or organic foods. Eat foods that build blood: Grape juice, molasses, beets, etc.
-Eliminate sugar, coffee and caffeine, alcohol, and soft drinks, as well as white flour, prepared foods and refined products from your diet.
-Use an herbal lower bowel tonic and have occasional enemas or colonics to keep their bowels evacuated thoroughly during body cleanses.
-Use herbs to cleanse and build the blood. Several of these mothers gave Periwinkle special credit.

Drink lots of red raspberry leaf tea.

Take: A tea made from red clover blossoms, chaparral, licorice root, poke root, peach bark, Oregon grape root, stillingia, cascara sagrada, sarsparilla, prickly ash bark, burdock root and buckthorn bark.

A few capsules daily of: golden seal root, blessed thistle, cayenne, cramp bark, false unicorn root, ginger, red raspberry leaves, squaw vine and uva ursi in a 100% pure vegetable oil capsule.

And a few capsules daily of: black cohosh, sarsparilla, ginseng, licorice, false unicorn, holy thistle and sqawvine. (Changease 100 capsules or extract ingredients: black cohosh, sarsparilla, ginseng, licorice, false unicorn, holy thistle and squaw vine. All encapsulated products are in a pure 100% vegetable based capsule).

GTT *(Glucose Tolerance Test):* Gestational Diabetes Testing.

This test is for the detection of decreased Glucose Tolerance during pregnancy. It is routinely used within most medicalized birth practices today without pre-existing symptoms being the ruling factor for prescribing the test.

Many women over the years have expressed their fear of even reaching this point of testing in pregnancy. It is because their care provider will ask them to come in after fasting over night, drink this horrible thick black sugar syrup and fast for a few more hours while they are poked with several needles. If a mom was not diabetic to begin with, her baby and her pancreas will soon be put at risk for blood sugar shock. This glucose drink has been compared to eating 25 candy bars!

Starvation diabetes is what most positive mothers are labeled with when receiving this test (not true gestational diabetes). It seems a cruel and unjustified process when the mother's nutrition is not taken into account, and then she is subjected to unnecessary tests such as the GTT when she could have (should have) been counseled to make a few dietary changes to keep her blood glucose normalized.

It is not that difficult to understand that a wee little baby inside its mother would be at risk for having diabetes in the future after being subjected to such large quantities of condensed sugar while her mother was fasting. It is hypocritical to ask a mother to starve herself during pregnancy when all anyone ever hears is, "Eat lots of small frequent meals." This may be one of the worst commonly administered prenatal tests I have ever seen.

My mother has been diabetic for most of my life. She struggled emotionally and physically while she was put through numerous experimental tests and procedures in the early seventies. I remember her being in a diabetic coma when I was four. I was mortified to find out later that the medical community she sought help from had not even a clue that diabetes could be controlled through nutrition! What a revelation when she finally figured it out, and especially after having been subjected to experimental insulin that has left her insulin dependant today. My grandfather, who was also insulin dependent, studied up on nutrition quiet a bit in those days, and my mother followed his lead, which has led her to becoming an extremely strong, healthy vibrant woman now in her sixties. This is because my mother now knows how to regulate her insulin and food intake to help herself feel balanced. Back in those days, it's strange but true, not a lot of people considered what they ate had any barring on their health.

By researching gestational diabetes over the years, because I grew up with a mother and grandfather who have diabetes, I realized that most of this particular disease can be prevented through proper nutrition early on, before birth and in childhood.

Hypoglycemia is a pre-curser to diabetes. When I realized I came from a culture that has a history of diabetics, I found I was susceptible to getting it myself unless I paid close attention to my food intake. I grew up watching my mother and grandfather give themselves shots three or four times a day and did not want to have to do that myself. I was aware of this situation and chose to avoid refined sugar and candy, and I decided to eat lots of whole grains, vegetables and, occasionally, fruit. Having had a few days, here and there throughout my life, when I was so caught up in what I was doing that I had forgotten to eat, I crashed my blood sugar levels and was hypoglycemic for a while. Then, realizing the importance of eating proteins and whole grains daily, I have not had many episodes when I felt like passing out from lack of food.

Gestational diabetes, if real, can be devastating to mother and baby. I do not, however, believe that large babies have anything to do with this diagnosis. I have witnessed a few babies, whose mothers where labeled with gestational diabetes, who were no more then seven pounds. In addition, I have seen big babies who were born to healthy mothers who did not ever show signs of **GD**, and they were over nine pounds, even some close to eleven, and they did not look like diabetic babies (Diabetic babies kind of look doughy with less muscle tone). Therefore, so called routine GTT testing that is done with most moms during pregnancy is outrageously dangerous and should not be done with starvation testing.

There are other ways of dealing with this situation. When a mother has symptoms like glucose in her urine take into consideration what she might have eaten within the last few hours. If she is thirsty all the time, dizzy, weak, has a poor diet that consists of refined sugar and white bread, then this could be a clear recommendation that a high-protein, less-refined sugar diet is necessary. She can be tested after eating well for a few days, then after having a breakfast of good whole grain pancakes and maple syrup, she can have a small finger prick taken an hour later, then again in another hour. That would be more humane to ask of her. Not a GTT fasting, starvation, syrup test!

Doing your own prenatal care, in hopes of preventing some of these conflicts, is something to think about. A simple way to do your own care is to remain focused on preventive measures and just listen from within. If you are keeping up with a good nutritional lifestyle, hygiene, exercise and drinking enough water you should be fine. Keeping a record would still benefit you if you want to pay closer attention to your "patterns" in each pregnancy you have, as well as having a record of your pregnancy and birth to use if you need to reflect on it.

Prenatal care is of importance to anyone having a baby, whether done by one's self or with a care provider, and should still be looked upon as "self care" as it benefits every one intimately involved, such as mother, father and child.

Through study, practice and sharing of information, we can prevent dependency on outside influences on our health care. When we educate ourselves and take responsibility for our own pregnancies, births and parenting, we are creating and preserving self-reliant knowledge, which can be shared for the benefit of community and family sustainability. It can also be rewarding and satisfying for the mother and all others involved.

Ultrasonography:

Today ultrasound is readily used without the education to back up informed consent of the parents. Little is known about the long-term effects of ultrasound on babies in utero, not to mention that the diagnosis from the use of ultrasound are more often false than not. Mothers and babies are subjected to high levels of radioactive sound waves (X-ray). It is like being cooked from the inside out (like in a microwave!).

Ultrasound was first used in World War II to detect enemy submarines. A high frequency wave is used with a fluid conductor to detect a solid mass in its vicinity, like a baby in amniotic fluid. The high levels of sound waves bouncing off the object in question can produce cellular change. With a fetus, which is most vulnerable in its cellular growth, it can pose certain risks the medical establishment does not want most mothers to know about. It makes a lot of money! To put it bluntly. How many ultrasonographs does it take to damage the fetus's cellular body, hearing, brain development and reproductive organs? There has been research studies done to determine this, but they have been "swept under the carpet," because women have become accustomed to the "luxury" of seeing their unborn child on the screen. Yes, I will admit there are benefits as well. Sometimes it is nice to know emotionally that our baby is in one piece and does not have mal-formations. It also can help a mother feel better if she has had several complications in the past. My questions are: "How many times does it need to be done in one pregnancy? Why are some doctors telling women that ultrasound is completely safe when we know it is not? And why give women more than one during a pregnancy, what is the point?"

There may be times when it is useful. Perhaps if there is a suspected miscarriage or the baby has not moved for a while, the use of ultrasound may put the mother at ease when she finds out what is going on internally. Though these few benefits may be gained through this technology, there is still an over-usage of ultrasonography on our unborn children today. The risks are many compared to the benefits of routine testing. I have heard many mothers say that their doctor has a scan done every month! Who is paying for this? Insurance companies? The risks of damage to the unborn are not even discussed among these women and their care providers.

My thinking on this is that this cannot be good, for anyone. More and more children are being diagnosed with forms of cancer and other disabilities that may well have been caused by this type of intervention. Why place technology above intuition? It cannot ever replace a mother's own inner voice telling her that her baby is healthy and fine. For millenea, we have been having babies without this device, how is it that in less then a century we are incapable of growing and birthing babies without technologies like this? Is it out of fear that we give away our sacred inner world where we grow our young? Has someone told us that we are incapable of growing a healthy baby without technological help? I do not know what the answer is; all I know is that this mechanical technique is not safe when over-used as it has been. It is up to every individual to make the choice whether or not ultrasound is needed in their particular situation. I, for one, would possibly want one (only one!) at some point during my pregnancy because of my previous miscarriage. But then again, I may not, depending on how much I work on my fear regarding my own body's ability to grow a normal and healthy baby.

Ultrasound Scans-Cause for Concern

First published in Nexus magazine, vol9, no 6, Oct-Nov 2002,

By Dr. Sarah Buckley:

When I was pregnant with my first baby in 1990, I decided against having a scan. This was a rather unusual decision, as my partner and I are both doctors and had even done pregnancy scans ourselves - rather ineptly, but sometimes usefully - while training in GP Obstetrics a few years earlier. What influenced me the most was my feeling that I would lose something important as a mother if I allowed someone to test my baby. I knew that if a minor or uncertain problem showed up (this is not uncommon), that I would be obliged to return again and again, and that after a while, it would feel as if my baby belonged to the system, and not to me. In the years since then I have had three more unscanned babies, and have read many articles and research papers about ultrasound. Nothing I have read has made me reconsider my decision. Although ultrasound may sometimes be useful when specific problems are suspected, my conclusion is that it is at best ineffective and at worse dangerous when used as a screening tool for every pregnant woman and her baby.

You can find abundant articles by Dr. Sarah Buckley online, just search "Dr. Sarah Buckley," there is a lot to look at, or you can go to her website: www.sarahjbuckley.com. Her philosophies on birth-related issues are greatly appreciated by many birth workers and us mothers. All four of her children were born naturally, at home, in water and were "Lotus" born! Thank you Sarah!

Age and Having Babies

Medicalized childbirth today considers women over thirty to be "high risk." The rationalization is that these women may have difficulties because their bones are too brittle, even *rigid,* or they're out of shape and not capable of having a healthy baby and birth. The truth is that most women, regardless of age if healthy prior to pregnancy, will do just fine. I have seen women over thirty give birth to their first children at home with support and encouragement and with no complications at all. The oldest mother I attended was over fifty, the youngest fourteen. All women who can conceive and carry a baby too term, with good nutritional habits and a positive attitude towards birth, will likely have no problems because of age. Regardless of the fact the medical establishment has labeled them as "geriatric mothers." If a "mature" mother goes to a doctor for care, she may be presented with some difficult decisions.

One is **Amniocentesis**. This procedure requires a test using a very long needle that is injected into the uterus through the abdominal wall to extract the amniotic fluid, while at the same time an ultrasound is being done. The risks involved in this procedure are many. One is the risk of accidentally causing internal damage to the placenta, stabbing the baby with the needle, infection, premature birth, miscarriage, and emotional stress from false positive results (which commonly happen). Most families would not abort the child regardless of the tests findings anyway. While the accuracy of the results is not conclusive, some may abort a normal healthy baby when the results are a false-positive, and vise versa. If the results are a false-negative, the choices are limited. Therefore, it is, needless to say, a wasted, expensive and risky procedure. This test is used to "rule out" any abnormalities in the baby such as Down's syndrome, hemophilia, sickle cell anemia, and other genetically related disorders. It is not the truth that just because a mom is having babies later in her life that her child would be at higher risk than any other mother who has a baby. I personally feel this procedure is just another excuse to do more tests! It makes women feel inferior and destroys their own inner wisdom, and all it does is profit the medical establishment. By doing this, there is fear in women's outlook on their own bodies and births, and they are more likely to place themselves into the arms of medicine to be managed.

If a woman is eating well, takes care of herself and happens to have babies later in her life, she is not at risk just because of age alone. I have supported many women having babies in their late thirties and forties and none of them had any problems.

Chorionic Villi Sampling is another test for women over thirty. In this test they take a piece of placental tissue to examine. This procedure poses the same, if not more, risks to mother and unborn child as the amniocentesis testing.

Weighing out the risks before subjecting yourself to any of these prenatal tests is important. Think carefully before consenting to unnecessary intervention that may cause harm to mother and child. A child may be born now and then with a disability regardless of what we do to prevent problems. Accepting our choice to have a child comes with many options. You are the parent, so your best own inner knowledge is your key to making these choices of what is, or is not, to be tested. You are the creator of this child, it is up to you to choose, not a stranger. There are many tests and procedures presented when pregnant. Research and education can eliminate unnecessary testing that may prevent other interferences later in pregnancy and birth.

NOTES:

Communicating & Making Agreements

Communicating and Making Agreements

Most of us need some sort of agreement with someone who can support us during our pregnancy and birth. If you are married and have a solid support system, great! If you are not married and want to get the support from a friend or relative who can be with you through the ups and downs, wonderful!

Whatever the situations, we all need a good support-person to be there to talk to when we need to talk, to go through labor with, hold our hand, or say the things that make us feel supported, nurtured and loved. If you feel you don't "need" anyone then that's fine too! Whatever the circumstance, we all need to communicate our needs and desires somehow.

When I was pregnant, I had a neighbor who was my support person; she was able to just "be" there for me and not tell me what to do or how to do it. That is what I needed most when I was pregnant. Since then, I have realized that most women just need to "vent" sometimes, and I am there for them just to listen and to support their feelings by validating them, not there to tell them what to do!

Not everyone can fulfill every need we have, so finding that person may take time if we do not already have someone. When we do find that person, figure out what it is you need from them; write specific things down and discuss it with them, have them agree or change things along the way until they can be fully with you and give you the space you need to be yourself, don't ever assume anything. Your perception, of the person you want to help support you may not be what that person is able to give. Make sure you are open and clear about your thoughts and visions regarding what you need from your support person. When labor begins, it is hard to say what may enter your mind, some things may arise that you had not thought of before. If you have done your affirmations and visualizations and discussed all possibilities with your partner then you've done a lot. Now you are almost there, strong and as prepared as ever but open and emotionally vulnerable to other's influences.

Most of us want someone who can just be there for us without judgment, and be ready to help us through our transition into motherhood. Even if this is your fifth, first or tenth baby, it is always going to be different than before. Your whole life will be changed! Your partner, and whoever else is there to share this experience and this sacred journey, will have a connection to you and that child for life.

A space of love and friendship is created at a birth. The unborn child should also have a say in who will be attending his or her emergence into this world. Let yourself listen to your unborn child, he may, or may not, like someone you have picked to attend the birth. Many times, I have been invited to go through a pregnancy and birth with a couple, or single mothers, and find a great connection with the family and also with the child. I can sometimes get a strong sense of who that being is even before the birth. Then when she comes, the feeling is as if an old friend I have not seen for a while comes out and looks up at everyone with strong knowing.

You will get the signals as to what you need to do in order to choose who will be involved at your baby's birth. In subsequent chapters, I list other valuable tools for communicating with your baby, so it will make more sense as we go on.

One of the most important aspects of prenatal preparation and birth is to choose the proper care provider, if at all, who will educate and listen to your families needs and welcome you into motherhood and help bring your child into the world with love and respect. A partner is so essential, even if it is not your spouse; you can create a support system that enables you to open and grow with the rhythms of life and the unfolding of all possibilities within you and your new family.

One of my favorite rituals is to create a circle of all the people who may be present at the time of the birth and then go around the circle and spontaneously rattle off positive words for the birth. Having one of us write down all the words said and then posting it up on the family's refrigerator so they can read it every day. This becomes a group affirmation which you can chant to create positive energy for the upcoming birth. Siblings should be involved if they can talk and want to be involved.

Here are some group affirmations from past births:

Flowing	Divine	Fortress	Emerge
Fun	Listen	Sound	Open
Fearless	Womb	Wise Woman	Softening
Joyful	Warmth	Vibration	Hands
Creation	Sacred Journey	Guidance	Heart
Faith	Forgiveness	Support	Gathering
Hope	Goddess	Angel	Unity
Protected	Creator	Greatness	Divine Connection
Love	Vast	Children	Spiral
Adventure	Family Involvement	Special	Waves of Bliss
Communication	Abundant	Fluent	Refreshing
Sound	Kisses	Movement	Oneness
Peaceful	Hugs	Birth	Peaceful Thoughts
Calm	Timelessness	Healing	Positive Energy
Inner knowing	Nourishment	Slow	Spontaneous
Intuition	Floating	Prosperity	Natural
Gentle	Dancing	Creator	Quick
Spiritual	Feeling	Relaxing	Fortunate
Surrender	Freedom	Self-Love	Appreciation
Trust	Remembrance	Dreamy	Giving Thanks
Caress	Warmth	Solitary	Bounty
Connected	Gratitude	Within	Birth

Your Group Affirmations Here:

This is one tool of preparation for your journey. This list will help, at least, to get you on the path with your support people. There are many resources out there for you to explore.

Practical Experiences to Draw Strength From

We all have had experiences in our lives from which we draw our strength. Even if you cannot find one off the top of your head, give yourself some time to meditate upon your past and the things that you have experienced, soon you will find that there are many things you learned from that gave you strength. While attending to your everyday life, you will see there are always challenges that you are dealing with and that you overcome.

This experiential learning is how we grow up in this world: we play with others when we are young and learn that hitting will not get us what we want; we will be put in the corner or worse--hit back! Touching the flame of a candle when mom is not looking will only hurt us; we may get attention for a few minutes and are either yelled at or babied, but the reaction is what teaches us how to either repeat the action and get burned again or try a different approach and possibly have a better outcome.

When we use a life experience to help us learn, we are redefining the past as well as making a new future for ourselves. Mistakes help us to evolve.

These experiences, and the strength we have gained from them, will help us take charge of our own education and help us birth our babies into our own hands. It will give us the strength to stand up against our fears and the persuasive pull of the birth industry telling us we are not capable of being full-blooded women who can have our own babies our own way.

This is the only way we are going to continue to exist outside of a test tube. The birth industry will never stop what they are doing; they make very good money from their work. Therefore, the only way we are going to get anywhere is if we take on our own responsibility to birth with dignity. So, look into your own heart and your own life experiences and find the strength to take charge of your own body and baby's birth.

We Were All Born

All over the world, most babies are born at home with, and without, professional assistance, and they are just fine. We can argue, of course, about certain places were mothers and babies are dying frequently due to disease and environmental hazards, but this is not because of birth itself.

Actually, the United States of America is at the top of the list for mothers and babies dying in labor and birth. This is because we have a technical approach to childbirth and treat it as though it were a disease that needs interference. If it is scrutinized, we will come to realize that birth is only considered safe when we have the money to cover liability for medicalized birth. If we can keep healthy and be aware of our needs--emotionally, spiritually, and physically--we are more likely to have a healthy outcome than if we just go to the doctor, get minimal education and have our babies "delivered."

I cannot say it enough: "No one has any authority over your body, and the birth of your baby, but you!" If you are willing to take on full responsibility for the creation of your baby's birth then you're doing all you can do to be a good parent from the very start, and no one can judge you for that. We need to remember that we are hiring these doctors and midwives to do a service for us.

You are paying and that makes you the boss! It is like any service you pay for, except this is usually the most expensive one—monetarily, physically and spiritually—that you may ever have to experience. It is the service of taking over the functions of your body, your baby's well-being and your birth outcome, which will affect both of you your whole lives.

Letting an authority decide whether you and your baby will have a good birth experience and that you will both survive it, is taking a huge statistical risk, and who wants to be a statistic? If you're going to be hiring these doctors and midwives, remember you are the one who knows yourself BEST!

There is nothing like a mother who goes into a prenatal care situation not knowing the language; all mothers should know and teach their children the language of doctors and midwives. If we educate ourselves, we are less likely to be experimented on or taken advantage of. Be Aware; you are hiring someone to have power over your life and your baby's life--that is a HUGE responsibility!

Pregnancy and Birth Wisdom

Listen with your Heart.
Listen to the voices of all your ancestors before you,
Ask them for guidance.
Keep your mind open, try new things that are good for you and baby,
Swim, dance and be present in the moment. . .
Nourish your body and mind with good foods and good books,
Your baby will learn with you, And you with your baby. . .
Be kind to yourself, take walks, bathe, get some time away from others,
Learn to enjoy being with yourself and your baby inside,
It is a special relationship while the baby is still inside of you. . .
You know what's best for your birth,
Be truthful and share your desires,
No one else can birth your baby but you,
Birth in truth. . . Stay away from negative talk about birth,
Your nervous system affects your baby,
Do not let media or family and friends give you advice that creates stress.
Research birth. It is one of the most important experiences of your life!
And your baby's life!
There is only one time when you will birth this baby,
So give yourself a lot of resources and good support.
Ask a friend or partner to touch you every day,
Get massaged and relax,
Your body and birth will respond to your needs more
If you get used to touch and letting go of negative thoughts. . .

Birthing naturally is an incredible gift to experience as a woman; enjoy your womanly body and the birth will give you strength in all of the rest of your life.

The wisdom of our Great Grandmothers is with you in every step you take to create a joyful pregnancy, birth, and parenthood experience. Be kind to yourself and listen with your Heart.

"Your children are not your children. They are the sons and daughters of Life's longing for itself. They come through you but not from you, and though they are with you, yet they belong not to you. You may give them your love but not your thoughts, for they have their own thoughts. You may house their bodies but not their souls, for their souls dwell in the house of tomorrow, which you cannot visit, not even in your dreams. You may strive to be like them, but seek not to make them like you. For life goes not backward nor tarries with yesterday. You are the bows from which your children as living arrows are sent forth."

~Kahlil Gibran, "The Prophet"

Wisdom's Children

We are wisdom's children, watching from up above,
Choosing our future mothers and fathers with love. . .
All we see down there is abundance,
A beautiful round sphere,
We would like to experience it there,
As long as the air is clean and the sea is green. . .
We are Wisdom's children, dreaming of this world,
Wanting to share in all the joys of boys and girls.
We are future children of the earth,
If we can be born, free, to explore this great place
With our minds and bodies intact,
We then can create what it lacks. . .
We ask our wisdom mother's too, please be clear,
If we are to be born free, we need you to be fully aware.
Our world is a great mystery and we are watching from above,
Until our time has come to be born out of love. . .
~ The Unborn Child

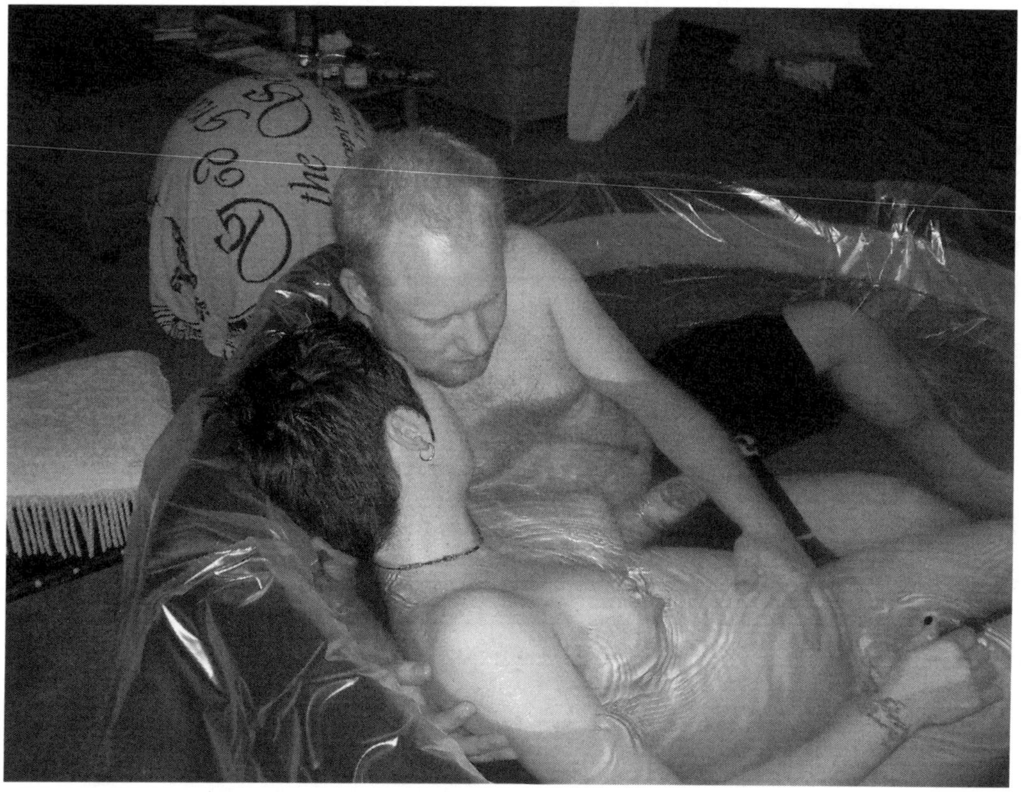

Kindle & Travis connecting lovingly in labor…

Redesigning Our Mind & Body Image

John H. Coates 1916

Body Image in Our Culture

Raising Our Children to Have Good Self Body Images from the Beginning

Trusting Our Inner Wisdom

Affirmations

Re-designing Our Views of Ourselves

Self doubt, The Epidemic of Our Culture

Sexuality and Birth in Society

Exploring Our Own Bodies

Self Examination

Sexuality, Breasts and Babies

Formula Feeding: Costs and Health Risks

Redesigning Our Body Image

Love your body the way it is. Learn to help your children love their bodies from the beginning.

In pregnancy there is nothing like loving your body, in fact I believe it was the only time I felt absolutely in touch and at ease with my body, completely. Being co-creator of a new being gave me the empowerment to finally take care of myself the way I should have been doing for years, but wasn't.

The reasons for this were family, society, media, peers, and my own past abandonment and rejection issues. However, typically for women even without all those supporters of "big bad body images," it is real and very common to have a negative body image.

Taking Care of Our Children's Body Image Future

I now believe that forcing a child to eat when they are not hungry is not good, and offering healthy foods at anytime is one way of making sure that they are getting what they need as far as nutrition. Even when my son was small, he knew when he needed to eat, right from the start I listened to his needs for breast milk. Later, at about nine months old, I would make food for him because, when he was hungry, he would tell me. If I offered him something he did not need I would ask him what he needed instead. Sometimes he would even point out to me what he wanted before he could talk. We learned how not to waste food since that was an issue. Making small frequent meals, or having one meal in a pot to eat throughout the day, was how we managed not to waste anything. Adding new ingredients to the main meal we ate for a few days was also a way to not waste food and get proper respect for the foods we ate. A few times during my son's growth spurts he would only eat veggies and fruit. Back then, I was a vegetarian and not a very good one. Tofu, fruits, pastas, veggies, beans, rice, and homemade breads were our foods. I realized. after awhile. I needed to learn more about nutrition; the best way I learned was by listening to my child. Grazing is how most species on earth eat; we should be no different.

Some days, I recall, Zack did not even want to eat. He naturally needed a day off from food, and this was good for him. He would drink a lot of water and soymilk (which, honestly, now I don't feel soy was that good), but after he was about 3 years old, soy was out. I got goat's milk, and he liked that better. Just realizing how some of us unknowingly program our kids not listen to their bodies makes me ill, literally! If I had been listened to as a child about what I needed as far as nutrition, I may have not had to suffer so dearly later in life; my body would have seemed good to me, and I might not have decided that starving myself was the way to take control over my existence.

Pregnancy and Body Image

Body Image is a noticeable problem for some women who become pregnant and have had self-esteem issues with their weight. Some of us are ok with the new body and some are not; it may take support and encouragement to create healthy self-esteem. Supporting moms and helping them to see it is their baby that is growing inside of them will help them love the belly that is their host.

Those who are weight conscious are not wrong for disliking their bodies, but most likely, their body image stems from the media and all the brain washing that has been done to us by setting up anorexic images as the ideal. These boyish, skeleton-like, frail forms are viewed as being beautiful and better looking than the historically healthy, round mamas we see in all those pregnant pictures in mothering magazines.

Throughout time, women have been curvy and luscious (that's healthy), not anorexic and energy depleted. However, we do not have to be fat to be healthy either. It is the balance between these two extremes that we should be striving for, and no matter what our shape or size, it is important to feel content within our own skins, right now, in this moment. That is what's important! Just realizing we are growing another human being inside of us is good enough evidence we are full of life and truly in balance with nature. That is beautiful!

No one's perfect and that's ok! Imperfection is Perfect; that is how we are created.

One thing I have learned through healing my eating disorders is that I strive now for perfect imperfection because our Creator created the entire planet, and all its inhabitants, to have some flaws. These are only flaws because we believe them to be so, because of mass perception, but to me those flaws are perfect in their natural way. So let us enjoy our imperfect selves and love our bodies however they are. Right now!

Some Body Image Affirmations:

"I love my body and its curves."

"Babies make bellies, and that's okay with me."

"My body is beautiful the way it is."

"Eating good food and exercising is the way."

"My body is a temporary vessel with which I nourish my children; my stretch marks are beautiful."

"I am a sensual, sexual, loving being, and that's why my baby is growing inside of me"

"I am a woman who is capable of enjoying my body however it is"

"I am able to experience my sexuality in a wholesome way that is caring and enjoyable for my self and my baby to grow"

"I AM PERFECT THE WAY I AM"

Exercise:

Take five minutes each day for yourself and slather some lotion, or oil, on each part of your body. Do this starting from your toes; tell them that you love them (aloud) "I love you toes! I love you and you give me stability, thank you toes."

Do this going up the body: calves, thighs, bottom, belly, breasts, arms, hands, face, hair and head. Tell every part what you appreciate about it, and also that "you love" that part of your body the way it is now.

Giving ourselves the freedom to love our bodies will help in labor and birth. This practice of telling our bodies at a cellular level "You are loved and appreciated," will indeed create the connection between all aspects of one's being. In turn, this will enhance the inner wisdom we seek while in labor and create a balance in mind, body and spirit. When this happens, it makes everything seem in the flow and in tune with what needs to be! Just Love It!

"I Am One With My Baby and Body "

Another great tool for loving our bodies more is to have our partner, or a good friend, give us massages. Relax, it may take a few times before you can really soak all that positive information into your muscles, tissues and psyche, but take the time, it works!

If you can do these affirmations and receive touch from someone you can trust, you will notice a huge change in your attitude towards your body. Creating a sacred space to express our dislikes is also good. When some of my clients tell me that they really are having a hard time with their growing body or that they feel fat, we can dilute this by applying positive healthy affirmations. Self-acceptance is the key. Even our dislikes about ourselves can be enjoyable, just by accepting them and not fighting WHAT IS in the moment.

"I Love and Accept Myself as a Whole Woman"

Feelings about ourselves can reflect how we live our lives and treat others. It also shows how we allow ourselves to receive happiness and nurturing from others who want to love us and want to support our emotional and physical evolvements. We need to be at peace with the world within and around us whatever the situation, and we need a friend or partner who will be there for us during the birth of our baby. So grab a friend, partner or midwife and let it all out!

Being at peace with ourselves is often "easier said than done," so give yourself credit for just trying to be in balance and trying to be honest with yourself. It's not easy. Some of us are in balance in some ways and not others. I am talking about that imperfect perfection. We humans have a tendency to beat ourselves up when we feel we have not lived up to some sort of standard, which is usually set by others.

In pregnancy, labor and birth, it is important to be "one" with your body and to find some sort of comfortable balance with your inner strength. You will need to trust your own intuition and listen to the baby who is working WITH YOU to birth.

Self-doubt is an epidemic in our culture.

As children, we are taught not to listen to our inner voices,
Not to love our bodies the way they are,
To be like someone else, not ourselves,
to please our parents, spouses, or society.
We are forced to eat when not hungry,
or not eat when we are hungry.
We sit before the television to keep occupied,
not getting the attention that we need inside.
Taught to listen to our teacher's even when they are not right.
We have relied on fast foods to grow our bodies.
Not getting enough fresh air or exercise.

We need to listen to our kids and empower them to be the best they can be. We can appreciate our children more, give them love and hugs everyday, share with them how to make good food and share creative activities, then they will have good self-esteem. It is never too late to give our children more love, more respect, and more joy so they can be healthier in their bodies, spirits and minds. These children will be the ones to create a better world in the future, with good self-esteem, and respect for their minds and bodies.

Trusting Our Inner Wisdom

Re-learning how to trust our inner wisdom comes from our hearts not our intellectual minds. We all have had moments when we had a knowing of some kind, an innate understanding of a situation or how to do something we were never taught to do, but intuitively … we just knew. This is inner wisdom. Taking us by surprise and showing us that we are indeed capable of many things we thought were not within our reach.

There's one huge example that I have experienced with my son many times. Somehow, through spirit, we are connected to our children. If we listen to our inner guides, we will know how to hear their calls. When using our intuition, we as parents can even know when our child is in distress, even if he's across town at someone else's house. I have experienced this with my own child when he was very upset with another child who took his toy or pushed him down. I had an overwhelming feeling, "mother's intuition," that I should go early to pick him up from his friend's house. Every time I felt that "overwhelming feeling," he was in distress when I arrived. Inquiring of his friend's mother what had happened, they supported what I had felt; that he had a scuffle or a battle over a toy and was very upset.

I learned at an early age to follow my instincts, I "went against the grain" of mass society and used my inner wisdom more than my intellect. I made instinctual decisions about motherhood. I remember numerous times when I let go of my mental, rational thinking and let my inner voice take over. There were a few times when that was not easy. Especially when other people were involved and tried to influence my decision. However, somehow I managed to learn to focus on that gut instinct rather then another person's opinion.

Usually these were cases when I was left alone for long periods because my mother worked a lot when I was growing up and I walked to and from school in a suburb of New York. On the several paths I took to school and home, there were many dangers for a small five-year-old female. I liked the time to myself on the walk through the woods. However, a few times I had to use my inner wisdom to get out of dangerous situations.

Once, I was walking and an older man appeared out of nowhere; he tried to slow me down to "talk" to me. I ran! He seemed nice and had a smile on his face, but something inside of me told me to run, so I did. Later that year, I remember someone saying that a man was trying to molest kids who were walking on that path between my home and school. We were told to start walking on the main road from then on.

I also remember being in the city one day with my mother; she had left me in the car while she ran into a store for something. I was about six at the time and waited in the front seat of our car. A man approached the vehicle and went to open my door, I instinctually locked the door, and I remember feeling scared with a lump in my stomach. I just knew he was up to something. My mother came out and asked me to unlock the doors, and I was frozen. I could not reach over quick enough to let her in, so she yelled at me and I started to cry because I was still feeling a little shocked about what had happened a few minutes before.

Communicating this to my mother, at such a young age when I was taught to "not disobey adults," or "talk back," left me afraid to tell her about what had just happened. I feared that my mother might get mad at me for not listening to the man who tried to take me out of her car. Babies and children live from their intuitive instinctual selves not their intellectual selves. If we as parents listen to our children, and support their instincts, we can learn from their pure wisdom how to parent.

Therefore, it is important to help our children maintain their inner wisdom, so they too can be aware of how to listen from within and use their instincts. This will enable them to become the best they can be as people on this planet, and make better choices for the rest of their lives.

Supporting our children to trust in their own inner wisdom is vital for their survival. We can ultimately create a place in this world where all of our children are intuitively intact from conception on into babyhood, childhood and then adulthood. We can listen to and support our children's dreams. We can practice natural parenting so our children can be connected with their source of inner wisdom and trust their instincts enough to listen from within.

Trusting in ourselves as guides and keeping the faith that our children have heard and felt just how much we love them, we must then trust they will choose their own best path in life.

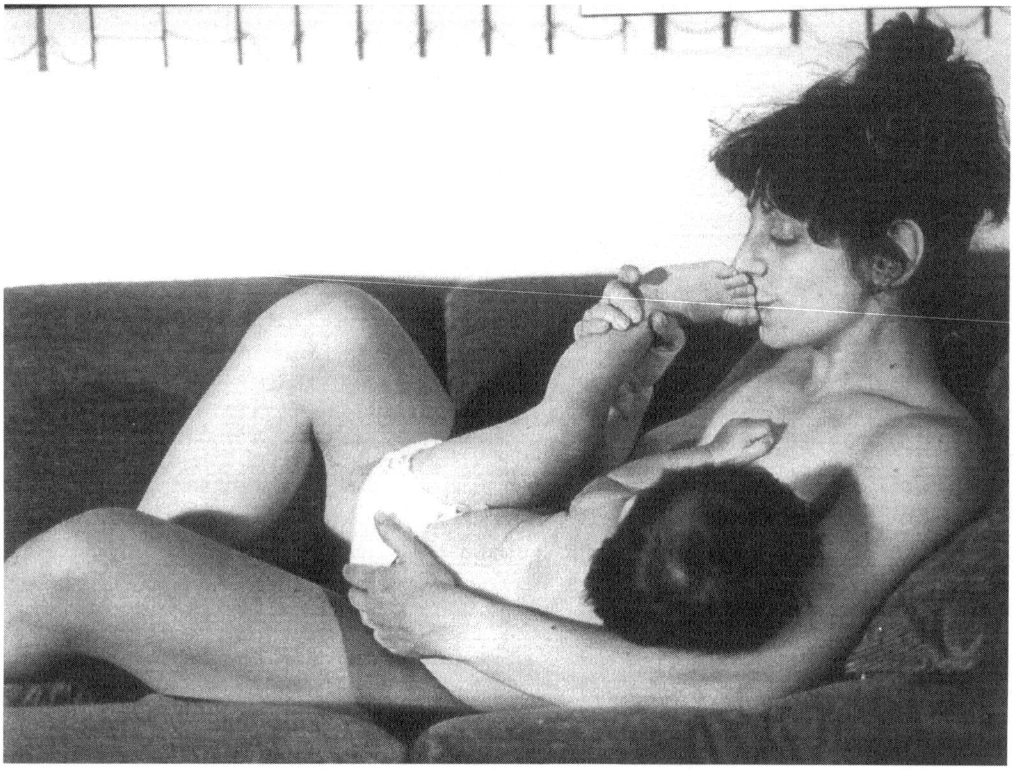

Donna Colelli nursing son Ciro 1986

Sensuality, Sexuality and Birth in Society

"As we have become increasingly self-conscious, we have developed a belief of shame. To one degree or another we feel shameful of our minds, our bodies, and our sexuality."

~Laura Shanley, Unassisted Childbirth 1994

In today's American culture, we have grown disconnected from our own bodies. All aspects of creating our babies have been separated from the actual pregnancy, labor, birth and parenting process much too often. It is making love that brings us closer to creation. Creating a new person is a beautiful experience and can be pleasurable if we allow ourselves to trust in our body's wisdom. Body image has a lot to do with our sensual selves, our sexual selves, and how we relate to others in life. Our bodies were created to live to their fullest potential and part of this potential is our ability to enjoy life and all our senses, which were given to us from our Creator.

Sensuality, sexuality and love are the way we create our babies. That same feeling of oneness can be a part of pregnancy and birth. It is not so much a mystery that when we are in the throws of ecstasy we can be making a baby. That pleasure, which creates our babies, can be the same pleasure we have in birthing them.

A part of loving our humanness is to experience pleasure in all of life. We were not created to suffer, but somehow we choose too. We are here to experience all of life and express our desire to create this world to be a better place in which to live. Sensuality and babies are very much the same. All mothers who have birthed and nursed a baby can say that at one time or another the pleasure of creating and birthing that child were seen to be one and the same. Nursing also gives both baby and mother pleasure; nursing hormones are released (via the pituitary gland) and create a sense of relaxation and euphoria. Some of us have orgasms during birth as some of us do when nursing our babies. It is a normal and natural event and can be enjoyed without guilt or shame. Because this pleasure merely exists, it is a normal and natural process of humanness.

It is not bad to experience pleasure from each other as long as it is not a forceful or an endangering act. Just relaxing and nursing, I experienced many orgasms. An orgasm is a contraction of the uterus, and after giving birth, we want the uterus to contract to keep from filling with blood and internally hemorrhaging. So it's pleasurable for the body to be doing what it should be doing; it's a good sign that everything is working properly. Nourishing our babies and relaxing while our body is getting back to it's original shape takes only a few weeks after a birth. All our hormones are working together to do the job they were created to do.

It is only logical that making love and having a baby go together. However, we in our culture have had so much shame and guilt connected with our bodies, and with self-exploration, that we're in need of re-remembering where we came from and need re-connecting to our great gift, which is to be happy and fulfilled in our bodies and being.

Having healthy, gentle births and babies is a good start in supporting our children to love themselves and their bodies, instead of being full of shame, guilt or hatred towards themselves and others.

Body Exploration

When learning about birth and woman's health care, I decided not to do anything to anyone I would not do to myself first. I learned how to examine my own cervix and looked at it many times during my studies to know exactly where it was and what it looked like. I was astonished to find that most women, even in their later years who had many children, did not know what their cervix looked like and had never felt it for themselves. It is one of the most liberating and practical things that a woman can do. First, ask anyone who gives you a pap smear to help show you with a mirror where your cervix is and what it looks like, or get a speculum yourself and by practicing with a mirror and flash light, you will learn when it is that you are fertile and how to keep track of your reproductive health. Learning about how to find your cervix through massage is lovely. Visualizing what the cervix looks like and imagining it thinning and opening support us when we are in labor. It works!

Unless you have seen it for yourself, it is very difficult to imagine what it looks like no matter how many textbook pictures you see. You can find it on your own, but it is usually easier the first few times to have someone else's feedback, so get your partner or a female friend to help you. Wash your hands. I find that my plastic speculum is easiest. They are usually in midwifery catalogs or you can sometimes buy them from a doctor's office, if you have a doctor or midwife that is supportive of your self-care learning, purchase one from them. They are about two dollars for the plastic ones and more for the metal ones, but those are cold! Eeek!

When finding your cervix, it's best to get in a position that you can reach it easily, sometimes even standing with one leg up on the bed or bathroom sink. Then reach up with your index finger and slowly move it around until you can feel a soft and roundish indent. That is your cervical opening.

Example: If you put your fist together and feel the outer part of the index and thumb, it sort of feels like that.

When using the speculum examine yourself visually, get a flashlight ahead of time and a mirror. You may need to elevate your hips on some pillows to get a good look and put a few under your head so you don't need to strain your neck to see it. Slowly slide the speculum sideways at first between your labias, holding them apart. Go gently, and once you feel a natural stopping point, stop! Hold the handle of the speculum up towards the front of your body, turning it slowly until you have a handle on it. Open it slowly and then lock it together to stay open on its own. Practice opening and locking it in place and closing the speculum many times before trying it inside yourself so you don't get pinched! Now with one hand your holding the speculum and in the other the flash light. The mirror is the tricky part, but after getting used to it you can do both. If you relax enough and do not contract your yoni muscles then the speculum will stay in place while you hold the flash-light and mirror.

Locating the cervix is usually hard at first, but if you can have a partner or friend help the first time you will get the hang of it.

I never go to get a pap exam without asking the nurse (the same one I have used for almost ten years!) to show me my cervix; it is the gateway for my children and my sacred body part, why should it be that strangers can see it and not I? Any time you go to get an internal exam you have the right to ask to see your cervix, hopefully whoever is doing the exam will support you in finding it and seeing it. On the other hand, why not just do it yourself, it is only practical to know what it looks like and how to find it on your own.

During prenatal visits, I often ask moms to examine themselves so they will have a good idea as to what's happening inside their bodies during labor without me having to "check" them. I do not do routine internal exams unless a mom wants me to for her own reasons. Very occasionally, this is helpful. I just feel it is intrusive and psychologically it can inadvertently cause the mom to feel like she does not know what her body is doing on her own.

Asking your girlfriend to help with your self-exam is one of the best ways to unite women in being supportive about learning together about self-care. Doing it openly, you will find some women friends who perhaps are not ready to share such intimacy. Finding others who are dying for an opportunity to explore their own bodies. And you have opened the door.

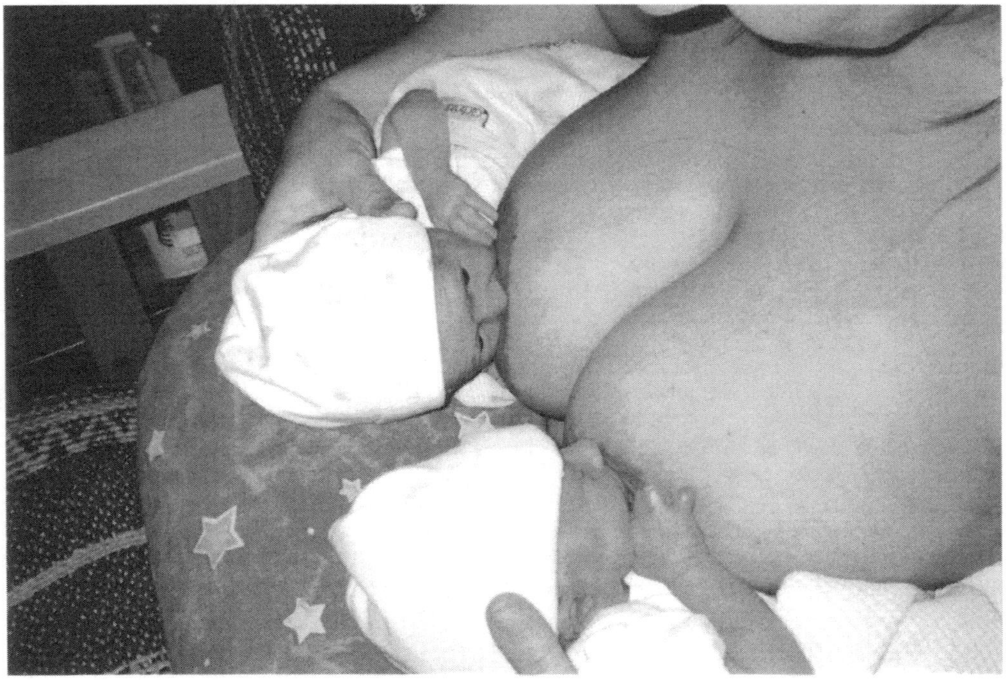

Nina nursing her homeborn twins Asher & Willow 2006

Breasts and Babies

Breast exams are also a part of knowing and loving our bodies better. I know some of us forget to pay attention to those girls in front "leading the way." Breasts have many incredible gifts to share, they are unique---every one, even a pair can be different from each other. Some are perky, some are hanging out, and some of them just live above the surface enough to get some sun light, they are all so different ... but one thing is for sure, they all need to be stimulated to remain healthy for their lifetime.

Doing a breast exam and massaging them each day will give you a sense of who they are and what purpose they serve in your life. Mine were always a "sex symbol" while I was growing up, all the boys wanted to do was to touch them. I ran of course, for several years, from such an invasion. I had not thought of my breasts as playthings. My first memory of breasts, in general, was of babies nursing on them, not mine of course but other women in my life. My imprint was "breasts are for babies not playing with." I even told some boys in my youth, "Hey these are for babies to get milk from, leave me alone!" They looked at me as if I was nuts!

When I had my son I breastfed him with dignity, I was not afraid of people looking at me funny, and I was not embarrassed to nurse in public. I took pride in going out to fancy restaurants with my husband and son and nursing him while we ate. I only saw smiles; no one seemed disgusted in any way. That was my perception. Lo and behold though, one of my cousins came into my house when I was breast-feeding and almost gagged! She said, "Oh do you want me to come back later?" (Like I was doing some sexual act with my husband.) I told her, "No you can come in, I'm just feeding my baby!" She actually said while I was nursing that she thought it was gross to breast feed and that she would never do anything like that if she had kids. I was horrified to hear such a remark. Here I was trying to do the "right" things for my baby and was insulted and shocked at such ignorance. However, that was her issue; her breasts were playthings to her and nothing else, just sexual objects that possibly did not even give her any pleasure. I just feel compassion for women like that who are not in touch with their own bodies.

Breasts are magical as well as essential to our existence. Without our ancestors' breasts, we would not be here today!

I was fortunate to be exposed to natural birth so young. Having the imprints of normal, natural birth and breast-feeding was, and still is, my image of how life works, that is, when we are working with nature and not against it. Also, the way our body is designed to manage many tasks was always of interest to me.

This imprinting of breast-feeding left me with a good outlook on motherhood and made me want to take care of my breasts. I have been doing self-breast exams for years now and encourage every woman to do her own. It, actually, is quite easy. Getting familiar with your unique breasts may take a few times, we all have lumpy days before a period, or they swell or have lymph glands that are more prominent than other's breasts. So before running to the doctors for a Mammogram, get to know your breasts the way they are, ever changing, during the course of the month. Some have little bumps around the nipple. Those are little whitehead looking things and it is normal; they just keep your nipples from drying out. A yeast-like bump is more around the breast itself and can cause sores in big-breasted women.

You can use some baking soda, cornstarch, or even a little bit of tea tree oil to wash the crease underneath the breasts. Do not use Talcum Powder as used in baby powder. It is toxic and not good for you! Talcum powder has been researched and found to have horrible side effects when used on the skin or even inhaled accidentally. Long-term use may cause certain types of cancer, thus this is obviously not good for baby's bottom either!

I have used Colloidal silver to wash underneath my breasts, and, after a few weeks, the irritations go away. Cutting back on yeasted bread and sugar really helps as does adding yogurt and acidophilus to the diet. Scrubbing the breasts with a lufa sponge can have great benefits as it stimulates lymphatic flow and circulation. To prepare for nursing, the lufa sponge will toughen up the nipples for suckling a wee one and also facilitate the flow of toxins out of the system.

Sure enough, if we get to know our breasts we will then understand ourselves in a different way. Sexually, I have gotten to enjoy my breasts more than ever. Now as an adult, I know my breasts better and respect the fact that they nourished my son for our breast-feeding months. My breast milk also gave him an incredible immune system that still benefits him to this day! I contribute his good health to my breasts, and all women who nurse will understand the benefits I am talking about.

If we know our body's well, our sons and daughters will also follow our example and learn how to take care of themselves through self-examinations and acceptance. Then in turn, they will be more conscious of who they are, and they will also love themselves enough to know when they need more care. Self-awareness is one of the best gifts we can give to our children.

Now back to the sexual part of breasts. It took me many years to learn to enjoy them sexually. I had to go through a lot of body-image healing before I felt like I could let them have pleasure. This took years, and with all the transitions I went through, I finally found my way back to my breasts. Because I was not breast-fed myself, I needed to find self-acceptance and forgiveness for myself for feeling left out. Having the strong desire to breast-feed my baby was also very healing. Every one of us, most likely, has had an experience with our breasts not feeling good in some way even if it is just getting sore before a cycle. They change constantly as we get older, and the ones who do not have breast stimulation are at risk for breast problems. They need to be exercised just like the rest of our body parts in order to stay fit and healthy. There is a higher rate of breast cancer for women who do not breastfeed their children. Breasts can become stagnant and therefore become a place where things can manifest, but if we touch them and have our partners and babies nurse on them, our breasts will be healthy and loved.

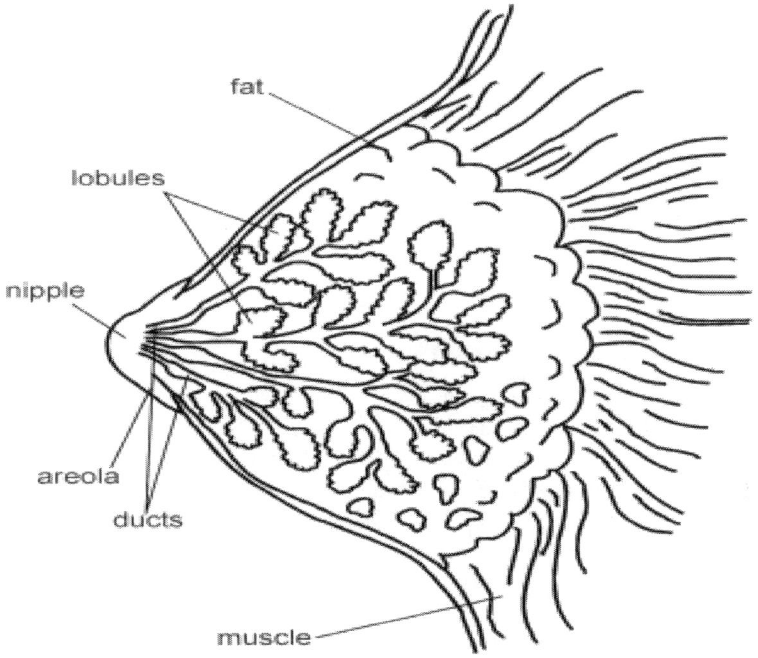

CROSS SECTION THROUGH THE BREAST

Breast Self Exam

First, trying to examine your breasts in the shower helps because they are lubricated by soapy water. Wash under each arm, lift and rest your arm on your head, wash in a circle around your breast where it meets the rest of your torso. Then put some pressure there while you wash, feel the grains and firmness of the muscles around that area. Now using your two middle fingers, firmly but gently move around the whole breast in upward then downward moves. If you have breast-fed a baby, or are now breast-feeding, you may feel little bumps, which are fatty tissue stores for milk later on. Try also around the nipples; pulling them and twisting them a bit and see how they react. Do they get hard, or are they still soft? A healthy reaction would be that the nipples get hard and erect. Try again, when you are lying down and feel the difference of texture and muscle tone. It is good to use lotion, or some Almond oil, when doing this so you can get deeper into the tissues. Breast care starts with knowing your breasts at every stage, and then if something becomes abnormal you will know. It takes a few months to get through all the breast changes in a cycle before really knowing them well.

Joys of Breasts and Babies

Breasts are incredible; they are equipped to do many things. Breast-feeding is one of those natural functions that is not only healthy for baby and mother but also prevents complications later in life.

It gives specific nutrition for the child's needs, without having to supplement.

It supports inner ear development and lessons the chance of ear infections.

Is gentle to baby's digestive system and promotes good flora (bacteria) for proper absorption of nutrients.

Provides balanced nutrition and prevents the likelihood of eating disorders later in life.

It remedies sick children and gives natural pro-biotic bacteria when the child needs it.

Is also good for skin, eyes, and other childhood problems when used as a topical anti-infection and anti-inflammatory remedy.

It can be used as a family remedy, which all will benefit from big and small.

It's good for parents and other children to boost their immune systems.

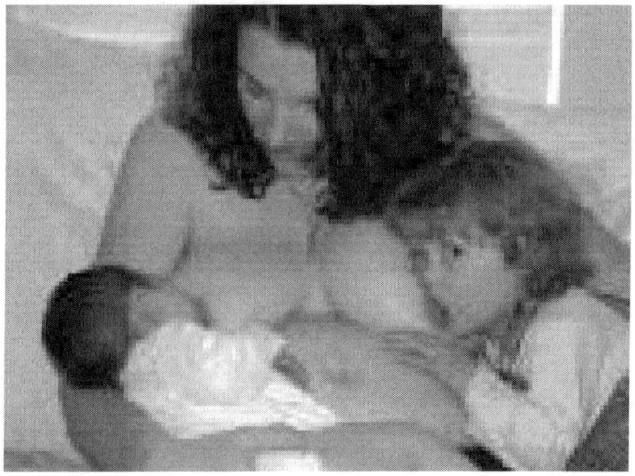

Patti nursing both her baby's Maya (2) and newborn Gemma a few weeks old 2006

It costs nothing and tastes great! You do not have to waste your time preparing bottles and risking infection to baby from a formula that has been processed through a machine. It may have sat in a can, or in an aluminum container, on a shelf somewhere in a warehouse for who knows how long!

Breasts are shaped to feed babies and other children too. Breasts are wise and equipped to adjust to a child's health needs. Breasts may also benefit other people's babies if needed. They will supply enough milk to go around if a friend is unable to feed her baby for whatever reason.

The breast is full of life; it is the ultimate way to nourish our young ones for as long as the child needs. All sizes of breasts can feed a baby well. The mind controls milk supply, so if you are relaxed and want to breast-feed, you can for as long as you like. You can feel safe in knowing that your breasts are feeding your baby what he needs and supplying your child's emotional, nutritional and physical needs as well!

Even adopted mothers can breast-feed their babies. My adoptive mother told me, when I was already a mother myself, that she had wanted to breast-feed me as a baby! I was so happy just hearing this that my inadequate feelings about not being breast-fed flew away. She did not have the support back then to do so, but now I have read books on the subject and also met a few moms who indeed breast-fed their adopted kids, and know it is possible. I hope moms who adopt babies nowadays are breastfeeding them. We adopted folk need all the emotional and nutritional healing we can get!

Resources: Breast-feeding Adopted Babies:

"Breast-feeding the Adopted Baby" ~ By: Debra Stewart Peterson 1994

Also: Le Leche League has a lot of information on breast feeding adopted babies and can give support and guidance to those seeking better alternatives to formula feeding.

From The Compleat Mothers' magazine: Volume 68, Winter 2003-4

The Cost of Artificial Milk

Coalition for Improving Maternity Services

Po Box 2346, Ponte Vedre Beach, Florida 32004

www. Motherfriendly.org call toll free: 888-282-CIMS (2467)

US families spend $2 billion a year on human milk substitutes such as artificial milk, otherwise known as formula. It costs an additional $1.3 billion dollars to cover sick-child office visits and prescriptions for respiratory infections, ear infections, and diarrhea in non-breast-fed infants during the first year. In the first year of life, it will cost more than $25,000 to treat lower-respiratory infections in 1,000 never-breast-fed infants compared with 1,000 infants exclusively breast-fed for at least three months. The excess cost of treating Type I Diabetes, (Insulin-Dependent Diabetes Mellitus) in formula-fed children is more than $1 trillion.Private and government insurers spend a minimum of $3.6 billion a year to treat medical conditioners and disease preventable by breast-feeding.

Fear & Birth

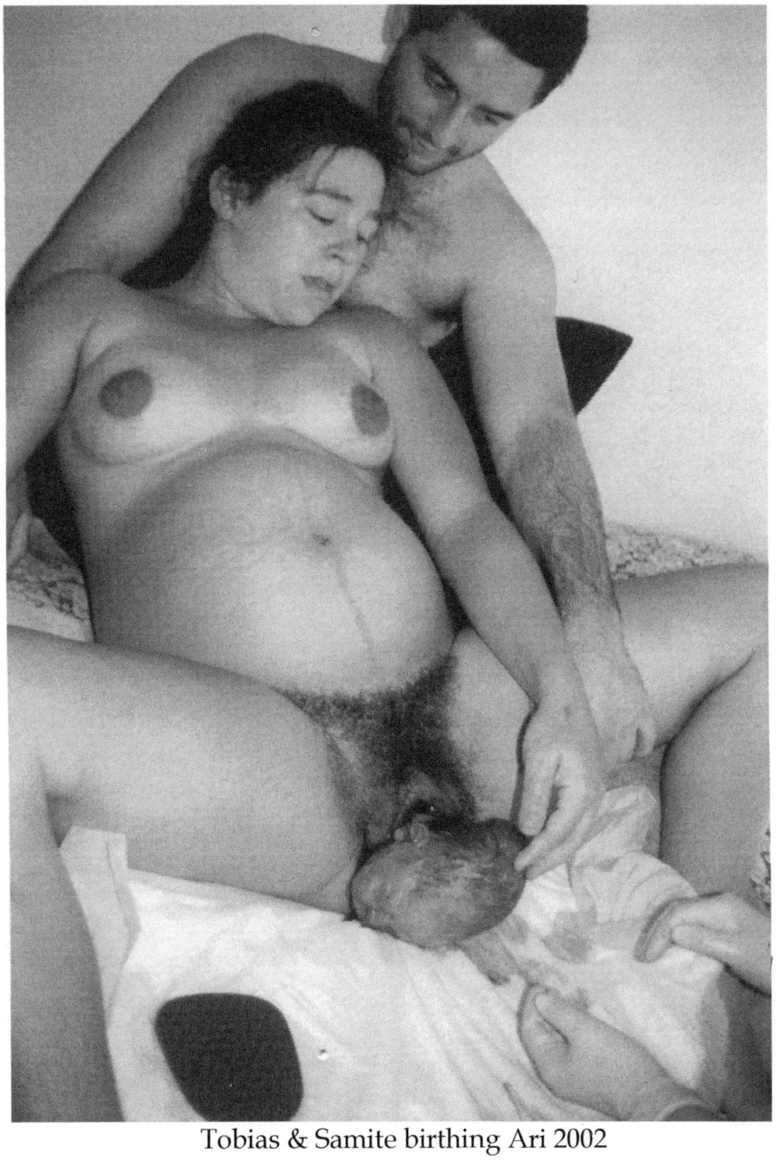

Tobias & Samite birthing Ari 2002

Painless Childbirth

Rituals to Release Fear

Breath Work

Relaxation

Communicating with the Unborn

Touch

Labor Perceptions

Fear Free Birth Affirmations

Post Partum Depression

"Pleasurable Childbirth," Quotes from Laura Shanley's website:

Painless Childbirth

"I know of no country, no tribe, no class, where childbirth is attended with so much pain and trouble as in this country." Thus replied a traveler, who had been many years in foreign lands, upon being interrogated as to the comparative sufferings of savage and civilized women.

***~From the Book "Tokology," A Book for Every Woman"* by: Alice Bunker Stockham MD. 1899**

"Tokology" from Taber's Medical Dictionary: "Tacology" -means the Science of Childbirth.

What is "Pain" and where does it come from? Pain is caused by a defensive reaction to fear, of some kind, in the course of protecting oneself from something in the mind. Pain starts with fear, psychological or subliminal. Then into the brain it goes, triggering a reflex to the nervous system causing a part of the body, which the mind is focused on, to become contracted. It creates a lack of oxygen to that body part depleting its reserves of needed oxygen. What happens then is that area of the body, say the uterus, struggles to oxygenate itself and has to work extremely hard to gather what it needs to do its task. Then it becomes exhausted and ultimately painful.

Of course, it is relative how, from time to time, the body fights illness by creating either a warning headache or inflammation of a body part. This is the body's way of saying, "Hey there's something going on with me; I need attention!"

Past issues of fear or mistreatment, which have not been dealt with, will come up during the birth. These issues can cause emotional upset, and then, birth may become painful.

If a mother were ready emotionally, spiritually and physically, she would rarely have any "true" fear, and therefore she would birth her baby without any "true" pain. She may be "crampy" or uncomfortable, and it may feel "intense," but rarely should there be true "pain." I personally experienced this phenomenon. I was perfectly fine throughout my early morning labor, fully dilated before reaching my midwife, then when feeling observed and in an environment that I did not want to be in, I began to feel some distress and discomfort. I prolonged my labor instinctively for my baby's protection and mine until I was in a room all by myself in the dark, then I gave birth painlessly and with little effort. Overall, it was a four-hour process, and one of those hours was disturbed by interference. The interference of other women making noise and the midwife distracting me by telling me something, which I can't even remember. During this time I had the most intense sensations I experienced during the whole labor. The labor itself, especially before leaving home, which I had not planned to do, and was upset about, caused me to feel more discomfort then any other part of my birth experience. Once I was alone in a dark quiet room, I gave birth with no pain whatsoever. It was 'intense' in a good way, and the most exciting and rewarding adventure I have ever experienced.

Learning from my own birth about the source of fear and pain, I have changed my way of teaching and supporting women with their childbirth experiences. I feel now after witnessing many births that women do just fine when they are left alone to follow their instincts, especially if they have the proper education and support to back up their instincts/intuition and their mental/emotional processes. Even so, when I am at a birth and present for someone else's experience, I am somehow a distraction, even though most of my clients who want me at their births have already developed a sense of well-being by working on themselves.

To prevent complications, during and before pregnancy, we need to work on ourselves, emotionally ridding ourselves of any negativity about our bodies, past history, or childbirth itself. Through affirmations, visualizations, re-birthing and re-learning what we, as women, are capable of, we will be able to create a fearless, painless birth experiences.

This may seem like a lot of work, and it is, but it's well worth it, and most of the time it can be done effectively and efficiently by doing just a few meditations once a week! Also just being alone with ourselves, as much as possible, will allow us to get in touch with our own strengths and intuition.

Don't get me wrong, I do not believe every woman should be left alone during labor and birth if, they feel they need support. Some women need other women to be present, to hold their hand, make tea, clean, and even help with the baby from time to time, but certainly not to "deliver" a baby or cause distraction. Since distraction can cause an interruption in the birth process, it may cause undue discomfort. Some mothers, like myself, benefit from being alone, because distractions can cause a protective response in the labor, and then the birth becomes painful because of the primal instinct to protect one's offspring.

Too many times, I have witnessed others telling a mom what to do in labor or taking an action without consulting the parents. Instead, they could support her to become more empowered by listening to her inner wisdom. Our job is to guide one another, to empower through self- realization and to educate about birth, then birth may be attended without interference or difficulty.

If we had more education as to the causes of pain and fear, then every woman would be educated enough to support her sisters the way they need to be supported and do their own births instead of hiring someone outside themselves and their families to do it for them.

Breath Work and Relaxation

Daily rituals for releasing fear during pregnancy and birth

"Persistence is the sister of patience. Patience alone will not carry us through. We must be persistently patient if we are to accomplish our goal." ***~Laura Shanley's "Unassisted Childbirth" (1994)***

Ideally, before even becoming pregnant, it is wise to learn techniques that can help in everyday life as well as when giving birth, but it is never too late to start. Breathing and relaxation sound simple, yet for some they seem impossible because of children to be cared for or chores that need to be done, right now! Usually these are the excuses for not taking the time out to inhale and exhale consciously. This little bit of focused effort can make a world of difference between being overwhelmed or gracefully getting through a day. Relaxation can also be achieved moment to moment by just breathing deep and full breaths.

Breath is the essential life force of every living thing on this planet. It can be stunted in stressful situations like labor, especially if a mom is stuck in an emotional issue. Taking the time to breathe may sound silly, but if done in awareness and in a focused way, it can bring relaxation and can rejuvenate one's entire being.

It is vitally important to relax during labor and birth, but this is easier said than done. Most of us have a hard time doing this because of outside interference, but it is possible to suspend time for a few moments, and in labor, that is what happens.

Mother Nature does not use a watch nor does she need to keep time of the interval between contractions during labor or birth, so learning to relax will enable you to be "still in the mind" and let things happen when your labor begins.

Below are two techniques to help you learn to breath and relax. They can be done anytime, upon waking, before going to sleep, or any time throughout the day. Find a moment to yourself in a quiet space, preferably somewhere dim or dark, even under the covers of your bed.

Turn off the telephone and put a note on the door so that you will not be disturbed. By the way, this is a really good thing to do while you are in labor and giving birth.

Kindle going deep within herself to birth her baby 2006

Breathing Technique:

1.) Clear your nostrils a few times by holding one nostril closed, and then taking three deep breaths through the other nostril making one quick blow out each time. Clear out both nostrils before beginning.

2.) Take in a slow deep breath as far as your natural air will go, then let it out slowly until emptied completely. Do this a few times until you feel that you have developed a natural flow.

3.) As you inhale, close your eyes slightly but not all the way, and then set your hands on your belly so you can feel the smoothness of your breath coming in and releasing out.

4.) Picture a white dot between the top of your head and your brow.

5.) Focus on the white dot as you breathe.

6.) Visualize this white dot slowly opening with each breath and getting bigger each time you exhale.

7.) As it opens, you become more and more relaxed.

8.) Keep breathing slowly in and out for five minutes.

9.) When you feel you have mastered this breathing technique, take five minutes twice a day to do it, or as many minutes as you can a few times a day, every day.

This technique will condition your breathing to automatically move freely even while in labor. Remember, let your breath move freely in and freely out and it will deepen your relaxation.

Relaxation

1.) Put a few pillows under your legs if you feel comfortable lying on your back. If you prefer to lie on your side, have one for holding beside you and another to put between your legs,

2.) Starting with your toes, tense and contract them with an inhale and let them go with an exhale. Then do the same with your feet, calves, thighs, and continue this exercise moving up through your entire body. Be aware of each body part as you inhale and exhale being sure to use smooth, deep and unforced breaths.

3.) Once you reach your head, move it from side to side with your inhale then let it drop into the pillow with your exhale.

4.) At this time, focus again on the white dot between your brow and the top of your head, inhale and let it open with the exhale.

5.) Now, let your body sink into the pillows and bed, breathing freely focusing on only that white dot on your forehead … breathing in, breathing out, breathing in, breathing out …

This relaxation practiced two times a day (or more if you can) with your breathing will enhance your mind and body to work in perfect balance during your labor and birth.

Artist;Anne Pyretek 1998

Connecting to Baby

Taking time to connect with your baby is an important way of understanding your inner-self and what your baby needs from you. Together you will be able to listen to what is happening at all times during labor and birth. Getting to know your baby before birth is a special time of bonding and a natural progression on your path toward parenthood. We are parents to our babies before they are ever born. We have a unique relationship with our baby while she is inside our womb. Once the baby emerges into the outer world, it is another type of parenting relationship.

When I was pregnant with my son we spoke everyday to each other, he would tell me stories of the womb and comfort me when I was nervous or had self-doubt. I listened to him through our special inner connection. Usually when I was without distractions from daily life, in the car or sitting on my couch, I could hear his voice laughing and having fun with me. I will never forget this very spiritual connection. If I was sad, he would tell me that I was okay, that he was there with me and that he loved me. I can remember dancing in my living room to some drumming; he tapped to the beat of the drum and followed my movements around the room. Once the music stopped, he stopped, and I felt him relax into my pelvic floor, taking deep breaths with every move I would make; he also would inhale and exhale with me.

By the end of the pregnancy we had bonded so well, I knew when he was awake or asleep, what he liked to eat and drink and how he wanted me to talk too him. He liked bed time stories, so I would read bedtime stories to him every night, he really liked the *"Good Night Moon"* book, and after he was born we continued reading it for several years, and he fell asleep every time.

When we were in labor, he moved with me and I with him, and no conflict arose from our synchronicity. We were communicating the whole time and had no fights of power or resistance.

Working together in labor with your baby is important for having a safe, flowing labor and birth. It is easy if you listen to your baby's "voice" before he is born.

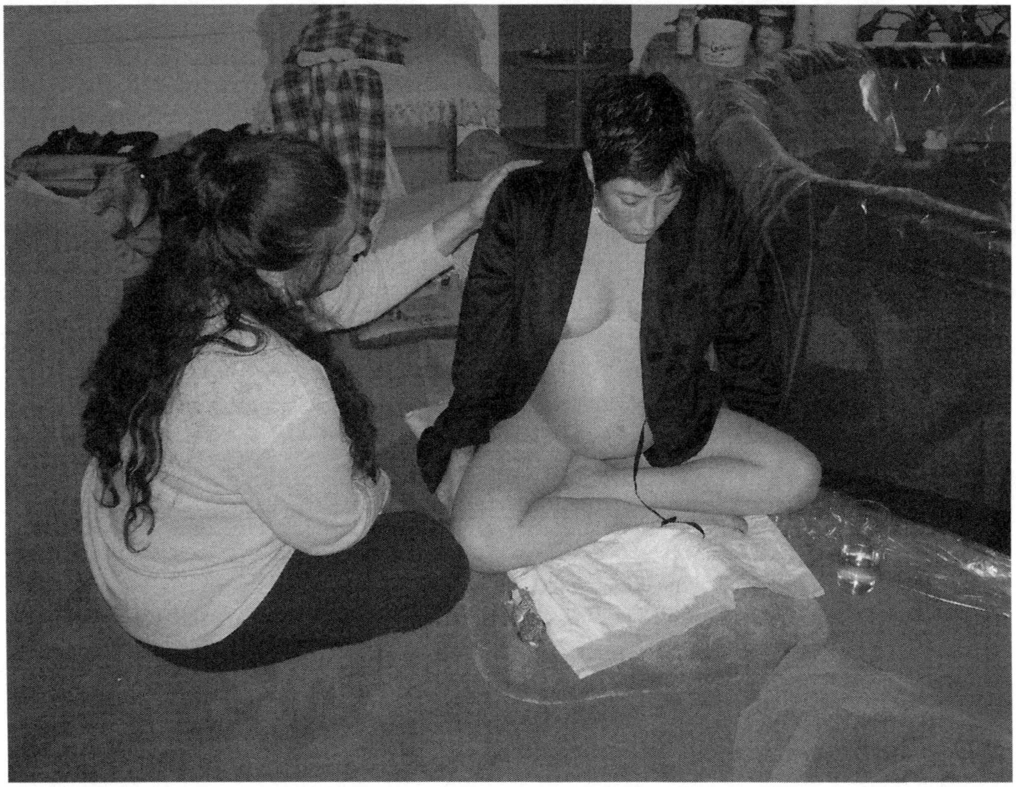

Kindle in labor getting some reassurance

Touch

Being touched is something we may have had to work through, as mom always says, "There is good touch and there's bad touch," but even though we are adults, it is still an issue in our societies today. We can benefit from slowly regaining our trust in ourselves, and our birth process, through massage.

Massage is an ancient art; it is a technique of healing and soothing muscles and emotional pain, it can bring great trust and joy into one's life. During the time of gestation, we are being massaged throughout pregnancy by our mother's uterine hugs. Being squeezed gently for the whole time we are inside our mothers wombs, this is a preparation for labor and birth, a preparation for being touched and loved when on the outside of the womb. This is nature's way of stimulating the nervous system and hugging the baby so he can grow effectively. We need touch to survive; if we do not get touched after being born, we may possibly die, either emotionally from the natural yearning to be held and loved, or physically from the natural way our bodies need to be held and massaged for the proper functions of our organs. Massage is so essential; we just cannot live without it. During our lifetimes we are hugged and kissed, caressed and cuddled, stroked and patted, or at least we should be. If not, we begin to distrust others and ourselves, we desensitize from others and become depressed. We need touch to live healthily and function optimally!

When we're pregnant, getting touched at least four times a day will help in eliminating fears, discomforts, anxieties, emotional pain, and physical ailments. If you have to go get a massage from a professional therapist, it is worth every dime. Some therapists may be covered under health care plans. Have your partner or a friend give you neck massages, shoulders and back massages, each day you need to be touched. At the very least try to get some sort of massage 3 times a week. Each day, hugs, kisses, rubs, and pats, from family and friends, are needed. Your baby will also benefit from your being touched, because you're happy hormones will circulate happiness to your baby as well. Feeling loved is just a needed thing, we all need to be loved and appreciated, what better way then through loving touch!

Labor Perceptions

When we think of the word labor, we think "Work." It stems from the very meaning of "hard labor," strenuous physical work, but truly it does not need to be a struggle; our bodies were made to do this kind of work, we have done it for hundreds of thousands upon thousands of years. In our minds, we can choose the struggle and have a hard labor, or we can choose it to be a pleasurable thing to experience. I believe and hold true that most of the work in giving birth is before it even happens. Prenatal education, self-care and persistence in affirming to ourselves that it is pleasurable is the only real labor you will have to do. When labor does come, it can be a flow of mother, father, family and baby to enjoy with laughter and contentment. If for some reason we do not feel this to be possible then we need to do more work within ourselves! When you remember that birth is not an illness, and its labors are "not for nothing," then re-thinking how birth can work for you is easy.

Any fear we have can attribute to any pain we have in labor, be it a previous birth that you were not satisfied with and have issues to work on, or other factors surrounding the environment you are exposed to. If these issues are not dealt with, they may arise once again, and it is best if you deal with them before you become pregnant or during your pregnancy.

I recently heard a story of a mom who had a Cesarean birth with her first baby. For her next pregnancy, she wanted to give birth on her own, without a midwife or doctor present. She realized she had fears from the first birth. She feared that her body could not open, because her last doctor told her that her cervix was dysfunctional, and that is why he gave her a C-section. She ran into that thought repeatedly during her labor with her second child. The labor took three days, because that doctor placed that notion in her mind. She kept telling herself, "Maybe they were right, and I can't open!" and then she turned it around and told herself, "Yes I can open, I am made to give birth to this baby!" After saying this to herself repeatedly, her labor would progress until another negative thought would appear; she kept turning her thoughts around until she finally told herself and her baby that it was ok for her to open and let her baby out. When she finally decided she could do it, then her baby came with no problems.

The power of suggestive thoughts, and the imprints we create for ourselves, is of great importance as a tool for positive change. It is helpful to work on these thought patterns before giving birth so that any negative thoughts are transposed into a positive affirmation. Use mantras, prayers, and chants for birthing without fear and without pain.

Throughout the ages, women, in all cultures, have been birthing babies. In other places in the world even today, women are able to work right up until they birth, then back to work they go! The reason for this is cultural beliefs that affect our consciousness more then we know. When we let our culture dictate our beliefs, we become a "product" of that culture and rarely a part of the greater reality. I am not suggesting we go right back to work after birth. I am merely suggesting that cultural beliefs condition us and how we make choices and function.

Post Partum Depression, also called the "Baby Blues"

Post partum depression or PPD, is a common occurrence in many (about half) mothers after the birth of their baby. This is thought of as a behavioral imbalance. Most medical care providers will medicate with anti-depressive drugs. This in turn creates more difficulties later in life for both mother and child. Nevertheless, it is quite normal to have some "imbalance" after a child is born. It is normal to have a huge shift in emotions. Hormones may be part of the cause as they fluctuate to assist in the production of "Prolactin Hormone" for milk supply. New mothers often have many fears, from their ability to care and provide for their child too difficulties with the father. PPD may be caused by a numerous array of environmental and social challenges. A birth that was not satisfying, drug induced, or operative may heighten the risks for PPD. A "let down" feeling after a "birth gone bad" may tend to create emotional anxieties in a mother who does not have the tools to carry herself out of blame, shame, fear and guilt for what happened in her birth.

PPD is thought of in terms as mild to severe and can be treated through natural means. PPD can come up anytime after a baby is born, even years later. It is not talked about as much in our culture as in others, and this is the reason why it is thought of as a shameful feeling, or something to hide. In turn, many women suffer alone in shame and guilt for their natural feelings. In fact, if hidden or not talked about, it can get worse even to the point of feeling suicidal.

After a child is born, numerous things change within our bodies and minds. Chemicals, for instance, are released during labor and birth to signal hormones that set up an instinctual response throughout the body to begin our parenting. These chemicals may be interfered with by the drugs used during labor and birth and may not be released at all. Sometimes a mother has had issues about becoming a mother or about her own child-hood. She may have many mixed feelings about the child, her own parenting skills, or even the planet not being supportive of her needs. This can inhibit the flow of hormones, causing stagnation and mental confusion.

Sometimes a mother has no idea what is happening, she may feel angry, sad, and mad at her loved ones and may sometimes even feel violent toward her baby. Compassion is lost in these violent episodes in the mother's mind, and only the mother herself knows how she is feeling after the fact. This is the worst-case scenario, but it may happen when a mother is not getting support in her emotional transitions into parenthood and not taking care of herself properly.

I did not have this dilemma after my son was born, but have supported many women through their hours of need. PPD is very real and should not be ignored!

PPD can be dealt with nutritionally, through exercise, doing affirmations, and getting emotional support from other women who can understand the normalcy of her feelings.

Herbs such as Saint John's Wort, Lemon balm, Mother wort, Skull cap, Cat nip and Valerian root used separately can sometimes relieve depression while taking other precautions with proper nutrition, exercise and rest. Utilizing the Placenta PP, by eating some of it, or all of it, over the course of a few weeks is also beneficial for reducing the risks of PPD. Mother Nature really did think of everything we need!

It is overwhelming enough to have a new child to take care of, but by taking care of ourselves as well, we lessen the risk of PPD later.

Having a good, reliable support system is essential for PPD moms; it allows the freedom to feel and move through her feelings without suppressing them. There are support groups online and twenty-four hour hotlines for assistance with PPD. *(Numbers can be found under resources)*

I Am the Master Of my own Reality

I Create my own fulfilling Birth Experience

I Am open to receiving pleasure . . .

I Am the best provider for myself and my baby . . .

I Am willing to work on my past, so I can birth with ease . . .

I Am healthy and full of positive energy . . .

I Am full of love and its potential to create my own great reality . . .

I Will listen to my inner wisdom and enjoy my birth . . .

I Will transform any doubts into positive thoughts . . .

I Am the life giver and receiver of this new being . . .

I Am grateful for this baby's creative force in my life . . .

I Am open and birth with ease and pleasure . . .

The Universe in all aspects of my being supports me . . .

Here are a few quotes from women who gave birth with pleasure, and allowed themselves to feel pleasure while giving birth, fully embracing their body's wisdom.

~From Laura Shanley's website Unassisted Childbirth.com

"At about 3 AM, I got a real feeling that the baby needed to be born, and also a great surge of energy, the first I had felt. Then I made a very astounding discovery. I was able, through prayer, to get knowledge directly from God, that birth is a sexual event and involves the same mechanisms that the beginnings involve. I was able to get my labor started again, and I was in hard labor within 15 minutes. As long as I was alone and able to yield to the sexual joy of the birthing, I was able to experience wonderful orgasmic feelings and no pain at all." ~ From Pat Goltz, in the newsletter, The New Nativity, edited by Marilyn Moran

It was then I began to scream, but not with pain - with joy. With release. I felt an enormous all-body orgasm as I bore down, again, and again, and again, crying out with lust and happiness. The baby was coming, and so was I. I pushed an enormous last push with every fiber of my being; the head and shoulders appeared. By then I was sobbing. I reached under the baby's armpits and pulled out ... a child. A living, breathing infant ... born perfect. Perfectly beautiful. My daughter." ~From Awakening, by Jen Bradley

"I returned upstairs with some of Stella's dance tapes. Belly dancing to the music, I found that the contractions were much more bearable. Oddly enough, the more obscenely I thrust my pelvis back and forth the less it hurt. I was amazed! Why hadn't I known that these movements were linked to the act of birthing, I wondered. Moments later, I discovered that all the pelvic thrusting I had been doing in my life - dancing to get a date, making love, and now, giving birth - was integrally connected. All that thrusting had gotten me pregnant, and all this thrusting would help bring a new life into the world. While the drums banged in my head, I was serene knowing that I had found the secret to life: the glorious pelvic thrust." ~From "The Glorious Pelvic Thrust," by Maria Young Alders (Mothering, Winter 1994)

"Birth is always intimate and sexual, although the intimacy and the sexuality can be masked. My own personal experience of the births of my children confirms this. My feelings throughout my wife's labors, I can describe only as those of a very close, physical-emotional, sexual union with her and what I felt to be the transcendent force flowing through her. The sensation was warm and soft, like making love, but was also strong, forceful and awesome. Each time the experience changed my life and allowed me a glimpse of the transcendental."

~Lewis E. Mehl, M.D., quoted in "Psycho physiological Aspects of Childbirth," in "The Psychology of Birth," by Leslie Feher

History & Birth Politics

History and Politics of Medicalized Childbirth

Propaganda to get rid of Midwives at the Turn of the Century

The Implications of Media on Birth

Solutions to Drugs and Violence in Our Society

Politics, Birth, and Beyond

"Culture has been doing it's best to destroy the safety and beauty of normal childbirth for many generations. It has tried hard to demonstrate the wonders of science upon the greatest miracle of nature. It has failed to understand the simplicity of truth and unhesitatingly introduced the complexity of falsehood."
~ DR. Grantly Dick-Read 1959:284

In the beginning of human kind, we birthed our babies instinctually; neither thinking nor knowing what a powerful thing it was to follow our instincts, we just did. Not questioning nor thinking that by following our instincts we were co-creating the world harmoniously with nature. We were just doing what our bodies were made to do, a function of woman and man to co-create new life in this reality of existence.

It was not until humanity became conscious of our power to manipulate nature with intellectual reasoning, that every instinct was manipulated for man's greed. We knew, as women do, that all man's greed would become a power, in the form of oppression, over instincts and intuition for control over society. Yet never, did we imagine, that they would have the power to destroy as much as it has.

The 'Woman's Holocaust," or what the church called a "HOLY-CAUSE," was set in place in order to eliminate evil by taking over the "unnatural" functions of women. This happened because we women, supposedly, sinned by creating man in the first place. Do we sense another vicious cycle here?

Unaware of the chaos they were creating that would last several hundred years, the church run by men decided it was not the place of women to "control" their communities with farming, praying to the Creator for their abundance (the church wanted to take credit for that one!), and own land or facilitate natural functions: bleeding, healing, supporting the dying and birthing. Thus, the church had millions of women murdered in order to place fear and superstition in all concerning natural things. The Matriarchal system thus broke down and was taken over by the church. Birth, it just so happened, was one of the main focuses of the power women have in society, as well as healing, harvesting the crops and caring for the dying. Men almost totally replaced these functions and regulated it by their own fears of being inferior to women's wisdom (Magic Powers)to heal. Even in a time of religious power, God was used as the scapegoat for women's sins. Supposedly, God created women as imperfect creatures who should not be in power of nature, and thus the church wanted to take over any natural power she had in childbirth.

I do not believe it ever started as a war of the "sexes," but I do believe that most men in authority knew if they could get rid of the powerful women healers in their society they would have much greater control over that society. Throughout her-story, women have been the symbol of life, the womb is the sacred vessel of all existence in almost every culture we can gather information from. This was a great threat to our religious systems of the times, and still widely is not recognized.

I also have noticed, in my studies, that women contributed to the mass destruction created by the "holy cause." Some chose to be alongside the murdering and stealing, most likely to save themselves from prosecution. The war over power was not a ballot of consensus, it was a forced decision made against the common people in order for the government to gain more respect through fear--kind of like how our government still works.

Before there were religions that dominated the people, there was the religion of natural prayer. We had rituals to give offerings to the earth for it's bounty of food in the harvest season, we had dances to the sun for giving us light to grow our crops, and to moon for its power of rest and rejuvenation and for the moving of the tides. We learned from the earth and gave thanks to its existence. Our religion was indeed a religion of natural things and our unknowing of how it scientifically worked did not hinder us from revering its power as the hurricanes, earth quakes and natural disasters did their own jobs instilling reverence in us. When we became thinking beings and began to understand our potential to create other realities, our consciousness shifted its paradigm, and man began practicing his dominating force over nature so our natural power became less and less important.

You are a part of Nature, God, and this planet we share.

"Because the Medieval Church, with the support of kings, princes and secular authorities, controlled medical education and practice, the Inquisition (witch hunts) constitutes, among other things, an early instance of the "professional" repudiating the skills and interfering with the rights of the "nonprofessional" to minister to the poor."

~From the book "The Manufacture of Madness" (by: Thomas Szasz M.D. 1970):

Three witches hanging, from the title page of a contemporary pamphlet on the third Chelmsford witch trial, 1589

Long before there was technology and organized medicine, the witch-hunts were begun. Dismissing any peasant population, mostly Pagans, worshippers of natural forces and practitioners of male and female balance, from their traditions passed down from other family members. This constituted the dogmatic church's role in the demise of all natural knowledge that had been passed down for centuries through the spoken word. Out of fear of loss of controlling the kingdoms through the church.

Thus, it created a space for the wealthy to take over healing and all medical practices became controlled by the church, hand in hand with state officials. It was seen as a good business opportunity.

Poorer populations were left to manage their own births and illness for many years to come, which was a blessing in disguise. This allowed preserving of knowledge to be passed down for a while longer. The women were also not allowed to seek medical education, or even formal education at that time, nor could the poorer population afford it. This did not turn out well since most lay healers were women, and their rights became less and less as legislation passed against lay healers in the years that followed. While the "witch hunts" were far from over, the traditional healers of the times could only administer their true knowledge in secret, which made it extremely difficult, and if caught death was on the horizon for themselves, possibly even family and friends would be brought to accuse them to save their own lives. Making the churches accusations even more real to the general public

Even though this all sounds like the female healer went extinct, and in some areas this is true, women are still the main care providers in health care, birthing babies, and being there for the dying in most parts of the world. Even through the hundreds of years of torture and murder to take over that innate power of woman, the church failed to understand the power of Mother Nature herself. I believe this so-called "cleansing" actually began because the men in power at the time were running low on their resources to hold down their kingdoms. Women of those times were landowners and land workers who would actually be the ones to control the crops and essentially control the kingdom's people. In many societies women were actually the leaders of religion and led their communities peacefully. Unfortunately, someone somewhere had an idea that they could do better, therefore, started the crusades of the inquisitions, which lasted thousands of years…

And in our modern day we are still faced with the ramifications of our past…

When the empire was growing weak, they caused a series of rumors to be spread against these so-called sinners or "witches." In fact, there was a bounty on such witches, and anyone who would turn one in would be given a reward from her estate. This certainly created a "turn on your neighbor" effect, which continued through many, many years.

After this began, it just seemed appropriate to continue the scandal that benefited the kingdom's wealth, but not necessarily the kingdom itself.

By the mid 1800's, male physicians began to realize that birth could be prosperous for their profession. Not many male physicians of that time had ever even seen a birth, but they had courses over a day or two that allowed them to examine manikins to prepare them to attend births. In addition, they performed human dissection on living pregnant women, most of them slaves, who were purchased to use as live experiments. Women who had died under their care where freshly cut open to reveal the inner workings of their uterine anatomy.

Many upper class elitists of that time wanted more "fashionable," "trendy" ways to relieve pain and expedite labor and birth. We have to remember that back then women were fighting for "equal rights," the feminists of the times were struggling for better treatment in general and equal opportunities. Thus causing a demand for "self-ownership" of the female body. In turn though, it caused another chain reaction in relinquishing the rights of women in healing and birthing. They had no idea what was to come!

Male physicians also needed to practice their newfound tools brought over from Europe. Forceps and "the crochet" were used to extract a baby when labor was too long or hard, then the baby would be pulled out in pieces. Also, plant derived drugs, such as Ergot (like today's synthetic Pitocin) could induce labor and remedy a hemorrhage. Which for thousands of years women knew about and used appropriately.

Back then, it was common to "bleed" a laboring mother of her blood--sometimes even several pints! The theory behind this was to rid her of demons, diseases and the supposed sins that she obviously possessed because of the "curse" of labor and birth. This was in all actuality not that long ago.

Leeching was also still very readily used by placing live blood-sucking leeches on the mother's body in order for her to be cured of her "ailments" associated with childbirth.

The "New male midwives" were competing with female midwives for the dominance over birth. Socially, at that time of course, most women were not usually allowed to enter into medical school, and they were defiantly not allowed to practice medicine in the greater portion of the United States. It was considered indecent for a woman to attend births rather than stay home and have babies--while being attended by a man. The new male dominated profession of childbirth became a fashionable thing to do with the upper class and working classes, who could afford it. The poorer under-privileged, which were the majority, were still in the care of midwives, and they had better outcomes at the time of birth than did the upper-class with the new male midwives.

In 1828, male midwives were trying to become their own profession and wanted to re-name themselves to separate themselves from the female profession of lower class midwives. An English man suggested that they call themselves "Obstetrician" which is a Latin term meaning *"to stand in the way."* Midwife means, *"With Woman,"* also derived from Latin meaning "med-wife," or "wise woman" not suggesting that nature need anyone standing in the way, but to have someone who knows what it feels like to give birth with you to share their wisdom and support.

Most Obstetricians of that time only worked with the upper class and paying patients, but midwives continued to work with farmer's wives and the immigrants who lived rurally. Most of the Obstetrician's patients called upon them for the use of their tools, not understanding the risks involved; they wanted them to use any means to expedite labor and extract a baby who was taking too long. Most wealthy women preferred the "well care" of a midwife, compared to the male physician, and it was, and still is, a popular "fashionable" thing to do. Most of these women in the early years of medicalized birth had a midwife for most of her labor and only called upon the male physician in difficult times, which were rare. It was an "option" left up to the mother and her sisters when to call upon them for assistance.

Usually, it gave women a chance to make more choices within their lives and gave them more power over their bodies and births. Birth was still highly regarded as the domain of women and an intimate event shared within the female and family arena.

Upper class women of those times wore girdles that cut their circulation off, deforming the pelvic bones, as it was also "fashionable" to be weak and frail. Because of this, many women were unprepared and too unhealthy to have good birth outcomes, Obstetricians were needed to do something to help in labor and birth, especially in these unfit situations; it was unusual that they would just hang around holding a hand and comforting a laboring woman. Their job description was to medicate and manipulate birth. At the same time however, some midwives were taking over the "female" jobs in hospitals and attending training programs to become physician "helpers" as this role was becoming popular. Women were not respected by most male physicians for having any kind knowledge or familiarity with female issues.

They were left only to help the unfortunate single mother or widow in childbirth. These great women are now known as Nurses.

Nonetheless, eventually, incredible women from all over the world came here to America to start their own Women's Hospitals with maternity wards, which usually, were privately funded by the women themselves. At the turn of the last century (20th), many schools of homeopathy and natural medicine were becoming extremely popular and were the standard for a short time. They were teaching the medical students preventive natural medicine, also these schools were mostly run by women from other countries who wanted to preserve their knowledge and pass it on, helping others become reacquainted with their Grandmother's wisdom. Shortly thereafter, western medicine set stricter guidelines so that these preventive medicine schools could not afford to remain open. The distinction between midwives, obstetricians and the female "women's" doctor was a separatist's way of competing for power and money. Only certain classes of people were allowed in certain hospitals. A poor woman would receive free care in a hospital to train male medical students, who were using the poor mother and child for experiments and tests. As today we have "teaching hospitals" that do the same things. However, do not be fooled by your local elitist establishment, most of the doctors you will commonly see for care ARE students.

The upper class also were subjected to experiments but in a nicer environment created to advance the cause of the medical profession and their reputation for an easy pain-free medicated birth. Reputation was, and still is, the goal of medicine.

A good example of the medical establishment's propaganda and hype to help gain the respect of their communities was by "saving" lives. If a mother or baby were in distress and were saved, they gained much more publicity for their cause. If a mother or baby died, which was very common in those days, but if they did 'all they could,' they were still the heroes, thus it was "God's will" (This happens still in our birth culture today). Therefore, the word spread and when transportation was made more and more available, women began to go into hospitals to have their babies under the impression that it was safer with the newfound tools and drugs that were being more popularly used by upper class women. It became a "trend."

Every class of women wanted to join the trend. Still though, most women gave birth at home with midwives. Because the "traditionalists" still existed for many years after "the shift," midwives were still needed and did not disappear. The majority of the "Migrant Grannie Midwives" became less available to the people because between 1930 and 1950, state by state, they outlawed midwives and the Grannie midwives did not have the education or money to fight to gain licensure.

Nurse Midwifery took over, and schools became more popular, many woman who could afford it (or it was state paid in some places) began a new profession in midwifery. Being regulated by the American Medical Association (AMA), they were "allowed" to practice in the home only with a doctor present. In a hospital, they were usually merely an "assistant" to the doctor to use for his convenience.

Midwives have continued to remain the best-known source of maternity care and birthing attendants all over the world. We are one of the very few countries who do not have a standard care system that utilizes female care providers for their pregnant women from the beginning of pregnancy. This makes us rank higher in complications and mortality rates for both mothers and babies than most other poorer countries in the world. In most places, when a woman finds out she is pregnant, she sees a midwife. Some of these midwives work in home birth, some in the hospital. They do not do routine C-sections, (except Brazil where the rate is up to 90%, for trendy sake), nor intervene unnecessarily. Only in the westernized areas of some countries do they practice this approach. However, they are becoming more and more aware that this new method is killing their people.

Most of our mothers in this country do not realize that our system of maternity care is one of the weakest in the world, that we have one of the highest infant and maternal mortality rates out of over 28 other poorer countries. We need to start re-thinking what it is we are doing to our children and ourselves. We have the resources to better ourselves and learn more about our options and not be fooled any longer about what is right for our babies' births. It is time to stand up and take a chance on having a more humane childbirth—it is a worthy goal.

In 1910, more than half of all babies were still being born at home with midwives, and they were having better outcomes than physician attended births in the hospital. There was an "anti-midwife" campaign to promote physician attended births, and they started a lot of propaganda in order to get rid of midwives. Went out of their way in fact. In this pursuit to eradicate the midwife in America, the American Medical Association (AMA) stated, on bulletin boards and advertisements for hospitals, many false accusations towards home birth and midwives.

Here are some from *Yvonne Lapp Cryns Film ~"Home Sweet Home-birth" 1997*

Midwives are. . .

"(Earning) $ 5,000,000 ... which should be paid to physicians and nurses for doing the work properly"
~ Ziegler, 1913

"A relic of Barbarism"
~ Delee, 1915

" ... Filthy and ignorant and not far removed from the jungles of Africa." `~Underwood, 1926

"The typical old gin-fingering guzzling midwife with her pockets full of dirt and her brains full of arrogance and superstition."
~Gewin, 1906

These statements from physicians were and still are stigmatizing most American women and men today. We are taught to fear the "natural" and place our trust in the false reality of "authority."

If it were true that midwives made that much money back then, why were they not allowed to attend political meetings and conferences to defend themselves? Since money has always dictated who had more rights and also the ability to hire an attorney to support their position?

Even when health official's statistics proved that midwives had better outcomes than did the physicians of the time, money played an important role in keeping the midwife down and allowing the physician to take over the role of birth attendant.

"Early 20th century mortality rates were lowest in localities where there were midwife attended births, and highest where there were physician attended births."

From the film "Home Sweet Home-birth" ~S.Suarez RN, BSN, JD, Researcher, and General Counselor of the North American Midwives Alliance of America

Of course no one would publish that on a poster advertising the dangers of hospital births, because the midwives did not have the money to do such things to defend themselves.

A national conference was held at the White House in 1925 to discuss the records of physician-attended births and midwife attended births. The statistics clearly showed that home births with midwives were safer than hospital births with physicians. I am assuming that the AMA got a "slap on the wrist" and were told to do a better job in representing the USA health care system to the rest of the world.

At this time you see, the medical scientists were promoting very expensive drugs and tools to sell overseas to other countries. They could not afford a bad reputation. Still this is the way it works to this day.

In fact, still to this day, there are no statistics to prove that healthy women are better cared for by physicians and have better outcomes in hospitals than at home, with or without midwives.

In addition, unbelievably, these manipulations of advertisements included the support of drugs in labor and birth, promoting their safety and magical applications, to rid mother from any pain. They did not mention however, the "ill effects" they had on mother and baby, just that it cured women of the "curse" of childbirth.

Statistics showed that drug use in labor and birth actually increased the mortality rate at the turn of the century. It was not uncommon that women would return home with no memories of their birth, less function of their bodies and other neurological damage from the drugs and procedures used, and childbirth was to blame! Also, there were the long-term complications associated with these drugs. Infections caused by hospitals, and harm done to the mother and baby's nervous systems that were never mentioned. They did not inform the woman using these psychedelic drugs about the risks to her and her unborn child. Today, it is still "customary" not to explain the implications of such drugs used at a birth. We may think that today we have better outcomes than in any time before, and that drugs are safer, but the truth is that drugs are not safe and never will be safer for mother or baby. Our outcomes need improvement compared to the outcomes of other countries that utilize a preventive care system, and who are not as "privileged" to be able to afford such intervention.

Recently a "new" old Amendment was reinstated in Washington State. It is called the "New Health Freedom Bill!" This bill states that numerous studies have been done on alternative care in America, and that over 50% of the people receive "alternative" care from practitioners of various educational backgrounds and certification. Since our western medical methods of care are not satisfying most Americans, the house of representatives has passed this bill for its citizens. It was passed in January of 2004 and is called the "Practitioner Freedom/Consumer Protection" measure. As long as the practitioner informs their clients of any training or background, "non-licensed" practitioners may care for those seeking them, and they may use references to advertise their services openly.

This actually was never abolished, though in the past 60 years or so our government, hand in hand with medical association, neglected to inform the "general public" of the Ninth Amendment, which has always been a part of American heritage. The Ninth Amendment describes that the "Natural Laws" must remain "unhindered by man-made laws," thus they cannot and shall not, interfere with these natural laws in place of man-made rules and regulations. However, over the years, medical propaganda has led us to believe that healers are in fact only those who have an M.D., Ob., Gyn., label on their door and a license on their wall. So far, no one has ever proven that natural traditional healers are dangerous, and medical doctors with degrees are not.

Adopting, or re-instating, this Amendment can mean that not only are we taking more responsibility for our own health care, but we are also able to help each other birth our babies in a more desired, loving and humane way without the man made laws breathing down our necks while birthing these sacred lives into our own hands.

An "Unhindered," healthy society is one that utilizes its potential to create sustainability agriculturally and socially without the aid of unnatural, outside interferences. "Unhindered" is a term used a lot nowadays in childbirth, and there are plenty of grass roots parent-run organizations that use this word "unhindered." It has great empowerment in the birthing community.

Unhindered pregnancy means that a woman does her own care, she does not need to depend on someone else outside herself and her immediate family to perform "procedures" of any kind or to be "over seeing" her through labor and birth. This is most empowering to the mother, and her baby and family benefit from this unhindered philosophy. This term has only been used since we have been "meddling" into the private worlds of each other, not realizing that our societies have taken the approach of controlling natural things to manipulate us for greed. "Unhindered" verses "hindered" childbirth will be our new health care debate for this century.

Unfortunately, we are facing a drastic choice when we realize our history is foretelling our possible future. We have been shown again and again that the medical community is "not all together there" for our well-being when it comes to natural things like birth, living consciously, preventing illness or dying with dignity. Today there is no study made that proves that birth and death are safer in a hospital setting.

"... Physicians in general may often have a strong dislike of people: "To cut and puncture a person, to take his or her life in your hands, pound the chest until the ribs break ... these and thousand other things may require something stronger then objectivity. They may actually require a measure of dislike." ~From: Melvin Kooner, MD, Ph.D "Becoming a Doctor, A journey of initiation in Medical School" (1987:373)

Because we are well aware of our nations crisis in health care, does not necessarily mean that we all know what to do about it. We are bound by medical coverage, insurance companies, our jobs, specific rules about maternity leave, or the government's rules about getting back to work if you're on housing or food assistance. This is only made to fool us into thinking we have no choices. If we begin to create our own politics around birth, no one can stop us.

We must just do what we know is right for ourselves and our children, regardless of other's influences. Wouldn't our future be better if we stay home and care for our little ones? Wouldn't they be better people if we gave them the love and attention they need from us in their most influential time of life? Is it important to place a child in day care, or in someone else's hands, in order to get back into the work force? Is it a cultural belief, or a government-set standard, not to care for our own children we bring into the world? Is our health care system really benefiting us, or themselves?

These are some questions I have heard over time. When mothers can stay home and take care of their children, there will, more than likely, be a lower incidence of violence, drug use, and a better attitude towards life in general. A child needs his/her mother, which is a need, not a luxury. Too many times I have seen parents place their new born baby into someone else's hands to care for while they get back to work, and then wonder why that child is so defiant or not connected to them. Well, it is only logical that a child would shut down his or her emotions towards the ones who abandon him or her. It is a mechanism that all children have ingrained in their emotional state of being, a primal defense reaction, to "reject" those who reject them.

When a child feels that rejection, it is often acted out later in life, sometimes through violence towards himself or others. In order to prevent, or at least minimize, this from happening, we need to stay home with our children and care for them ourselves, with much love and nurturing. I am not talking about not ever leaving your child anywhere. The benefits of someone in a family or community who can help assist in caring for our children is very important. I am mostly talking about mothers who feel they cannot be with their babies because the society or government dictates that they should go back to work or school and leave their young and vulnerable children with strangers.

Do whatever it takes. Live in a tent if you need to. Save money, go to a warmer climate and eat from fruit trees, try finding a new place that is less expensive to live. Until your child is old enough to be on his own, you have the opportunity to teach her your values and better ways in which to live, so when you go back to work you will be confident that your child has learned well and can take care of herself. There are many ways to deal with these situations in life, but if we are going to have children then we need to be responsible for their future well-being, and that starts by raising them, schooling them, and taking time to just be with them--ourselves. This may all sound ridiculous, and it may be, but I feel that raising our kids to have good self-esteem and be healthy happy people is worthwhile even if we need to change our own ways of living. Sacrifice a lunch out or a new dress for our little ones.

Before there was organized medicine, there was wisdom to help us care for ourselves. Women are still here for each other, and we are the supporters for family evolvement, and the ones hold the knowledge of our ancestors.

We made it this far with little interference. Have we lived to become "superior" over nature?

I do not believe so. I believe we are one with nature, and that Mother Nature is the cure, the knowledge and the wisdom we need to live fully and in peace with the rest of the world.

A Prayer for Families

Loving and Merciful God,
We pray for the many needs of families:

For abundant love,
For forgiveness and reconciliation,

For a living faith to face the challenges of each day.

Jesus, you were born into a human family
And became our brother.

You know well what families need to nourish
Both children and parents

In long-lasting bonds of love and respect.

Help families of all shapes and sizes
Turn to you as their source of life.

May your spirit encourage husbands and wives,
Mothers and fathers, brothers and sisters.

Give us all the eyes to appreciate one another

And to be grateful.

Amen.

~ *From Creative Communications for the Parish (1993)*

Desensitizing Ourselves from Mainstream Media

"Women today not only possess genetic memory of birth from a thousand generations of women, but they are also assailed from every direction by information and misinformation about birth."
~Midwife, Valerie El Halta,

Who doesn't sometimes wonder where the media gets its information? Moreover, why do television sitcoms only reveal this dark perception of childbirth?

Women are strapped down and drugged; babies are pulled out or slapped on their bottoms. It is distressing for the young viewer as well as the potential mother to be. This is creating fear of birth, and imprints what birth is like from that point of view, which is not true at all. This is not funny, even though it's meant to be, and cannot seem funny when it's brainwashing our children (the next generation) to believe it is true. Too many women and children are watching unrealistic programming each and every day. It is harmful to say the least.

Have you ever seen a gentle natural birth on public television? I saw one once, but it was of wolf pups being born on *Wild life America* when I was a kid. Somewhere out there, there is a reason why people are placing "notions" that childbirth is a drama, and we are to be poked, strapped and drugged willingly. Are the drug and medical supply companies sponsoring these shows? Most likely. The message is that women are incapable of giving birth without a doctor telling them what to do. It is a dangerous, visual, subliminal disease, thousands experience each day, and these thousands of new, young minds will forever think that birth is supposed to be that way.

We need to start showing our young ones the truth about birth; that birth is a natural, and incredible, family experience to be enjoyed, that babies do not have to be pulled out of their mother's bodies, that it is beautiful to give birth, and that it is not a disease to be managed.

It is not always going to be easy to re-program ourselves and not let our children be subjected to violence on TV. We can start in the subtle way, not brain washing ourselves by watching lies about birth or reading about wolf/human babies and two-headed aliens. It is not even about truth, it's a fraud made to make money off our fears and create superstitions and fear about natural things.

Not watching TV would be a start, and then avoiding such propaganda all together would help to alleviate the fears we have been subjected to since we were kids. Then we may be able to absorb the beauty of birth and its potentials for our children's lives.

I may seem a bit angry, and I am! It is about time we see what is really happening to our kids, and FAST! It is not going to stop or even slow down until we begin to nourish our minds from the start with positive images. Everything we watch on television, or hear from our friends is a code, an imprint that stimulates receptors in our brain. Television propaganda is a new form of desensitizing us from our human potential. If the television networks refrained from this "birth drama," their ratings will surely suffer, and then money will not dominate the programming they show. It will, in fact, lessen their need to show their viewers violent birth-related stories and gain a new sense of what we really want to see on TV. Possibly something may change. Maybe advertising drugs for pregnant woman for depression, and all those other so-called "safe" drugs and baby formulas, will cease to exist in advertising anymore.

Any births shown could be more gentle and normal, empowering women and children instead of making it seem like we need to be dependant on a "system" to take those powers from us. This could all be possible, but we have to start by turning off these programs. Maybe we could make our own local stations in each community, educate our children with materials we select as a group and in a more sensible way. Program it with what we want to have our children see instead of chancing their minds to broadcast stations that we are not involved with, and who are brainwashing our kids without our consent by what they view.

My own view is not necessarily the "right" view, but a start. I do not have regular TV programming and have not seen what is on the television for quite sometime. When I have watched it though, usually at a friend's house, I have witnessed a gross negligence in programming. Why do you think they call it "programming" to begin with? It is propaganda for controlling masses of people all at once. It's a way to make money and a way to keep us from seeking the truth outside of our own homes. We stay in tune with what is unreal to desensitize us from reality, it is a disease of the mind not to see beyond our own televisions, or computers, into the larger world we have outside our homes. I can attest that this writing on the computer is addictive. I have been sitting here writing for months now on this thing, and this is the first time I have even had this type of technology in my own home. I feel like a micro waved hunk of meat. Working like this makes the rest of the world seem non-existent; I have sworn that when I am done with this project I will put my attention elsewhere for a very long time. I need to go on walks everyday, which I like to do anyway, because when I sit in front of the computer for too long, it starts to mess with my mind and body in a way that shows me how it can dramatically effect a persons' life.

City kids, I hear, are suffering from rickets because they sit in front of the computer all day instead of getting out in the sunshine. It is easier to stick our kids in front of a television or computer than to go outside and play with them in the fresh air, or take a walk. Even just playing with our kids inside in the winter instead of allowing them to "veg" in front of a TV screen would help circulate their minds more. Reading is an ancient past time and could be a wonderful way to help our kids heal from all of this TV propaganda.

I always had one rule for my son, no television during the day. He would spend most of his time playing outside during the day and after dinner, sometimes, we would watch a movie I selected. I rarely had cable or satellite programming, but when I did have it briefly one time, he was not too interested in it anyway. He got used to our routine of keeping active during the day and rarely watched movies. Today my son is active in outside activities rather then sitting in front of a radiation screen desensitizing him from life. He loves to read and tells me that he has to go read so not to disturb him; I thought he was kidding a few times but he was serious, he really benefited from all that time spent in my lap with books.

When I was growing up I had a mother who worked all the time, I was alone when I got home from school and to keep myself occupied I watched television. My little brain got so stagnant I later had a harder time finding myself. I can attest to the fact, first hand, that it damages our minds and desensitizes us from the real world. It was a survival mechanism for me, but it defiantly caused more harm then good. I am repairing my self from years of radiation still!

"You're braver than you believe. Stronger than you seem. And smarter than you think".

~Christopher Robin; in Pooh's Grand Adventure

Drugs and Violence

We hear many stories in the paper, in our schools, and from neighbors, it is everywhere: drugs and violence is an epidemic in our society today. How do we begin to help our children become gentler and less dependant on substances?

Beginning with conception there is an answer. Imprinting of behavior happens when in the womb; every cell is developing with the energy in the mother and father's environments. Thoughts and actions are deeply subjective to the unborn fetus.

Being parents is not an easy job; it begins with our own self-healing and branches out to our kid's lives. If we can become more aware of the impact of our own lives on our children's future behaviors, we can then discover that this is how we create our situations.

No one would say its ok to pull our babies head from side to side violently, or put an injection of deadly drugs into our child, but much too often we do this during the delicate time of birth. Our baby's system is receiving its first outer stimulation and this imprint has an affect on our child for his/her entire life.

The new baby's brain is connected to the whole sympathetic nervous system, which relates to every other body system there is, so during gestation and at the time of birth, it is vitally important to minimize the stress on such a delicate primal mind. Many of our children's first imprints are violent and drug induced, this is creating a hostile and crude beginning that our children are playing-out repeatedly in their lives today.

Almost 86% or more of mothers in the hospital are having some type of drug for labor and birth, which forces the mother and baby into a stressful situation that can be extremely harmful. Another 80%or more use Epidurals, which means those babies are being subtly or majorly brain damaged from the lack of oxygen from those drugs, and from the supine positions (lying on the back) the mothers are in. Most of the time Epidurals are accompanied by inductions because of the forceful effects on the uterus, these drugs make it unbearable to the mother and to baby; it becomes painful and drugs are thought to be needed to help the mother get through the birth. In addition, an astounding 28% or more have it all plus a C-section, which is one of the most dangerous procedures for birth there is. Inductions cause more pain in birth and more stress on the baby. Lacking in oxygen the baby panics and so does mother, she is in so much pain from the induction that she usually then wants that Epidural. This numbs everything from the neck down, or from waist down, depending on which type she is given. The baby also receives these drugs and becomes passive. The mixed messages given to the baby cause a dependency on such stimulants later in life so when things get rough these children need something to calm them down, as stated in studies made by scientists on birth. Researchers and advocates have clearly shown the association between birth industrialization and social drug use a generation after.

Today most American women are giving themselves and their unborn babies to science to manage. Birth does not usually require such scientific assistance, it is a function of the human since the beginning of humans, we have not changed that much since our first ancestors walked the earth. Some survival mechanisms have certainly changed, we no longer need to walk slumped over to find ground foods, we no longer need to chase our pray to eat meat, we gather our groceries standing upright, and only need to look straight ahead when we're walking, so survival is easier than before.

However, birth is the same today as ever in time, although most of us are disconnected to our birth heritage. Women still carry their babies in their wombs and need to move for labor to flow well. We need to squat or stand to have our babies come in with gravity to help facilitate the birth. In addition, making noise is an age-old helpful tool for birth, not much has changed with that!

Only when we suppress our natural instincts during birth does it become unbearable. Usually if a mother has good support and education to assist her in her journey, she will have little discomfort, no pain at all and will give birth easily. When birth is interfered with, it is hard and painful and needs assistance because it was interfered with from the start. If consciously managed by parents or "hands-off" practitioners, it rarely gets out of control and then those babies are born without violence and drugs, setting a good example from the start for our children's future choices.

Not to say if we do everything right, that once in awhile we may have a child that uses drugs or experiments with violence. It is just a matter of risk assessment. If we do eat well and get good prenatal education, support from caring people and have joyous gentle births, we are setting the stage for more gentle loving human beings who will not make the same choices in their future as we have seen happen in the last few decades. These gentle human beings will be able to change the things we see wrong in our system today and possibly make better choices then past generations.

Learning where we came from helps us to understand and change the way our babies will be birthed in the future.

Let us go back and research how you were born, and what type of situation it was. Was it a home birth? Hospital? Drugs? Forceps? C-section? Were you breast-fed?

If possible get your birth records, talk to parents and relatives, sometimes you need to tell people when you ask them that it is important to get the real story. Most of us do not want to upset each other so we tell little lies to make up what happened, but this does not help us. I have a particular difficult situation from my birth because I was adopted from a culture in the Middle East where they don't have social security numbers, or keep their records for very long. It is almost impossible to gather information about my birth and actual events that took place, who the father was, exactly where my biological mother was from, etc. Nevertheless, because I have been diligent in researching my culture and asked my adopted mother and grandmother about my biological mother's life, I was able to get some information that helped me tremendously on my healing journey. If we can get at least the basics of who, what, where, how, or other little tid-bits, then it can help us understand ourselves a whole lot more than not knowing anything.

Questions like (these are questions I have asked myself), Why am I so moody sometimes? What causes me to push people away who care about me? Can I ever have a decent relationship? Do I have difficulties relating to others? Why am I so isolated? Why do I have a problem with patience? Am I controlling of others? A lot of these issues stem from conception and births because the imprinting of our personalities begins there.

These questions, about who we are and where we can go with our selves if we take some time to recognize why we are the way we are, can transform our lives and create a healthier life for our children. It takes dedication to change and to support our children the way they should be supported to become healthier individuals. It starts with us.

Our brains start developing immediately within the first weeks after conception takes place; the primal nervous system is storing information and recording it in the cells that are developing in the nervous system, and the brain stem. Even before that takes place, the cells from mother and father have imprinted in all the emerging cells that surround the growing embryo. All our cells have memory and contain information that branches out in the growing "baby to be." We all come from these cells and thus our realities manifest from their surroundings. The inner worlds of cells stem from all other life on earth, therefore we are capable of changing the inner world of our offspring through our own thoughts and realities.

I do not feel any of us parents want to create a child full of rage and violence, but we do inadvertently by our own feelings and self-doubt. Imagine a world free of violence and free of outward interferences that could cause any harm. When you conceive a child, their world is created inside of you from the beginning of time itself. You are creating a new world by creating a human being, a loving gentle being that can only conceive of love and prosperity.

Are We Truly Awake?

Knowing the implications of violence and birth are we willing to let go of fear? Subjective programming? Are we willing to re-locate our attention on all the great possibilities and potential we have been given. Hopefully so. It would be sad to be awakened just to fall back to sleep in such a short lifetime.

If we can assume, just for a moment, that we are clear and free of illness and disease, of any mental imparity or physical abnormality, that we can give birth freely and with our inner wisdom to guide us, without needing outside assistance that may cause stress or violence upon us or our babies, would we believe in ourselves and our Creator and accept this gift of free birth? A calm, peaceful, loving birth?

The experience in itself would be worth the slight chance of needing a hand, if so, we have two hands. Are we truly awake yet? Can we fathom a place of beauty on this great planet? Enriching it with more balanced and peaceful human beings? I hope so. I wish so. I pray so. It would be nice to see it in this lifetime.

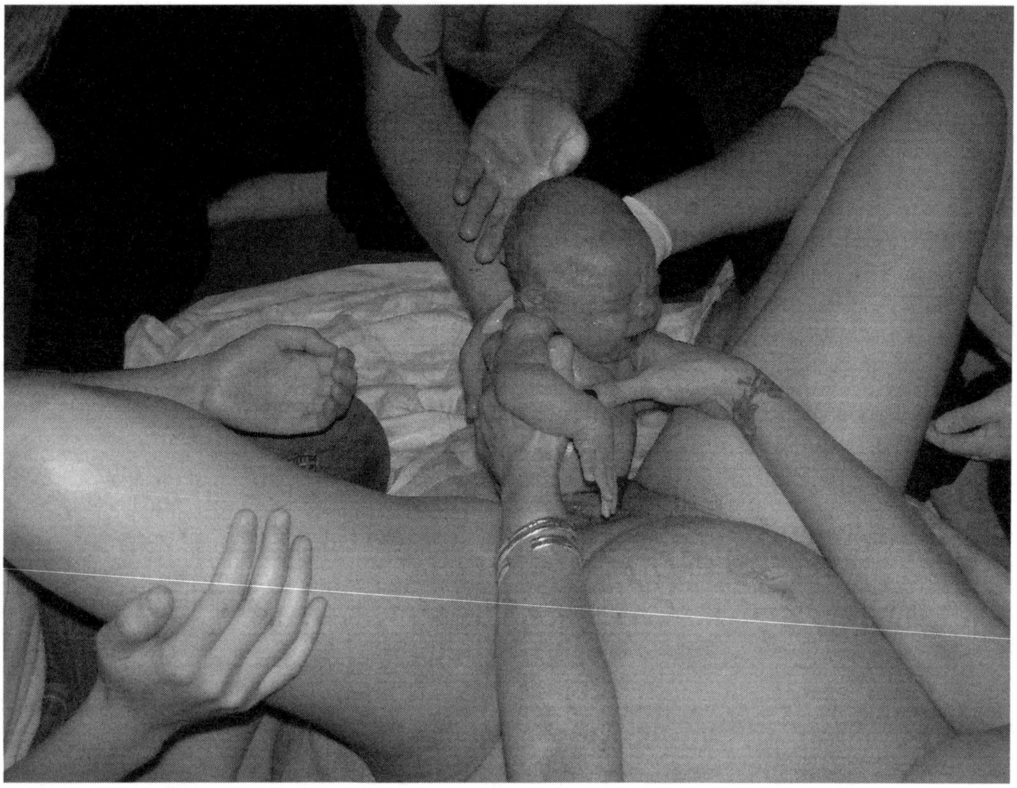

"Reach down and get your baby Kindle!"

Expectations:

When we embark on a new experience it is normal to have expectations, of course we do. Though we may not fully realize in our conscious minds, it is normal to dream up some idea that will make us feel better about the great mystery about to be experienced. It is from these pre-conceived ideas and chatter from media, society, our mother's friends, and our own mothers that we form these expectations. This chatter in our minds dictates what things should be like, then we create expectations; not that it has to be that way, it's just a perception that has been implanted in our sub-conscious. We can change this. Unbelievably, our human minds are designed to change perception, therefore changing outcomes. That is why I explained earlier in the first part of the book, that we are the only species with a unique ability that has been given to us, a great challenge of choice, 'free will.' To find our strengths in ourselves for a greater potential, we must find within ourselves compassion for all of life. We also have intellect. It is vital to try to understand this concept for our parenting to be progressive and for us to teach this to these new beings coming in, so they can create a better place in which to live fully. We can learn how to change our expectations and perceptions of how things can be. The first step is to re-program the mind, this takes some practice and practice makes perfect, right? We will have space in this book for practicing. Take notes on the blank pages as you go. One of the most helpful tools I have used with clients and myself over the years is affirmations. If you have worked with these before it is easy, if not, it will take a few times to get used to the idea. It really is very powerful to change a thought pattern, literally, for the rest of your of life. I will set into categories a few tools and how to use them. In another chapter, I will discuss using affirmations. Be kind to yourself, and patient, it is not always easy to improve our minds. We have had too many years of outside interferences that have polluted our true essence, but now we do have the tools to help improve our planet and one by one, we will!

NOTES:

Fathers & Partners of Birth

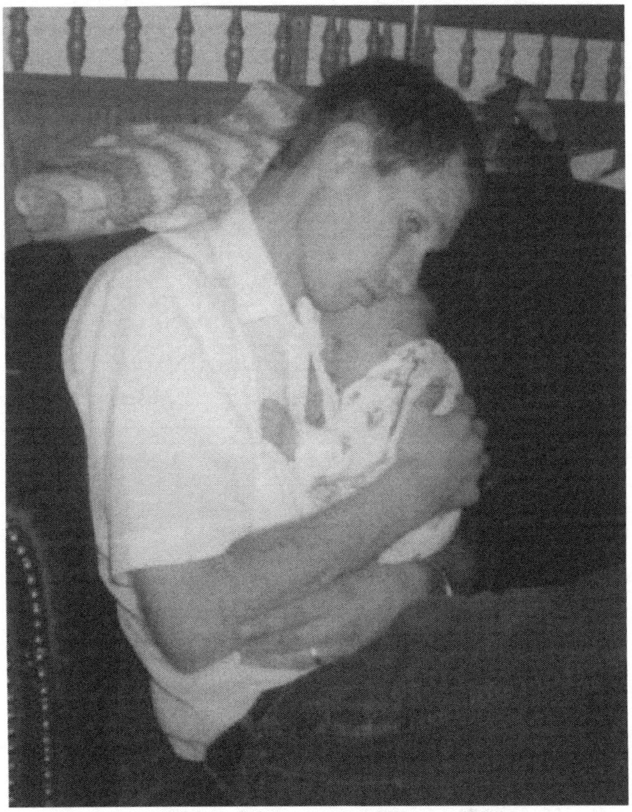

Bob with new son Royce 2004

Fathers Being Active Partners in Birth

Lotus Birthing

Preserving the Placenta

After Birth Rejuvenation

Repairing Tears

Media and Fathers

Using the Placenta for Healing Post Partum

Fathers and Partners of Birth

Instead of fathers and partners just being on the "birth team," holding mom's hand when she pushes or counting to ten while she is holding her breath, the birth partner can actually be more significant. In conscious birthing practices today, more and more fathers are learning how to support their wives in birth. "Catching" their baby with the mother or midwife's support, instead of just counting down or panting with her, is one of the "birth partner's" roles. Partners in birth are beginning to recognize that they are a part of that child's creation and have the right to be more involved and help with birth "hands-on."

It is a given that when a father or partner support a mom through pregnancy and birth, they are going to have an experience of a lifetime. The joys of co-creating a new life during the birth experience are as close to the actual process as anyone can get without having a baby oneself. When fathers take the initiative to share the birth experience, they are truly going to have a sense of what we go through.

Over the years, I have been honored to witness fathers and partners being re-born themselves through birth, and time and time again it has been my experience when birth is shared, all people present grow and are transformed as a family. Working hand-in-hand with fathers during the prenatal period has been my greatest experience as an educator and birthing assistant. They study and learn to do things such as palpate the growing baby, and birth is becoming a joyful experience instead of an isolation experience, as some fathers feel. There is nothing more pleasing than to see fathers birth with their wives or girlfriends, and be a part of the birth instead of being just an onlooker. Taking responsibilities as the "partner" in birth is an amazing job; it can only bring joy and accomplishment to the whole family and give strength to them for the rest of their relationship and lives.

Fatherhood at its Best

~ By: Belden Johnson (Fatherhood wisdom circle)

A man loving himself and his future children enough to heal himself of his past wounds before he chooses a woman to conceive another soul.

A man nourishing himself by choosing a good woman and committing to a consciously loving relationship into which to warmly welcome (the) wished-for children.

A man nourishing his woman by speaking total truth, by taking 100% responsibility for his reality, by supporting her highest good as well as his own, by co-creating equally with her the safe nest of home and family.

A man who tells his eight-month pregnant wife how beautiful she is.

A man who creates lullabies to sing to his baby in the womb.

A man who wants a home birth and is present during the labor and delivery.

A man who protects children, male and female, from genital mutilation and sexual abuse.

A man who chooses to work half-time so he can parent half-time.

A man who changes all the diapers.

A man who loves skin to skin contact with his babies.

A man who welcomes a family bed.

A man who carries his baby in a heart-to-heart Sling or Trekker.

A man who plays piano with one hand while holding his baby with the other.

A man who kills his television and reads his children stories.

A man who wrestles with his children and always lets them win.

A man who coaches co-ed sports teams for his children and, when they ask who won, tells them it was whoever had the most fun.

A man who will gladly teach and gladly learn.

A man who listens.

A man who says it's okay to cry, be afraid, and be angry without violence or blaming.

A man who celebrates his children's differences from him and encourages them to become whoever and whatever they wish to become.

A man who, when the time comes, can let the birds fly the nest and bless them on their way out into the global family.

These images are true and real. Such fathers are now among us.

Bless them and their fatherhood ...

Fathers are also the creators of that being and deserve just as much respect and encouragement as do the mothers. Over the years husband and wife-assisted birth has become a more desirable way to give birth--in the "original" way. This is the way of the new world family, to birth their children in the same way they conceived them. In peace and calm, birth takes place more easily than it does when others are present. Everyone participating in a birth with the ones they love--be it spouses, good friends, or family, will gain wisdom and knowledge through witnessing life emerge during this great experience of creation.

Preparing for the journey of being a birth partner, you will find there are many things to learn. First, it is wise to get a good education about pregnancy, labor and birth. Thus, you will be there not only to support and encourage, but also to help prevent complications. You will become a positive sharer in the joyous event.

When a father is not prepared for the birth, he often feels helpless when his wife is in labor. He doesn't know what to do to make her happy, or how to console her, when he hears her make sounds that sound as if she is in pain, when she seems irritated, "out of sorts" or just does not know what she needs or wants.

It is difficult to know how to deal with these things. I have heard men discuss these feelings of frustration and helplessness; nevertheless, with good education and inner-work, a father, or partner of any kind, can be of good support and nurture through this transformation of new life. Sometimes moms forget the father's feelings, as well as those of everyone else participating in the blessed event. This is normal, and with preparation it is much easier to stay centered and not take it personally.

During the pregnancy, it is easy to learn and become more connected to the birth process. This is the time for inner work and the healing of past issues in the relationship, or in the partner's own past. Married couples often have some issues to work out emotionally before a birth. Sometimes realizing that these issues are just a part of marriage, and that all of us have them, is reassuring to some degree. If a couple is planning a birth without another assistant, then these issues have to be healed for the birthing mother to be able to trust and have faith in her partner to be there for her in the ways she needs. In the event that these issues are not worked out, and the mother feels that she cannot feel safe with her partner, then she may choose to birth on her own. In any case, when the mother and father are not having an easy time with each other, I have seen births go awry. Emotionally putting our energies into one another is a process that needs attention before the birth takes place. Getting mediation and support to go over issues is essential, because during labor the mother and baby are number one priority, and no issues should have to emerge between her and her partner if they are dealt with in advance.

One couple, I worked with a few years back, neglected to clue me in on some of the issues that were coming up in their relationship. During the labor, I realized that they were not getting along. They were actually arguing in between contractions! I called my assistant, and when she arrived I went into meditation to feel what was going on between them. It seemed to me that the whole marriage was on the verge of collapse. When I talked to them about it, the mother said she felt the father was disconnected and did not really want the baby. He denied that accusation and held her in his arms. While they went over her childhood issues of separation and isolation, I could feel the healing happening and the labor becoming more productive. This is just one example of the power of birth; anyone invited to a birth must understand its complexity.

Other emotional issues can affect a labor as well. One mother-to-be had a vision of sharing her birth experience with a few friends. The morning of her labor (on her due date), she called and told me she was experiencing some mild sensations. I went over, an hour or so later, and found her friends hanging out, playing loud music and watching a movie in the living room. I felt the chaos unfold when I talked to the mother, and one of the friends, about her labor slowing. I suggested to her that it might be a good idea for her to either ask some of the people to leave, or for her go off on her own to be alone with her baby. I left the decision up to her and went home to prepare for her birth. The next day she called again expressing her frustration with the whole scene at her house. I reminded her that she needed to express her needs and desires to her company or ask them to leave for a while.

That afternoon I went to check on her. The same friends were still there, and there was still no progression in her labor. The friends were concerned but, not really prepared for the sacredness of birth. I took the mother aside, held her, and assured her that she did not have to worry about hurting her friends' feelings by asking them to leave. Finally, the mom decided to ask them to leave, and an hour later she called me again in active labor. When I arrived this time the whole environment had shifted, no longer was the energy chaotic or distracting. The father of the baby and the mother's best friend, were now the only ones present. It seemed, the mother magically made up her mind to create the birth she truly desired. From then on, her labor stayed steady, and she had her baby within a few hours.

Partners in birth must realize its implications. It is not a party, but a sacred journey. It is a celebration, but without the loud music and noisy guests. I feel that anyone attending a birth should be prepared to leave his or her emotional stuff outside the birthing bubble. You are there to support the mother when needed, not to affect the process as it unfolds. To be invited to a birth is an honor. It does not mean you are in charge; rather you are there to surrender to the process, to give energetic and emotional space for the birth, and to witness and allow this sacred event too unfold in the mother's own time--not yours. It is not your birth, and if you are a part of it in anyway, you must respect its flow and flow with it, not take anything personally, and be open to receive the mother's silent or not so silent directions.

Travis holding his beloved in active labor 2006

Media and cultural influences on fathers

Too many times over the years I have heard comments from fathers, or people in general, that men do not know how to feel or be connected to their babies. It is a mother's "job" to birth, and fathers would not or could not know what to do without another man (doctor) or a midwife present. Actually, fathers have instincts too! If we raise our men to feel disconnected from women, or feel that they are inferior to women, because they cannot physically give birth, we are losing the most precious chance of creating more compassionate men on our planet, who also have the inherent instincts of birth. I have seen many fathers who help in birth, who catch their own babies, who create a space where their woman is protected and help their woman give birth with a feeling of safety. Men are so important; they are the creator of that being as well as the woman herself. They need to take care of themselves and learn with the mother, so they can be a part of the awesome experiences of birth.

During pregnancy, it is ideal to have a partner who is willing to eat well and take walks. He can support your needs emotionally and physically. In labor, he is there creating a sacred space to receive the child you both made together. Fathers can and do deliver their own babies, that is a part of who they are. The instincts and intuition of men are not as appreciated as they should be in our culture. Male doctors take control of the laboring mother while fathers are sitting in the corner. Meanwhile, another man or woman (a doctor) takes over the father's role, which the father of the baby should be encouraged to have.

I have heard stories of men feeling helpless and unprepared for the birth of their baby, and this feeling of helplessness is promoted by the health care profession as well as the media. Fathers can learn to palpate the baby and do exams with their wives during her pregnancy; this creates trust, knowledge of anatomy and how birth works. We all need to educate ourselves if we are going to have children.

Fathers have the right to touch their wives if both want this, and, of course, if the relationship is solid why not! I have attended births where I do nothing but support the father in delivering his baby with his wife; it is the most incredible thing to witness. I have also seen greater outcomes with mothers and babies if the father is the only one touching them.

I believe, in our society today, that fathers are the best midwives for their wives, and the midwife's job is to educate and support the birthing family, not to take the father's role as "care provider." Taking paternal responsibility to a new level also creates more trust between the mother and father for the rest of their lives. If fathers were placed on the priority list as primary care providers, we may see more fathers taking their rightful place in the home and being present for their wives and children. Maybe these men would start taking better care of themselves when they share in the pregnancy and take time to educate themselves for their birth experience. Maybe if fathers start to catch their own babies and be there with the mother to imprint on them in the first few moments of life, we would have more respect, compassion and connectedness for each other, and for life itself.

Fathers are a very important component of birth. They are the ones who helped create these little beings, and so they also should be the ones who are responsible in helping that child emerge into this world. It's just logical. Most fathers I support during pregnancy and birth are so into it that they do not feel fear, or even need me by the time they are ready to give birth. I wait down the road, sit in the corner, or help in other ways by supporting, educating, making tea, boiling water, helping clean up, or just being a friend. Daddy performs the necessary checks and catches baby. After all, I am not the father, he is!

Sometimes, for whatever reason, the father does not want to catch baby. I educate them on why I feel it is important, but I cannot make him do it; so then mom has to catch the baby herself! This is also very powerful, and I can help her with this. However, mothers can deliver their own babies without any help at all. It is done all over the world!

Of course, there are certain situations when neither parent is the first to catch baby. In this case, within a second or so after the birth, I hand baby to mom. It is all up in the air, but is a very good try.

If fathers, as the primary source of that new life, can be as involved as possible during birth, then we can also become more understanding and compassionate as people. In remote areas of the world, where there are no doctors or midwives, fathers often share the responsibilities of birthing. Sometimes they also need to breast-feed their baby, that's why they have nipples too! Stay with me here! If they were not meant to function, they would not be there. Male lactation is not my specialty, but I do tell men that they have the ability to breast feed if needed. If mom needs to go back to work, or is unable to breast-feed, why give a baby formula that can cause health problems. If dad is baby watching, then let Father Nature do his job! See *Laura Shanley*'s "**Milk Men" article on her website: unassistedchildbirth.com**

So now, we know fathers give birth too. It is up to everyone out there to encourage and support men in pregnancy, labor and birth so they can experience the incredible wonders of their own creation.

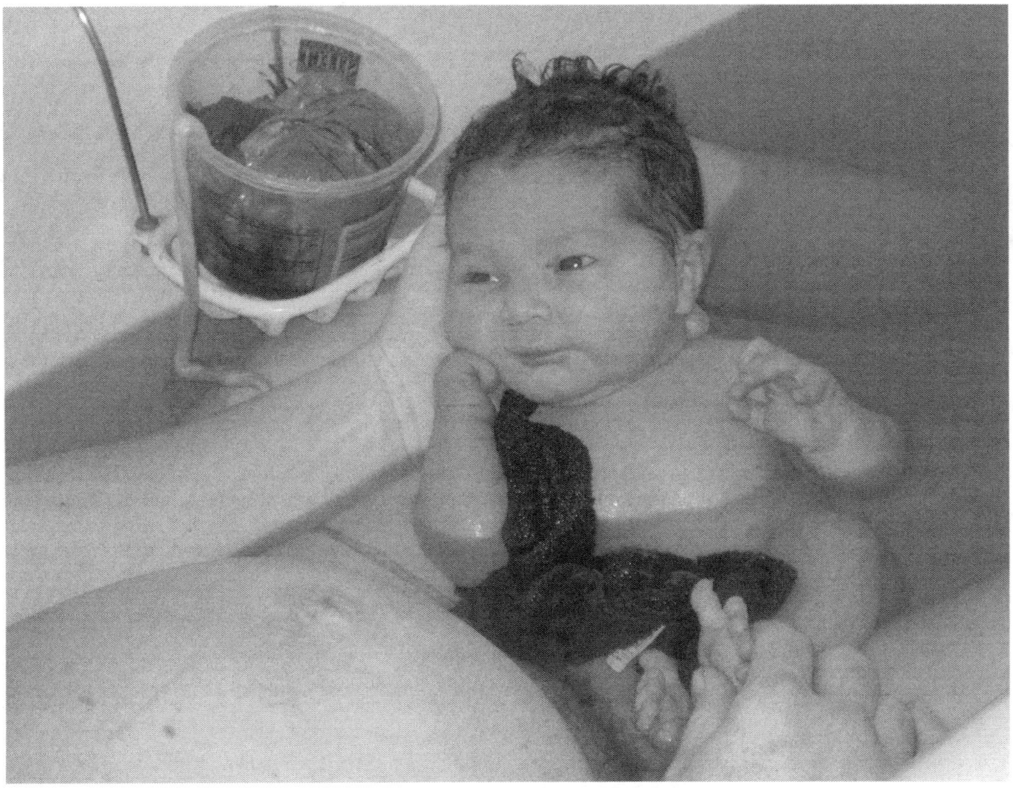

Gemma Lourdes Nagel, still "attached" First Bath with Mom Patti Nagel

Lotus Birth

Fathers and Partners 'After Birth' Work

In some cultures, the placenta is a sacred and respected organ, life giving to the baby even after its birth. In our culture however, it has been detached and discarded as a waste product, sold to medical or cosmetic corporations, and simply not respected and used properly in the way it is intended. Most midwives know that using the placenta postpartum as a remedy for a hemorrhage, or for preserving it for the child's healthy future, is an essential part of the birth process.

A definition of Lotus Birth: "It is the natural normal process in which the placenta and baby remain attached until the cord dries and detaches naturally in its own time."

Again, Mother Nature does think of everything! The natural unfolding of this process is for a good reason. After the baby's birth, the placenta is attached normally to the mother for a few minutes to an hour; however it can be longer. While attached to the mother and child via umbilical cord, it is still providing the baby with oxygen and nutrients, as well as setting the stage for the child's unique transformation and unfolding into the environment. Some babies do not breathe right away. This is common, because entering into a different atmosphere takes time and patience. The baby will get the oxygen she needs for as long as the placenta is still attached to the mother. However, for some reason in our culture this is not obvious. Our rush to get things over with and move onto the next "patient" is a typical attitude in our American ways of birth. The rational is that the baby no longer needs the placenta and it is disregarded as not having any purpose. Therefore, it is detached and thrown away, or sold usually without informing the creator of the placenta at all, the parents.

I have also heard the rationalization that the placenta needs to be detached soon after birth because it will give the baby jaundice if it stays connected. Personally, I highly doubt this since we have a unique system that needs no hindrance: it was created the way it is for a reason. The placenta will know when to balance the RBCs (red blood cells) through the oxygen exchanges at the time of birth, without having to be disconnected manually. If the cord is tied and cut, or even just tied, the RBCs in the newborn will indeed multiply quickly and likely CAUSE jaundice. This type of hasty act, cutting the cord too soon, creates an antibody reaction in the baby's system to over-produce red blood cells because the baby's white blood cells are not mature enough to combat such an invasion. With too many RBCs in the baby's body, the accompanying build up of Bilirubin in the liver ducts causes jaundice.

When the placenta is hastily detached from the mother, the baby's liver, nervous system and circulatory system take a few days to adjust to the environment, If the cord is left intact, the placenta will know when it has done its job and the cord dries up. This happens naturally within the first 24 hours after birth if left alone. Our bodies are capable of transmuting these messages even without our personal opinions.

Interfering with the delicate newborn's system is only asking for trouble. We do not have all the answers for why and how it all works, but we do know that it does if we just leave it alone and have faith in the way we are created by our Creator.

Detaching the baby from its life source and then doing "life-saving acts" in order to save the child has become the normal way of birthing in our society. When instead, if we leave the process to unfold on its own, there are less risks of fetal infection because the intact umbilical cord can keep the baby free of infections, and the baby's respiratory functions develop more gently and efficiently. Newborns do not have their own immune systems at birth; they depend on their mother's colostrum, then breast milk and their environment to keep them safe in the first few months of life. Exposing the newborn to cutting and surrounding him with strangers puts him in distress and leaves him at risk of infection.

Parents rarely know how unsafe it is to cut the cord so soon after a birth, but in hospitals, and even at home, cords are cut too soon leaving the baby open to various problems. Then they discard the placenta; the very thing designed to help heal the problems!

The placenta can be dried and preserved for later use. It is the original cell of the child and has healing properties for both mother and baby. In so many ways, the placenta can give life. It can help balance hormones after birth, rebuild cells to heal disease, help heal wounds, and rejuvenate a sick child. So many healing properties are gained and diseases prevented from this temporary organ of birth. When people throw away, or bury, their placentas, they are throwing away vital medicine that has been known in nature to help the creators who made it. Lotus Birth is a safe gentle way to practice conscious birthing and to preserve the life-giving placenta with respect.

To Preserve Placenta

After a birth, place the placenta in a bowl with a sieve and put a cotton towel, or cotton diaper, underneath to promote drainage. Extra blood and fluids may be used in the garden as fertilizer. Relax with the bowl on either side of you so that the baby can nurse comfortably. After a few hours, take the placenta out and change the towel, dump any blood into a separate bowl.

The blood can be used, if you wish, to paint a picture of your birth or make baby foot prints onto a keepsake certificate (instead of using toxic ink). This way you will have your baby's DNA, and also the baby's unique footprint, on paper for identification. Placenta prints are fun, and siblings of the baby can help make a keepsake for the whole family. It takes a few days for the baby's cord to fall off (typically 3-6 days), but after even 24 hours the cord is usually totally dry all the way to the baby's umbilicus. Some of my clients prefer cutting the cord after the first day when it is dry and brittle. Sometimes, they cut just a few hours after the birth when the cord is cold, and others leave it attached until it falls off naturally. However you choose, it is important that the placenta be preserved for the future of mother and baby's health.

While it is still attached, you can start putting herbs such as comfrey, rosemary, lavender, and golden seal onto the placenta to help dry it, and then add some sea salt as a preservative. You can just use salt if you wish, because it is the simplest way of keeping it dry and clean for shelf life. If you know how to make Jerky, then preserving your placenta is the same process. Although, you will not have to hang it up to dry and do not want to heat it, as it loses it's properties. It needs to be turned a few times a day until the cord is dry and detaches naturally, then the placenta can be placed in the sun or near a woodstove to help dry it. But no artificial heat. Turning it twice or more daily, and after it is totally dry inside, cut it into small pieces. Use the cord for a teething device for the babies' first teeth; it has stem cells which can help baby get through the pains of teething and build immunity to the world outside. Practices in other cultures vary, but this is the gist of Lotus Birth, and the benefits are tremendous for the health of your child, and you as well. There are many resources out there for Lotus Birth; you can find some of them at the back of book.

After Birth Rejuvenation

Eating a bit of your placenta as well as preserving it for later will give you a healthy perception of your own body's capabilities to supply what it needs to heal. It can serve you and your baby for the rest of your lives. You made a super medicine!

A small little raw piece of your placenta is swallowed just after it is born; it will not taste like anything if it is swallowed whole. Swallowing it whole activates your body's hormones helping them to balance and become ready for breast-feeding. It also helps to prevent hemorrhage. So enjoy your bodily reproduction qualities and do what the rest of the species do, eat your afterbirth!

A friend just recently told me about a friend of hers who ate her placenta everyday in a smoothie. She reported that it made her feel incredible, and she wished she had more since it gave her strength and helped her to heal after her birth.

Repairing Tears

If by any chance there is a Yoni tear after a birth, there are a few things too consider. One is where the tear is. If it is a small surface tear, which some of us call "skid marks," then it rarely needs any repair, just bathing and cleaning the area with healing herbs is usually sufficient, keeping the legs together for a few days also aids in healing **(See post partum bath herbs in alternative modality section).**

Prepare your herbal infusion before birth. Make compresses out of your moon pads and put them in the freezer, to use after the birth to keep down any swelling. Post partum-bathing herbs can be used for a few days, or weeks, after birth for bathing and cleaning, and after using the toilet. You can start by putting the cold compresses on after the placenta is born, this will expedite the healing process.

During the prenatal period, good nutrition (get those EFA's!), Yoni massage and visualizing that there will be NO tears at birth can prevent any severe tearing. In the rare case when it does happen, there are a few things to do.

One is preparing a Yarrow, Comfrey, Rosemary, Witch Hazel brew, and then spray the area with it. Use it warm (not hot and not cold), room temperature to the touch. This combination acts as both healing agent and as a temporary anesthetic. This can be prepared ahead of time and set aside in case you need it. In addition, giving mom a dose of ***Bach's Rescue Remedy*** may help mom to relax during this time. Homeopathic ***Arnica*** may also be given before the birth of the baby, during the *Active* phase of labor. ***Arnica*** is known to heal muscles and tissues which have been traumatized in some way, it may also prevent profuse bleeding, help heal babies head, and just accelerate the post partum healing process of mother and baby. Many midwives use this as a preventive remedy, though some say it has no effect and do not use it. I have seen it work, but maybe it is just because I believe in it's effects.

If the tear is deep and long inside the labia or yoni area, the best thing to do is cleanse it with these herbs and keep the legs together for a few days. After each time to the bathroom spray the area with the above herbs until it is healed. On average, this takes a few days to a week. Another way to repair perineal tearing if it is substantial (longer than a half an inch or so), is with ***Super Glue***, yes super glue! It is easy and works great. In most cases, this can be a safe alternative to suturing, since the sutures will make new holes in the tissue and create a greater risk of infection or more tearing. ***Super glue*** has been used as a 'quick' repair technique in war, survivalist training and in the medical field for many decades.

Bringing the tissues together you will see where they meet naturally, wait until any bleeding has slowed and swelling has gone down while using the herbal compresses, generally within six hours after the birth, but you can wait until the next day after a good rest. Then get a sterile gauze pad, the ones that are non-stick, wash your hands, no need for gloves, if you are the father, just clean hands. You can use an iodine solution for more security, mixing a quarter amount and the rest warm water. Get a blow dryer that has a cool air setting, a flashlight and mirror so mom can see what you are doing if she wants to be aware of what is happening down there (I know I would!). Take the super glue out and puncture the top with the pin that is usually on the cap. First, do a little squirt test onto a piece of paper or something that can be tossed away later. This is to make sure you do not glob it on her Perineum and get her stuck to anything! Make sure just a tiny little dot comes out of the tube at a time. Holding the tissue gently together, as it connects naturally, you can dot down with the glue, using the non-stick gauze pad to make sure it does not drip onto other parts of her bottom. The dots should be a little less than half a centimeter apart along the area that is torn. This takes only a few minutes to do well. Then use the blow dryer on cool air setting, a few inches away from the area, waving it side to side, to get it to dry quickly.

After a few minutes, put the herbal cold pad on. Just be patient and keep your legs together for a few days. The glue will dry and fall off on its own as the tear is healing. After the first day, check the area to see if it is holding together, sometimes another dot of glue may be needed. Most of the time however, it is healed up by the second day. Yoni tissues heal quickly, especially around the perineum. On the inside there may be some superficial skid marks, as I have said, and they usually repair themselves within a few days. Using your post partum bathing herbs twice a day will help accelerate healing.

If for any reason you feel that the tears are so bad that you need extra help, go within the first day after the birth to get them repaired by a more knowledgeable perineal suturer. I say "knowledgeable" because some medical nurses and doctors do sutures on other parts of the body and may do well, but the perineal, Yoni area is a different thing all together, you want someone who has done it many times, and can give you a suture job that will not leave you with long-term discomforts. You can do this by calling around to out patient clinics, or your family practitioner. They are usually happy to help in birth related situations and give references. Trying to sew it yourself, unless you have this skill already, can be dangerous and also you are making new holes that may cause even more tearing in that area if not done properly.

If you are well nourished prior to birth, you should not have any of these problems. I have only personally repaired two of my own clients ever! We repaired one with super glue and one with sutures, because that one was a labial tear, which went right down to the root. Both healed up, but the super glue one did magic within two days.

Perineal tearing is common, and can look worse than it really is. If by any chance a tear goes right down to the anus, please do not hesitate to get more professional repair done. I have not had a client with one this bad, but I have heard about moms who did and did not have it repaired. Go with your instincts and do what you feel is right for your situation.

Severe tearing can be prevented, most of the time by not pushing forcefully, getting good nutrition prenatally and just listening to your body's rhythm in labor. Birth slowly, and let each movement of the baby stretch the area without force. Use your intuition and look down there, after all is well with mom and baby, to see if anything seems like it needs attention.

Nuchal Cords

Around 22% of babies are born with a "Nuchal Cord" wrapped around the neck, torso, legs, or a combination of these. It is very common. Do Not Panic. If the baby is coming out with the cord loose, it needs no manipulation. If you feel gently around the baby's neck, as she is emerging, and it is tight but still able to move through the birth canal, just loop it over the head or slide it over the torso of your baby as the baby is being born. There is no huge danger if you cannot get enough slack of the cord to do so, just leave it and let the baby come out the way it is. Do not make any remarks to the mother if this is happening, she may tense up and restrict the process and oxygen flow to the baby. If the baby can come out with it still around the neck, just gently unravel it within a second of the birth, and rub the baby like you would anyway up the back to bring oxygen toward the heart and head. Keep the baby between the legs for the gravity to help facilitate oxygen from the placenta back into baby after this type of cord compression. This is another reason to leave the placenta and baby attached, for its oxygen to replenish the baby after being reduced from the cord entanglement. Optimally, cords have reserve oxygen between the cord compression and the baby; this is nature's way of giving the baby what she needs to get through the birth canal with enough oxygen.

Some babies may seem a bit blue or grey at first, then after the birth most babies will pink up within a minute or two, reabsorbing the oxygen lost. Do not panic as you will cause mom to panic and hold her breath in fear, which holds back oxygen from the baby, and sends stress hormones throughout her body, so just breath and be calm, let baby come as he needs to come and just be mindful of gentle cord handling when he emerges. Fathers and Partners of birth are blessed to be invited and participate in the most amazing creation of life. We can give respect and honor our roles as partners in birth by listening to our own inner voices. When doing this, we are then set free by our own conditionings and thereafter have more patience, faith and honor for this sacred life.

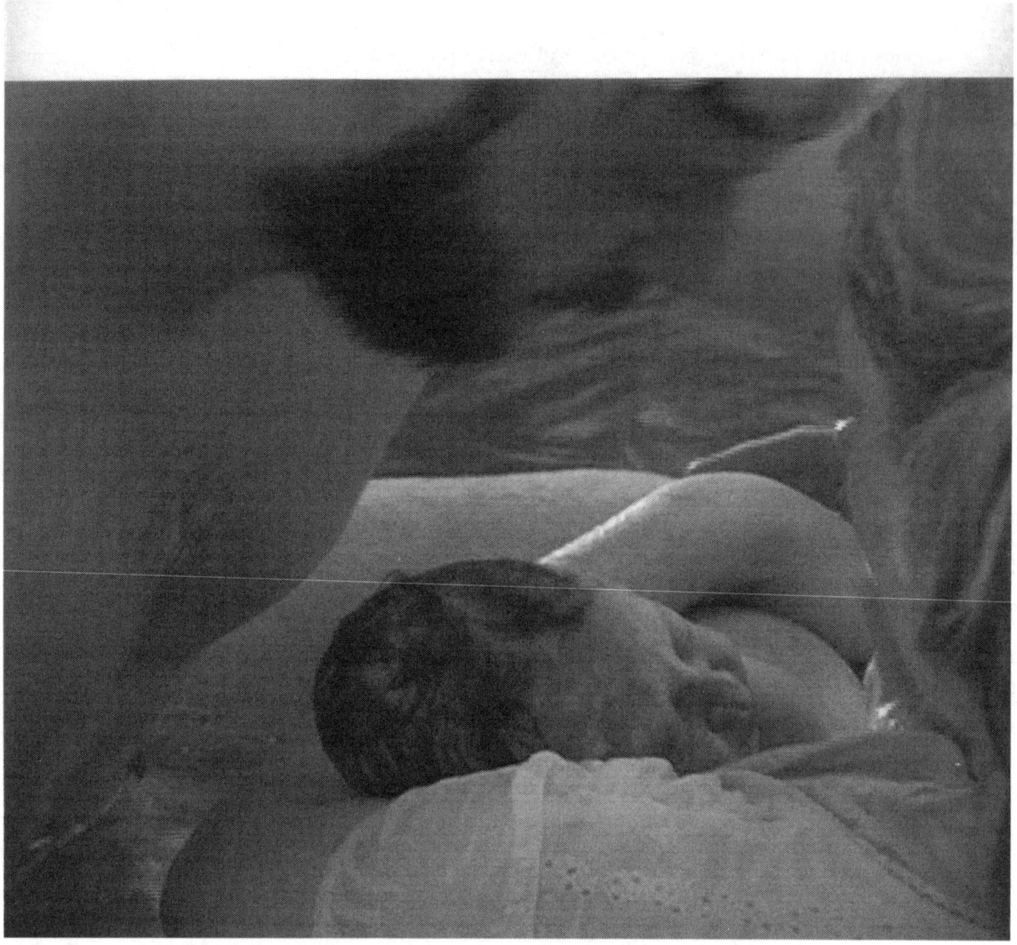

Anna Spring DeHaan Welcomed into the world by her parents January 2004

Myths & Midwives

"... rather than still hold myself as a victim, in that I became a healer. This is what I learned from my father's people. That when we take our journey in life, inevitably we are going to trip on a rock here or there. We must as a people stop, pick up that rock and remove it from the path, so those who come behind won't trip also."

~Spiritual midwife, Jeanine Parvati Baker, author of "Hygeia," "Prenatal Yoga," "Conscious conception," and "Proponent of free birth." Quote from "A Clear Road to Birth" ~Film by: Judy Seamann 1994

Myths and Midwives

We are, "with woman," calm and centered; we listen not only with our ears, but also with our hearts wide open. Through our own experiences, we can understand what is being said or not said, and know to listen from within. We run to sit side by side when called to do so. We are tired, yet honored, to stay away from our own home, in another's home, for days on end. Women are not just midwives, but healers, we are one with nature, and we are one with birth, death and lifetimes of wisdom. We are here for all women and their families without prejudice.

"With Woman" is what midwife means, it is an ancient path for those who can listen to the spirits of the unborn and the dying, we are the ones who guided all here now on this earth; we would not be here if it were not for our wisdom. Every woman is a midwife.

There are myths about midwives, "old wives tales," that come from ignorance and rumor. I have heard that we are not educated from media, society or doctors trying to slander us. That say we are only in it for the money and of course, we are not capable of helping each other birth. It is an old tactic to scare women away from each other, back into the male arms of medicine, even into the female arms of patriarchy who encourage us to surrender our bodies, and babies to technology.

Midwives are wise women and men. Oh yes, men too, there are male midwives out there, how do you think the Obstetrician got started? Well male attendants are not new, but they are surely different now.

In the beginning, before even midwives existed, it was the men who watched as their wives gave birth, it was men who knew our strengths, our wisdom. They acknowledged us for it and paid us respect.

When we began to live in more populated communities, women took care of each other while the men were out hunting.

"You are a midwife, assisting at someone else's birth. Do good without show or fuss. Facilitate what is happening rather than what you think ought to be happening, yet still free and in charge. When the baby is born, the mother will rightly say: "We did it ourselves!"
~The Tao Te Ching (a 2500-year-old saying)

We all have the answers for ourselves, if we listen closely. It is the fear in others that has created such problems of distrust within the circle of women. We are bound for extinction if we cannot heal from our pasts, mistakes and ego-filled notions. As women, midwives, men and all feeling beings, we have the right to be in peace with nature, and no one has the right, through their own fears, to manipulate us into anything else but the truth. The truth is that midwives are in all of us. We all should be "with woman," understanding her strengths and supporting her in hard times, respecting her for where she is coming from and where she is going. She is everywhere, in you and me, in the earth. After we are gone, she will still be here, so let us stop fighting her. All the evil that has been done to women emerged out of fear of her strength, her wisdom and her power of life and death. We are no longer in a time of superstition, or are we?

Midwives Tales

Well let's just say that it's the oldest trick in the book.

Woman were revered until men grew fearful of her strength.

She became the "Witch." Blamed for wrong doings, for her healing powers.

Burned, and hung her alive in front of her children.

More and more women, and their loved ones, were murdered for some sort of sin.

Nine million were murdered and then,

There were no women without fear left to begin.

Somehow, out of the dust

There was a midwife to help new birth, new hope.

With strength and wisdom she carried from the grave,

All life was saved.

Male medical doctors saw this power in awe,

They wanted to be like the old midwife they saw,

And dressed in gowns to gather her secrets,

Turning her wisdom into mischief,

The male midwife so did appear,

All was again full of fear,

He made tools and cutting devices

To control and leave the woman to his whim,

Soon the power over nature began.

Now many years later, dominating with their minds,

We are still fighting against their crimes,

Taking back what was always ours,

A woman's body not a technological farce.

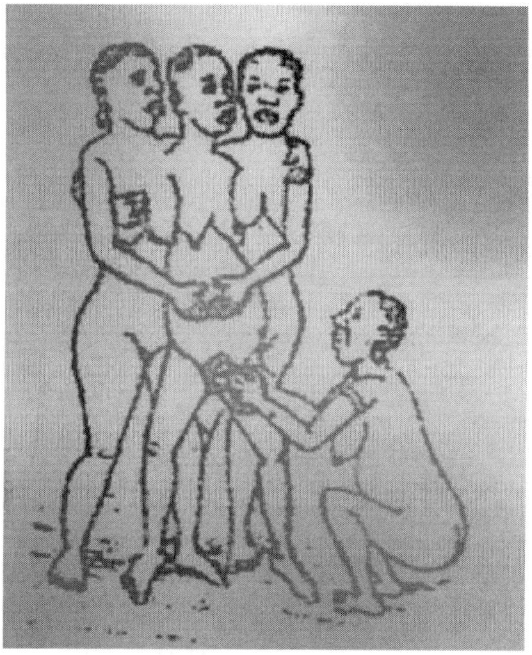

The Midwife within You

Midwife may be understood in many different ways. One who is at service to her female comrades, or who sits by the side of a loved one who is passing from this world. Midwife is universal; every language has a term for her. She is within all of us. The Midwife has also been taken out of her context and placed into a system, which does not recognize her various talents.

The current definition of a modern midwife is "One who is legally bound by state regulations." She has lost her original identity through prosecution. We need to preserve her dignity, by finding her within ourselves, and sharing that part of ourselves with others.

We are all midwives. Every woman who sits beside another is a midwife, every man who sits beside his wife, is a midwife. All of us have a midwife inside waiting to be utilized. Even young children can tap into their own inner midwife. In a child's mind, the definition of midwife is not yet tarnished by mass media and society. The young child is the best midwife there is, they have not lost their instincts of compassion or understanding of ones emotional being. If we can re-connect to our inner midwife then we will surely benefit as a people.

Midwives and Working Together

"As men became more involved in birth, theories regarding how pregnancy and labor occur became less magical and moved to more scientific and mechanical explanations."
~Anne Frye's "Holistic Midwifery" Vol.One (1995)

In our days of realization, we as a community of women are working for the betterment of each other and the future for our children. We can start to work on more accepting levels, than on an authority "trip." Unfortunately, the standard for a legal midwife is still for the benefit of the male dominated system at large. Midwives throughout time have been in a social war competing against one another to be in power over birth.

Today, midwives situation is still similar to the times of the witch burnings. We have been placed into hands of male hierarchy. It happens even now with one another competing to be better than our sister midwife, with labels and rules to place us once again in a subservient role to the system at large. Instead of seeing midwifery as a right of women to utilize and support one another, we are just another money-making asset to the government. We need to start seeing midwives and birthing parents as people! Midwives are simply women helping women, and families, through a transition of life, into motherhood, and fatherhood. It is life that we serve, a temporary system, which does not come with us when we leave this world, but our wisdom will always be a part of our spirit, and ultimately a part of our children's future human rights.

Natural things have been ruled over for the purpose of patriarchal rule, control, and greed. Throughout time, herbs from the earth were used to help heal and remedy common ailments; healers who gained the knowledge and wisdom from their Grandmothers and Grandfathers cured even ailments that could have been deadly.

Massage, herbal healing, energy healing and other modalities of health were banned, called "bodily sins," "voodoo," and "witch craft." All healing was regulated and controlled by the government and the church. As midwives were banned and killed for their knowledge, women healers have also banned themselves through fears placed on us long ago. We have left our Grandmother's wisdom behind to follow the sorcerers (or the government) of this time. The rules and regulations have been placed on us once again, so they can control what happens in our natural lives. It is just another way to suppress women and profit from our wisdom.

In order to have a sustainable situation long term, midwives, with one another and the people we work with, need to have a relationship in order to create a better future for this new generation. We can teach each other about personal growth and responsibility; about birthing in harmony and balance; and about making our own best choices without depending on rules made by the government, who gives the same guidelines for every woman.

Midwives, who do not teach other women to be self sufficient in their families care, or who have an attitude of authority over the ones they work with, should not be in this role.

With nature once again, we are all midwives and have the heredity of all the wise women throughout time behind us to help each other birth our babies with integrity and respect. No one can tell anyone else how to birth, where to birth, or with whom to birth. Women are made to birth, and unless the whole planet has ceased to exist, we will birth until the end of human time. That may come sooner then we think if we keep messing with birth the way it is now.

While we are still in physical bodies, women will birth as our ancestors have always birthed. We would not have survived this long if birth did not work. There are arguments about midwives being safe. Well, birth is safe if not interfered with, even by midwives. It is another way to control women through other women. If we place ourselves above nature and into a patriarchal role, then we are, by our own hands, dooming our future women to give up their rights. Working with women is just that, we work with families and share what we have learned. Yet, we are the apprentices at the birth. They are the ones having the babies and birthing, not us.

Finding a midwife who is not disillusioned by rules and regulations is a challenge. We have been drawn into this system thinking it is better to be under a ruler than to be totally outlawed. By the way, there are still some states that outlaw us on various levels. Even certain types of midwives are outlawing their sisters from their given paths to be birth keepers because of such hierarchy.

Who knows best, mother or midwife?

By Laura Shanley

"While the idea of non-intervention is certainly not new in the midwifery community, many midwives still believe that birth needs to be "assisted." It is not uncommon for a midwife to break a woman's water in an attempt to speed things up, or tell a woman when she can and cannot push. All of the women I know who have given birth unassisted have known when to push, and most of the time their babies were born with very little pushing. I theorize that most women begin pushing long before their babies are ready to be born, simply because a midwife has told them "it's time." At the very least, women wear themselves out unnecessarily, and often they damage their bodies in the process. If a woman is at all in touch with her instincts, she will know when and when not to push."

From the book, Legal Guidelines for the Unlicensed Practitioners

By: Lawrence Wilson, MD (1995)

"The situation changed with the passage of the licensing laws between 1910 and 1920. Now we rank last in health care statistics among the developed nations. Not accidentally, we have some of the most restrictive and confused health care regulations in the world."

Searching for a midwife who respects your needs

Once on the search for your ideal midwife, there are ways to adjust and carry forth-new ideas--as things do change over the course of working on one's self. I have always made it a point to discuss my own philosophies about birth in the beginning of a client relationship, and I encourage my clients to share their feelings, beliefs, ideas and desires as well as stories from previous births. This is how we work together to bring this new being into the family with love and respect, and also how we support all the needs and dreams of parents. I ask my clients to read and research, supplying materials on birth options, and then after pondering these options, the parents tell me what they want from me as their supporter. In the beginning of the relationship, we discuss emotional concerns and lifestyle needs, then when the parents are fully aware of their choices and desires, they can decide whether to continue with me as their birth assistant or choose a different level of support. Sometimes, after all the research, they feel confident enough to do their own birth. Then I am not needed at all! We leave everything open until the end of pregnancy to give the freedom of educated and clear decision making instead of feeling pressure to remain unchanged. No decision is without room for change. It is just natural that we grow during a pregnancy and realize many new things about ourselves. Often the more we grow our babies and learn about birth, the more capable we feel. To be a facilitator in that growth, we must leave room for our clients to grow and move on without us, if that's what they desire.

Some of my clients want me there for support, education, and my skills. It is not about power or control; it is about choice, education and freedom to change ideas and make different decisions if they are needed. It is my job to guide, support, and supply my clients with educational materials so they can make good choices. It is not my job to tell them what to do. Unless a birthing family wants me to do more, I am just a guide facilitating the process, working with them to support the decisions they make, that affect the whole family, not just the actual birth process. It is wise, as a midwife, to be an activist for self-reliant education above all.

I recently had the honor to be hired by a couple who knew they did not want me at their birth. This couple came to me to gather the information they needed to birth their first baby on their own. The mother is young, in her mid-twenties, and a nurse at an outpatient clinic, so she had seen what birth can be like in a clinical setting and knew that she did not want that for her birth experience. The father was also in his twenties, healthy, educated. They were well-read people. I agreed to support them however they wanted as long as we had clear communication. That is my main requirement for anyone with whom I work. It took a few visits before they were sure they wanted to do their own birth, and they wanted me to educate, gather supplies, and use my birthing pool. Throughout the pregnancy, we worked together every couple of weeks doing prenatal checks and education. Before the due date, we got everything gathered and the pool set up.

They called me in the beginning of their labor to let me know her water had broken and what was happening. I was on call for them, so I stayed a few blocks away at a friend's house so I could be available if they felt they needed me. After about three hours, the call came. They had a baby girl and everything was fine! I went over on the second day after the birth to check on them, and see mom and baby. It was really a joy to be able to be there for them without interfering or managing things. They did an awesome job, she had no tears to repair, the baby looked great and was nursing fine! They shared with me the video of the actual birth, and I was proud of how calmly they flowed throughout the whole thing. What a fantastic way to come into the world!

I love being at births, don't get me wrong. There is just such a fine balance between being an authority figure and being a supporter empowering women and families to birth naturally using their own instincts. I love my job as a free birth activist, and for all its worth, I believe that women need to care for themselves more and depend less on others who do not have an emotional tie or connection with them. This may be developed with a midwife who is meshing with the families' divine plan. Even then, the parents are the only ones truly responsible. We can help each other as woman-to-woman, man-to-man, family-to-family. We can support, gather resources and share our knowledge thus preserving it for the future of our little ones, for their children's children and so on, before the knowledge disappears completely.

The Future of Midwifery

By Laura Shanley

Many people have asked me if my goal is to put midwives out of business. To the contrary, I would like to see the profession flourish - albeit in a different form. In the future, I envision, midwives will be educators, helping women to reconnect with their innate knowledge and power. They will do their jobs so well; their services will rarely be needed at birth. Some midwives are already moving in this direction. I often get letters from midwives who are supportive of unassisted birth. Melanie, a student midwife, wrote to me recently saying,

"I'm a student midwife and even if it would mean I'd be out of a job I think women do have the ability and definitely should consider unassisted birth. I became a midwife because I believed that birth was natural, not a medical condition. However, the more research I did the more I realized that midwifery was just as medical a field as obstetrics. Just when I was about to reconsider, I found out about the Association of Radical Midwives. In a way, ARM encourages unassisted birth, but certainly not without research. To be honest I'd only like to see my clients come to me once, and then feel confident enough to go it alone."

Unfortunately, not every midwife shares Melanie's enthusiasm for unassisted childbirth. Just as some doctors believe all babies should be delivered by doctors, some midwives believe all babies should be "caught" by midwives. In doing so, they limit a woman's choices and undermine her ability to take charge of her own life.

When all is said and done, the only person capable of deciding how, where, and with whom a woman should give birth is the woman giving birth. Women, not midwives, are the true experts of birth. For those who are brave enough to recognize and believe this, the rewards are beyond measure.

We need NO labels !

Midwife, Nurse Midwife, Lay Midwife, Certified Midwife, Direct Entry Midwife, CPM, LM, RM, Obstetrician, Gynecologist, Herbologist, Massage Therapist, Cranial Sacral Practitioner, Bradley teacher, Lamaze teacher ... the list goes on and on. All labels, all professions working for the same populous: people wanting better health care, better births, and better new beginnings for the ones we bring into this world.

It all sounds so separatist, like we are not all one, not working together for the cause of creating a better place for all our moms, babies and families. I would love to see everyone of those labeled people join together at a big pot luck at my house to share their stories and embrace the one sitting next to them who does not have a stamp on their name, or is not as schooled as another, but has the same purpose: working with women and their families. All of us need to start realizing the bigger picture, we are the ones who will be able to help our neighbor with the broken bone, or the cut that needs suturing, we are the healers of our time, here and now with no labels.

"The Traditional Midwife"

"The contemporary traditional midwife is a woman capable of adapting to and bringing into harmony the tradition of midwifery-the Wise Woman Tradition. Born from the time honored knowledge, practice, understanding and wisdom, the fundamental truths of the childbearing ecosystem and women's sexuality are handed down orally, woman to woman, without hierarchies of information or ignorance."

~ By: Sher Willis, Nan Koehler Solomon, and Nancy Duncan
(from: Midwifery Today Magazine,1991)

Every woman's journey is different. I suppose I stumbled upon midwifery, or it found me. While I was growing up, several people told me I should be a midwife. Whether or not any of these people intuitively knew I was destined to be involved with birth, I feel blessed to have been chosen. Women are created to support one another through major events in life. This is our natural 'programming,' and even though we have been misled to believe other wise, this will always be true.

I have met many midwives, and we all come from different backgrounds. Some midwives have never even had children themselves (which is another issue all together), but all of us have one thing in common, we love women and we love babies. We are not afraid of either, and even with some not so good experiences we continue our work as helpers and educators. It is amazing to me that we even survived after what we, as women, have been through, but that is the way of the mother; we are survivors, and women were born to birth babies, male and female babies. I suppose it's because of our genetics, women are made to be strong so we can endure birth and long hours of work, feeding, gathering, and taking care of families--multi-tasking is our forte. So as a woman, myself, telling another woman that she needs to be managed, or does not know herself well enough to birth without me, is an hypocritical statement that should be re-evaluated by midwives and all women who are seeking better care for themselves and their families.

Male Birth Attendants

There are male physicians and advocates of woman-centered birth who have helped us back on our feet. Dr. Grantley Dick Reed, Michel Odent M.D, Michael Rosenthal M.D., Marsten Wagner M.D., Dr. Laboyer, Igor Charcovsky, Dr. Gregory White. In addition, there are many other male advocates for more gentle birth practices and woman-centered birth. They are speakers and educators, men, who are listened to more by women, than women will listen to women. It is because we are conditioned at an early age to listen to our fathers, girls are taught to be passive and boys are taught to be the one in charge. Thus, our patriarchal imprinting begins at an early age.

We are now in a situation that needs addressing. Male dominated childbirth will never create a gentle culture. These medical "pro-midwife" males will not be around forever to support our cause. It is time to listen more to ***our sisters*** than the authoritarian male. Time to teach our children different models of behavior, and time to create a tradition of gentle, humane childbirth practices.

We can see life as a sacred passage and not a technically managed event. I do not feel this is a battle between male and female birth attendants. I am not advocating against male midwives, for if he is a gentle, caring conscious man, he may do well for the mother and baby by being with them. I feel that every one of us has a purpose. Women, naturally, have more birth wisdom than a man who cannot give birth through his body, but he can be as compassionate through his heart.

Patricia Cloyd Carter was wife to General Ellerbe Winn Carter of the Army and mother of nine children. The first two were born in the hospital, so with that experience behind her, Patricia decided to birth alone at home with the rest of her seven children.

She inspired many women around the country and even internationally with her book. Women wrote to her for advice on how to give birth unassisted, in a time when hospitals were just beginning to take over childbirth rights. Many women benefited from her story, you will too!

Patricia Cloyd Carter was also a pioneer in her community; she started one of the first free Libraries in her small Florida town of Tallahassee, and was an activist for women's education and civil rights movements. Her stories are humorous and extremely real, that's why I like her.

Photo courtesy of **LOOK**

THE "DO IT YOURSELF" MOTHER AND FAMILY. Left to right: Molly, Teddy, Lila, General Carter, Mary Winn, Clare, Mrs. Carter holding Douglass [4 days old] Patricia, and Winifred. Eldest son, Robert, 19, is now with the Army in Hawaii.

The Easy Way

"Place of Birth"

By: Patricia Cloyd Carter
~From her book: "Come Gently Sweet Lucina" 1957

Under the first classification comes the choice of place. I think no one will deny that the impulse to seek and prepare a private, secure and familiar place in which to bear one's young, is an instinctive impulse.

"My room becomes a Cathedral. While the first warm glow that heralds the coming of a child is still present, I go to its peace and security. Humble tho it may be as luxurious surroundings go, I find in it all surcease from the trials and tribulations of life out in the great world at this time. It glows with a warm radiance of remembrance that dulls the splendor of rich furnishings in other rooms, in other homes, in other places. It is HOME! HOME! HOME! And I am at peace as is the mother bird upon her nest. In this room I can BE, I AM. In other rooms for the birth of a child I would mark time. This room is my chapel wherein I can meet myself face to face, and sometimes that is beyond myself. Here I am not forced to meet myself as I am to myself, and myriad other little "selves" around me at the same time, coming between me and my personal horizon. I do not need to share myself with all and sundry, who though they willed it not, would be destined to take part of me away from me-my joy, my triumph, my love, my strength. My life springs. Here I can bathe at the source ~ the fountain of Being

Anatomy & Physiology of Pregnancy & Birth

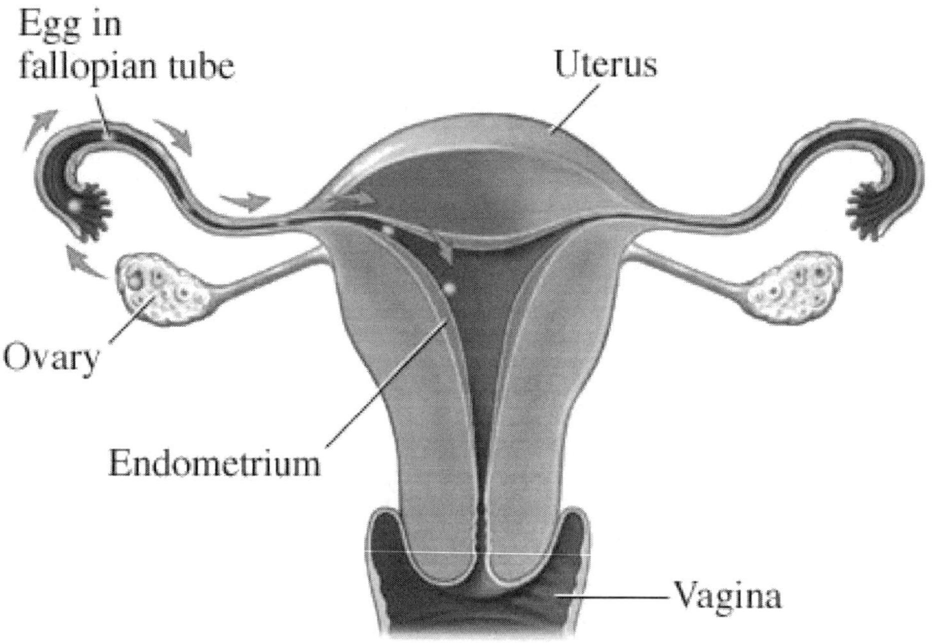

Anatomy and Physiology

A Brief look inside Mother and Baby

Throughout the centuries, with little knowledge of our "technical/scientific" anatomy, we, as women instinctively knew how the body worked. We were able to diagnose and cure disease. We grew and birthed our babies, and we dealt with the changes in our bodies, and in our emotions, as they happened.

A Little Look Inside at Conception, Pregnancy and Birth Process.

Conception usually takes place around the fourteenth day after the first day of your last menstrual cycle. It varies in every woman and can be different every month. This is just an average time when ovulation occurs. After the ovum meets the sperm in the fallopian tube, many changes begin to happen. Once joined, the fertilized cells, egg and sperm, are now called a "Zygote" and are traveling through the fallopian tube toward the uterus while they continue to divide.

Division takes place rapidly to ensure a speedy and safe formation and implantation into the uterus. Hormones are signaled, by the pituitary gland, too create more progesterone. This hormone helps the endometrium (uterine lining) to thicken in order to catch the egg and nourish it as it implants into the uterine wall. Alternatively, it waits until next cycle to be shed, through menstruation.

Emotionally, at this time a woman will feel many new feelings signaling her that something has taken place. Inside her soul, she knows that a new life may be beginning to grow. Intuition is the best pregnancy test there is.

Once inside the uterus, the Blastocyst, which it is now called, burrows into the uterine blood-filled environment. Nerve cells start to form, and it begins to grow rapidly. The Blastocyst will be nourished by the uterine blood until the placenta has grown and rooted itself into the uterine lining.

Four weeks after fertilization, the cell, until now called a Blastocyst, now becomes an Embryo. Inside the safe, warm and secure environment of the uterus, it has developed the space to expand in size and rapidly evolves.

Some women become very tired and irritable at this time, maybe even hungrier; there may be a sense that something has taken place. Emotional changes are occurring as well, and the intuition/mind may be consciously trying to tell us that we are pregnant.

When I become pregnant, my signal was uncontrollable eating. Prior to this, I had not had a menstrual cycle in almost two years because of an eating disorder, and this usual first sign of pregnancy was not available to me. When I couldn't quit eating, I wondered why. However, I knew intuitively it was because I was pregnant. The following month, my breasts got a bit sore, and then I had a little nausea until my eating patterns became more balanced; once I had adjusted to eating regularly, I was feeling fine. My boy would not let me go a day without eating greens and protein, so my diet was rich in those.

Once the Embryo has embedded into the uterus, the placenta starts to form and the placental hormone, human chorionic gonadotropin (HCG), begins to send signals to the mother's glands that she is pregnant and ovulation and menstruation do not need to take place for a while. HCG is the hormone pregnancy tests are looking for in the urine. As early as a week after fertilization, and a week before a missed period takes place, this may be detected in the urine. On the other hand, in the blood, it can be found as early as a few days after fertilization.

Once the placenta starts to take over the hormonal functions, the rest of the mother's body need not produce any more hormones for the growing embryo. Until about the eleventh week, the yoke sac is attached to the umbilical cord and nourishes baby's blood supply, and will continue to do so until the bone marrow, spleen and liver take over.

Even at three weeks, the Embryo is forming primitive nerve, heart and brain cells. It is beginning to look like a fish with a long tail. But genetically it is already becoming a member of the family. Genes, selected at the moment conception took place, are starting to create family likeness in the growing baby.

At four weeks, the heart, not yet covered in a protective layer of skin, is visible outside the Embryo's body. The head is starting to take shape because the brain is growing. All central nervous systems are still forming but apparent, and the skull is slowly starting to look more human.

At five weeks the embryo starts to show signs of eyes, nose, and mouth; it is only about a half-an-inch long but all its organs and brain are functioning.

At six weeks, the Embryo is growing arm and leg buds, little webbed fingers and toes are not yet totally formed but on their way. The Embryo is almost to its eighth week of gestation, when the Embryo will be called a Fetus and noticeably male or female. Now all it needs is to finish growing.

Now the Fetus is about 7/8 inch long and 1/30 of an ounce, but looks human and has all its organs primitively formed.

By the end of the third month, facial features are apparent, the little fingers and toes are no longer webbed, ears are forming externally, and the inner ear is starting to develop audible sound within the Fetus. This is the time to sing and have gentle sounds surround you.

Now in the second trimester, the next set of three months (being three sets of three months total), your belly is starting, if not already, to show. Depending on body type and genetics, your belly may show from the onset of pregnancy or not until later in the second trimester, but either way the belly will grow if your baby is growing well.

By twenty weeks, most moms feel movement; it varies from little flutters to noticeable flips and turns. I felt my son do a full flip when I was eight weeks pregnant, it is common for moms to feel movement later in the second trimester, but anytime is possible.

By the sixth month, your baby will begin to form vernix, it's that white creamy substance we have all probably seen or heard about. It helps the baby from being wrinkled and nourishes the skin while continuing development.

The skin is also starting to become thicker and less translucent. Although fully formed, the baby, if born at this time, has a very slim chance of survival.

In the seventh month, the baby is starting to grow body hair. It can hear magnificently and is reactive to sudden sounds. Every sound that is heard, the baby will be imprinting on. Loud sounds may frighten the baby, and you may notice a lack of movement when this happens. If classical music is playing, you may notice the baby reacts by simulating the movement to music. Classical music has been researched in fetal brain development and is helpful with creating positive receptors in the brain. You do not have to put earphones to your belly. Your baby will hear the music just find if it is being played in the room. The amniotic water in the womb provides a good conductor for sound, in fact, everything sounds louder in there.

When ultrasonography is used on a baby, it sounds like metal being hit under water. If you ever heard that, you may not want to subject your unborn baby to such traumatic noise during this time of inner ear development and brain formation. It is a good time to start reading to your baby. The baby's brain is continually developing, and the stimulus it receives will determine how the brain receptors grow. The brain stem may connect differently depending on the sounds in the environment. Thus, creating a healthy environment with soothing sounds will help your baby's development and impact her entire life.

Now in the eighth month, the baby has been already growing his brown fat stores. This helps the baby conserve energy, and, if in the first few days the baby is having a hard time nursing, the baby will utilize the storage of fat, but not for too long. After the birth, the baby will need to be kept warm and nurse so as to preserve as much of the brown fat as possible. Babies will need this fat for nourishment while sleeping, to help keep warm, to maintain blood sugar levels, and for energy maintenance.

At nine full months, or the beginning of the tenth lunar month, the body may be beginning to show some signals of preparation for labor and birth. For the last few weeks, most moms feel excitement, nervousness and anxiousness. It is normal to want to get it over with, and with the belly being it's biggest, it is sometimes difficult to sleep comfortably. A few weeks to a few days before the birth, the baby is likely to be "engaged" in the pelvis.

This causes frequent urination, but just keep pumping that water down so you do not get dehydrated. Some women have more mucus discharge the last few weeks because the baby's head is pushing on the cervix loosening the mucus plug. It is normal for moms to lose their mucus plugs weeks before labor, but it also happens during labor. It really depends on if the cervix is actually dilating or not before the onset of labor, and sometimes it is mixed in with other fluids and is not seen at all.

Mine came a month before my son was born, and I was four centimeters dilated for the last month of my pregnancy. This could explain my quick birth. Please be patient, babies will not stay in there forever! They come when they are ready, not always when we expect them. Do not give into any pressure to induce at this time, baby needs the extra days or weeks, too settle down into the pelvis and stretch your muscles and tissues as well as mold their heads to fit into your pelvic outlet.

Do not rush them out; this will save them from having any subtle damage to the brain and to your body as well.

Healthy babies weigh between 6 and 10 lbs, but vary. I have only seen maybe 6 babies born less than 7 lbs, and 10 babies born over 9 lbs so that's the average. My son was 8 lbs 2 oz at birth, which is the most common weight I have seen with my client's babies. The similarity of length is also common, 19 to 22 in. is average length. Head circumference averages about 13 to15 inches, and the chest will be about the same in a healthy full-term baby. They are all different but usually vary within those ranges.

Placental Systems

Inside the uterus the baby gets nourishment from the placenta, oxygen, and whatever mom puts into her system. The placenta has a maternal side and a fetal side. The fetal side is where the baby is wrapped in two layers of membranes called the Amnion and Chorion. These membranes protect the baby from anything that comes into the uterus. Bacteria, air, etc. are present, however, it is very unlikely that anything will get in there because a woman has another protective mechanism called her labias. The mucus plug is also blocking the entrance to the uterus, and the yoni is very protective at this special time, so it is unlikely for anything to get up there. In addition, these membranes hold fluid, called Amniotic fluid, this is essential to the growth of all systems and bodily functions. While the bubble-like sac is clearing fluid out and bringing new fluid in, it also acts as a practice place for breathing. The baby breathes in the natural hormones inside the fluid filled sac and then breathes it out as waste. The renal system (kidneys and bladder) is what constitutes fluid volumes through fetal urination. The placenta continually gives the baby nourishment and oxygen from the umbilical vein and two arteries in the umbilical cord. The amniotic fluid, which comes from the baby, goes back into the placenta and out through the mother's kidney and urinary system to help in fetal waste removal. This is how baby survives before being born into the atmosphere.

Labor and Birth Unfold

Signs of labor vary from woman to woman. In every mother, it is different every time. I will go down a list of common signs of labor, taking into consideration that none of these signs are going to be absolute, and every labor pattern is unique.

Contractions (which I call expansions or sensations throughout this book) Increase in strength over a few hours of time and become closer together. Feeling expansions are different for everyone. Some women feel them intensely and some do not, but this is one of the only clear ways to define whether you are in labor. I have had a bunch of moms who have shown no sign of any labor, and then all of a sudden they looked at me and began to birth their babies, just like that. This is actually very common when a mom has no fear or is so relaxed her baby can slip out without a fight.

Patience helps when you have a sign of labor but you're not sure if it will continue. Sleep (most important), drink a glass of water, eat and then off to bed for a rest. If you still feel expansions and sleeping through them is difficult, best guess is, you are in labor!

I ask my clients to relax at this time. Getting anxious will only prolong labor and make the mama tired which often stops the labor, so it is wise to get rest early on.

Amniotic sac breaking is sometimes a sign, but not always. Some women have leaks from the bag of water for days, and some bags do not break until the baby is actually coming out. Some babies are even born in their sac "born in the caul." So when your water breaks before expansions start, it does not mean you're going to give birth that day, it is possible it could be that day, or may be a day or two later, or more. If you just relax and drink, eat, rest, and keep a clean pad on, it will happen when it's meant to happen. There is no danger to you or your baby after your water breaks, unless you are in the hospital where there are air born pathogens everywhere!

Pitocin is to induce contractions if your water breaks without good labor starting within 12-24 hours. This is the maximum time to wait in the hospital environment. At home though, we do not feel that it is always necessary to induce after-water breaks, we have waited up to over a week for a labor after the sac has broken. Amniotic sacs are made to repair themselves and can do so even after a huge gush. If there is a small tear in the bag, it can seal back up because the baby's head will usually block it from leaking any more. In addition, fluid is still entering into the womb via the placenta, so no worries.

For prevention of infection after your water breaks, keep hydrated, eat, rest, take some vitamin C 500-1000mg twice a day, change under pads often, and urinate frequently. In addition, I have seen moms who have thought their bag broke but it was just some other fluid coming out. If that happens and labor does not begin, it could be juicy fluid from stagnant sexual glands. I really feel that this happens more often than not, and women then rush to the hospital to give birth because this fluid came out of them, and in all actuality, it was just some other thing happening down there, but then they end up with pitocin and all those interventions for no reason at all! We sometimes refrain from sex the last few weeks and this fluid can build up, and with all the pressure from a baby on our organs, it can sometimes overflow and leak (So please pleasure yourself or have joyful love making to release any stagnation down there).

Remember every body is unique in growth, in labor and of course in emotions, and no one can say anything for sure except with patience, birth works! So enjoy pregnancy and its ups and downs, it can be a joyful journey into the unknown without feeling pressured by any authorities or forced procedures. Just eat healthily, get rest, listen to your own inner wisdom and communicate with your baby!

Sean & Rebecca's first baby's birth at home 2006

Labor and Birthing Positions

Naturally, without being told what to do, a mother will assume a kneeling, standing, or squatting position to birth her baby. In labor, the flow of sensations creates a rhythm of its own. Moving against this wave of energy may stagnate, prolong and make labor and birth much more difficult and painful. In a hospital or birth center, most likely women are told to lie on their backs to birth their babies. In reality, this position is only convenient for the on looker. Manipulating the birthing mother and her baby is much easier when she is down on her back.

Primitive drawings on cave walls let us know that traditionally women stood, squatted or knelt to have their babies. It is gravity that helps facilitate a birth, not anti-gravity. When a mother is on her back the pelvis becomes compromised and has less mobility to work with her baby's head that is moving through her pelvis. The female pelvis is designed to birth babies. However, when interfered with, the mechanics of the pelvis seem to close down or have less room for movement. So when in labor and giving birth, it is wise to move with the flow instead of against it--stand, squat, rest when you can, and remember that your body and baby need to work together to have a safe and joyous journey in birth!

Over Due, or Are You?

More then half of first time mother's go overdue. Perhaps the LMP (last menstrual period) has been miscalculated or the body also is "priming" itself more slowly than what the textbooks say to expect. Every mother and baby is different. Sometimes when a skilled person is caring for the mother, they will notice a steady growth of the baby without it correlating exactly to the dates originally estimated. There is no harm in patience and waiting for a baby to be ready to be born. In actuality, there is only harm in impatience and jumping to drastic induction measures.

Statistics show that the average length of gestation varies depending on race, age, parity (how many babies a woman has had), family history and physiology.

Unfortunately, too many babies have been forced into this world when not ready, and this can be extremely painful, scary, and dangerous to both mother and baby. Pitocin, the drug that is administered to induce labor is a synthetic oxytocin derivative. Oxytocin is the natural hormone that we secrete for birth. When synthetic oxytocin is used it creates intense and sometimes extremely painful contractions that are not normal and can cause damage to the uterus itself. During the last half of pregnancy, natural oxytocin from the mother's own hormones release slowly in order to prepare for labor and birth. This may happen over a few months, up to a few weeks or days before birth. When synthetic hormones are given to a mother and baby when they are not physically nor emotionally ready many complications can occur. Labor becomes abnormal because the mother and baby are not quite ready for labor or birth. The baby may not yet be entirely aligned in the pelvis and thus not ready for the intense contractions pitocin encourages. This puts a huge strain on the baby's whole body and may cause fetal distress that normally most of us want to avoid. The chemicals in the mother's brain, which have been artificially stimulated by the Pitocin, send messages to other areas of the mother's body to protect itself from the invasion. This causes her to panic, and it becomes extremely painful for most women. Once the pitocin "kicks in" the mother is usually on a bed with a fetal monitor strapped to her belly, which immobilizes her even more and the contractions are unbearable. The baby is also feeling these intense contractions and may not be in place or ready to be born. This will cause the baby's heart rate to speed up and then slow way down. Causing much worry amongst the parents and the staff of the hospital, and most likely the mother is propositioned to take more drugs to calm her down and help her relax. The excuse for this is that the baby is in distress because the mother is not coping with the pain well. The pain is there because it is not time for the baby to be born and the drugs, which have induced labor, are foreign to the mother and baby's system.

Before a decision to induce is made for any one's birth, there are many things to consider. One is how the mother is feeling emotionally. Does she feel any apprehensions towards giving birth? Could her dates be off a bit? Is the relationship with her partner supportive? Who is pressuring her too get it over with and just go get induced? Are there significant reasons for the birth to take place now? On the other hand, is this just impatience on the parents and care providers part?

After evaluating induction criteria, is it really worth the many risks for mother and child? Firstly, the statistics for complications after receiving an induction are many. The C-section rates for induced births are very high. More than half of all inductions turn out to be C-sections. More then 90% of inductions receive an epidural because labor is extremely painful when induced. The child in question will most likely need extra care after birth. The baby's system may not be ready to be born, therefore the child may need resuscitation and various other interventions at the time of birth.

A funny little story I experienced about seven years ago, was of a mom who thought her estimated due date was on Mother's Day. She and her partner felt absolutely sure of their conception date. As she was growing the baby, we palpated size and measured her each visit. The baby was growing fine and moved a lot. Her heart rate was always normal and the parents were sure of her EDD (estimated due date). Mother's Day came and went. Their friends, who came for the birth, came and went. After re-evaluating the situation I suggested that the dates were off and that they should not worry if the mother felt that the baby was healthy and moving well. The mom and dad were definitely stressed out just because they had a specific date in mind. I usually suggest that parents be generous with their EDDs because they are not always an absolute indication of when birth may take place. We counseled and did affirmations to calm the parents, anxious friends and neighbors. Weeks past, and still the baby was fine and growing steadily. Mom and dad relaxed and became a little calmer. In the wee hours of Father's Day, I got the call. Six weeks after her original EDD she gave birth within four hours to a healthy 8lb 4oz baby girl. Both mother and father were pleased they did not give in to the pressure to go get induced, although it was a challenge to keep faith and patience. Their reward, however, was an un-medicated, natural birth at home on Father's Day!.

Looking back, I really feel that they thought they were pregnant when the mom may have very well skipped a cycle but then got pregnant later that next month. However, I realized after this birth that dates should not be the answer. Mother Nature does her thing without calendars, clocks, or scientific proof.

Unfortunately the medical system, and even some midwives, are told that due dates are everything, that if a mom goes past her due date there must be something wrong. This is just another example of not trusting in the natural process of life.

We can prevent this from happening from the beginning, by getting educated. Then, by finding a support person who is not going to jump to any conclusions once a date comes and goes. It also goes the same for early babies. The standard textbook time for early babies is three weeks before a due date. In many cases, the baby is just ready. Lungs are mature and both mother and baby are just done. Before 37 weeks, gestation is thought to be dangerous because the child's lungs are not fully mature. And in some cases this may be a true problem that needs to be taken very seriously. Although in hospital, they will do C-sections on babies before 30 weeks, and induce labor at this early date if they feel the mother has some pathology requiring this procedure. None of these interventions are usually necessary. It is taking care of ourselves, and getting education, that will lesson the effects of these interventions on our children's minds and bodies. It is dangerous to interfere with Mother Nature. She has her own timing and logic beyond our own; however if we listen to her voice, we will know what is needed during our time of birth.

Communicating "The Language"

When working with midwives and doctors, it is helpful to know a few terminologies as well as the physics of labor and birth. Even if you are doing your own care, these things are still useful to know.

I do not feel that routine internal exams are always beneficial. Sometimes it is helpful to look inside one's self for clues as to the progress of labor and birth. Self-examination, whether it is emotional or physical, is key to understanding these internal findings for your own well-being. Every woman's body is unique and so these techniques are not always accurate, but rather a "guesstimate" about what is going on. It is good to know you can figure this out on your own, instead of having someone else tell you. You can feel from within how your own body works in relation to your labor and birth and then be able to relate your own findings to your care provider (if you have one).

During pregnancy and labor, there are a few average stages of progress that can help you figure when labor and birth are nearing. Some of these things, we have already discussed in other terms throughout this book. I am trying to cover each angle of all these situations, so this may all sound familiar.

Within the last few weeks, the baby and you go through some physical and emotional changes that are apparent.

The first thing you will notice is that the baby will settle down into the pelvis. For some moms and babies, this happens weeks before labor begins, and for others it might not happen until the day before, or even the day of labor. Prior to this, you may be feeling tired for a few days, then all of a sudden a burst of energy surges throughout your whole being, and your nesting instincts kick in.

"Internal Rotation" takes place. This is when the baby rotates into the pelvis to fit his head through the first boney "protrudents," called the Iliac Crests. These are your hipbones. Once baby nests into your "inlet," he will usually stay there until more sensations ease him lower. At this point more mucus or even a small amount of blood may appear, your mucus plug may be loosening up. You will be able to breathe better since the baby is farther down into your pelvis and out of your ribs, but you will have to urinate more because of the pressure on the bladder. These signs are good to notice and will assure you that things are progressing well.

"Dilation" is one way of checking yourself for progress. The cervix is the gateway to the uterus so doing internal exams at this time may be dangerous as there is the potential to push bacteria and pathogens from the outside environment into the uterus, thereby contaminating the baby's environment. If it is your own fingers, and not in a foreign environment rarely would infection occur.

The cervix begins to open and thins out ***(Effacement)*** slowly during the last few weeks of pregnancy. Because of the baby being lower in the pelvis, the baby's head will put pressure onto the cervix and begin to open it. Dilation is a controversial element, like many birth-related things. If you listen to your body and go with it, it will open well and labor should not be unbearable at all. The first stages of dilation are sometimes in late pregnancy, you may find your mucus plug has moved out of the cervical opening because your cervix is softening and getting ready for labor. If you do an internal exam on your own, you may feel it softening and opening a bit, sometimes a lot!

Without any, or with very mild feelings of expansions, you may be ***dilating*** and ***effacing***. This is normal and good, it makes for a slower transition, and once in active labor the dilation time is shortened.

During active labor, the cervix will open all the way, making more expansion and pressure, and you will feel a difference in sensations that clue you in to the fact that you are almost ready to give birth. At this point, the baby is filling up your entire pelvic inlet and moving down towards the outlet, slowly to stretch your muscles and bones, and his or her skull bones are also molding to fit through your pelvis. At this time, it is good to take a break and rest, expansions usually get less frequent and more intense so it is not wise to push unless you feel the overwhelming urge to do so.

I have heard so many horror stories of moms pushing for hours, or that they were told to push just because they were fully dilated, this is not needed. Full dilation has nothing to do with being ready to push. This idea was started in the early days of hospital births when the mother was too drugged out to know what was going on. They had her lying on her back so the only way for her to give birth was for her to push forcefully (with or without the help of the doctor pushing manually on her abdomen) or for the doctor to use forceps to pull the baby out by the head!

You do not need to force your body to push when it is not ready to do so. Pushing forcefully will only cause more harm to the baby and to your bottom! Respiratory problems and fetal distress are common when there has been forceful pushing as this causes the baby to have less oxygen. For the mother, the risk is a higher incidence of tearing her yoni tissues.

Episiotomies, the surgical cut between the perineum and the anus, are also not needed if one is patient and lets nature take her course. Episiotomies are painful, take longer to heal then a natural tear and can cause permanent damage to muscles of the yoni and anus. In addition, holding of the breath while pushing has caused mothers to have other problems such as high blood pressure, breaking of the tailbone, hemorrhages, brain embolisms, death from over exhaustion and heart failure. If you listen to your body, you don't need exams, and if you don't have exams from others then you do not have the sub-conscious feeling that you do not know what you are doing and need someone else to tell you what to do.

By the way, when women are subjected to unnecessary internal exams, manual manipulations and intervention in natural situations, their bodies are not flowing normally with labor because of the intrusion. If you want to do your own internal exams, to find out what is going on in there, you will be in power over your own birth instead of having someone else's schedule or rules being in power over you. Not doing any internal checks is even more empowering, because you are trusting in your natural abilities and therefore, you are listening to the primal calls of birth in it's most raw state!

"Effacement" is another technique to determine how much progress is going on; it is the thinning of the cervix. As a cervix dilates, it also thins out. Normally the cervix is full; it looks like a small plump donut, with a little hole in the middle. The whole uterus is pulled up by the expansions causing the cervix to open and thin at the bottom, and as the cervix begins to open, it also begins to thin in order to accommodate the opening and stretching of the uterus. Effacement is not as easy to check yourself as some other things, however, to feel the cervix you can move your fingers around it and after checking a few times, you will notice a change in the thickness.

Also doing this yourself is better than having someone say, "Oh, you're not progressing because dilation and effacement are not moving as fast as our text books say they should." This is just another way to control birth and make you feel inferior to your own body's capabilities. All women labor and birth differently, and just because we have a way to measure progress in labor through dilation, effacement and the station of the baby, does not mean that this is going to be the same for everyone.

"Station" of the baby, is measured by feeling the head of the baby in relation to your ischial spines, which are basically the boney pelvic parts on which we sit (sitting bones). The head will be "minus station," that is it will be above the spines or "plus station." below the spines. Some babies do not drop into the pelvis until labor is in an active phase, others will drop down very low early on, and some are even through the ischial spines well before Labor even begins. Therefore, to determine the station of the baby you also have to get in there and feel where the top of the baby's head is in relation to your ischial spines. This is not something any of us moms want to worry about, so don't! It really has no bearing on your progress unless you have CPD (Cephalic Pelvic Disproportion), which is a very rare condition that affects less than 3% of women. Even then, this does not mean that the baby cannot fit through; it is just a slower progression. Most babies slowly and successfully stretch the bones and muscles to fit through the pelvis. The impatience of some doctors and midwives will lead them to label someone CPD, and then they can perform an unnecessary cesarean sections and be off to play golf, or whatever else it is they might prefer to do. So, do not have an internal exam and you will most likely be fine.

I had a client who told me her last baby was a cesarean because her doctor told her she had CPD. We worked together, and she had a 9 lb baby at home with no problems. This diagnosis is also confused with the fact that mothers in hospitals are usually lying down with monitors strapped on their bellies not allowing them to move freely, thus causing the pelvis to have less mobility to move with the descent of the baby. Bones are flexible when they are allowed to be. A woman's pelvis is designed to birth babies through it; do not let anyone tell you otherwise. It is impatience of others that causes inflexibility!

"Active labor," according to the textbooks, is from about four centimeters to full dilation. This cannot be true, because many moms, including myself, were 4cms or more way before labor even began. Therefore, to me, active labor is when mom has the feeling that she is actively about to give birth. It cannot be measured the same way for every woman, some moms will be only a few cms dilated for hours with little sensation, then all of a sudden they feel like pushing baby out. This is common in moms who let labor happen and do not fight it. When we fight labor and are too eager to get it over with, or afraid, it often slows and even stops for a while. This is fine, as it gives the mother time to relax and rest before pushing her baby out. Then labor will begin again when the mother is ready. And sometimes the mother and baby need time to get emotionally ready to meet each other, so resting until you're clear enough to continue the labor is a good idea, an exhausted, anxious mother is no fun!

It really is ok to take your time in birth. All aspects of pregnancy and labor are made to emerge slowly, not forcefully. Pregnancy is a time for inner growth and change for all involved, for the mother, father and child. Labor is the initiation into parenthood and finding your true self.

Birth is about beginnings and hope of new days to come, so why rush it! Be at peace within yourself and enjoy every moment of this transition and creation of new life. It will all come when it is ready without stressing out about it.

Enjoy your body and birth! It took 10 full moons to grow that baby, and it will take however long it takes to birth that baby healthily. You have made it this far, so why doubt yourself now? Give yourself as much time as you need.

If all babies were born in faith and in nature, we would have many more beings who knew themselves and felt like whole people. They would then create a better world, as they would no longer need to struggle to find an identity; they would know who they are from the beginning of life. Violence would not dictate their behavior, and their spirits would be intact. Their natural emergence would be the sign that their life and purpose on the planet was not a mystery, and they would fill the world with new life, and new hope.

"God has given us new Birth into new hope." ~1 Peter 1:3

We do not know what we are meddling with as far as these little ones are concerned. The next child born may be a great poet who can transform the world through her words. A new prophet may arise who leads us out of suffering and fear. But if we continue to induce these beings, we risk damaging their primal minds and then we, as a people, lose the magical chance of creating beings who bring their sacred gifts into our lives.

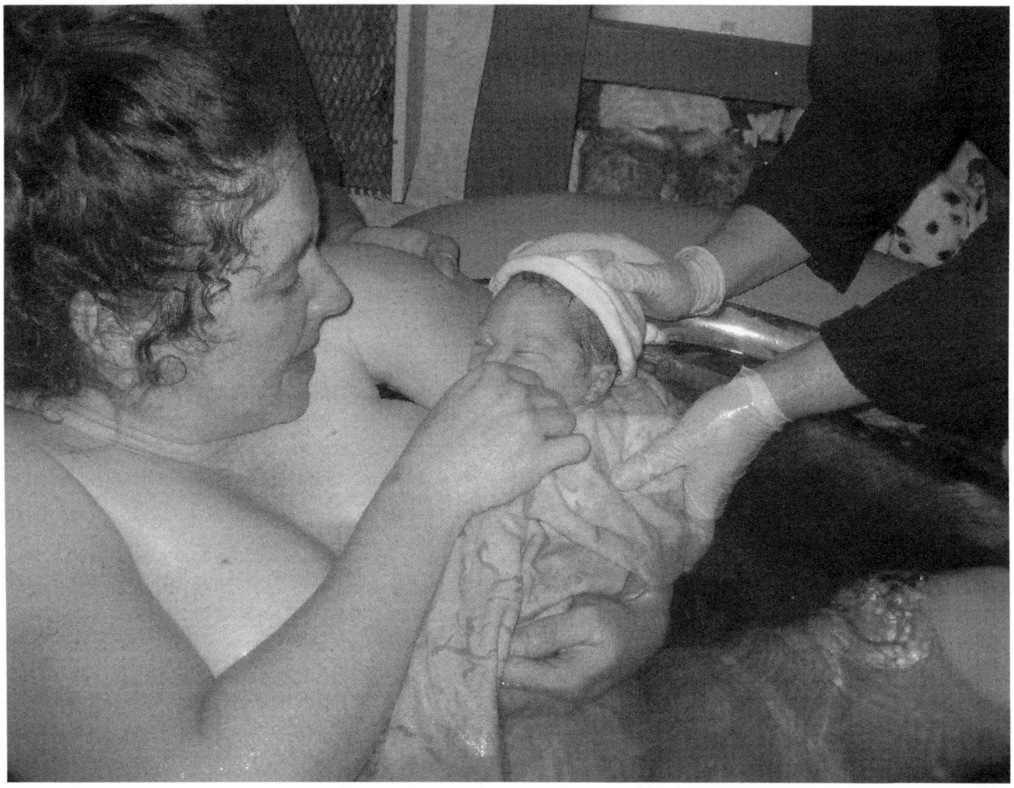

Patti meeting Gemma for the first time 2006

Anatomy of Babies and Breathing

Though babies need not breathe straight away after they are born, most do. If yours does not, check the umbilical cord by gently holding it in your hand and feeling its pulse. If there is a good pulse, which is most likely, then do not worry. Just keep massaging baby and talking to her. I do not suggest ever cutting the umbilical cord after birth; the baby is less likely to panic if she has the original organ of survival still with her.

She will slowly be able to try out her new environment without having to be rushed. It is never necessary to cut the cord, and by leaving it alone for just an hour or two enables the baby to breathe in her own time without being subjected to possible injuries because of someone else's impatience. I have heard stories about premature babies being left attached to their placentas, and they survived because the cords were not cut. The placenta and cord have reserve oxygen and nutrients to support the baby in her journey into the environment.

To learn how to breathe on his own, he needs that slow transition time. We are not meant to be disconnected from our original food and oxygen source right away. I have witnessed babies survive difficult situations just because their cords were left intact. So if you are working with someone, be sure to research this and communicate your desires to prevent any undue harm to your baby.

There are important benefits to the mother also. Firstly, it allows mom's body to get the signals that baby is out and ok, then when the baby's lungs have been profused with oxygen, contractions will increase to release the placenta. There are fewer hemorrhages and less feeling of panic. Mom can relax with her baby and breastfeed knowing that they are gently separating from the intrauterine life. If by any chance, the cord is very short and it is hard to get around, try to lie on one side and scoop the baby in your middle until the placenta is born. After the birth of this amazing organ, which has sustained the baby's life for all that time, give it a look, place it in a bowl or on some chux pads and see its beauty. If it is not rushed out, it's likely that none of it will get stuck inside, but if some does, your body will expel it naturally within a few days. Breast- feeding also helps to get rid of anything left inside the uterus. If postpartum bleeding becomes a problem, literally bite a piece of your placenta off and swallow it whole, even just a quarter size piece will stop a hemorrhage in no time. We are the only mammal that does not utilize the placenta in some way; most mammals eat it, as it prevents hemorrhage, revitalizes the mother, and gives her the nourishment needed to breast feed her young for several days without having to leave to search for food. For mammals in the wild, it is also wise to clean up after birth so other animals are not attracted to the newborns.

The placenta is a multipurpose organ that is of great importance. Do not throw it away or bury it! Your placenta is medicine for you, your baby's future immune system and your family's well-being **(See lotus birth for preserving tips).**

Affirmations for Labor and Birth

My body is designed to birth this baby.

My pelvis is flexible and will allow my baby to enter.

My bones and muscles are designed to protect my baby when she moves through.

My birth will be as slow as it needs to be to allow my baby to be born safely.

My body is in tune with my baby.

Together we will know what to do to birth well.

My baby is conscious and can tell me how to move to facilitate her/his birth.

My body will accept pleasure in labor and birth.

My heart is open to receive pleasure.

My mind is open to receive wisdom.

My hands are open to receive my baby into them, with love …

Labor Dance

As women flow, New life emerges,
Changing all we know.

My love sets his seed so deep,
While maturing earth it so reaps
Ten moons pass my belly ripe
Somehow night seeps through into light

Morning breaks full of vigor,
My water breaks
On my knees, Feeling at ease,
Moving with the breeze,
My belly heaves.

Oh so wonderful, Time has come,
My fruit is ripe and I almost done
Dancing along throughout the day,
Peaceful sounds come my way,

A bird sings outside my door
For a spirit is ready to be born

So I dance
Moving along
Stand, squat, sway, my love holding my arm
A beautiful sound comes over me,
Then my love and I bring our baby up gently into our arms,
A cry, a sneeze, she is finally born ...

Priority List for Life

Building your Priority Lists in Life

Resolving the Past

Creating a New Future

Human Potential

Listening to the Unborn

Perspectives on Birth

Taking Back Our Human Birth Rights

Priority Lists For life

Priorities can be a very useful tool for making life a bit easier. We can set our goals by focusing on the most important to least important values in our lives.

For example:

Simply creating a calm space, to really focus on your list, might be your first priority. Then, when making your list, don't get caught up in wants and desires, just stay with the basics:

My first priority of the day is to make my bed, clean myself, brush my teeth and drink a large glass of water. After doing this, I eat a healthy breakfast so I can make it through my morning without getting low blood sugar.

After stating your most basic priorities, then move on and set priorities for all the different aspects of your life, like health-related priorities, relationship, money, etc.

A general list for pregnancy and birth

I will nourish myself emotionally, spiritually, and physically.

I will drink at least six glasses of water a day.

I will eat small, frequent, high protein meals throughout the day.

I will write my affirmations 3 days a week.

I will talk to my baby everyday and massage my belly.

I will walk at least 4 days a week.

I will be honest with myself, and my partner, about my needs and desires for the birth.

I will meditate and write affirmations once a day.

I am open to all new ideas.

I will ask for help around the house.

Creating a beginning list, from basic to complex life situations, is a good start for re-creating our lives and making life a joy to live. Doing this simple priority list will help organize life's daily needs, and prioritizing goals will make them easier to accomplish. Tomorrow morning, after doing your basic routine, write your first priority list of the day. Sit for a minute with a piece of paper and a pencil and write down the activities that you are committed to. Then write a separate list for the things you know you should do for yourself.

Need List:	**Self List:**
Make breakfast.	Take five minutes to write affirmations
Take out trash.	Bathe with soft music and candlelight after kids go to bed.
Clean house.	Read my book.
Do laundry,	Set time aside with my partner for a massage.

Check off each thing you have accomplished for that day, and then write your list each evening for the next day. If you like to get things done, but feel that you are neglecting your personal self-care, this is a good way to learn how to prioritize your life and set goals, which can then be easily accomplished once they have been committed to paper.

Resolving the Past to Create a New Future

It is easy to say, yet another thing to do. However, with self-realization tools we can re-create a new life for the future. I, for one, had an enormous amount of work to do within myself (and still do) before I could actually conceive of having a decent life. Simply being adopted left me with issues that I still work on today. I gather strength from meditation, affirmations, priority lists, and just reminding myself that I deserve a good life has helped a lot.

In pregnancy, many issues from the past may arise, as we are so open and vulnerable, both emotionally and physically. It is wise to recognize these issues when they do come up. Before the birth takes place, it is best to start the healing process, so we can be clear and focused on the tasks of parenting ahead.

It is true that when we take time to heal old wounds and let them go, we then have more room for greater things to emerge within ourselves. In pregnancy and birth, these issues will usually arise because we are in a very open and life-creating state of being. Dealing with them helps us become better parents.

Children learn from example. For instance, just the way a mother handles life's trials and tribulations sets a pattern for her children to react in a similar manner. So she can either pass on dysfunctional patterns or great knowledge and wisdom when she acts, and reacts, in a more gentle loving way.

Therefore, by using the tools we have already discussed here, and practicing self-forgiveness, we will have a much more clear and focused path for birthing and raising our young.

"As Human beings, we can have the best of both worlds. We can retain our self-conscious personalities while at the same time becoming aware of our inner selves. To do this we must first rid ourselves of the unnatural emotions of fear, shame, and guilt, for they are like clouds preventing us from seeing who we are and what we are capable of doing. This can be accomplished through Love, Forgiveness, and Understanding."

~Unassisted Childbirth (By: Laura Shanley 1994:8)

This is one example of a mom who did not work on her past issues:

At the age of 38, first baby, had several abortions and a history of sexual abuse. She didn't tell her partner about any of these issues. When they conceived a child, she chose to go to the doctor for her care, and, of course, the doctor did not have the time, or inclination, to deal with her past or even asked about it. Therefore, she ignored the abortions, her guilt and fears from the past. When she went into labor, a rush of fear started to stagnate her contractions. At the hospital, they put her into a hospital gown and continued with their routine procedures, which includes vaginal examinations. She had an extreme reaction to these invasive procedures, and labor became very painful. Because the emotional issues were not dealt with prior to labor, her fears started to circulate through her entire body. Instinctively, she held back to protect herself and her unborn baby from the situation. After awhile the hospital staff decided to put her on Pitocin (a synthetic hormone that increases the intensity of contractions). After the Pitocin kicked in, she was helpless against the strength of her contractions, yet she fought them because they were too painful. By this time, they had strapped a fetal monitor to her belly to keep a record of the fetal heartbeat. Tied down, with the pain increasing, she had no control over the birth. Then, they administered an Epidural (a spinally injected form of narcotics to numb from the waist down). This rendered her even more helpless. Next came a catheter in her urethra because she could no longer feel when she needed to urinate. Because the drugs posed a risk to the baby and could deprive him of oxygen, a fetal scalp monitor was placed vaginally inside the mother. They literally screw this contraption into the baby's head, or, sometimes, a suction cup holds it in place, having to break her water artificially to do this procedure. Adding to the distress, preformed a C-section. The mother was left feeling raped by the hospital staff, and this added another layer of fear and helplessness to her already disturbed past. These inadequacies followed her into motherhood. Not knowing why she felt so unhappy, she took it out on her baby by disconnecting from him. Upsetting as this may seem, it is very common in these situations. Because we are thinking creatures, we can rationalize these procedures, but at the same time, our primal body says something is wrong. After all of these things are done to mother and child, the ethereal body starts to take over. It is a survival mechanism, and we detach ourselves from our situation and often from the people in our lives. Blame and guilt riddle our subconsciousness. By resolving past issues we can take back our power to choose what happens to us. Sometimes even then things can happen, but the chance is lessened when we work on ourselves to heal our wounds: emotionally, spiritually, and physically.

For Our Children

This great gift, we have so much ignored, needs to be noticed and cared for more.
Our children are the ones who will live in this place when we are gone,
So it is up to us to create a new world with a new dawn.
Open up your heart and soul,
This is the most important human potential for our world.
Our potential could be used much more fully if we just listen to what can be gained.
We could be our own leaders,
Set ourselves free.
We can be the standard of what we want to see.
Our kids will be honored and respected.
Their lives are sacred and loved.
They are our power, our potential, and our gift from God.

Human Potential

Our Creator gifted us with enormous potential, and most of us rarely use even a quarter of it. Our bodies and our brains are full of cells that can transform and manifest our lives into a divine reality. Minds can be re-created through perception, action, acceptance, and acknowledging our potential to create the world around us from within us.

Human potential is rarely measured in our school systems today. Good grades are the criteria by which our kids are measured, and the system does not look beyond their performance in school. We are not living up to the optimal human potential on this level. These artificial standards imprint the priorities of a community on its children. If we feel getting good grades is better than a child being compassionate, knowing himself and having good self-esteem, then we are defiantly not teaching our children about their true human potential.

I, for one, never got good grades, I disliked school and focused more on survival in my youth then anything else. I loved animals, being in the woods, and physical movement; roller-skating, bike riding, swimming, gymnastics, and all the emotional releases I could find through staying with myself. My son, however, once in "real school" loved it. He got good grades easily, loved to read, and socialize, but I never pushed him into school and always left the choice up to him whether to continue home-schooling or go to other alternative school systems. My focus of parenting was to encourage my child to listen to his intuition, express himself openly, and to be compassionate to others. This supported him in all other areas in his youth. Making friends was easy for him, even in a different country where they spoke a different language, he just knew himself well enough to make friends and accept others as they are. This also affected the other aspects of his life, and he is still learning about who he is and what he is capable of in his existence.

All of our parenting styles are going to be different, but one thing is for sure, most of us just want happy healthy kids! Nurturing our children to be inwardly happy and self-reliant is our greatest gift to them as parents. We can instill greater values in them than the minimal standards set by society. This is one tactic to create a dependency of society and therefore we are easily controlled by it.

Teaching ourselves how to re-gain our human potential is a journey itself. However, it is an important one that we all may benefit from. Basic human potential, as I have come to realize, has to do with the mind and the conscious reprogramming of perceptions. The world manifests through thought and actions, cause and effect. The influence of media and society caused us to be conditioned one way, however, we can choose to become reconditioned by using tools such as affirmations, visualizations, meditations, sound, song, and movement. By using these tools, we can erase unconscious conditioning and create more sustainable reactions to our environment. Thus we choose the "cause" that will condition the desired "effect" in our own lives. We can re-learn how to fully utilize our human potential and how to use our minds and our bodies systems more efficiently and effectively; as opposed to the standard ways we have been taught.

During and even before conception, pregnancy, labor and birth, your baby has already begun being conditioned through your emotions, the sounds in the environment, and the conditions of her birth. This conditioning continues through your actions and reactions towards your child, and the effects of the media, the school system, and churches. By the time your baby is an adult, and thrust out into the world on her own, she will have had years of unconscious conditioning already behind.

When we realize that everything we do and say instills in our little ones the blueprint by which they will live their lives, then we see how necessary it is to be careful with our words and deeds. Too many times I have seen young children already judging others for how they look, the culture they are from or the economic status they belong to. This is not because the children have made up their minds to be prejudice; it's parents, media and society who have instilled this prejudice in them at a very impressionable age, when all words and actions cause an effect on their little open minds.

Once, when I was with a friend and her daughter, who was 9 yrs old at the time, the daughter looked at some people and said, "Oh, look at those stupid people!" I was shocked and asked her why they were stupid? She replied, "Because my mother said so." These were people in a passing car, how did she impose such an opinion on them? I believe it was because they had a crappy looking car, and her mother insulted people with cars that looked like that. This goes to show that we have as much responsibility towards our children's mental health as we do towards their physical well-being.

It is important that we instill in them freedom of perception. When my son was young, I made it a point to watch what I said and did around him so that I would not impress upon him any prejudices or preconceived notions that I may have held. As a result, he is a fearless, accepting, compassionate young man with good self-esteem—as much as a seventeen year old could have! Of course, there are times when he is negative about something or someone, and now, at his age, he will need to find out for himself what those feelings mean. However, we still discuss how he feels or sees the world, and hopefully this will help him respect other people and remain open to his potential.

Imprinting these thought patterns begins in the womb. Talking and reading to your baby is important. Nourish him with good literature, music, relaxation tapes, and exercises, and above all, have a gentle birth. These things will create a positive beginning that will affect your child's entire future life.

With our understanding of imprinting and human potential, we can make this a better place for our children in which they can fulfill their dreams and desires. We can learn how to set a good example and imprint more mentally and physically healthy patterns in our children making them more self-reliant in mind and body. They will begin their lives knowing no limits to their human potential and become the ones on our planet who make better choices.

Remember, the child you are creating has wanted you and your partner to be his parents, even before conception. For some reason you are the chosen ones. This spirit has come into you and through your body, and now it is up to you to give this child the very best you can in education and care!

Communicating and Listening to Your Baby Inside

In other sections of this book I have gone over affirmations, visualizations and such. Meditation is one of the best-known ways to help one's nervous system heal, and it helps us remember who we are. Just sitting and breathing in the proper way can do wonders for high blood pressure and bodily ailments. Take a few moments a day and sit cross-legged as best as you can. Do not force yourself into any contortions. If you can't sit cross-legged, sit in a chair with your feet comfortably on the floor and your legs relaxed and open.

Take in a deep breath through your nose. Don't force it and stop when it feels natural to do so. Exhale slowly at the same pace as you inhale, do a few breaths to get a good rhythm, taking it in on a natural count (about four seconds), and letting out fully the same way. Now close your eyes until they are only open a crack, relaxing them with each breath, take in at least 20 breaths while doing this. After you feel like your breath has been "tuned in," and it is happening naturally without effort, place your hands on your belly, relaxing your arms on your legs, and visualize light streaming from your hands into your belly. Send Love and Light intentionally to your baby, and ask your baby to give you a sign that he hears you. Some of these kids may be sleeping, but they will hear your inner thoughts and suggestions. In your mind, discuss your day's plans, how you are feeling, etc, and ask your baby for feedback. With each meditation, see if you feel you are getting a response of some kind. It may not be movement, or it may be movement, it may be another voice coming back to you through your mind or your heart. When you are in tune with your baby, somehow you will hear an answer. Sometimes, you will hear a really loud voice that seems like another person--who is already born and has a physical voice of his own--is in the room with you. I had that happen when I was pregnant with my son. It actually scared me the first time I heard it. It was amazing! Therefore, you are not crazy if you hear a real voice, it is just your baby letting you know that she is there with you, awake and listening. Doing this exercise twice a day (if not more), will give you and your baby lots of oxygen from the focused breathing exercises, and will create a relationship between you for the journey you are about to embark on together.

Getting out of survival mode

We are so fortunate to live in a place where we do not have to wake up with bombs going off around our houses. In other places in the world, like the country I was born in, there are gunshots, bombs, and militia walking around and patrolling the towns and cities on a daily basis. We are in a culture of luxury; we worry about money, work, having a car, and getting to our favorite television program on time. This is not to make anyone feel guilty, but it is just another way to see our lives in a better light, being grateful for our freedoms. We, here in the U.S., have an abundance of resources. I have heard too many times that a person is suffering in our town or community and has no place to live or food to feed their children. Why, when we have so much land and so many resources is anyone left out in the street? Personally, I feel if we have a choice to be free from responsibilities, whether it is intentional or not, we make our own lives the way we have created them to be on our own. There is no reason why any of us here are starving or out of work. The greatest potentials we as humans have, come from the fact that we create our environments from our minds. If we want to manifest a life of ease then it takes work to get there!

"Or do ye suppose that the Lord will still deliver us, while we sit upon our thrones and do not make use of the means which the Lord has provided for us?"
~ (Alma 60:21)

Utilizing the resources we are blessed to have can bring about change in our existence. If you cannot find a job, well then plant a garden! At least this will feed the family, and it is a lot of work.

When we are choosing to have a child, a lot of us ask, "Can we afford it?" That is the biggest question I have heard, even before asking ourselves, "Can I love this child?" or "Am I ready to spend all my time caring for this child?" The big $ mark is one of the first things I have seen people worry about. Not to say that it isn't a valid question to ask ourselves, but it is the least of one's worries if the child is wanted, loved and cared for well in other ways besides material possessions. In the U.S., there are resources, co-operatives, and places to get information and help. We are over- loaded with the storage of food and clothing for kids. There are many churches, food banks and sheltering services that can be of help. There is no reason why any of us need to be without these basic provisions.

Learning to utilize this world's resources is the first step to understanding our place in it. No one should be left out in the cold to suffer unless they choose to do so. This does not mean we should not lend a hand if we see someone starving in the streets. I feel that when we are called and inspired to help someone, and they are asking for that help, that it is our duty to supply it.

After my son's father died (in 1992), I chose to leave the town in Massachusetts where I was living. I packed up and told no one where we were going. My mind was cluttered with pain and worry, I barely had enough energy to take care of my two year old son. We moved back to the Catskill Mountains, and lived out of my car for three months. I chose to do this because I had too much going on in my mind to bother with paying bills or cleaning a house. I wanted my son to be free and be a kid for a while, while I figured things out. It was very healing to live in nature, and it soothed my spirit and mind. My mother and friends were angry with me for not telling anyone where we were going, but I felt, at the time, that it was the best I could do for my son and myself. We spent a lot of time by the riverbeds. I watched Zack as he played in the water and explored life, as all kids should be allowed to do, especially in these stressful situations. Slowly my sanity set back in, and fall was approaching, so I found a two family house to rent for the winter. I had little money, but I found things to do to make life sustainable.

From the few months camping out, I had saved some money that I used to buy bulk food and materials to make items to sell. I also found a part time job cleaning and babysitting. I traded childcare whenever I could so I could work, and sell the things I had made. We lived a simple life for many years so we could have the bare necessities. I realized, one day, that I had not bought myself anything in almost five years. I got my clothes from the community free store, and Zack was fortunate enough to receive most of his from grandparents. As time went on, I realized that I had been in survival mode most of my life. It was not that I did not have things when I was growing up, on the contrary, I had more than enough. For some reason, though, I did not accept the gifts I was given until I was much older. Maybe I didn't think I deserved it. I always thought of the country where I was born and all those people starving and being killed in the streets everyday. It left an impression on my soul. I often made my parents angry by giving away my things to other people less fortunate than I. At about age twenty-eight, I realized for the first time that I did deserve what the universe was giving us. I began to tell myself that I was worth having some luxury in my life. I had been struggling just for the bare essentials, having little time or money to do anything else. I never went out unless someone else could pay for it, but I always had enough to help someone else if they needed a hand. Go figure!

Once I accepted that I was meant to have things, and became more grateful for what was given to me, I drew in more and more resources. Finally, I was able to receive, not just material, although that was a part of receiving, but also emotional love and friendship.

Now years later, I have found my balance with the material and emotional aspects of my life. It is known that when we ask the universe for something, it is likely to come our way ("when we ask, so shall we receive"). Often we need to do some work on ourselves to be fully open to receive what is needed and desired because it does take a lot of self-worth and motivation to accomplish this.

Being in survival mode is a whirlwind of events that only create more reasons to survive. If we gain a sense of freedom within our choices to make a better life, if that is what we desire, then that will happen. Through hard work and persistence, anything can happen.

Affirmations I have used:

(Giving Thanks to Sarite' Sanders for her guidance)

I deserve to be loved and appreciated.

I am open to receive great gifts from the universe.

I am worth the time and effort to work on myself.

I will be open to all new possibilities.

I will receive love and acceptance from others.

I deserve to have some comfort in my life.

I give thanks for all I already have everyday.

My life is full of mystery and I will enjoy the adventure.

I create abundance through hard work and persistence.

My life is full of joy and love.

My children are my teachers.

The Goddess is within me in every step I take to becoming a happy woman.

Cougar Hot Springs "My Healing time" 1992

A New Perspective on Birth

"The right place to give birth, would be the right place to make love"
~Dr. Michel Odent from "Water Babies" 1986

In this century, we, as a civilization, can look back and see evidence of decades of experimental trials. Medical break-throughs and medical flops are all there if we want to see them. For over a hundred years now, women and children have been subjected to these experimental research games.

Man-made rules have nothing to do with natural laws. I will say that any man-made rule does not ever apply when it has to do with birth, death or planting seeds. These are, and will always be, natural laws. Anyone who chooses to birth responsibly should receive the love, support and empowerment of those around her.

Dr. Gregory White attended home births for decades; he did breeches, twins, V-bacs (vaginal birth after Cesarean) and has stated that most women (95%) if given education and support do just fine in birth with no interference.

"If we would just leave women in labor alone, they do just fine; it's the meddling that causes problems!"

~ An interview with Casimer Beileky, MD. (Physician for over forty years)

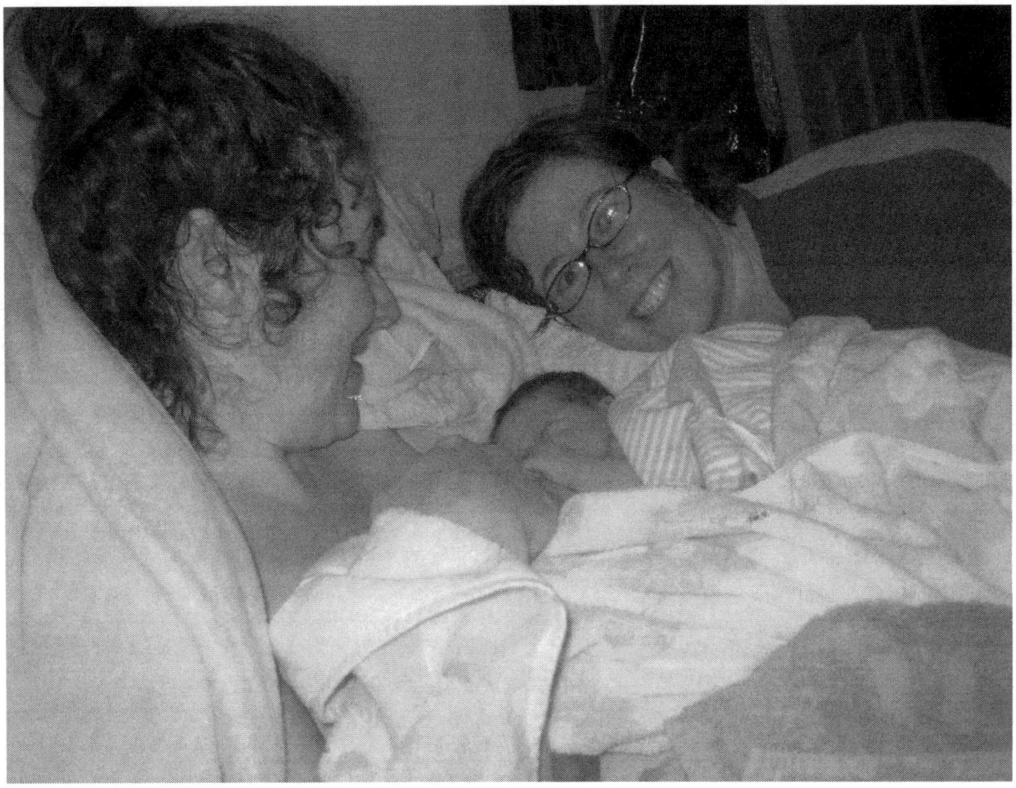

Patti Nagel with new baby Gemma and her friend Kim who assisted her at birth.

Taking back our birth rights

Natural forces that be,
Our human minds cry to be set free,
We seem to be in Samsara Land--
A hellish nightmare that we did not plan ...

This is the way of the human mind,
To fool ourselves by thinking this is it,
What is before our eyes is all there is.

Life is not so very long,
So why are we playing with Mother Nature's song?
We should be in her arms with trust
What has happened to our sisters is wrong.
We cannot allow this any more,
Stand up and speak; do not leave the door.
Be kind
and care.
Birthing is a natural affair.

I feel deeply, that being connected to all living beings is an essential part of helping women. Therefore, they have not just good birth outcomes, but a life-changing growth experience that reaches the whole family. Birth is a sacred event. It echoes across the world. It is a vibration, a wave of life force that enables us to progress and create a more positive future for ourselves and the entire planet.

In our industrialized societies today, we are spending more money on birth than almost every other country in the world, and not getting any better results than do other places that are less privileged. Not that I feel it is a privilege to have an Epidural stuck into my spinal cord, or forceps applied to my baby's head, or tubes stuck in all my orifices, but a lot of women feel it is their right, and they deserve this special treatment. What did these women ever do to deserve this type of abuse? How could our babies have done anything to deserve this treatment?

Birth is an everyday, normal event that needs no fuss or tending. The medical establishment however, seems to have lured and manipulated this sacred event into a medical phenomenon, as if it was a rare disorder or plague. It just so happens that we have been here for over hundreds and thousands of years before the medical establishment even existed. Our new perception on birth practices today may enlighten even the most dedicated western consumer. I have spoken with doctors, nurses and health care workers about birth and, astonishing as it may be, they all have a keen sense of what the problem is. It is just how to solve the dilemma that needs attention.

If we, as a people, start to educate ourselves about birth and take the responsibility of caring for our young, and ourselves, then we may get somewhere. If we decide that we are willing and able to birth, care for our children, and die with dignity--at home--then we will be able to dictate how the medical profession cares for us when we truly need more assistance. If they know that we have a vested interest in our own health, and want better care when it is truly needed, then we will receive it.

If, on the other hand, we just stand around and do nothing, we loose out. Our lives will not be fully lived; our potential will be lost. If we continue in the illusion of powerlessness, believing that we are not the creators of our own reality, then our children will not have the wisdom to create better choices for their own future.

As a people, we all may benefit from learning and practicing conscious birthing together. Women and men, already have the knowledge needed, if we just give ourselves a chance to explore our minds and inner wisdom. Then a new reality will surface that can solve many of the problems we have today. We are not helpless here, as we are led to believe, unless we want to be. We do not need to be dependant on other so-called "health systems." We can co-exist with them, and not let them overpower our own judgment.

We can work together with the new technologies to better our civilization, instead of being ruled by them. I feel that over the years technology has given us many great things. When it comes to birth though, we have to realize that the potential has been misused. Making a better place to live on our planet has nothing to do with destroying and manipulating nature and our natural functions. We do not understand how it all works together, and any natural function of the body, which is manipulated, can, in turn, cause an effect later in history that can be devastating.

For example, it takes about 1000 years for us to adapt and evolve into a new genetic form. If women keep allowing themselves to receive unnecessary Cesarean Sections, in 800 years women's pelvises will adapt and no longer be able to give birth naturally. If this sounds astonishing, it is. Our genetic makeup is adaptable. Over time it all changes--our eye color, hair color, the pigment in our skin, our bone structure--all starts to change and adapt to whatever environment we end up in. If we all come from the same place, from Eve and Adam, and they are our true parents, then it begins to make sense. Over time, we had to migrate to survive the changes of the earth. After migrating across the continents, the weather and environment changed and had an impact on us. Our bodies had to change, to be able to survive (See "The Real Eve" at discovery.com).

If we continue to allow the medical system to take our babies by force, through drugs and surgeries, then future generations will have to adapt. Even in the last 100 years, we can see that the medical birth industry has brain washed most women to believe that they are not capable to birth without medical procedures. It is already happening. It is up to us to stop it so our children can be born and live free!

"God did not create a meaningless world!-"
~Lesson 14 "A Course in Miracles"

NOTES:

Living Simply

Kelly Courage pregnant with Osha 1999

Living Simply

Preparing Yourself and Your Family for Healthy Experiences in Life

If we could only be closer to the Earth,

Then we will find,

All the Wonders that are so divine.

Within the Trees and Mountains is the Truth of our Existence,

Then we will See how Beautiful this Life can Be.

SIMPLY.

I have often thought that living simply is like a preventive measure to hundreds of possible complications. Being raised mostly in suburbia, I sought the solace and safety of the woods for most of my youth, taking solo trips into nature by bike or foot, and then spending time in the trees, contemplating life. When I was older and on my own, I re-entered the lifestyle I had always wanted for my sanity and my soul.

Re-raising myself, as a single mom with a child, was all consuming. To make things as simple as possible, I gathered resources and knowledge. I wanted to fulfill my own creative urges by living as simply as I could with as little distraction as possible, in any circumstance I found myself.

With basic preventive care and knowledge, while utilizing the natural elements in our everyday lives, we can live fully and with less stress than in conventional ways. Living simply may vary according to our needs, expectations and desires. It can be as simple as growing a garden, using cloth diapers or even going diaper free! That could make a difference in one's stress level and emotional well-being. If we could only see this world as a finite space, use its resources sparingly, and share any common knowledge with others, we could bring about a great change--a change in the quality of our own lives, as well as for the betterment of our planet.

My little garden 2006

Rising with the Sun, Going down with the Moon

Rise with the Sun, say a Morning Prayer,

Wash your Face and Teeth,

Comb your lovely Hair.

Be Alone for a Moment,

No one else is Awake.

The Planet is still, Mostly Quiet,

And You're Up, getting Ready for the Day.

When the Day is Done

And you're feeling Good, All is in its Place,

Dinner's made, Kids all fed,

Now it's time to Read a book and put them to Bed.

Time to say Goodnight to the Sun

And Hello to the Moon.

When Moonlight peers into the dark lit Sky,

It is time to say your Evening Prayers and go "night, night" …

Simple living tips:

A standard priority list for living simply can be found in the ***"Priority Lists for Life."*** Here is another list for simple living and fulfillment in everyday life.

Reuse everything you can:

Start with reusing plastic containers and grocery bags. Use them for storing food in the refrigerator, as garbage bags, or for cat litter disposal. Any plastic containers that food comes in can be reused many times. This will save you money and reduce the amount of trash going into the landfill. Just clean everything in hot soapy water, and you have instant "Tupperware" without having to spend anything extra.

Cotton Towels:

Buy some cotton towels for hand cleaning, dish drying, or napkins. These are more durable and can be washed and reused many times. Paper products are usually used once and thrown away (again, ending up in a landfill). I am proud to say I have not bought paper towels or napkins for more than 18 years now, but have not yet figured out the toilet paper problem. If anyone reading this knows of an alternate to TP, please let me know. I suppose using washcloths, as I did for a few years when I had no money, would do the trick for the TP dilemma. For some of us, reducing our paper consumption will mean a time of adjustment. It is well worth the effort to save both money and resources, as billions of oxygen-producing trees a year get used for paper.

Cotton diapers:

Use them for menstrual pads. I have never used tampons. I feel they are dangerous because our blood should flow out and tampons stop this natural flow and allow blood to dry inside, which, in turn, can lead to infections. Toxic shock syndrome is an infection that can result from tampon use. I have seen this in a few women over the years; they could have died if the fevers and infections were not remedied quickly. Today those women know better and do not use tampons anymore (hopefully!). Also, I have always felt that buying factory-made disposable pads was a waste, and they are unhealthy because they are made with chemicals. I invested in about a dozen cloth diapers and cut them up into over fifty strips of absorbent and re-usable "Moon Pads." Now I never run out, and always have something to use. It is no wonder why so many women these days have yoni (vaginal) problems; pads and tampons are just another monopolizing, propagandic product to avoid.

Make your own Baby Wipes:

Making your own baby wipes is inexpensive, easy and safer for your baby. Avoid all the chemical store bought wipes. Using a washcloth with warm water to wash your baby's bottom is optimal, cleaning wash clothes and reusing them is also affordable and easy to do. For traveling mamas and babies, just prepare a few wash clothes in some warm water and gentle baby soap, store them in plastic bags in a container then use the plastic bags for the dirty ones, and later wash them. There are some recipes for making your own baby wipes, but I find that this method of wash cloths is gentle on the baby and also easy and inexpensive. Search online for "homemade baby wipes" for more alternatives to store bought chemical filled ones.

Go diaper free!

Many women are learning, through web sites and support groups, how to manage babies with their natural elimination patterns. It makes sense. If we do not put a diaper on a baby, we can learn their natural elimination times during the day. Babies also learn quickly when and where they should eliminate. They learn that when you take them to the potty, that's when they should go, so it's a good practice that needs more attention. There are many cultures that do not use diapers--this is the most natural thing in the world.

If you are going to use diapers, using cloth is better because of the reusability issue and the chemical problems of the store-bought brands. Of course, cloth diapers are more time consuming, so consider going diaper-free. It is even better because you do not have years of changing dirty diapers ahead of you. I have heard from some moms that it might only take six months to become familiar with their babies' elimination schedule. In addition, taking babies to the toilet is easier than changing diapers or dealing with rashes that can harm a baby's bottom and maybe even his/her ego. Would you want to sit in your own waste for any length of time if you didn't have to? Probably not! Maybe it is a cellular memory that we have from our babyhood that causes some of us to dread having our first babies because we have to change dirty diapers. We just feel somewhere deep down that it just is not right. **(See more resources in Appendices.)**

Eating Simply:

As much as possible grow what you need to eat, buy only what you cannot grow, and find a co-operative food club so you can buy in bulk. These are great ways to eat better and conserve resources by reducing the transportation of various food items. Being more conscious about food can save time and money, making life healthier as well, by eliminating the need to go shopping everyday. Learn to preserve fruits and vegetables in the fall for the long winter. If you are lucky and live in a warmer climate year round, just eat off the trees and out of a garden!

Recycling:

Recycle what you can by reusing it, or taking it to a recycling center rather than having it end up in our landfills. Now recycling can even be done at the local market or at the landfill itself. Having separate containers to sort out glass, plastics, paper and metals, can be very rewarding. I have also learned that some glass and plastic containers can be used for insulation in some types of home building. Where I live the building codes are pretty lax, so the using of this type of material is allowed. If you are building a home that needs light in places that also need privacy, use glass bottles to make the windows. In addition, in the old days, they used whatever was not usable any longer in the walls of their homes. This was common practice that afforded warmth and reduced waste.

Composting:

Composting is another beneficial way to save garbage from the landfill while creating a more fertile earth. Keeping a bucket just for food scraps in your kitchen can make all the difference between having a healthy garden, trees and berry bushes, or not. I usually just do a simple compost by digging a hole in a sunny area so the heat can help break things down. I add food scraps to it each day. Every other day, I put more dirt on top of it and turn the soil to mix the scraps of food in, and then I add water to help it all decompose. After that, I add a little ash, a few wood chips, or even a bit of straw to keep moisture in, this helps it break down faster. After a while, start turning the whole thing every now and then to help the decomposing process. I have done this for years with great success. After only a few months, you have mulch for your trees and bushes and healthy fertile soil to add to your garden. There are commercial Composters you can buy, but this is just another product and has little to do with living simply. I choose the simple way to compost—the way our ancestors did.

If you compost there will be less smell in your kitchen, and less waste to haul out every week. You will be returning to the earth what is hers. It's like making an offering for the food we receive. We become part of the natural cycle. Mother Earth provides us with food, we use what we need, and return the rest thus providing Her with the material she needs to make better soil for us to grow better food. It is the way of nature, and composting can be our way of giving thanks!

Reuse Water:

Reuse your bath water or dish water! Use it to water your garden and house plants. If you are using mild non-caustic soaps then your plants will love you! Bath water contains dead skin, among other things, and is a good fertilizer. Even diluted baby poop is good for the plants and your garden. Adult waste is only good after it breaks down over a couple of years, but can be added to your compost to have fertile soil later **(See books on *"Human Manure"* for references).**

Living Simply Within Ourselves:

Just connecting everyday to the trees, animals, birds, sounds of the wind, the mountains or oceans can be another way of living a simple life. Just being ... this is a part of the simple way to live, which we all can benefit from, mentally and spiritually as well as physically. Nature keeps us in tune with our source, our essence of life. Those little *"Zen Sand Boxes"* are not necessary, but are relaxing. You can just sit on your porch, even if you live in a city, and connect with the earth. You may hear people and traffic, but you can still identify with the natural forces; it will all blend and become a part of your life experience.

Cleaning Without Toxins:

Using natural elements for cleaning could be considered another way to live simply. Cleaners like vinegar and hot water, as well as biodegradable soaps, are a gentle and safe alternative to harsher more toxic chemical cleaners. They work just the same (sometimes better), are cheaper and can even be home made. I have used hot water and vinegar for years, as well as simple soap *(like Dr. Bronner's)* to clean toilets, sinks and the bath. When using chemicals to clean our homes, we are exposing ourselves, and our children, unnecessarily too ingredients that may have dangerous side effects. Fibromyalgia, chronic fatigue syndrome, migraines, skin allergies, rashes and respiratory ailments can be some of the side effects from using the more harsh store-bought cleaners. Even simple laundry detergents and dish soaps can easily be made at home from ingredients found in the kitchen. A capful of white vinegar, a spoonful of salt, about four drops of biodegradable dish soap and a shake of baking soda makes a great laundry detergent. Hydrogen peroxide **(a mild antiseptic and cleansing agent, as a 3% aqueous solution)** can take stains out of clothes and carpets if left to stand for about five to ten minutes before washing. There are great books out there for making your own household cleaners. Try a search on the internet for *"Natural Household Cleaners."*

Clothing:

Choose consciously what you wear. Clothes made of cotton, linen or hemp that is non-restrictive is more comfortable and will allow your body to breathe. Your skin is the largest of all your organs. In the early days upper-class women wore restrictive and suffocating corsets, which increased the likelihood of miscarriage, sickly babies and fainting, all in the name of fashion. Women who could not afford corsets wore loose, natural fiber clothing. In addition, because they performed manual labor on their farms and in a factory (not the healthiest environment) they actually had better outcomes with their pregnancies and births because they got exercise! (Go figure). Because of current fashions, many women today are also restricting their blood flow (for example, by wearing tight jeans), and some of today's synthetics do not allow the greatest organ of our body (our skin) to breathe.

Societies that do not wear clothing live longer and are much healthier than we are in our culture. The reason is that we need to take in oxygen to survive. If we are restricting our intake of oxygen then our bodies need to break down more cells to gain the oxygen we need. When we go without clothing as much as possible, our skin draws in the remaining oxygen we need, instead of utilizing the stored cells in our bodies for it. I am not saying we need to join a nudist colony to stay healthy, but when at home, or just in our own back yards, we can try to go without the restrictions of clothing as much as possible in order to let our bodies breathe.

Bras:

These new "corsets" can be stifling. Bras just do not allow the breasts to flow properly, plus finding the perfect bra can be an adventure. Try one that is less restrictive and made of softer breathable cotton. Bras without the under-wire are also more comfortable. The wire is restrictive and can lead to breast infections later. I have found some that really help me such as wireless cotton sports bras, and ones that are not too tight, but give me support. The rest of the time I just go without (I'm a 38C). Under the breast is another world that goes unseen unless we look, and we have to take care of this hidden area. I have a personal belief that wire bras have led to more and more women being diagnosed with breast cancer. Now this could be purely coincidental, but it makes sense. Lymphatic toxicity and cysts are two conditions that could arise from the metallic toxicity & the lack of blood flow caused by a bra with wire.

Toys:

Children's toys can also be simple and safe. One thing I remember when my son was little, and I did not have a lot of money to spend on extras, I used what was on hand to entertain him. Of course, there were a few things grandparents would buy and send us that I did appreciate, but sometimes they were things that I had to throw away before he saw them, like plastic! Or, the forever-daunting gun shaped items I had to whisk to the trash. Children like to put things in their mouths and can choke if a piece of plastic is chewed off and swallowed. I had lots of books for us to read, wooden toys that were not preserved by chemicals, and kitchen tools that seemed to please my son just as good as any other toy on the market. Monitoring what our kids play with is sometimes difficult, but we can try to eliminate the toxic ones by just weeding through the toy box every month and replacing them with our attention and time.

"To forget how to dig the earth and tend the soil is to forget ourselves."
~Gandhi

Food:

One of the first five female physicians in our country, from Chicago, at the turn of the 20th century, Alice Stockham M.D., was a women's health educator, activist, and world tribal researcher. She writes in *"Tokology, A Book for every Woman"* (published in 1899):

"Most womanly problems are easily remedied through proper nutrition, loose clothing, exercise, and cleanliness."

Dr. Stockham attributes most ailments to our digestive system. At the turn of the century, she linked the effects of preserved foods to a sluggish digestive system. She saw a clear distinction between healthy migrant workers who grew their own food and the unhealthy upper class who could afford the processed, but less healthy foods. Most Americans were suffering from poor nutrition because of over-population in urban and suburban areas. Fewer people were getting fresh food out of their gardens because the food industry was trying to accommodate the growing population. In addition, it was becoming increasingly more convenient to buy what you needed from a grocery store. The overall health of those people changed dramatically. Dr. Stockham found that approximately 8,000,000 pounds of baking powder a year was being ingested by the American population. That was a hundred years ago, now it is three times that amount! It forms a sticky substance within the intestines causing a lack of proper absorption of nutrients in the digestive system. Therefore we over eat because our bodies are literally starving from lack of absorption. That is the largest American nutritional dilemma.

More and more people were starting to live in cities and suburbs back then. Food with preservatives have a longer shelf life and could be shipped farther and wider. With a growing number of people living this way, there was less and less room for growing fresh food. Moreover, as the number of women working outside the home increased, gardening decreased, and more food had to be bought rather than grown. Not realizing the enormous, long-term impact it would have on society's health, convenience was allowed to change the traditional way of living. This all became a pattern for the modern and more "improved" lifestyle we know now. Lack of fertility, poor general health, and a greater desire to make money to accommodate our industrialized lifestyles had become a trend. Overall, we can help each other and the planet by leading more simple lives. If we can reduce, or eliminate, our superficial needs, we can create a healthier, self-sustaining and more affordable world in which our children can live fully.

Creating Our World

The future is not something we enter... The future is something we create.
~L.I. Sweet

Our Creator gave us the gift of consciousness, and sub consciousness (an intuitive and psychic part of the brain), to utilize for the betterment of our community and ourselves.

Over time, we have turned our consciousness into an enemy by not listening to our intuition. Intuition has been ridiculed by some as just coincidence, a vivid imagination, hog wash, or simply not worth listening too. That is the reason why most of our realities are broken and twisted. Who in their right mind dreams of a reality of war, violence, and hatred? If that is our only potential in this world, we are very lost and far behind in our evolution. It is known that when we work with our consciousness, using both sides of the brain (the logical brain and etheric (spirit) brain), we can do magical things in our world. By manifesting dreams, and the gut instincts of our primal consciousness, we can improve conditions on our planet by creating a better world within ourselves.

Over time, male imperialist propaganda has led people away from their intuition, instinct, and knowing of reality, calling it evil or witchcraft. The Church and State condemned the common people for using their folk medicines (song, dance, prayer and herbs), and natural intuition for their survival. Over the course of only 300 years, 9 million men and women (of which women were 85% of that figure) were burned, drowned, hung, tortured or dismembered in front of their children for using their natural conscious minds and their intuition to create their reality, to grow food, and remedy illness. This battle to suppress the common people has lasted until today. This does not include The Spanish Inquisition!

Without the knowledge of the conscious mind and the natural world, our ancestors would not have survived for so many hundreds of thousands of years. Nevertheless, because of the social and political changes within the Church and State, we were not allowed to practice our natural skills any longer. This was the government's way to control the masses and move them into cities. This gave them power over a large amount of people and turned them into a "work force," fueling an economy that only empowered the wealthy. Once the population was concentrated into cities, it was also easier to control their minds through hatred, greed and fear and trick them into wars that were for the profit of the elite and powerful.

The loss of our intuitive voice has become epidemic, yet it can be regained. We can create a more holistic reality for everyone. Rather than feeling separate (which is how we've been conditioned to feel), we can realize that we are a part of something; a united force. Together, our manifested realities will be able to change how things are happening now. How? If even a quarter of a society's population realizes it's potential to manifest a new reality, then we will begin a trend that then becomes the standard way of being. Having our babies at home, being responsible for educating and caring for ourselves, breast feeding, and using more natural means to raise our children are examples of trends that can become standards. All we need to do it, is to do it!

We need to listen more to our consciousness, our intuition, our hearts and our gut instincts, and we also need to speak out about it!

"You gain strength, courage and confidence by every experience in which you really stop to look fear in the face"
~Eleanor Roosevelt

It all comes down to listening to our inner wisdom. Our minds are full of incredible gifts from our Creator in whose image we are made. Remember? We were created to create, so why is it so hard for most of us to believe that we create our own realities? All around us, we can see that everything out there is created by someone's mind; houses, cars, clothing, shoes, books, towns and cities. Everything we have is created by the power of the mind. These physical realities are "perks," in a way, to use for our comfort. However, our ability to create them on the physical plane has confused us and given us a sense of superiority over nature. This is not the way to create a "superior reality."

Understanding the capabilities of our mind, limiting society's negative influence, and ridding ourselves of disempowering beliefs that prevent us from achieving our fullest potential, takes work. We can manifest a new reality for ourselves and our children by changing our perceptions of ourselves and our world. It is actually an easy thing to do once we cut through all the years of conditioned, negative attitudes we have inherited.

Birth is the beginning, and it is the first thing in a child's life to be manipulated. It has been taken over by powers that control and destroy our young minds, and it has been in the wrong hands for far too long. It needs to be put back into the Creator's hands; Mother and Father. The child's reality, for his whole life, depends on his prenatal and birth imprints. The first, and most important, hands to touch that child should be gentle and loving, and not some stranger's gloved hands, or worse; a tube, a tank, or metallic guides. None of those things will be imprinting the Love of the Mother, Creator.

Women have been led to fear birth and to feel incapable of birthing naturally. Our reality has been twisted, and we, and our children, have suffered as a result. The medical establishment has taken control over our natural processes because it makes them a lot of money and gives them a feeling of power. We have been sacrificing our children's rights, and OUR rights to fully experience being a woman and mother, for the sake of someone's new car or mansion. All the while, we have been living in fear and in poor conditions. Now is the time for change, for us to take control and manifest the reality we want to see—a reality of peaceful co-existence with each other and the natural processes of life.

Doing the work in this book will help you unravel the mystery of your inner reality. In time, you will realize that not only have you had the power to change things in your life, but also to improve those lives with whom you come in contact. It does take some work and responsibility to begin this journey of self-realization. It is a commitment that will change your own future and that of your children. You can place yourself on the path, be willing and open to do the work and share your knowledge with others who may benefit from what you have learned. It is all up to you!

Simple Home Care Supplies:

Reusable cotton towels, cloth diapers, wash cloths: All these are for cleaning, moon rags, washing, drying, to use as napkins, scrubbers, and underneath the baby when training yourself about *"Elimination Communication …"*

Vinegar (white distilled): for cleaning, **Apple cider vinegar** for making tinctures and for taking internally for cleansing purposes …

Herbs of all kinds

Reusable strainer: cotton, bamboo, or wood

Glass Jars: Mason storage jars, gallon glass juice jugs, these are to store tinctures and teas, and other homemade remedies

***Note:** Stay away from Aluminum cookware and teakettles. They may be the cause of Alzheimer disease and mental impairment. Try cooking in Glass, Porcelain or steel. Eating many Calcium rich foods with Magnesium will help eliminate these metals from our bodies.

Homeopathic family kit: With a basic book, Hyland's has good ones for basic family care.

Hyland (800) 624-9659

Herbal remedy books to refer: Good ones I have used for years: Jeanne Rose's *Herbal body book,* and her *Modern Herbal book,* both have recipes to make your own lotions, salves, baby care, and pet care. Also Susan Weed's *Wise Woman Herbal* books and *Modern Herbal* by David Hoffman. There is an abundance of herbal and homeopathic resources out there, I suggest looking online for used books under natural health care. Try *amazon.com, abris.com,* or *BarnsandNoble.com.* There are many resources to find books.

Seeds to save for gardening: Save all seeds from anything organically grown and without genetic modification so they will reproduce repeatedly, or stock up on your seeds through an heirloom company.

Start a study group: Learn with others how to make your own medicines and baby care products--preserve the knowledge. Spin your own yarn. Make what you can at home for your family, this will save time and money and is rewarding for the whole community. Even in cities this is possible--an abundance of knowledge can be found anywhere.

These are simple, survival skills. We can continue to depend on stores and products, but it's nice to know how to do for ourselves if those things do not last. If we are broke, or just want to save money for something, at least we will have the resources to have what we need for our family's health.

Simple Birth List

Most births do not need unusual things. You can use what you've got around the house, rather then going out and buying a bunch of stuff you will never use again. Sometimes however, some of us just like to get specially made birth items and may possibly use them, or pass them onto a friend who may need it for their birth. I will list a few items that you may already have handy or may want to purchase.

Towels/Sheets:

These can be old towels that you do not care if they get dirty. Just dry them on high in the dryer after washing them in a mild detergent, for about half an hour. Stick them in a clean garbage bag or sealed case until needed for the birth. About 5-10 are usually needed by mom for getting in and out of bath, wrapping baby in after birth, and changing the towel around baby several times until he is dry. After a birth, most babies will need warmth, depending on the climate in which you birth and the time of year. It is always nice to dry a baby after he is born; the fluids a baby has on him can act as a cooling agent and can cause a chill. So changing the wet towels a few times after a birth is common, until baby is warm and dry.

Chux Pads:

Chux pads are those cotton/plastic adult undergarment things that you can buy at most pharmacies or grocery stores. They just protect furniture from getting stained, by blood and other fluids. A towel or sheet with a large trash bag underneath can do the same thing. A shower curtain can be placed on a mattress then a few layers of sheets over that to protect your bed from being stained. Many parents do these things instead of buying a bunch of factory made chux pads, which cannot be reused. There are, however, flannel chux pads that can be used repeatedly. These are nice because they can be washed and reused for changing pads, and then later for a potty training under pad. These can be bought in most midwifery catalogs or birth supply companies. They are flannel, or cotton, on one side then a heavy plastic on the other. High quality materials are used for these because they are meant to be reused many times.

Good food and fluids:

At any labor and birth you want to have good food and fluids handy. There is nothing like having to rush out in the middle of a labor to go grocery shopping at the last minute! For some, this may be a good distraction, but for a middle of the night birth you want to be prepared so you will be nourished and hydrated during labor, birth and postpartum when most people just want to eat and snuggle up with the new baby, without any extra hassles. Easy things to have on hand, at all times nearing a birth, are miso paste to make soup, protein powder and juice or milk to make a shake, Chlorophyll for an iron supplement (if needed), clean water, herbs, homeopathic remedies for various things, and whatever you may want to eat and drink during this time.

Household "Instruments":

If you are doing a Lotus birth, you need not worry about sterilizing scissors or string to tie and cut a cord. This is often the biggest concern at births, but in reality, this is the least of any concern. No cords need to be tied nor cut. However, if you want to have something on hand for this, then any household scissors will do. Just sterilize them in boiling water for at least 20 minutes from boil time. Cotton shoelaces work the same way. There are plastic cord clamps out there that may be bought for clamping cords. I do not suggest tying or clamping cords, this is really least important thing on this list. Some parents like to make their own cutting devices out of Jasper, or other hard stone materials. This is nice but really, no cutting is necessary.

Placenta Bowl:

Any bowl will do. Plastic, glass, metal, clay, whatever you want to use for the placenta is fine. Some people like to use both a sieve and a bowl so blood can be drained off the placenta while it is fresh. Then after a few hours, the bowl is removed and the placenta is placed in a cotton diaper or chux pad while it dries **(see Lotus Birth in Fathers and Partners section)**. I have seen a few hand made placenta bowls throughout the years, and they are keepsake items made especially for this by the birthing mother or her friends. Newspapers are handy at a birth for many things. One is for cleaning up any fluids around the birth area, or for handling the placenta.

Gloves:

If you are doing your own birth without any outside people involved, gloves are rarely needed. The only reason midwives and doctors wear gloves is so they do not give you any of their own bacteria, and so they do not contract any of yours. If you are the father, or household member, just wash your hands when handling any birth related things. If you are squeamish about fluids or placenta then gloves may come in handy. Latex gloves can be bought at any pharmacy or grocery store for home care use. Some women are allergic to latex so ask, or test one out, before handling a mom during labor and birth.

Salt:

Salt is always handy. It can be used for re-hydrating a mom during a long labor. Cell salts are best: Celtic Sea salt, and other sea salts may also be used in the bath (it helps clean it of bacteria) when mom is in labor and in her post partum bath as well. It is good to use in drying the placenta once it has detached from the baby. Normal table salts with iodine are avoided for these things. You want to try to use as much un-processed salts as possible.

Fan:

Sometimes moms in labor get really hot and need extra air flow. Especially in the warmer months when air is dense or humid, it is nice to have a fan to keep mom going with extra vigor. A nearby window may suffice, but having a hand held fan or electric fan is always a nice luxury. Hormones, and just the fact that labor increases the metabolism, make for a sweaty mom. Cooling her off with wash clothes, or some sort of breeze, can help her to remain energized. If she feels the need of air, a fan or window will be needed.

Wash cloths:

Washcloths are also very useful in labor and birth. They can be used for compresses on the belly, face, and body; for cleaning any messes on the floor, toilet, or carpet; for wiping the fluid from a newborn's face after the birth; and just for keeping in bowls of water for different uses. I like to have one bowl of cold water and one of warm water handy. Sometimes I use herbs in one bowl for the mother's bottom to help facilitate stretching as the baby is crowning. A cool washcloth can be used to wipe mom's face to help her feel refreshed, or a warm one can be used for cleaning off any blood or sticky stuff. Dried blood can stick to the skin and be very uncomfortable if left for too long.

Bulb Syringes:

Bulb syringes can be handy for some purposes, but are not usually needed for birth, and when used to suction a newborn baby it may cause other difficulties. In addition, the bulb syringe is made of a toxic rubber substance, which can cause an allergic reaction when it encounters the baby's mucus membranes. Newborn babies have an automatic reflex to rid themselves of any mucus, more gently then a rubber bulb syringe will. Babies cough, sneeze, and spit up or swallow any un-needed mucus from their airways at birth, without any manipulation. If the baby's breathing is delayed, you can massage up the baby's back or suck once, swiftly over the baby's nose and mouth, with your mouth. This will release any mucus from the upper airway.

Manufactured bulb syringes can, in fact, cause a new born to gag and pass out if handled inappropriately, which happens quiet often in hurried birth situations. A bulb syringe, if stuck into a baby's throat too deeply and aggressively, can hit the vegal nerve in the back of the baby's delicate and short throat, causing the baby to choke! Besides, babies are nose breathers, and the plugs of mucus in the nose are usually squeezed out during the birth process, or sneezed out shortly thereafter. Trying to stuff a bulb syringe into a tiny newborn nostril is just shoving the mucus further in, causing the baby to have breathing difficulties. When this happens, it will sound like a snort when the baby tries to breathe.

However, bulb syringes can be handy for other uses. One is for squirting the herbal wash onto the Yoni area after birth. Another is for basting a turkey at Thanksgiving! Normally, at a gentle birth, babies do not need anything to get the respiratory system in action other then their mother's warm arms and her breast to suckle. Birth itself is supplied with all the natural mechanisms it needs to be successful--if not interfered with.

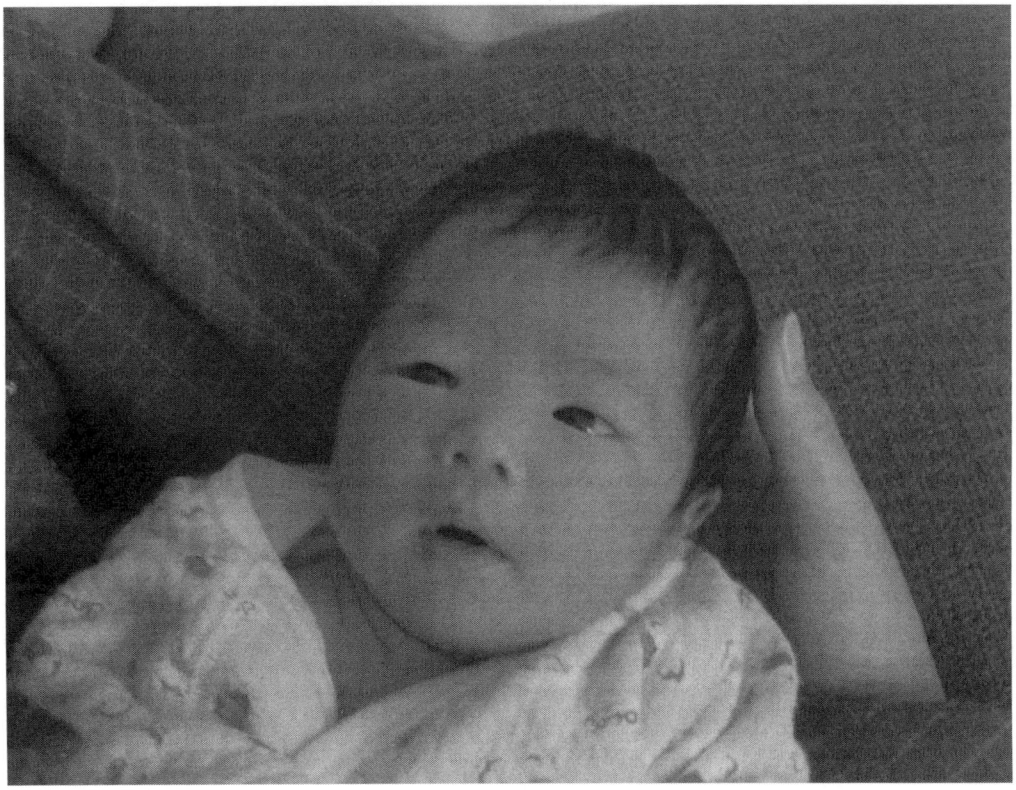

Hanami Sato born at home March 15,2006

Care for Newborn Babies & the Whole Family

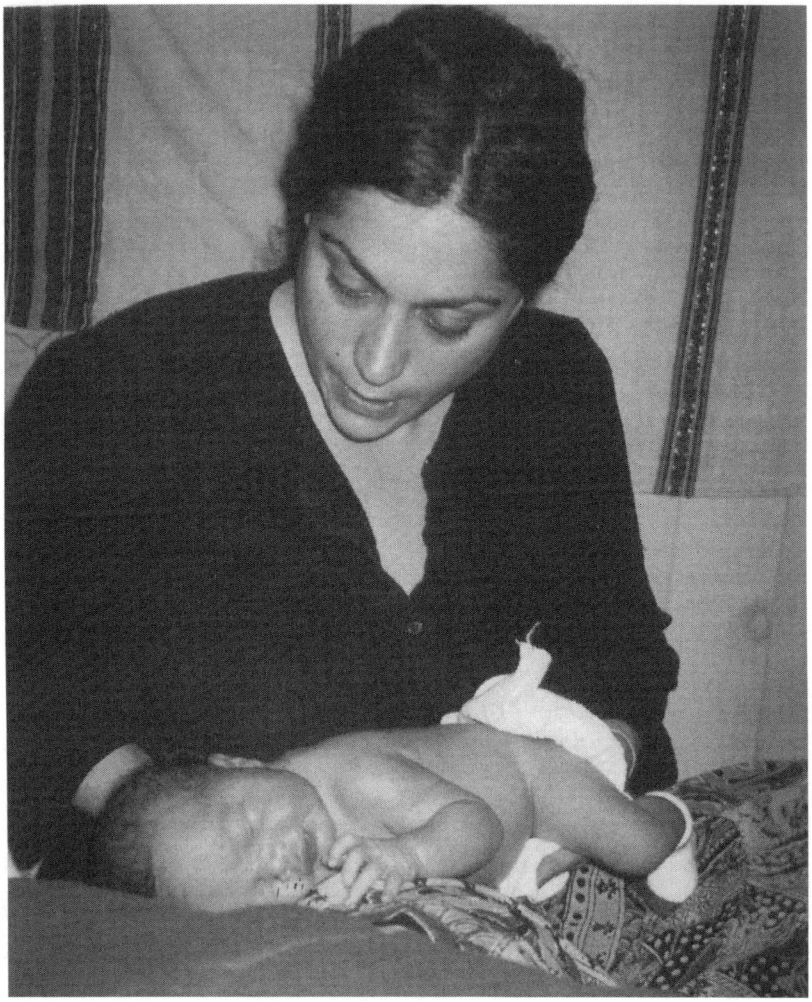

APGAR Scoring

First Few Days of Extra-uterine Life

Leaving the Cord Uncut

Breast-Feeding

Post-Partum Care for Mother and Father

Helpful Friends and Neighbors

Baby Development, in Early Days

Immunizations

"Attachment Parenting," by Joy Shanley

Natural Baby

Diaper Free

Circumcision Decision

"A Jewish Woman Denounces Circumcision," by Laura Shanley

Care for Newborn Babies

And the Whole Family …

Bless this child for a safe emergence into this world.

Through the womb of the Mother, come gently sweet one.

O' Mother Goddesses of Birth: Artemis, Kwan Yin, Athena, Yemeya,

Lakshmi, Mother Mary, Ubagami,

Bring your wisdom here to this baby on Earth …

Keep her safe and healthy from any interference.

We give our thanks for your guidance for this new life,

We ask for our hearts to know what to do for this baby we Love so much,

And want to protect and cherish her …

Blessed Be!

In the last few moments before the birth of your baby, you are alone with him or her before one becomes two. This is a special time, your last time alone without an external child. After this your baby will forever be an outer reflection of your creative life force. There are many ways, in which parents choose to care for their children. It is important to remember that before we had diapers, Destine Ointment and formulas; we had nature. Nature provided us with simple and reliable sources of caring for our young. Here we will explore the wisdom from the ancient ones to care for our new babies, our whole family and ourselves.

Like with all things;

have fun, explore and be open in learning!

In the 1950s Dr. Virginia Apgar created a system to quickly check the baby's well-being in five specific areas. This can help you to determine quickly and easily if your baby needs extra attention.

Use your five senses; by looking, listening, touching, smelling, and tasting (not really tasting, but it's a sense so I thought it would be useful), you can assess your baby's condition.

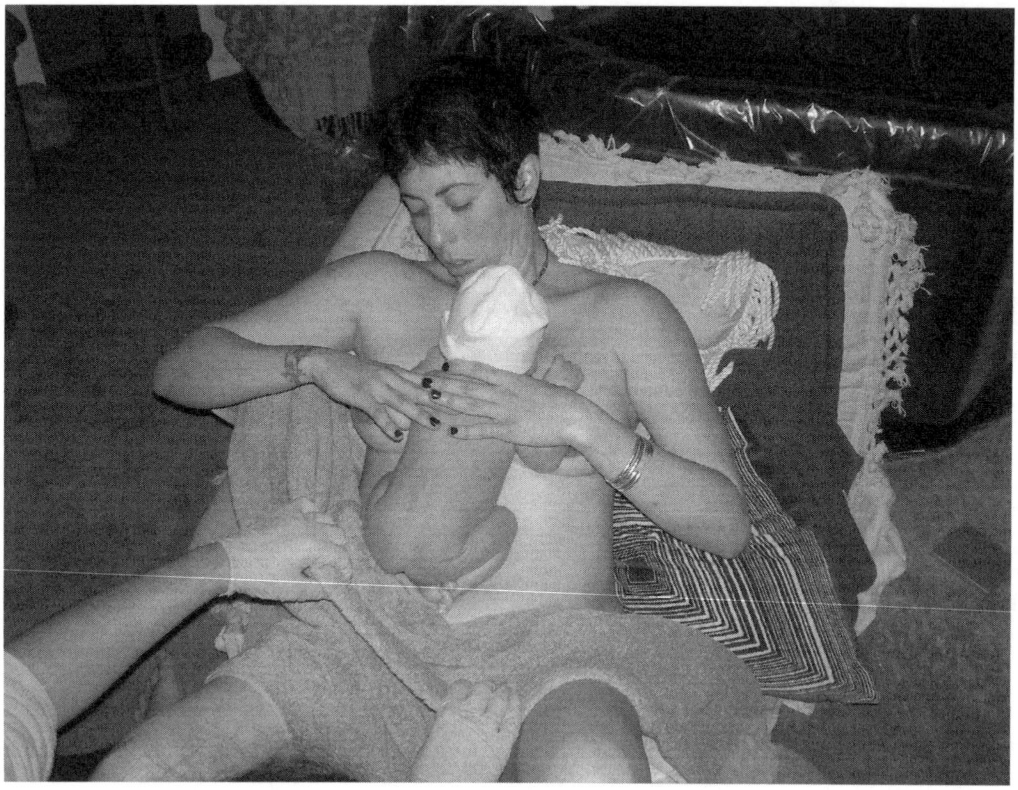

Kindle examining Tristan for the first time

APGAR SCORE SHEET

Circle which assessments apply (when you can) and add up after all is well ... this may be needed for birth certificates where you live.

APGAR	MINUTE		
CIRCLE APPRO SCORE	1	5	10
HEART RATE			
absent	0	0	0
< 100	1	1	1
> 100	2	2	2
RESP EFFORT			
absent	0	0	0
weak cry	1	1	1
strong cry	2	2	2
REFLEX STIM			
absent	0	0	0
grimace	1	1	1
cough/sneeze	2	2	2
MUSCLE TONE			
limp	0	0	0
some flexion	1	1	1
well flexed	2	2	2
COLOR			
pale/blue	0	0	0
ext blue	1	1	1
all pink	2	2	2
TOTAL	___	___	___

Add your score up by counting which signs apply to the one-minute assessment then the five-minute. Within the first minute, you only want to look, listen, and feel your baby, no need to worry about writing anything down ... just being aware of the baby's first sounds, breathing, and over all appearance will allow you to assess his/her condition just fine.

This is an evaluation of the baby's overall well-being, and can help you to determine if any other assistance is needed. A score of 8-10 is excellent, 4-7 is guarded, and 0-3 is critical. If you are conscious of your baby's attitude and other signs of well-being, and you feel she is doing well, then listen to your instincts and do what you have to in order to be at peace with it. Not all babies are totally "with it" at the time of birth; it depends on the labor itself. If the baby is exhausted from a long labor, it may take a few minutes to get him going. If it was a fast labor and a bit shocking for both mother and baby, it may take a minute for your baby to come around. Not all signs and symptoms are alike for every baby and mother, but your intuition and awareness will dictate what needs to be done, if anything.

First, look at your baby. Within the first few minutes after the birth, it is common for the baby to look a bit off-color (a pale blue to light pink is ok, but white is not very good), and sometimes breathing is delayed for a few seconds so do not panic too soon. Feel the baby's chest and umbilical cord, is it pulsating? If so, she is going to be fine. If your baby looks white, keep her below the cord; this will assist the placenta in oxygenating her. Within the first minute, while connecting with your baby and massaging her, you can talk to her, "Welcome baby, we're so glad you're here!" This will get her attention; she may look at you and respond within seconds of the birth.

Listen for shallow breathing, touch her, massage her and talk to her, if she responds even a little, then that is one sign that she is going to be fine. Keep massaging up her back so the fluids may drain from her airway, tilt her head to the side so any fluid can pass, she will swallow, cough, sneeze or spit out any fluids on her own. Then put her to the breast and look at her color. Within the minute, she should "pink up" and breathe more deeply. Sometimes this takes a few minutes, but if she is breathing and responding, she's fine. She may need to cough or sneeze a bit more. This is good; her reflexes are working to rid herself of mucus. Breast-feeding also helps to stimulate breathing and drainage from her airway, as well helping her to swallow whatever comes up instead of breathing it in.

While you are nursing her and talking to her, you can play with her arms and legs to stimulate her muscle reflexes, if she is content she may pull back, note this in the reflex column.

This scoring system is designed for quick action, if you sense that your baby is not doing well, there are a few ways to deal with it.

First and foremost, remain CALM. Breathe deeply, and let it out fully and slowly. Any anxieties, or unnecessary action, will alarm your baby, so remain centered and be mind-full of how you act and talk to the baby.

If your baby comes out, has no reactions and does not breathe after being massaged, then suck over the nose and mouth once with your mouth; a quick one-time inhale from you, like a siphon. This should get the mucus unclogged. Most of the time though, babies will cough or sneeze a few times to unclog themselves. If within the first 30 seconds to a minute, the baby is still not breathing on her own, give her one quick deep breath into the nose and mouth, then give her a second to react. Still no response? Continue this "suck/blow" action as follows. Suck over the nose and mouth, wait a second, massage, then blow over nose and mouth. Leave a three second break in-between to let the baby exhale your breath before doing another slow but full breath. Wait, suck, blow, massage and keep your baby warm while doing this. Do Not tilt babies head back like an adult, a newborn's throat is very delicate, and this action can cause a pinched trachea. Keep the baby's head at her body level when attempting CPR.. DO NOT CUT THE CORD! (Prior to giving birth, it would be extremely helpful to take a class in neonatal CPR.)

Calling 911 is not recommended for neonates (newborns). The logical reasoning behind this is that newborns have a different system than ours. They are made to be able to store energy and oxygen for a longer time than we are, they come around more quickly than we do, and at birth have much more time to be resuscitated than an adult has. Therefore, if you are alone, calling 911 is just wasting your baby's time. You should be working on her. You can revive your baby easily with the suck/blow technique I just described above, but if there is another person in the house to call 911 while you are working on your baby, have them call if you feel that is what needs to be done.

Do not panic! As I said before, the baby may take a few seconds to a minute to get going.

To Cry or Not to Cry?

In the movies, the awaited cry of a baby is usually welcomed and a good sign that the baby is healthy and alive. However, babies do not always cry after they are born. In most of the homebirths I have been blessed to be at, the babies did not cry at all after they came out. Sometimes they just give one big whale and then are content and quite. In gentle births, especially the water births I have seen, babies come out and are very aware, smile, look around and then nurse. Therefore, if you have a baby who comes out after a gentle birth and does not cry right away, enjoy the peace while you have some! Eventually all babies will cry, especially when they are teething.

Babies cry from stimulation of the lungs at birth or distress. After a difficult birth, babies will usually cry because they are under stress from the events that may have taken place for the last several hours. If a mother has been pushing for a long time, if the birth was induced, or the umbilical cord was cut too soon, then most likely the child will be upset and crying is one way of releasing that anxiety. In some situations, a baby may cry even if the birth was gentle and uninterfered with. This may be the child's way of opening up his/her lungs to take the first breath of oxygen. That has been the scientific conclusion that I have read repeatedly over the years in my textbooks. However, when a baby cries it is most likely due to the environment in which she is born. If it is chaotic and confusing to the baby then I can see why she would cry. When a child is born hearing familiar voices and in a calm, loving environment, there is contentment at the time of birth. The baby will not be fearful or panicky, but will feel welcomed and will not need to bellow out in fear or unhappiness.

List for Partners in birth:

Keep calm, breathe and let nature take her course. Massage your baby, talk to her, touch her, and keep her below the cord if she is white. Place her to the breast as soon as possible, place a hat on her head, warm her with a towel, and keep massaging up her back firmly but gently. Encourage the mother to talk too and hold her baby; do not cut the cord! Encourage mom and baby to nurse, while you check for new bleeding. This signals the placenta is about to be born; do not pull on the cord to speed things along. Listen to the mother, and give her some "electrolyte drink." Have her eat a bite of food, check the cord to see if it is still pulsing, and be patient. Let the placenta come through and guide it gently, this may take up to an hour, then put it on a chux pad or in a bowl to sit beside mother and baby ... wait a minimum of three hours before cutting the cord. If bleeding seems to be a bit much, cut a small quarter size piece of the placenta off and have mom swallow it whole and raw; this will stop any unnecessary bleeding almost immediately. Look, listen, touch, talk to mom to assess her condition, ask her to urinate on a chux pad to empty her bladder, this will help slow the bleeding. Do not let mom get up right away unless the bleeding has balanced out, and she feels steady enough to get up. Have her take a few deep breaths and help her get up slowly if she has to go to the toilet to urinate, then support her to the toilet. Keep mom and baby warm, mom hydrated and yourself well nourished!

New Baby Poem (of the Kwakiutl Indians)

From Diane Steins "Casting the circle, A book of Women's Ritual"

When a girl is born by her mother, she is washed by the midwife who takes care of the woman who has given birth. After she has washed her, she wraps her in warm covers. Now the mother of the child takes a little mountain goat wool and puts it on the narrow strip of cotton cloth. Then she prays to it and says, "Now great supernatural power of Supernatural-One-of the Rocks, look at what I am doing to you for I pray that you please, have mercy on my child and that you give her success in picking all kinds of berries on the mountain; and this, that she may have success in obtaining properly and be rich like you, great supernatural One; and this, that you protect her that nothing evil may happen to her when she goes up (the mountain) picking berries on the mountain; and this (against) sickness. Go on, please listen to my prayer to you, supernatural power of the

Supernatural-One-of-the-Rocks," say she."

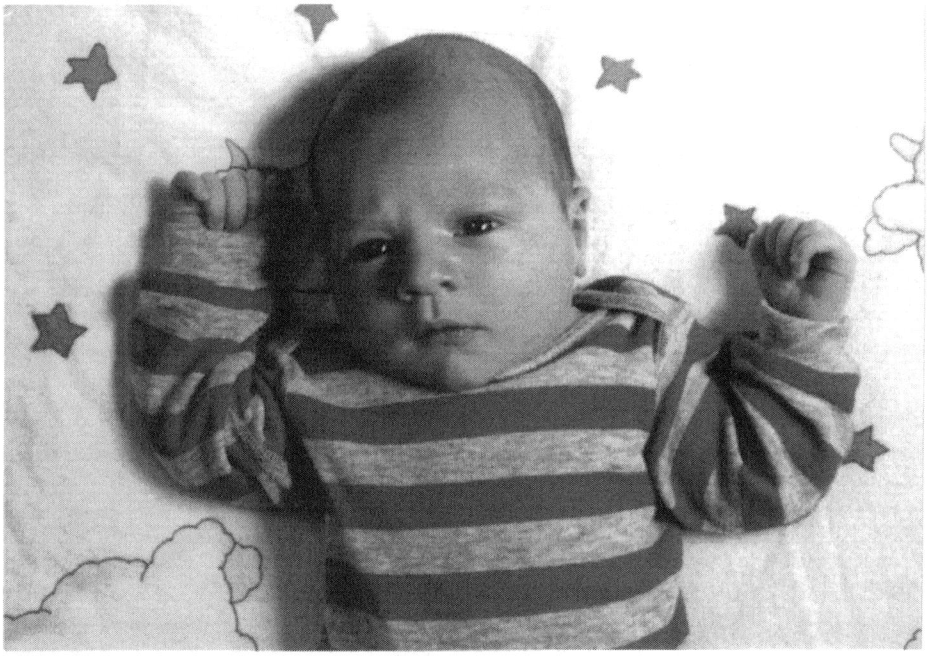

Zack one day old September 22 1989

Your Baby within the first Few Days of Birth

Some babies are really tired for a few days after their birth. Moms are also. "Just take it easy" is easy to say when hormones are raging and your energy may be high from the exhilaration of new life. For both mother and child, endorphin levels are high enabling them to connect and heal. When a birth becomes interfered with, these endorphins are less effective but can still aid in postpartum healing if the mother and child are allowed to have space away from outsiders and interferences. For some, just getting used to the new baby is a challenge in the first few days. Taking herbal baths to heal and recuperate is gentle to you and baby. Baby can also take a bath with you if you wish, and this will help accelerate healing the cord; there is no need to worry about the cord getting wet because the gelatinous cord cover (Wharton's Jelly) protects it. Leaving the baby's belly exposed to the air will also encourage the cord to dry quickly. If you have the cord intact with placenta, the herbal bath will help facilitate drying **(See herbal remedies)**.

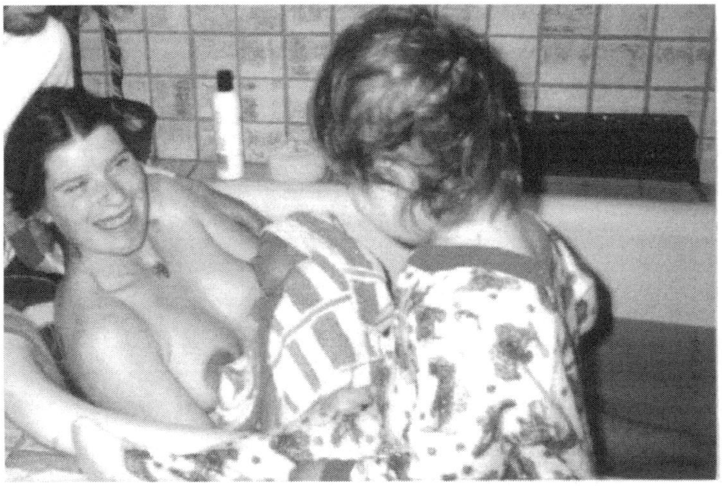

Yarrow meeting his sister Cedarrose for the first time

In most cultures around the world, they have a postpartum code: moms and babies do not mix (sometimes up to three months!) with strangers and people outside of the family. Those who are ill do not even get to look at the baby, and there is good reason for this. The newborn's immune system is just beginning to build its own tolerance to the outside world. The baby needs ample time, up to a month, to be able to fight off any infectious illness on his/her own. A newborn's immune system is already used to your home, your other children and your pets, but when outsiders come in with their germs, or other kids with viral infections, then it is a different bacterium that your baby does not have any immunity to. So take care not to over-do visitors or be running around doing errands too soon. Especially in the winter months when viruses are rampant … stay home and relax, nurse your baby and take phone calls instead of exposing yourself and the baby to undue illness.

Your baby will get the needed antibodies from your breast milk, but this will take a few weeks to get stored up in her/his system, so be patient and take your time re-socializing. Breast-feeding takes patience and within the first few days, you and baby will get the hang of it. If you are a new mother and have never nursed before it does take a while to learn, and both of you will be learning together, so relax, it is not always going to be difficult. Keep putting baby to breast; relax, breathe, and hold the breast underneath like a cup with the nipple in-between your index finger and middle finger to allow slack for baby to properly latch onto breast without causing discomfort. Sit back and relax so baby can breathe. A way to do this is to have the baby sit on your lap upright. In this position, the baby is eating the way most of us eat and there is less stress on baby's digestive system. Things are going down and not sideways as in feeding positions where your baby is lying on her side. In most countries around the world where mothers work with baby in tote, they feed them in this position. These babies do not exhibit the same colic that most American babies do.

After the birth of the baby if you had a gentle birth **(see Lotus birth chapter)** and did not cut the cord right away, your baby should not get jaundiced. Jaundice is a back up of bilirubin (an orange yellow pigment in bile) in the tissues surrounding the liver and is usually excreted within the first week of birth through the first bowel movements (meconium). Before birth, the mother is supporting the baby's liver's function. Newborns do not have mature livers, so if RBC's (red blood cells) are being pressured into the baby's system unnaturally before the RBC's are balanced out in the system (from a cord being cut before all the blood has been drained into baby), the incidence of jaundice can be more severe within the first few days of life.

This can be serious. Baby's liver is over taxed trying to eliminate the RBCs in the bilirubin from the liver; this can cause a yellow tinge to the skin and whites of the eyes (toxic liver). To prevent this from occurring, *DO NOT CUT* the cord and nurse frequently after birth. Your colostrum (first food in breasts) will help eliminate the bilirubin through the baby's first stools.

If the cord has been tied or cut too soon, it can cause a back up of blood in the baby, deferring the closer of the Foramen Ovale, the vessel which connects to the baby's heart internally from the umbilical vein that crosses over through the liver into the heart.

If within 24 hours your baby appears to be jaundiced, this can be a serious event that needs attention. Since the baby is not yet carrying a fully mature liver, she/he can become toxic and have liver damage if not treated. It is very rare, but can happen.

Jaundice is less serious after the first 24 hours since the liver has already been producing its own bile and can excrete it better. It is still vital that you nurse as often as possible to quicken the bilirubin out of his/her system.

Contrary to medical diagnosis of "Breast Milk" jaundice (they tell you not to breast-feed your baby when there is jaundice), it is actually vital that you breast-feed. It is the only way to move the bilirubin out of the baby's system efficiently. This type of jaundice may last a few days to a couple of weeks. Continually nursing helps, as well as getting a bit of sun vitamins. Lay your baby naked in the sunniest window for five minutes at a time, do not leave your baby alone as she may get sunburned. Be aware that your baby's eyes need covering, do this with your hand while holding your baby in your loving arms or put a cloth over her eyes. Doing this will aid in the absorption of vitamin D and A, which can help to eliminate the bilirubin.

Some moms have babies that always seem to get jaundiced no matter what they do, this may be genetic, I do not know. I do know though, by not allowing the placenta's nutrients, oxygen and blood to fully drain into baby can cause many serious problems. Also not breast-feeding the baby a lot in the first few days can cause more jaundice. Be aware and be conscious of your baby's needs that is all you can do.

I have heard some doctors tell women that they cut the cord to prevent jaundice, this is just not true, it was a theory for a while but now we know from experience that it actually will create more difficulties.

Alice Stockham MD. writes in her book Tokology, A Book for Every Woman" about such an accusation:

"By tying, a small amount of blood is retained in vessels peculiar to fetal life. This blood by pressure or irritation may prevent perfect closer of thefForamen ovale, and be a cause of hemorrhage. Besides, it must be absorbed in the system, causing jaundice and [aphtha], so common in young babes."

"Aphtha" ~"A small ulcer on a mucous membrane of the mouth, as in thrush."
***~Taber's Medical Dictionary* definition of aphtha**

After years of attending births, Alice Stockham MD, had not realized the danger of tying or cutting cords too soon, until she met a German physician who explained to her the implications of such a procedure. He told her about his experience with waiting to cut cords, that this lessened jaundice in the newborn, and that she would have better baby outcomes if she tried doing this. Thereafter, she tried this approach and found that the babies were not as lifeless and white when born and had better respiratory functions then when she tied and cut too soon. Dr. Stockham even adopted the cut without tying technique soon after that. By tying, you cause a back up of blood as we have discovered here, by waiting a couple of hours or doing a Lotus Birth there is no need to tie or cut at all. Dr. Stockham cut the cord after waiting awhile, two inches from the naval after all blood and pulses ceased, and then no blood was present in the umbilicus to worry about when cutting. With a lotus birth, you do not need to do any cutting, it saves the cleaning and any worry of infection getting into the cord, and after even just a day it will be able to be broken off a few inches away from the naval or left to fall off on its own.

"There is no evidence that cutting a baby's umbilical cord soon after birth is worthwhile at all, in fact it may create a series of problems."

Once the cord falls off on its own, you need not worry about it too much, only if there's still a bit of blood around the naval should you put some goldenseal powder on and around the stump. Golden Seal powder is an antibacterial plant and will disinfect the area just fine. Be aware of any chemical based detergents that may irritate baby's new skin. I have often suggested just boiling baby clothes for the first month after birth so not to risk skin allergies later. In some cultures, belly binding is another way to keep naval clean and protected from friction of clothing. Place an ace bandage with some drying herbs around baby's belly to keep the cord from herniating as well as protecting the naval from infection. This is not technically necessary, but add it as an option.

If you end up cutting the cord before its dry, it will take longer for it to fall off. Generally, a week is average but it can take a bit longer for the cord to dry and fall off. If it is cut, it generally takes longer and more care is needed. Sprinkle some Golden Seal powder over the entire cord stump a few times a day, let it air, no covering it with diapers etc, since moistness will be held in and cause infections, as well taking it longer to dry. Put the Golden Seal or other drying agent all around the base and shaft of the stump. It is not a necessity to bathe baby, but an herbal bath may benefit cord drying. Babies need their own oils to keep skin protected from cracking and drying. Babies are sometimes born with vernix (the creamy white stuff on baby sometimes at birth). This is a good natural protective cream that you want to keep on the baby, do not wash it off . . . rub some into baby's skin, and your own skin also, it is an amazing lotion.

You do not need to do much except the basics to care for your baby; they just need warmth and love. Breast-feed often, anytime you can during the first few days, and then on demand whenever your baby seems to want to nurse. Breast milk usually comes in around the second to third day after birth. When it does, it may be "filling you up" after the first week or two, however, breast milk will usually balance out to "supply on demand" just what your baby needs. In these first days of nursing, it is a good idea to feed your baby as often as he wants in order to help the breasts and baby learn what "supply on demand" means to them.

During the first few days, offer the breast any chance you get, your baby will benefit from your milk's condensed protein-packed nutrients found in the Colostrum, the first milk that is full of amino acids and rich in protective nutrients. Soon, you will learn when your baby is hungry and needs to nurse, and you will be able to have somewhat of a normal life again.

These first few days are fun, mysterious and tiring; be patient and you will learn together.

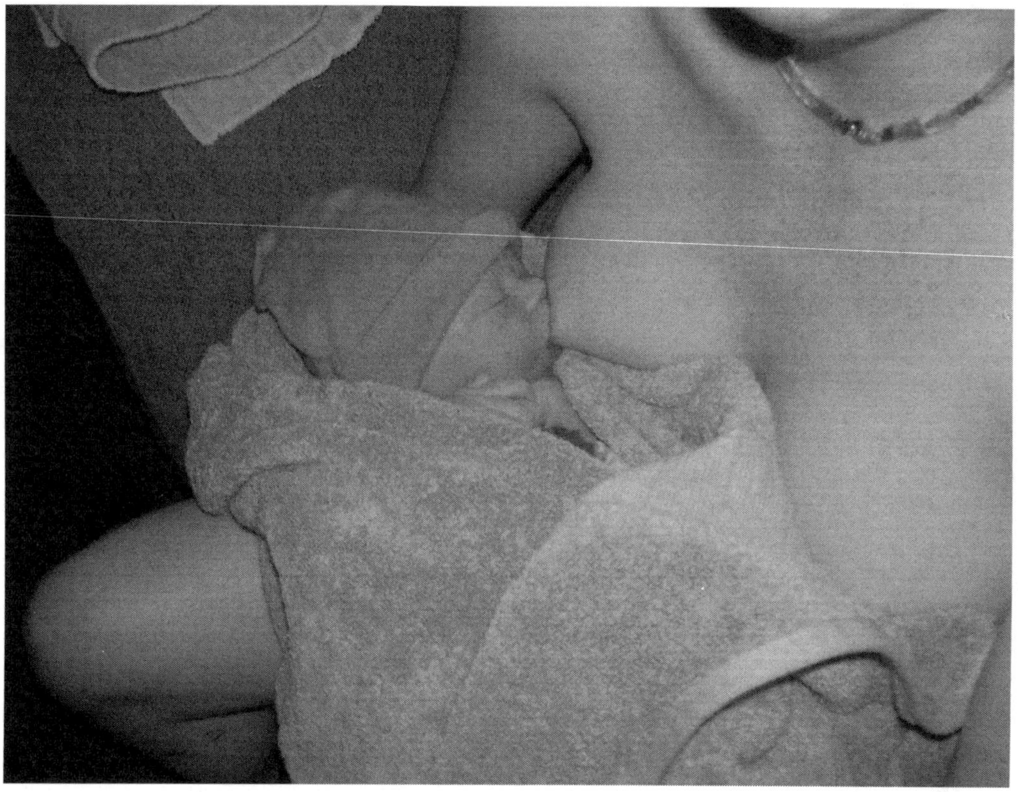

Tristan's first meal shortly after birth

Breastfeeding Wisdom

Offer the breast as soon after birth as possible, relax, and take it slow.

Hold breast like a cup underneath so baby can latch onto the areola really well.

Sit baby upright to facilitate proper latching on and digestion, placing a towel or pillow under baby to have an angle that you are comfortable in to feed.

Let baby figure out what it is there for, just offer the nipple as much as possible, if he does not get it right away it is ok. You are both learning.

Just keep offering the breast every chance you get; be patient, the first few

days are the hardest--it gets better!

Be kind to yourself, rest, take baths, and drink lots of water and de-caffeinated teas to keep hydrated.

Eat, sleep, nurse. That is all you have to do.

Ask for help with other chores around the house.

People want to help new moms; that's what we are here for!

Do not feel ashamed to get rest, which is your only job, relax and nurse baby, love baby.

Cuddle with baby. Eat, rest, drink, void, and nurse. Your time is now to relax, enjoy, bond with

baby. Soon your life will be back to normal with an added bonus …

Patti nursing Maya a week before birth

A Need List for Mom and Baby for Birth:

Medium towels: 5-10 for mom after bath, to sit on, and for keeping baby warm, and changing when needed to keep baby dry.

A few cotton baby caps: For keeping the baby's head warm. The head is where all the heat can escape from if not protected.

Herbal postpartum bath (see alternative modalities): 1 cup comfrey leaf, uva ursi, lavender flowers, red rose pedals, rosemary, sea salt (no iodine), garlic. Use muslin re-usable bag to simmer all herbs in a large pot and then pour into warm clean bath water. Add salt and garlic separately.

Arnica: 200, 30x, 30c, for taking just before birth of the baby, about an hour or so, to prevent shock, hemorrhage, and to promote rapid healing of yoni, and baby's head.

Warm Water: House needs a source for warming water and cooking.

Phone, cell, or CB radio: In case of emergency.

Access to driveway: Keep a clear path to the door nearest the driveway, and have the car readily available, close to the door and the back seat cleaned out.

Little Extras: Candles, incense, music, and pillows, low lights, phone turned off!

A Sign: On the door that says, "Busy having baby call to make an appointment. Do Not Disturb!"

Note: Hospitals, and even some midwives, routinely use an antibiotic in the eyes of your baby. The rationale for this is to protect the baby from any genital infections you may have, such as gonorrhea, chlamydia or herpes. If you do not have these infections, please refrain from these antibiotic eye ointments, they can damage your baby's eyes, as well as create short-term blindness, which can inhibit bonding and breast-feeding time. This procedure is done routinely in hospitals and can be denied if you so desire. Just tell them ahead of time that you do not want this done and sign a form so they are not liable.

If you do have any of these yoni infections, I highly suggest something for the baby's eyes so he will not go blind, which is rare but may happen with certain situations. Washing the eyes with some colloidal silver water is another way of handling this dilemma. Use a damp gauze pad of diluted colloidal silver water to gently wipe around the eyes. If your baby does exhibit any eye irritation, which sometimes happens with all babies and kids, put some breast milk into the cracks of the eyes and with a clean finger gently rub it in. Breast milk is the best probiotic eye treatment there is.

Postpartum Care of the Yoni

I use this word yoni a lot throughout this book, don't I? I feel it is a more suitable name for the female genitalia. Since yoni means "sacred space" and vagina comes from Latin, meaning "a sheath for a sword" (Icky!). I use the word yoni to show respect for women and our sacred spaces.

The postpartum care of the yoni starts before birth, I have gone over this a little in the *self-examination* section. Pre-natal Kegal exercises (squeezing the PC muscles) and labial massage help to prepare the tissues for stretching. Eating well and taking essential female oils (fatty acids) prior to birth is also very important.

Prepare for the birth throughout your pregnancy by eating avocados (good fats), flax (which promotes good digestion), borage (good for breast milk supply), and primrose oils (will help soften the cervix and tissues surrounding yoni area). They come in food sources as well as gel capsules. The best way to take these is through your food, but taking supplements towards the end of pregnancy is sometimes also very useful. Primrose Oil has helped prepare many women during labor because it helps prevent tearing; after labor, it promotes rapid healing and balances hormones.

Of the moms I have seen take these oils, about 98% do not tear. Some moms will always tear a little, but not enough to repair. However, in the off chance that you do tear during your birth, the herbs that I recommend in the *Alternative Modalities* section of this guide are good to help heal the yoni and all its relations.

Soaking in a bath before, during and after a birth will help soften and stretch the yoni muscles and tissue. Relaxing when you give birth also helps. Another thing to help prevent tearing is if you don't fight the stretching feeling, but rather allow yourself to breathe the baby out slowly. In the postpartum time, putting a cold herbal pad on soon after the birth will help to minimize swelling and promote quick recovery of any torn tissues. The tissue cells in the yoni are repaired within just a few days after birth. If you take it easy, don't overdo it, and keep your herbal pack on, then you will be healed up in no time.

Do not wipe with tissue paper for a few days, try a warm herbal wash cloth, it's gentler on your tender bottom and will not leave fragments of tissue behind to collect bacterium. Try a sitz bath or squirt bottle with herbs to clean yourself after urinating, it will be warm and can aid in the first few urinations and bowel movements, when most of us are afraid to let anything out of there. Urinating may sting a little bit the first few times, but remember you need to urinate to keep the uterus contracting well and prevent urinary tract infections. Squirt the herbal wash on yourself while urinating to alleviate some of the burning. Soak a few times a day to accelerate healing of the yoni, and you will be enjoying your time with your baby, nursing and resting.

Michael cuddling with Zack a few weeks old

Postpartum Care for Fathers

Fathers are amazing creatures! They do it all, they care for you and baby during and after a birth, cooking and cleaning, running errands, and caring for other children. It is exhausting work, but very rewarding. Fathers need to take it easy too. After a birth, especially if you did it yourself, emotionally and physically fathers can be drained of their energy. Ask a friend or family member to come over after the birth so dad can rest also. It is important that he stays rested and energized for later. The first week is tough, especially if dad has not had a baby before. He may be anxious at every sound and movement the baby makes. Try to get him support from another father for the first week. This way he can relate any fears or concerns to another more experienced father, maybe even his own.

Fathers are important people, they need to drink fluids and keep nourished. Resting and relaxing with mom and baby are essential to the father's bonding with his new family. I feel fathers are invaluable; they contribute even when they do not really know what to contribute. Fathers are full of knowledge and wisdom. Give thanks to ALL fathers who are supportive of your choices and are there for your birth; he will be forever changed and imprinted with your strengths and wisdom. Fathers will be able to learn more from this birth experience than any outside job they will ever have. Praise to all the fathers out there who read this!

Note: Remind fathers to go ahead and ask for directions. He may know where he is going, but not how to get there.

Helpful Family, Friends, and Neighbors.

"You shouldn't hold that baby too much, he'll get spoiled," "Don't hold him that way, do this, don't do that!"

There is so much good advice out there. I have heard it all from "If you put your arms over your head when you're pregnant, the cord will wrap around the babies neck!" to: "Your breasts don't have anything in them for a few days so feed him a bottle!" Too much information, I am exploding!

Helpful family, friends, and neighbors sometimes are not so helpful, especially when you just had a baby or are going to be having one. These remarks and advice, handed out so freely, are well intentioned but not necessarily good information. I believe that most people have no clue as to what's right for you. If you are reading this book, you are probably conscious enough to understand that not all good advice is good for you. You need to make up your own mind about whom and how you tell what you are planning for your birth.

I had a client, a few years back, who wanted to tell her ex-doctor that she was having a home birth; the mom felt that the doctor was her 'friend' and that she would be supportive of that choice. After a great home birth with no complications, the mom took her new baby (the next day), out to meet the doctor who had delivered her last two babies in the hospital years before. The doctor was so irate and called social services (CPS) on her. Soon, a visiting nurse went to her home to investigate the birth, and the parents were faced with the possibility of the state getting involved. That is just one reason why we should keep our personal information out of other people's air space. I do not feel that when a friend or neighbor gets involved with your decision-making, that it is necessarily of benefit to you.

When a family member supports you 100% in the decisions you make, they can be a great supporter of your birth and postpartum process. Family, friends and neighbors need to realize that it is a privilege to be involved in your baby's birth, and not a given. In some cultures, the mother of the expectant mother is always a part of the birth; that is different. Outside of cultural traditions that you may (or may not) want to follow, it is always a good idea to choose wisely the friends and family who will attend your birth. Having a supportive mother, or family member present is very special, but if that person is not supportive in your way of giving birth then it is not usually helpful to have them there.

I feel that having the wrong people at your birth can be dangerous. We are so open, and emotionally vulnerable, when we are pregnant that if we are not secure within ourselves, or with our birth choices then it just gets chaotic. So be wise and select your chosen support systems carefully.

Baby Development

In the first few weeks after the birth, your baby will be growing fast. In a well-nourished baby, you can expect a weight gain of up to, or over, a pound within the first two weeks. If your baby is not thriving and gaining weight as quickly as he should, he may need more nursing time and extra massage to stimulate digestive absorption. Some grow taller in the first week and even out their weight by staying the same, this baby may take longer to show weight gain.

Do what you do best: love and keep baby fed, warm and massaged; the rest is up to Mother Nature, and that will be shown in time. If you feel your baby is not growing adequately, is a funny color or seems lethargic, I would highly suggest getting him an oxygen level count and a heart check. These may be signs of a heart abnormality or respiratory distress. Sometimes they are minor and there is no need too worry, but sometime they are not, and it's best to find out.

Keep in mind, though, that not all babies grow at the same rate. There are many variables such as genetics, body type and family history of growth, and not all babies fit the standard medical charts. American charts are based our country's standard diet of meat and potatoes, then our growth charts for babies will reflect that standard. We do not have a standard medical chart for vegetarians or vegans, but they are relatively different from the average American standard growth chart. So take that into consideration, and do not panic. If your baby is urinating two to six times a day and has one to five bowel movements a day, he is probably just fine and absorbing his nutrition well. Breast-fed babies do not have to have bowel movements everyday, so don't worry and think your baby is constipated, it's only because breast milk is so nutritious that every bit of it gets absorbed into the baby's system and does not constitute a waste product that needs eliminating. Stools of newborn's change drastically over the first two weeks. For the first few days, even up to a week, it starts out very black because of the built-up waste while in utero. It is thick, black and sticky, and called meconium. After this, it usually will turn brown, then seedy-like, then sweat-smelling yellow. If this has happened, your baby is doing fine digestive wise.

A formula-fed baby's stool is a lot different: thicker, stinkier, and more frequent than the breast-fed baby. This is due to the natural elimination of the baby's digestive system, ridding itself of unneeded waste, which is most of what formula is. The majority of formulas out there are made from hormone fed cow's milk, which is not the proper enzyme to be given to a baby, or anyone for that matter! It is not absorbed well by the new delicate baby's digestive tract because it is not meant to be there. The baby may even vomit more frequently because he is not ready to digest such an alien form of nutrition. If any milk substitute is given, Goat's milk is the closest to human milk in the enzyme department.

Keep doing massage every chance you get, and relax while you are nursing to let your milk down in a flowing way. Sometimes your baby will only nurse for a minute and fall asleep, and then the next nursing may take longer. Some babies seem to eat all the time, and others only eat occasionally, but as long as you are feeding your baby breast milk, he will have all the nutrition he needs. Babies do not need any supplements if they are healthy and growing.

Remember, breast-feeding takes patience, time, and persistence, so do not give up! Your child's future health depends on you!

Immunizations debate

"The art of medicine consists in amusing the patient while nature cures the disease."
~Voltaire (1694 - 1778)

Immunizations were originally created to prevent viral infections and disease, to safeguard our children from childhood illnesses. However, most vaccines that are routinely given to infants have adverse side effects, and may do more harm than the good that was intended. Our bodies, if left intact, have their own unique ability to overcome illness without lab-made antibodies.

Mother's breast milk is naturally antibiotic, and it is the first "immunization" that the baby needs. In fact, Mothers, who have breast-fed their babies for a while, know that when they are ill their baby usually does not suffer from their illness. This is because the mother's milk is protecting the baby from viruses. Mother's milk even protects against the mother's own viral infections. If the mother is severely ill and has a fever for more than a few days, her breast milk may protect her baby from her own illness, it is the perfect preventative medicine for your baby.

"The link between autism and vaccines is certainly not a new idea. In fact, suggestions of this link have been in the national news for at least six years now. Just last year, a study, that reviewed data from the Centers for Disease Control and Prevention's (CDC) Vaccine Data Link, concluded that children who receive thimerosal-containing vaccinations are 27 times more likely to develop autism than children who do not."
~From Dr. Mercola's website (http://www.mercola.com/2005/may/4/amish_autism.htm)

Even through infectious viruses, babies have been known to fight off illness on their own with a lot of rest and good hydration from breast milk. Infant's bodies build their own immunities, but this can take a few months to be in full effect. Nevertheless, if breast-fed and kept away from strangers who are ill (like in waiting rooms of clinics), the baby's own antibodies can usually handle most infections.

There are, however, times when parents do not know what is going on with their baby. Educating one's self about preventive baby care is one sure way you will know what to do, or when to get more assistance, for a sick baby. Illness teaches the baby's body to fight against viruses and infection and helps create antibodies that will be activated naturally when encountering the virus later in life. When this happens on its own, the body will be able to produce the right antibodies to fight the illness; however, if interfered with by vaccines that trick the body into producing antibodies when they are not truly needed, the body gets confused and may quit producing its own antibodies. Therefore the child may get even more ill when coming in contact with a similar virus.

These book are available to help you understand more about immunizations and their effects, short and long-term:

What every parent should know about Childhood Immunizations By: Jamie Murphy.

How to raise a healthy child in spite of your doctor By: Robert S. Mendelsohn, MD.,

Both these books have invaluable information on childcare, immunizations and common sense tactics to treat our children at home.

"Attachment Parenting: A Natural Choice"

By: Joy Shanley

Parents have an infinite number of decisions to make and parenting styles to select from. "Attachment Parenting" (AP), for example, is one style gaining acceptance in western culture. The man credited for coining this term, Dr. Williams Sears, points out he did not formulate the concept of AP, merely just its name. Sears (1992) states, "AP has been around as long as there have been mothers and babies. It is in fact, only recently that this style of parenting has needed a name at all, for it is basically the common sense parenting we all would do if left to our own healthy resources." (p. xiii).

So what is AP?

There are six basic concepts to follow (Granju, 2001):

-Bond with your baby immediately after birth through relaxed, close physical contact.
-Extended breastfeeding.
-Practice responsive care giving for your child.
-The practice of carrying, holding, or "wearing" your baby.
-Co-sleeping or sharing a bed with your child.
-Respecting your child as an individual and never expecting them to follow any set timetable for development or progression.

This style of parenting strengthens the parent/child bond and furthers intimacy. As a result, children who are raised in attachment parenting-style homes are more likely to be independent, secure and happy. The style also promotes children's physical and emotional health.

Evidence for AP comes from doctors and medical experts, scientific research and observation across cultures, and parents first hand experience.

The moments after a child is born are critical for mother-child bonding. Obstetrician Michel Odent (2002) explains the biological reasons behind this phenomenon. During and after labor, both mother and baby release high levels of the hormone oxytocin. Oxytocin is considered the "hormone of love." Oxytocin is also associated with another hormone called prolactin, "the mothering hormone." Oxytocin plus prolactin creates an intense bond between mother and baby. Because of the almost morphin-like state(as long as other drugs do not suppress the hormones) once mother and baby make physical contact for the first time, an immediate intimacy is formed. AP supporters say there is a small window of time in which this bonding can take place, after which time establishing that immediate attachment is much harder.

As with childbirth, prolactin and oxytocin are also released during breastfeeding. This makes breastfeeding not only about nourishment but another chance to bond. Because of this, AP also believes in extended breastfeeding, which usually means breastfeeding beyond 12 months. The World Health Organization recommends breastfeeding for at least two years (Sears, 1992). Even with these recommendations, AP believers say there should be no timetable or deadline for mothers to meet. They generally advise the weaning method of, "don't offer, don't refuse." By doing this, a child, in most cases, will gradually and naturally wean themselves.

Extended breastfeeding is also advised for health and developmental benefits. Human milk contains natural immunities that fight diseases. It also contains nutrients that promote brain development. In fact, researchers in England concluded that babies who drank breast milk scored an average of 8.3 points higher on IQ tests at age eight than babies who drank only formula. Nearly a dozen other research teams found the same results, some even tracking children for 18 years (Sears, 1992).

The third aspect of AP is being responsive to children's cues. Conventional methods of parenting tell us to let the child "cry it out" because responding to the child would be rewarding "bad" behavior. Dr. Sears (1992) reminds us, "Newborns don't misbehave, they just communicate the only way nature allows them to" (p. 333). So ignoring a child's cries doesn't teach them to be a good, well-behaved baby, it teaches them that their only means of communication is not effective and therefore they feel helpless. They can't trust their parents to meet their needs. When a baby stops crying, it is not because they learned a lesson, it is because they got discouraged and gave up.

Many cultures actually "wear" their babies in slings across their shoulders or on their backs. This allows busy parents more freedom, while still giving the baby the physical closeness and comfort they desperately need and crave. Baby wearing does not exclude fathers. Having the father wear the baby allows bonding time for father and baby, and provides a much-

needed break for the mother. Studies have shown that babies that are carried by their parents for most of the day are more content and cry less often than other babies and toddlers (Granju, 2001). Baby wearing also fosters learning and talking. Because babies see things from the mother's point of view - instead of flat on their backs in a pram or crib - they learn and interact more with the world around them.

Another important aspect of AP is co-sleeping. While this is the preferred pattern of sleeping in most countries, it is taboo in western society (Spock, 2001). AP argues that co-sleeping is healthy and beneficial to the whole family. It bonds mother, father, and baby. Those who practice AP say co-sleeping is better because parents don't have to go to the other room to feed or comfort a crying baby, which is about two to three times a night during a child's first year. There is also a biological reason to co-sleep. Babies continue to develop the regulating hormone adrenal in their nervous system for nine months after birth. The mother's presence exerts a regulatory influence over the child's nervous system, promoting better sleep (Sears, 1992).

Author Jean Liedloff studied the Yequana Indians, a primitive tribe who lives in the jungles of Venezulean, and concluded their style of child rearing could be classified as AP. The Yeguana are a peaceful tribe who do not war and rarely show signs of violence. In her book, The Continuum Concept, Liedloff (1975) states, "One of the most striking differences between the Yequana and any other children I have seen is the former neither fight nor argue among themselves (p. 81). " She also recalls seeing a child throw one temper tantrum during her many visits.

Halquist (psychology MA, SEP, March 13, 2005) supports the beliefs of AP. Halquist, along with her husband Chip, have decided to raise their son Albin (who is now 20 months old) according to these concepts. When asked why she felt this was the best way to parent Halquist states, "Instinctively, it's the only way that felt right. I treat him with respect and gentleness and he gives that back to everyone in return." Responding to the criticism that AP spoils children by putting them in control Halquist states, "Children don't see things like that. Until they are about 18 months old, they do not even realize they are a separate entity than you. They only know 'I am getting my needs met' or 'I'm not getting my needs met." Halquist also adds that simply responding to a child's emotional needs could never be considered spoiling. When asked if Albin ever throws tantrums when he doesn't get his way she answers, "Albin wants to do the right thing. When I don't allow him to do something he doesn't push it just to get his way and be defiant. His needs have always been met so he doesn't need to push just to get his own way." She continues to say, "AP is difficult in the beginning. It requires a lot of time and energy. But, once you get past the first several months, the baby you have as a result, will definitely be worth the time and energy."

AP supporters believe if children learn how to form deep, meaningful attachments when they are young, they will be able to do so later in life. Halquist agrees with this. She states, "If people are growing up able to form solid attachments to others, it will be harder to engage in any violence or harm against them." We may also see a decline in rates of divorce and depression. Overall, those who feel a connection with others living in this world will be much happier and healthier."

Many doctors and medical experts claim AP parenting spoils children and make them harder to discipline later in life. They argue it puts the child in control and does not show the child who is boss. Burton L. White (1985), the director of the Center for Parent Education in Newton, Mass., says, "I believe that part of the problem is that parents have already adopted a style of responding to their babies demands that has led to the unhappy social behavior" (p. 71).

However, a direct observational study conducted by Mary D. Ainsworth and Sylvia Bell at John Hopkins University thwarts this misconception. Ainsworth and Bell set out to find if responding to your baby's cries encourages or discourages crying behavior. After over a year of observation, the researchers found that the mothers who consistently and promptly responded to their infant's cries had toddlers who cried much less and for shorter durations (Weisbluff, 2003). Letting the child know their cries will never be in vain and that they can trust their parents, makes for a child who cries less.

Another common criticism of AP is co-sleeping. Richard Ferber M.D. (1985) writes, "Sleeping alone is an important part of learning to be able to separate from you without anxiety and to see himself as an independent individual (p. 39). Sears (1992) rebuffs this argument as well, "Why hurry a baby into independence? A child's needs that are not filled leave an empty space that can come back later as anxieties" (p. 312). Sears goes on to say if you simply create a secure nighttime environment, when it does come time for your child to leave the bed it will come easily and naturally.

This can also be seen in a cross-cultural study on co-sleeping conducted in Norway. The study found that the indigenous Sami tribe practiced co-sleeping as well as self-regulation of food, which allows children to determine how much they eat. Other Norwegian families did not practice either of these concepts. The study concluded that Sami children were more socially independent than their Norwegian peers, showing that co-sleeping does not foster long-term dependence on the mother and father.

As argued throughout, babies are born with a biological need for closeness and physical contact. Being responsive to these instinctive needs helps children become secure, happy and independent. Those who advocate for AP believe that raising children this way will not only lead to more secure, happier, and independent adults, it may also help solve the larger societal problems that plague our culture today.

References: *Attachment Parenting By: Joy Shanley*

Ferber, R. (1985). Solve Your Child's Sleep Problems. New York: Simon & Schuster.
Granju, K.A., & Kennedy, B. (1999). Attachment Parenting: Instinctive Care for Your Baby and Young Child. New York: Pocket Books.
Javo, C., Heyerdahl, S., & Ronning, J.A. (2004). Childrearing in an indigenous Sami population in Norway: A Cross-cultural comparison of parental attitudes and expectations. Scandinavian Journal of Psychology.
Liedloff, J. (1975). The Continuum Concept. New York: Warner Books.
Odent, M. (1992). The Nature of Birth and Breastfeeding. Westport, CT: Bergin & Garvey.
Sears, M., & Sears, W. (1992). The Baby Book. Boston, Mass: Little, Brown and Company.
Spock, B. (2001). The First Two Years. New York: Pocket Books.
Weisbluth, M. (2003). Your Fussy Baby. New York: Ballentine Books.
White, B.L. (1985). The New First Three Years of Life (2nd. Ed.) New York: Fireside.

Natural Baby

There is a lot of information available on natural remedies, natural soaps, and natural this and that's. You can make your own baby wipes, soaps, ointments, lotions and health care products, and doing so is both rewarding and better for ourselves and for the environment. Nothing is truly 'needed' for the new born baby except love, touch, a voice and eyes to stimulate brain development, breast milk, warmth, and rest.

How about going diaper free? Parents today put diapers on their babies thinking it is the way it should be, but when we actually think about it, it does not seem logical. Keeping the urine and fecal matter close to our baby's skin is unhealthy; the bacteria and waste that grow in a diaper is not something we want our baby to be sitting in. It is much more efficient and reliable to know a child's time to eliminate. This takes patience, as all things do with babies. Just keeping an eye on your baby will teach you when your baby is about to eliminate. There will be a particular facial expression or a sound that will let you know when it is time to place a bowl under your baby or bring him to the toilet. Just imagine, within six months or so, your baby will be potty trained!

This will save you years of wasting plastic, washing in bleach water and filling our landfills with stuff that will not be gone for hundreds of years. No more changing diapers, or dealing with rashes and dry bottoms that look diseased. There are great web sites and books on why this is the better way to practice what is called *"Elimination Communication."*

***Diaper Free, Gentle Wisdom of Natural Infant Hygiene* by: Ingrid Bauer**

Circumcision Decision

Most men of the world are "intact," (90%) NOT circumcised. However, in America it has been a common practice and moneymaker for the medical establishment for far too long. Within the last forty years or so, it has become the norm in American hospitals to take the foreskin of a newborn within a few hours after birth. Unfortunately, millions of baby boys have been circumcised unnecessarily. In religious practices, it is done at the age of eight days, and even then it carries a certain spiritual aspect that has nothing to do with medicine or money, but it is still controversial and a real risk to the child. There is no medical reason for taking a God-given body part from any child. I do not feel that it is either humane or logical. Many parents do not realize that the risks involved out-weigh the little, to no benefit, associated with cutting the foreskin.

It was not until the 1950s and 60s that foreskins were placed in skin banks. The foreskin has an extremely good cell-reproducing rate; it will grow easily if grafted onto another body part. Many war victims, that lost their faces from chemical burns and fire, were used as experiments. The foreskins, taken from newborn babies, had an incredible effect on growing new cells that would reproduce rapidly ... thus, foreskins became a new market in American Medicine.

Nowadays, we routinely do these circumcisions, and even pay for them. We are not informed that someone else is making money off our baby's body parts. We are paying for our baby boys to be sexually assaulted at a delicate stage of life, and then someone else is making money from it. Everyone is paid, except the baby; he is mutilated and robbed.

The American Medical Association has no sufficient evidence that this procedure is of any benefit medically. Most medical coverage will not pay for circumcisions because of liability. Removing a newborn's foreskin is a great risk to take. There have been many lawsuits. There is no guarantee that it will be done in a way that will not cause long-term harm to your child's experiences: emotionally, physically and spiritually. Some men, who were circumcised, have been critically injured for life. Some of these men have regrets and anger towards the procedure and feel raped. There have even been men whose male parts have been so deformed by botched procedures that they have been cosmetically changed into a female organ! It is very difficult to asses how much foreskin there is to remove from a newborn baby and therein lies the problem. Now, think about it, is circumcision worth the risk? I do not feel so. Babies do not have the voice to say "No" and parents need to protect their babies from any harm, that is our job, so why is it ok to dismember our baby boys when we do all in our power otherwise to protect them from dangerous physical abuse. This is what circumcision is, physical and emotional abuse.

Research and re-think your decisions if you want to have a gentle birth and baby who is intact in more ways than one. Emotionally we need to re-think what we are instilling in our children's minds from the beginning of their sacred journey here on earth. Do we want them to be programmed in the first hours of their life that what is in store for them is pain and mutilation? Or do we want them to feel loved and protected? The choice is yours.

You can find resources on organizations to help prevent newborn mutilation in the back of book:

Here are some statements from:

"Doctors Re-examine Circumcision"

~ Thomas J. Ritter, M.D. & George C. Denniston, M.D.

What the Experts are Saying ...

"Submitting your son to the procedure to prevent urinary infections makes only a little more sense than buying insurance against being gored by a unicorn in Riverside" ~Eugene Robin, M.D. Sanford Univers

"The risks of newborn circumcision are an under reported and ignored factor in this argument. Most often a poor surgical result is not recognized until years after the event." ~James Snyder, M.D. Past President, Virginia Urologic Society

"I'm opposed to inflicting an (elective) operation on an individual without his permission." ~Howard Marchbanks, M.D. Family Practitioner

"My own preference, if I had the good fortune to have another son, would be to leave his little penis alone."
~Benjamin Spock, M.D. Author, Baby and Child Care.

" ... No one is aware of the deep implications and life lasting effect (of circumcision). The torture is experienced in a state of total helplessness which makes it even more frightening and unbearable!"
~Dr. Frederick Leboyer author, "Birth Without Violence

A Jewish Woman Denounces Circumcision

By: Laura Shanley

Several weeks ago, I had the honor of attending a blessing for my friend Julia's baby, Madeleine. Julia is a Mormon so the blessing took place at her church. The blessing began when Monte, Julia's husband, took Madeleine to the front of the chapel. Then as Madeleine lay peacefully in Monte's arms, several men formed a circle around them and said a prayer. Many babies, I'm told, cry all through their blessings, but Madeleine didn't utter a sound. She was as peaceful and happy a baby as I've ever seen.

After the blessing, Julia stood up in front of the congregation and talked about her wonderful home birth. Clearly this was a subject that was quite foreign to most of the members. She spoke of the trauma surrounding her first birth (an unnecessary cesarean), and the absolute joy of giving birth naturally this time, with only her husband and friend Jenny by her side. Then, much to my surprise, Monte stood up and he, too, testified to the wonders of home birth. Many eyes were opened that day.

As I sat there, I thought about what a wonderful gift this blessing was to Madeleine - two loving parents and numerous church members all saying a prayer for this newborn baby. All babies should begin their lives this way.

Ironically, I had spent much of the previous week conversing with various people about a "blessing" of another sort - a bris, a ceremony held for Jewish boys on their eighth day of life. The difference, however, between a Mormon blessing and a Jewish one, is that at a bris, a circumcision is performed.

I was raised as a Jew and yet I never even considered circumcising my sons. Reason told me that God or nature doesn't make mistakes. Obviously, there is a vast intelligence behind all of life, and just as our eyes have eyelids to protect them, foreskins must serve a similar purpose. Why then do people choose to circumcise?

To answer this question it helps to know a little about the evolution of self-consciousness. According to psychological historian, Gerald Heard, for as long as humans have been on this earth they have been evolving psychologically. Contrary to what many people believe, there is a purpose to this evolution and that purpose is to create a rational, critical, thinking human being who is capable of understanding both herself and her non-physical source. For it is only when we become fully aware of ourselves as individuals that we can truly become co-creators with God, or the larger consciousness.

Before we developed a self-consciousness, we were more like the animals. We felt connected to God (and when I say God I don't mean "the man in the sky") and to each other. But without a strong sense of self, we were limited emotionally, spiritually, physically, and psychologically. Hence the need to break away from the "safety" of the herd mentality and develop a self-consciousness.

Self-consciousness, however, brings with it its own set of "problems" or challenges. Fear is a natural consequence of becoming self-conscious. We fear ourselves, our world, and the non-physical source we are slowly becoming distanced from. No longer can we rely on instinct alone to guide us. We must think for ourselves, and sometimes that's frightening.

Awareness of self also brings with it a sense of guilt and shame. A baby is not ashamed to be naked, nor does she feel guilty about taking up a good amount of her mother's time. But as we grow older and grow in self-consciousness, things change. A nine-year-old will generally cover her body in shame, and a thirty-year-old will often feel guilty about having her own wants and needs met. These are beliefs that come with the awareness of self. They can, however, be overcome.

What, you may be asking, does all this have to do with circumcision? Circumcision began at a time when humanity as a whole was growing up and entering a new level of self-consciousness. Sexual guilt and shame were strong, and those who were able to suppress their sexual feelings were looked upon as virtuous and God-like. Sex was dirty and babies, which were a result of sex, were thought to be dirty as well - unless they were cleansed of their mother's sin by either Baptism or circumcision. There are actually Jewish writings stating women are "unclean."

Circumcision was also a way of dominating the individual and subjecting him to the control of the group. Individuality is frightening to those whose identity is totally wrapped up in the group. Losing a member means losing a part of what they consider "the self." And so, just as the cutting of the hair in the military sends the message that the individual is now the property of the state, the cutting of the penis sends the message that he is now the property of his religion or the institution.

Thankfully humanity is evolving and many of the barbaric rituals of the past are no longer being carried out. Among many Jews, Muslims, Africans, and Americans, however, circumcision is still prevalent. Why?

The first answer is ignorance. Many people are unaware of the realities of circumcision. Inaccurate "studies" of the supposed benefits of circumcision are still being quoted by doctors and religious leaders. However, all of the so-called benefits have now been disproven and even the American Academy of Pediatrics, the American College of Obstetrics and Gynecology, and the Pediatric Urologists Association have all stated that circumcision should not be performed routinely; the former stated that "there are no valid medical indications for circumcision in the neonatal period."

In fact, not only is circumcision unnecessary, it is also dangerous. According to anti-circumcision advocate Frank Garcia, on any given day at least one hundred routine infant circumcisions will result in complications, irreversible surgical trauma, penile loss or even death. Meatal ulceration, or inflammation of the urinary opening happens to half of all circumcised infants. This condition does not occur to intact infants. This is because without a foreskin, the delicate glans is constantly exposed to urine, feces, and abrasive diapers.

Sexual sensitivity is decreased when a boy is circumcised. The foreskin contains many nerve endings which of course are destroyed when it is removed. However, the exposed glans is also affected. According to Dr. Dean Edell, over 75% of the glans near surface nerve endings are destroyed in the years following circumcision by friction between the glans and clothing. Layers of nerveless skin cells, at least ten times thicker (and therefore less sensitive) than the normal glans surface, are grown by the denuded glans to protect itself.

Dr. George C. Denniston writes in his article "Unnecessary Circumcision" (The Female Patient, Vol. 17, July 1992), "If there is any possibility that the foreskin can contribute significantly to sexual enjoyment, is that not a cogent reason for rethinking our motives for this ritual procedure?" It goes without saying that circumcision is a very painful procedure. M. Pickard-Ginsberg, a Jewish man who regretted having his son circumcised wrote in his article "Jesse's Circumcision" (MOTHERING No. 11, Spring 1979):

I can still hear Jesse's crying...begging for someone to stop the pain...screaming of being violated. Elizabeth, with tears streaming down her face, soaked a washcloth in wine, which Jesse intermittently sucked. His little hands clutched my thumb. Sharon's "Om's" occasionally drifted between screams - bless her. Steve (the urologist) was explaining that Jesse's foreskin was unusually tight; a dorsal slit was necessary. He asked how we were, while holding the hemostat on Jesse's bloody penis after each cut. Hemorrhaging was important to avoid.

Why didn't we stop him? Shock?

He cut again. Pulling back the foreskin, Steve revealed the tip of Jesse's penis, which was the color of raw liver. This was a circumcision? Finally, he put the bell clamp around the tip of Jesse's penis and clamped it. Jesse let out a scream we will never forget. It crescendoed up and up until his mouth hung open, face distorted, and no sound came out. Pure anguish.

Twenty-five minutes had passed. A sacred boundary had been crossed. Never again will a son of mine be circumcised without medical reason.

As was traditional, we said a few blessings and served cake and wine. To me this seemed barbaric. What had Jesse gained from this "tradition?" What meaning could it have for him? How could Elizabeth and I justify violating his body? We couldn't and can't.

M. Pickard-Ginsberg is not the only Jew who has taken a stand against circumcision. Jews have been debating this issue for years. Nelly Karsenty writes in her article "A Mother Questions Brit Milla" that she was stunned to realize that questioning this ritual is the ultimate taboo among American Jews. In Europe, she says, many Jews reject circumcision as an archaic and barbaric ritual. She speculates as to why American Jews seem to accept it so readily.

Perhaps, she writes, it is because "circumcision is seen as a symbolic loyalty oath stating that one belongs to the Jewish tribe. It is easier to do so by circumcising one's son than by demanding of oneself to pray three times a day or to observe the dietary laws or the Shabbat each week."

In Europe, she says, Jews have divergent approaches to this issue just as they do with other aspects of Judaism. Or maybe, she writes, it is because brit milla (circumcision) is one of the major ways in which Judaism differs from Christianity. Therefore many Jews feel that rejecting circumcision implies an embracing of Christianity.

As I stated earlier, many Jews are simply ignorant of the realities of circumcision. They still believe the inaccurate studies concerning cleanliness and disease. And of course, some believe that circumcision has been mandated by God. There are even those like Dr. Henry Romberg who insist upon traditional methods such as the use of fingernails as cutting instruments and the taking of the bleeding penis into the mouth to suck the blood.

The good news is that circumcision is going the way of the tonsillectomy. In the 1970's, 90% of American males were circumcised. Today less than 60% are. Only 15% of males are circumcised world-wide.

When all is said and done, circumcision is really a human rights issue. What right do any of us have to permanently remove a normal, healthy, sensitive part of another person's body without their consent? I have no problem with an adult male who chooses to be circumcised. I do have a problem with an adult who makes that decision for a child. I have known too many men, both Jewish and Christian, who resent the fact that they were circumcised.

While writing this article I dreamt that my newly married sister, Janet, was having a blessing for her newborn baby. In reality, Janet has yet to conceive (as far as I know!). Janet is a loving and creative person and I'm sure she could put together a beautiful blessing ceremony for her baby. I only pray that if she does have a son someday, she will love him enough to leave him intact. We all have a right to wholeness.

Postscript: *This past December my sister gave birth to a little boy. She and her husband decided not to circumcise him.*

Circumcision does not prevent urinary tract infections; it actually makes them more exposed to any infections of the glands, since the foreskin protects the inner glands of the penis from infections. In fact, during the first week after circumcision, there is more care needed to protect the exposed glands from bacteria. Circumcision does not prevent masturbation, that's why it's there, too protect and facilitate in pleasure.

The Penis is fine the way it is. Not until the child naturally needs to explore himself, by touching and self-fondling, does the foreskin need to be massaged back to help facilitate the growing penis. This happens around three years of age and correlates to the time of normal healthy self-exploration, for boys and girls. Therefore, it is not necessary to remove the foreskin for any reason.

If we are trying to prevent violence in our society, we must realize that we cannot inflict violence onto our babies and expect them to understand our intentions. Let us keep our boy's intact and keep helping them be gentle.

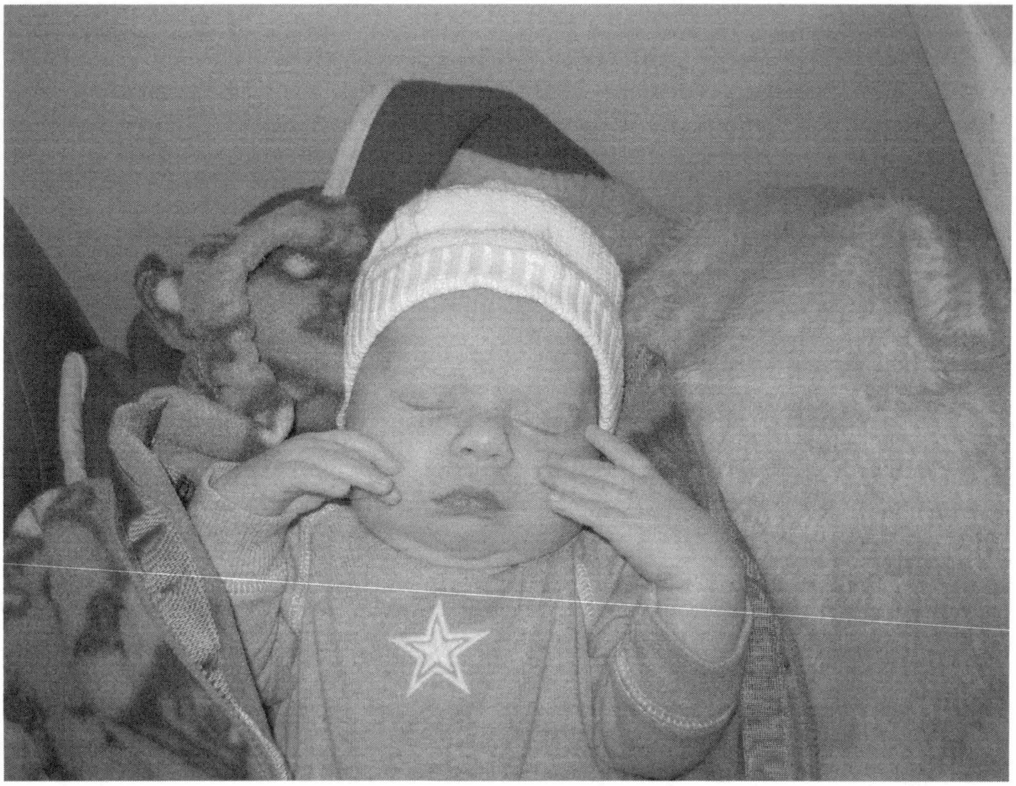

Tristan a few months old

Yey! I am INTACT!

Warrior, Goddess, Queen

(inspired by and dedicated to all of the mamas in my life)

By Lara Catone

I gave you breath, when you took your first, it was in the form, of a healing scream and at first glance

I fell in love like deep, in ways I thought, only possible in movies and dreams . . .

I am a Woman, I have given birth, over and over, in my life, over and over, I reciprocate, what the earth

births for me, but never anything, as miraculous as this, when you were in my womb, I carried you

as if you were me and I would fantasize---endless days of sun swept skies, we'd ride horses through

rainbow flowered fields, I'd lay on my back in the sand on a moonlit eve and then I'd dive down to the bottom of the bluest sea where I'd set us free, I'd soar into the night and pick a bouquet of the brightest stars---

All so you would have beautiful dreams, when you were conceived and I could not believe that you chose me . . .

I could not believe that you chose me, I decided I'd save you, make every day safe for you, I will bear every burden that encumbers you I will add it to the maternal armor I wear across my chest

I am your Warrior Woman, that conquers through . . .

unconditional, uncompromising, unrelenting love that marches in spit rags and diaper bags, that sacrifices hair cuts and getting dressed up and lots and lots of sleep,

I am your Goddess when the rest of the world shuts you out I'll be your omnipotent being, I'll give you warm raindrops and sugar flavored tears I'll be your great healer through scraped knees and your first heartache we will laugh away nightmares,

Daughter, you are my Princess

I will drape you in white silk and hematite rings I will braid your hair we will look in the mirror and vow that we are beautiful beings the earths great creators and we will always love ourselves

I will name you Glory,

Son, you are my Prince, I will garnish you in red velvet and white dove wings I will hold your hand you'll be my wise little man and together we'll whisper mantras, that we are gentle beings that we respect everything that gives light and in peaceful visions we will take flight,

I will name you Integrity.

I am your Queen and I rule my mighty matriarchy so you can climb backyard trees and swing from branch to branch gleefully, so you can rest your baby head on a pillow of peace and know nothing of fight or fear you give me breath, you give me breath, you give me breath

every time I look at you I remember

why I am.

Practical Thinking, Embracing Our Bodies & Souls

Practical Thinking

Embracing Our Bodies & Souls

When we think of pregnancy, we think of a healthy, normal everyday process. Understanding the normal, healthy and fruitful aspects of pregnancy and childbirth can ease any confusion over the practical, logical, and basic things to do.

Being that pregnancy and birth are everyday events, we can begin to change our perceptions and see them as ordinary and not as medical conditions (illness) that need to be managed. When we become pregnant, we do not need to change much. Our bodies are designed to adapt to our baby while she grows. Our body will let us know when we need to eat more veggies, or less dairy. If we learn to listen to our bodies, we will know when we need to rest or when we need to take a walk; it is very simple. Re-learning the way our bodies work is an inner exploration and sometimes takes time, but ultimately we already know what we need too do if we listen from within.

Practical care for the pregnant mom means simple, basic preventive care; it is easy--as nature intends it to be---and doesn't need any outside interference, manipulation or managing. Good health starts with basic, simple, logical, practical knowledge. It starts with good nutrition, hydration, mind and body focus … letting our bodies share their wisdom with us, by relaxing and not fighting it. Understanding our own limitations, our perception around birth, and how to change those perceptions, comes from inner wisdom and practice of that wisdom over time.

Women are intuitive and inherently knowledgeable about their bodies and births, and if we encourage and support women in these sacred events; we are setting an example for all young girls to gain wisdom for their future. It is not until we, as children, are invalidated by others, that we become detached from the innate wisdom of our own feelings, intuition and bodies.

Example: When we are young, intuitively we know that something is bothering us. We may express to our parent(s) that we feel bad or have an emotion that needs attention by saying, "I don't feel good," or maybe crying or being weepy. A destructive answer is, "Oh, its nothing honey, just go lie down," or "There's nothing to cry about." This is an invalidating answer to the intuitive expression of the child's emotions or needs. Instead of exploring the problem, the child learns to ignore it, or worse, distract herself with television, food, or some sort of destructive behavior. This sets a poor pattern at a young age, and the result of this is that we learn to distrust our own feelings and intuition, and to surrender to others' authority over us. As adults, we then have been programmed for years to ignore our own primal feelings, and in childbirth, this is a problem. We feel compelled to seek out an authority to tell us what to do rather than attend to our own inner knowledge and wisdom.

Solution: When children ask for validation, a healthy response is to ask them, "What do you feel? How can I help you? Do you feel upset about such and such?" This will help them create their own solution to the problem, letting them decide what the right course of action would be. This will set in motion a positive pattern and create more self-reliant individuals, so as adults, they will believe in themselves and their own inner knowledge. The result of this scenario would be a grown woman who knows her boundaries and can freely express her needs and feelings. She will know how to listen from within and give birth without interferences.

Learning to re-learn: It is simple, once we begin to understand the fundamental process. Get into a class on how to make your own medicines, or take a home study course on herbs and natural healing. Get books on homemade remedies. There is an abundant amount of resources out there to begin self-study. It is easier today, than ever, to find things on the internet. Just type in a search for a school of natural medicine, herbalogy, or bodywork, whatever it is you need to re-learn for self-care. It will make the difference later when you do not have to run to the doctor for something you can manage on your own. With our children, it will make a huge impact on the way you parent; your child will benefit from your knowledge and respect you more as their teacher and caregiver. Taking responsibility for ourselves is an important aspect of human life.

Birth and God

I was just visiting some friends the other day, and they asked me if I knew why most religious/spiritual people seemed to have total and complete faith in God for everything in their lives except birth, and even sometimes death?

I wondered that myself after serving communities that presented themselves as believers of a greater power, and I do not know the answer. I believe in God and the Goddess as many, pertaining to all natural things; I also feel there is a great plan for all of us here on this planet. No matter how many horrible things are happening here, I still have faith that we are all here for a reason and that birth is the beginning of new life, new hope and a new world--hopefully a kinder, more loving one.

Feelings can arise when I discuss birth with strangers. They tell me of their calling to be in spiritual groups or a new faith of some kind, but to them birth is dangerous, and faith has nothing to do with it. It doesn't make sense unless you look at it from the standpoint of history and the Church's persecution of women, which I wrote about earlier in the book. The church cut women in half, separating us from our instincts and our healing gifts, and then teaching us and our children that we, as women, were "not right" in some way, and that natural things were evil. As we watched our mothers hanged and tortured and our wise women burned, we learned to fear our natural processes, our instincts, and our natural, God given, talents and gifts.

Birth is a gift from God, and it is perfect. Just as our bodies, our wisdom and our natural instincts are perfect, and it is time we let go of our conditioning and remember our source.

There is no mystery in birth as there is no mystery in death; these two events are just a part of life. There is however the mystery of when both these events will take place, and how they will unfold.

I believe the mystery comes from the unknown of living in-between these major events. The sense of mystery in life itself is that we cannot control (though we try very hard to do so) our lives, our births or our deaths. It is truth in a large way that all natural things are mysteries. We don't really know why, what or how? It just "is" this way, and that is where faith comes in. It is time to apply our faith to the natural processes of our lives, and trust that we have been given what we need to birth our babies simply and naturally as we were intended to do.

When I am afraid, I will trust in you.

~Psalm 56:3

If everything is based on our Creator, birth is good and there is a reason for everything that happens in our lives. We were created to give birth, and we are perfect in doing this because our Creator is perfect in creating us and structuring all the events of our lives--even when they are not always what we want.

Yes, that question is a difficult one to answer. We cannot say for sure why our Creator gave us challenges, but if we do have faith, we can surely see that our experiences are to be learned from, and we need not take them personally, and we should not blame others or ourselves.

People rationalize what happens to them, for instance: "Well, I was created imperfect so I had to get induced," or "They had to use forceps because the baby would not come out." Even more excuses are given when we are not living fully in our faith that the natural world was created perfectly and follows a divine plan that we do not understand. I suppose, even in these circumstances when we do not trust in our own divinity, or ourselves, that it is a part of the great and mysterious plan of life.

It is the same with death. I have witnessed a few deaths in my life where someone is trying to save the dying in order to play God. If a person is going to have to be on machines for life, or have brain damage that leaves them with no life to live, why are we playing with their plan? I can say from personal experience, that saving a life when it is not viable is more cruel and unjust than just letting it go, and having faith that there was a reason for it.

When a baby is stillborn, we need to grieve; we need to find it within ourselves to accept the loss and not blame others, or ourselves, for the natural death of the baby. If someone intentionally causes harm to that baby, or the baby dies because of neglect or interferences, there is another way of dealing with that loss; and we need to learn to accept our decisions based on whatever we put our faith in, be it the law, medicine or nature; it is our choice.

"The doctor, in defending his position concerning medical intervention, is actually defending a whole belief system - a system that says: There is no God or spiritual reality. Whatever nature has produced is inferior to what the official technologically based establishment has produced. Nature is ignorant; technology is supreme. And even if God does exist, with all my years of training I'm smarter then He is!" ~ Laura Shanley "Unassisted Childbirth (1994)

Spirituality--a sense of belonging to or being connected to a higher power of creation, be it Goddess, God, Jesus Christ, Buddha, Mohammad, or any other Divine Entity--is right. They all teach self awareness, forgiveness, trust in the self, thank-fullness, prayer, ritual, and that death is a re-birth, and birth is a type of death for that soul entering this world. Let us live by our faith and trust that our lives are unfolding perfectly as they should. When we truly live according to our faith, we will no longer be willing to give the authority over our lives, our births and deaths to another human being because we know that the ultimate authority in our lives is the Divine.

A Personal Doctor Drama

I was sick a lot as a child, I was not cuddled early on in my babyhood, and I had not been breast-fed so my immune system was compromised. Every time my mother took me to the doctor, I was in fear because I knew intuitively that their medicines were not the best thing for me. I was on antibiotics for most of my childhood because of recurring inner-ear infections. Antibiotics not only destroyed my immune system, which I have built back since, but left me emotionally drained and susceptible to mental confusion, which is common in children who take antibiotics too long, probably because of the mercury preservatives in them, which does cause mental impairment.

I was fortunate, however, to have a grandmother who took care of me frequently, and who was in touch with a more traditional medical doctor who used homeopathy and herbs to treat my ailments. His treatments did more for me than those of the allopathic doctor my mother took me to see.

When I was raising Zack, I had no Insurances or Medicaid so I made sure I studied and researched how to feed him and take care of him appropriately with homemade baby foods and herbal medicines, which I frequently made myself. I decided pretty early on that my son would not need drugs to live healthily. I knew from my own experience that allopathic drugs are deadly, and to this day, I am still healing from their effects.

Once, when Zack and I were visiting my in-laws, Zack came down with an earache. I had dealt with earaches before and knew what to do. I put warm compresses on it, mullein/garlic oil drops, and had him rest on that side so it would drain. For some reason, my sister-in-law freaked out on me for not taking him to a doctor. In front of my son, my nieces and nephew, she insulted me and told me I was neglecting my child. It took all the power in me to not do something I would later regret. However, I maintained my inner strength and did not allow her to bully me into taking him to the doctor, which I felt was ridiculous as children get earaches, it is a common childhood ailment. Then my mother-in-law took up the cause and tried to persuade me to take him to the doctor the next day; I really did not want to and told her he would be fine and that most ear infections clear up on there own after forty-eight hours or so.

I overheard my sister-in-law and mother-in-law on the phone the next morning; they were discussing getting a court order to make me take Zack to a doctor. I was outraged to say the least. I told my mother-in-law that all the doctor would do is stick the ear scope in his ear for a second and then prescribe antibiotics. She insisted I take him because we were flying out the next day, and she didn't want his eardrum to burst!

Now, my son at this point had never had an antibiotic for anything, and he was almost ten years old. Zack was naturally upset and finally told me that he would "go to the stupid doctors' office" to make everyone stop fighting!" I told my mother-in-law that we would go, but that Zack was not going to take the antibiotics. She replied, "Just do what the doctor says, and he'll be alright!" I was outraged, felt bullied and powerless as a mother.

My mother-in-law decided to warn the doctor before we even arrived that I was not into antibiotics and to talk to me about it. However, I sensed that the doctor realized that I was educated in this area, and he did not try to tell me anything. He took a quick look inside my son's ear and said, "Yup, that's an inner ear infection, here's a prescription for two different antibiotics."

We went to the pharmacy, and my mother-in-law bought the medicines because I conveniently had no money for them. I informed Zack that because he had never had antibiotics before, he really needed to think it over before taking them. I would not force him into it, and that the side effects of antibiotics deplete the kidneys, and they are hard to get out of the system. Nevertheless, of course, I left the decision up to him; he had already been through enough drama.

My mother-in-law pushed Zack to take the pills and drops, and he finally agreed to take one pill to get her to leave him alone. It made him so sick, so fast, that he vomited for over an hour; the vomiting, however, unclogged his ear almost all the way! Well, that was $80 dollars well spent.

The bright spot in this story was my father-in-law who remembered his mother using garlic oil and warm compresses on his ears when they were infected, and he told me that he trusted my judgment. He even went to the store and bought some colloidal silver for Zack!

Zack took no more of the medicine that the doctor had prescribed; however, he did take the Colloidal Silver, and that cleared up the infection overnight. On the plane the next day, Zack had no pain at all. This is an example of nature curing itself while the "doctors amuse us with treatments."

Several years later, Zack went to visit his grandparents on his own, and they took him to a dentist because he had a tooth coming in, and it was sore. They gave him painkillers! Later my son told me "those were good drugs," that made him numb, and he learned to associate being numb with feeling good! Needless to say I was furious.

I can understand how hard it is to live simply and with nature when so many people in this world seem to be against it and unwilling to understand or respect others in making their own choices in their raising children.

"I will always be forever standing in my truth, and accept the things I cannot change, and change the things I can, and hopefully have the wisdom to know the difference."

Alternative Modalities

Basic Remedies for Common Discomforts in Pregnancy
Massage
Mayan Uterine Massage
Homeopathy
Ayurveda
Utilizing Your Dreams
Yoga
Water and Birth
Dance
Song
Sound
Blessing Ways
Birth Alter
Visualizations
Meditations
Prayer to Our Creator
Acupressure
Acupuncture
Self Hypnosis
Energy Healing
Reflexology

Alternative Modalities for Pregnancy, Labor and Birth

AND FOR EVERYDAY LIFE

"Only nature cures. The task of the physician should be to help nature's efforts, not combat them"
~Hippocrates

In this chapter, you will find many systems that you may want to research further for your own unique needs. Although not the standard systems in American culture, more people are recognizing these modalities to have great value for their health.

These practices are recognized in many cultures for bringing improved physical, emotional and spiritual health, and they may prevent complications in pregnancy, labor and birth. They also may serve you as preventative, and help maintain your health for the rest of your life.

Not all these suggestions are for everyone, but finding your unique needs and determining what will work for you is your choice. Finding the proper person(s) to guide you for further learning of these modalities is an important part of your continuing education.

Corsica 2001

Common Ailments in Pregnancy and their Cure:

Basic preventive care is based on nutrition, exercise, emotional healing, getting good support from those around us, and educating ourselves with material that is based on healthy living and natural birthing practices. There are some common complaints of pregnancy that can be remedied through these means. Here are a few common discomforts and their cures.

Nausea and vomiting: Good hydration and nutrition can prevent these common obstacles in pregnancy, eating small frequent meals throughout the day and drinking a protein shake with extra vitamin-filled foods such as almonds, bananas, kelp, spirulina, and molasses can alleviate nausea and vomiting. Vit. B6 also is helpful. Some essential oils such as, Lavender, Rosemary, Bergamot, and Spearmint may help relieve nausea. Pregnancy tea listed below will also give relief.

Hemorrhoids: Swollen rectal tissue can be irritating and even painful if not dealt with, or prevented. Usually this will diminish after birth but sometimes can turn into a recurring problem. Keeping hydrated, walking and swimming several times a week may help prevent hemorrhoids from getting any worse. Using witch hazel as a compress, and homemade ointments of witch hazel, comfrey, and calendula also help prevent itching, and inflammation. These little hemorrhoids are associated with the liver being stagnate. Acupuncture may bring relief, clearing the liver pathway to excrete waste, and using an infusion of dandelion leaf and root may also help.

Varicose Veins: Varicose Veins are common amongst pregnant women, and sometimes they appear, then go away later, after birth. However, some of us have them even when not pregnant. These are related to Liver stagnation, poor circulation, and other vascular difficulties, as well as heredity. These are not necessarily dangerous if a woman is taking good care of herself. They can be painful, however, if not attended to. Walking, wearing support hose, drinking plenty of water, taking EFA's (essential fatty acids) such as borage oil, primrose oil, black current oil and cayenne pepper can help promote better circulation and healing of the veins. Some women may benefit from hawthorn berries, which are known to support the circulatory system, heart, lungs, and nervous system. If the swelling or pain gets unbearable, after trying these suggestions, consult with an alternative source such as a homeopathic practitioner, or naturopathic doctor. This problem rarely needs special attention if taken care of with nutrition, exercise, and supplements. Swimming is an excellent remedy for Varicose Veins!

Heartburn: Eating small frequent protein-filled snacks in between meals is helpful. Eating live foods, such as sprouted seeds, breads and papaya enzymes, can keep heartburn at bay. Drinking pregnancy tea and exercising helps to alleviate heartburn.

Tiredness: Getting enough minerals and vitamins in our diets is helpful in getting the energy we need to make it through a full day without feeling overly tired. It is good to get short naps at siesta time after eating your mid-day snack, and then resume activities with another protein-filled nutritious food break. Having enough iron, calcium and other trace minerals is useful to keep up with busy lives. Adding molasses to protein shakes and alfalfa and nettles to your pregnancy teas will also help keep up your energy.

Constipation: No one likes to feel constipated. There are ways to improve digestion and elimination by eating small frequent meals, chewing food well, keeping hydrated, and exercising. If our bowels are not moving well then we can become ill, tire easily, and just feel clogged up. To prevent constipation, it is good to follow your pregnancy nutrition and hydration program. Adding more fiber to the daily menu, such as whole grains, vegetables, and fruits, as well as drinking at least a half a gallon (3 liters) of water a day will help aid digestion and elimination. Drinking a small glass of prune juice a day can help add the necessary enzymes to facilitate a bowel movement. In addition, a bulk fiber supplement for stubborn digestive tracts can be found in health food stores, but are not to be used everyday during your pregnancy. Eating your EFA's, essential fatty oils, each day can help also, flax, borage and primrose may help the digestive tract by keeping it lubricated. Some people like to take cod liver oil, or castor oil, to keep their digestive system moving. However, during pregnancy, it is best if all your nutritional and health needs come from your food. Doing some simple exercise, such as walking or swimming, a few times a week will do a lot to gain regularity. Getting a massage each week can also be of help. In addition, making sure your food is chewed well before swallowing it will help a lot as there is less work for your stomach to do to breakdown and absorb your nutrition.

Headaches: Headaches are common in pregnancy today. Unfortunately, most pregnant women do not get the encouragement they need to take care of themselves. They are expected to do what they usually do and even more. Women today are expected to be like Super Woman. Especially in the first few months of pregnancy, so many things are changing in one's body. Blood volume is rising, hormones are shifting, there is a growing baby inside who is pushing all the mother's organs up and into another place than they're used to being. The body shifts to make room for the growing baby. During this time, if a mother is not getting enough rest, is over worked, not drinking enough water, not eating high protein vitamin rich foods, taking time to relax, she is likely to get headaches. These headaches are a warning. They signal the mother "You need to feed me better, take it easy, drink more fluids and do the things that are good for us!"

Migraine Headaches can also become more frequent, especially if the woman had them before she became pregnant. The cause of these can be tension, a previous injury, a mineral deficiency, caffeine consumption, poor diet, and/or low glucose levels. Emotional factors also are a precursor to migraine headaches. Keeping hydrated, eating a high protein diet, using less dairy, exercising and drinking more water may help eliminate headaches all together. Meditation is also very useful with Migraines, it helps facilitate the whole nervous system to slow and calm down. To minimize or eliminate any of these common ailments, get enough protein, eat small frequent meals, chew your food well, drink enough water, get a lot of fresh air, walk, swim, dance, get massages and laugh each day!

Body, mind, spirit work is also essential for over-all health and preventive care and maintenance.

Massage

Touch is essential to human life. With touch, we can overcome fears and emotional stagnation. Energetically, we flow better when touched. With love, massage can bring a person back into touch with her body, and healing takes place. Getting a massage from a partner, friend, therapist, or even yourself, can improve health and awareness of emotional and physical states of being. Massage improves the lymphatic flow of bodily functions. It can promote better digestion, move toxins out of the system and create a relaxed state of mind and body. With massage in your lifestyle, you will notice an overall health change that benefits you long-term. After the birth takes place, massaging the mother helps heal her muscles as well as smooth bones gently back into place. In some Asian cultures, a massage is performed within the first day of birth to promote healing of the circulatory system and rid the mother of stagnated blood or disease. Turmeric (an Indian Spice) also is made into a paste and rubbed on the new mother for drawing out any infections and purifying her body and spirit. Her uterus is also massaged back into place within two to three days, or sometimes up to a month, after the birth.

Infant massage is known to help in the development of the child's body and mind. During birth, the baby's body is naturally massaged as the baby passes through the birth canal; thereafter a gentle massage helps facilitate clearing the lungs and expelling fluids. Massaging your baby, a few times every day while breast-feeding, changing and cuddling, may help release any related fear or trauma associated with pregnancy and birth. This helps form a relationship between baby and parents in a safe, nurturing environment. Breast-feeding also gives babies a sense of well-being, and it is, of course, the best nutrition in the world. Talking to your baby while massaging him is also a good way to build trust and open the pathway receptors inside the baby's mind. It is well known that babies who are talked too and rubbed during pregnancy are more aware at the time of birth. They grow better, develop more quickly both mentally and physically and relate to their surroundings and parents with much more "knowingness." Infant massage, and related modalities for helping our babies become healthy beings in mind, body and spirit, will be the root of their entire life.

Mayan Uterine Massage

The Mayan people have used this ancient form of massaging the belly and uterus since the beginning of their culture. Many other cultures around the world use this technique as well. The alignment of the uterus brings balance to the body's physical and energetic mobility. By massaging the abdominal area, finding the uterus and moving it into place, reproductive organs are kept healthy and the vital life force energies are kept flowing and not left to stagnate. If left out of place, floppy or retroflexed, the uterus can build up with disease, so uterine massage is another part of self-examination and preventive care. It is easy to do yourself with a bit of practice. Lie comfortably on a bed or the floor with your knees supported up with pillows or blankets. Have some lotion or oil nearby, and with your dominant hand, find your pubic bone; the top of the pubic bone has a ledge. This is above your pubic hairline. Once found, put a small amount of pressure straight down toward your back, and feel around for another muscular ledge. It will feel like a strong organ, and you will be able to feel around all its round edges. Move your hand around it once or twice, so you know where it is. Take some lotion and use both hands to massage your whole belly from your right to your left in a circle.

Do this a few times before retreating back down to your uterus, this will loosen up the belly muscles, and give you a deeper sense of relaxation. Once you feel more relaxed and are ready to do your uterine massage, take a few deep breaths and ask for guidance. Find again the edges of your uterus. Massage from the pubic bone upward to the belly button with one long and deep stroke; go to the edges of the pubic bone and do a diagonal stroke up toward your naval. Then the other side again, do each side three times, then rest for a few minutes. Now with both your hands on your uterus, relax, breath deeply and focus on love and healing. Visualize light radiating in and around your uterus.

If you want further instruction or to find a therapist near you, look up "Mayan Uterine Massage" online, or on bulletin boards in your local health food store.

Homeopathy during and after pregnancy,

~By Mati Fuller, DI Hom (pract).

Pregnancy is a time of great change, both physically and emotionally. In many ways it is a joyous and exciting time, although the physical and hormonal changes can be uncomfortable. Most of these changes, whether they are physical changes or emotional instability, can usually be eliminated or greatly reduced by the use of homeopathic remedies. We often find that women suffer many annoying problems, especially during and after pregnancy, because allopathic medicine simply does not have much to offer in terms of safe and effective medicines during pregnancy or while nursing. Because I personally know how it feels to suffer from female problems that allopathic medicine can't do anything about, I am very interested in helping women overcome these kinds of ailments so they can enjoy their pregnancy and post pregnancy time more. Here is a list of common female problems that can benefit from the use of homeopathic remedies:

> *PMS, cramps during menses, irregular periods, bleeding too much, vaginal infections and pelvic inflammations, sex drive too high--or missing, cysts, fibroids, tumors, excessive bleeding, bladder infections, swollen breasts, breast lumps, pregnancy problems, infertility, abortion/miscarriage, morning sickness, fatigue, bleeding gums, constipation pain, heaviness, digestive problems, heartburn, emotional ups and downs, fear after pregnancy, bleeding, infection, aching, bruising healing of episiotomies or caesarian section, cracked nipples, too much milk, not enough milk, mastitis galactocele, bad tasting milk, post partum depression, lack of sleep from nursing, and relationship problems.*

Homeopathy is a form of gentle healing that can offer safe, gentle and effective help for all these ailments, and more. The main principle of homeopathy is the concept that "like cures like." The word homeopathy consists of two parts, homeo, which means similar, and pathy, which means sickness. Therefore, when someone comes in for a remedy, we have to look for a remedy that covers a similar symptom picture, because this is the remedy that is most likely to bring the body back into balance and stimulate healing. The homeopathic remedies do not just remove the symptoms, they actually assist the body's own immune system in such a way that the healing happens from the inside out, and the symptoms of disease or discomfort simply disappear. This is why homeopathy is called holistic healing. The most obvious advantages of homeopathy are the facts that the remedies are inexpensive, non-addictive and safe for anyone, including babies, children and pregnant women, when used correctly, and they have no negative side effects.

When you book a homeopathic consultation, you will also find it refreshing to be able to tell somebody your whole story. All your details and concerns are important parts of who you are and how you experience your reality, so the consultation often takes several hours. When the total picture of the situation has been uncovered, a homeopathic remedy can be found that covers this picture as closely as possible. Homeopathic remedies are made from many different substances, like plants, animals and minerals. The medicinal property of a substance is released when the substance is diluted and "succussed," (which means that the bottle is vigorously knocked against a hard surface). This process "potentizes" the remedies. The higher the potency, the more times the remedy has been diluted, succussed, and the more of the remedy's healing properties have been released. Only a minute dose of a homeopathic remedy is needed to affect the body's immune system (vital force). The remedy stimulates the immune system in such a way that the body is able to overcome the sickness, or imbalance, more quickly, and it also makes the body less susceptible to sickness in the future.

All the homeopathic remedies have been tried first on healthy people, and the symptoms they created have been carefully written down. This is called a "proving." Proving make it possible for the homeopath to know exactly what symptoms a remedy can cause in a healthy person. When we know this, we can pick the same remedy in homeopathic form to heal similar symptoms in a sick or imbalanced person. The role of the homeopath is to be your ally in your process towards greater health. Sometimes, the first remedy you get will be perfect, but that is not always the case. The choice of remedy is based on the information you give, and many times, you need to have several interviews because more information is needed. Homeopathy is like detective work; you and your homeopath are looking for clues together, and the healing becomes a process that can change your life. The goal in homeopathy is to restore the natural balance that has been disturbed, because when the balance is restored, the body is able to heal itself and the symptoms of disease simply disappear.

If you are considering homeopathy to help you deal with problems during or after your pregnancy, it is always best to find a local homeopath that can see you in person, so they can observe you during and after the consultation. I live in Crestone, Colorado, so if you have the opportunity to come and see me in person, that would be preferable. If there are not any homeopaths available in your area, I also do consultations by phone. If you are interested in a consultation, or you would like more information about homeopathy in general, please visit my website: homeopathyonline.biz

Making your own Ointments (Salves)

I thoroughly enjoy making my own ointments, its fun and rewarding to know that this easy process saves me time and money from store-bought medicines, which most likely have other ingredients that are not good for me. Homemade ointments work really well for many skin problems: rashes, burns, cuts, dry skin, stretch marks, kids skin stuff, cradle cap, eczema, scrapes and just plain old dry skin. They are useful in everyday life, and can be made easily in your own kitchen.

You'll need a glass coffee pot or Pyrex measuring cup; bamboo or reusable cloth strainers; bees wax; lanolin (optional); olive, peanut, walnut, or almond oil; vitamin E oil; herbs; and essential oils.

Simmer herbs in your chosen oils for an hour, or two, depending on the herbs used: if they are hard roots, two hours; if leaves, flowers and stems, less time is needed ***(see herbal preparation books for more specific ingredients and proportions).*** Strain into the glass coffee pot, or Pyrex measuring cup, and continue simmering the oil on low heat, and then slowly add the bees wax. After the bees wax begins to melt, add a solidifier like lanolin, coconut oil or a solid butter (mango, avocado etc.). If you do not want extra solidifiers in the ointment, a natural bees wax is good enough. Add your essential oils. Stir for a few minutes until it all mixes in the infusing oils. Then pour into glass containers for cooling and storage. Keep caps off while the ointment cools and solidifies. Store in cool dry dark place for up to three years or longer.

It is easy and fun to make your own ointments. I have never measured my ingredients, I just learned through doing it repeatedly. It will take some practice to get the amounts down, but there are great books out there that can help you. Many health food stores, herb companies, and cosmetic suppliers will carry the ingredients.

Ayurveda

Ayurveda is the most ancient and complete system of medicine. Thousands of years old, Ayurveda has incorporated all modalities of health, preventive care, and health maintenance into one system. It consists of nutrition, daily routine, massage, herbs, energy, chakras, psychology, stone therapy, movement, prayer, song, and smiling.

It's roots are from India, and its name is derived from two Sanskrit words: "Ayu" (life) "Veda" (knowledge), thus Ayurveda translates as "Life Knowledge." Ayurveda practitioners, are often found in holistic communities around the world, use the five elements of the universe (space, air, fire, water, and earth) and relate them too our body's systems. The practice of Ayurveda is based on life-long learning and the cultivation our "essence," which we share with others on this journey. In this system of health care, bodies become stronger and more balanced through proper nutrition and exercise, sticking to a daily routine, awakening early before sunrise, meditation, and getting enough rest. Nutrition is specific to the body type, or "Dosha," and in this system there are three: Vata, Pitta and Kapha. Combinations of all three are in each of us, but we are more dominant in one than another, and usually people are diagnosed with a combination of two types, such as: Pitta/Vata, or Kapha/Pitta.

Your Dosha is determined by a practitioner who looks not only at your body type, but also asks questions about taste, movement, ailments and diet. A large part of the practice of Ayurveda is that there should be joy in life, and over time, this modality can help you not only be healthier, but also have a more satisfying relationship with yourself and your family.

There are great Ayervedic cookbooks on the market today. They all explain the fundamentals of the system, and how to find your body dosha and what foods, herbs and spices are for your specific type. Once you get involved with Ayurveda, you are well on your way to creating balance and harmony on your life path.

NOTES:

Dream Work

I learned, early on in life, that dreams are the doorway into my subconscious mind. Dreams are so helpful in getting the answers to our questions when no one else can understand where we are coming from. There are different levels of dream states. One is the standard dream that relates to our everyday lives, it usually makes sense because we are dreaming about getting up in the morning and accomplishing some sort of task that we may have been thinking about just before going to sleep. It could be about a friend, partner or nothing in particular, it just makes sense to us the next day when we awaken.

The second type of dream state I have experienced is the deep sleep dream. It is more vivid than the standard dream, and has more meaning, sometimes even profound meaning. I usually remember these deeper meaning dreams the most and will think about them for days, until I realize what they may be signaling in my life. In these, I can usually move at will and feel feelings, talk to others in the dream, and consciously think about what is happening around me. I can even change the scenario with my conscious mind by thinking I want to do something different, if it seems like I need too. Sometimes, I make new dreams out of the present ones and change the scene or people by just concentrating on what I would like to see or where I want to go. Then, all of a sudden, I am in a different environment.

Another type of dream, but more than a dream, is a feeling that I have left my body, and my spirit has gone to another place in time. It is even a place where I speak a different language or have a very different body, when I can see myself in a mirror or some sort of reflection. These dreams seem like I am living an alternate life. I usually will fly a lot in these types of dreams and awaken with a fresh new look on things.

In my early years, I experienced many dreams like this, usually starting out with that falling sensation. I had the first one, as far as I can remember when I was four, and I remember it like it was yesterday. During my waking state, early afternoon at my dads house on my weekend visit, I climbed out onto a small, second story balcony and accidentally fell, landing in a rose bush. All the neighborhood kids gathered around my limp body, hanging from the thorns of the bush. Some were concerned; some were laughing. Then I had the sensation of floating up and out of my body and I saw everyone below gathered around me. I kept going farther up, it felt great to be out of there! Soon the earth began to get round. I felt free. As soon as I felt like I was totally free, a huge male presence stopped me and like a large hand and said "NO, you are not ready yet! You must go back."

In an instant, I felt intense sadness and sorrows at having to go back, and suddenly I awoke back in my little body. I opened my eyes and saw my dad leaning over me--I was in the bath. I looked around and realized that I did not remember anything from the time I left my body hanging in the rose bush until I awoke in the bath. I had scrapes all over me, my dad was concerned, but I told him that I was ok.

In my early twenties, I started to experience leaving my body again. It happened a few times very vividly, and I had intense experiences with it. I never noticed a silver cord connected to my body though, as some people have stated from their experiences. I did, however, have two spirit guides, one on each side of me, guiding my spirit like chaperones taking me out for the evening. They awakened me from my slumber, but my body stayed asleep. I went willingly with them, and soon we were flying across endless mountains, the sun was bright, but not blinding. I found myself stopping at places like waterfalls, and there were other people walking around, but no one could see me. Once, we went to a place that looked like an M.C. Escher drawing of staircases. This was cold and dark; I did not want to go in, so when I made up my mind that I did not like it there I flew back up through a tunnel of light and met my guides at the other end. They took me out a few times within a few months. I felt electrical surges in my "crown chakra" (top of my head) a few of these times when leaving my body, and I also remember that I was not afraid at all.

Since I have been out West I have not had these experiences, but I have had incredible dreams, and I am much more aware of their meaning.

I sometimes write my dreams down first thing when I awaken in the morning. This helps me to go over them later when I have had some time to process what they may be about. Dreams can help us in so many ways, if we listen to our inner voices and ask for guidance before going to sleep, we can get answers to many of life's questions.

Working with our dreams takes some practice and dedication. After repetitive sleeping rituals, such as asking yourself before going to sleep to be given an answer to some question, you will soon see the answers in your dreams. Writing each thing you remember when waking, even if it's only one thing, trains the mind to retain information from dreamtime. I have dream journals from years ago, when I read them now I can distinctly see the progress of my life.

In helping others with this dream work, we are allowing ourselves to connect with each other on a completely new level. Eventually, we will be able to communicate with others through this dream state.

During pregnancy, dreaming usually becomes very vivid, and many women have shared their dreams with me over the years. During pregnancy, sometimes fears can come out in dreams, or a vision of the birth may arise in dreamtime. Sometimes questions are answered, and warnings about certain situations surrounding the pregnancy or birth can come through our dreams.

One story, I recall from a few years ago, was a couple's dilemma over some dissatisfaction with their midwife. The young mother had a dream about the situation that guided both her and her husband to do an unassisted birth. The last week of the pregnancy, they told her that they were planning to do their own birth. Of course, the midwife was a bit upset, but the parents needed to follow their intuition. After the birth, they came over and told me about how incredible it was to be able to be totally connected and at peace with their experience. They had felt that having that particular midwife there would have taken that experience from them, and they were glad to have listened to the dream's message to do their own birth.

It is important to listen to your visions and dreams. They can clue us into what we need to focus on in our life, help remedy a fear, change a particular scenario, or bring to consciousness other things we need to work on that we may be unaware of.

For instance, a mom has a dream about having a horrible birth. She awakens with a sense of fear, and then later realizes it is not necessarily what has to be. Nevertheless, she had a warning, if she did not start to work on her fears surrounding the birth, it could happen. Instead, she can choose things to be different by releasing her fears and getting good support from her partner to have the birth she truly desires.

Sometimes, dreams can show us just what we need to learn for that moment in our lives. However, with those signs we can create a more suitable outcome by just listening to the warnings we get from them.

Our paths are not unchangeable; we can manifest changes in our destinies by realizing we can, and then also taking the steps to re-design our thoughts and perceptions of reality. Through our higher selves, we have the answers.

Yoga

Yoga means to "yoke" or to "unite." Movement, breath, meditation, and balance are obtained through yoga. It is another essential part of being connected to all aspects of ourselves: Spirit, mind, and body.

Doing yoga is something you can pick up at anytime; it is not difficult if you start out slowly. Getting books, videos, or going to a class is easy nowadays. Yoga is everywhere! Most of all, utilizing the breath is what can be useful in any daily activity and especially in labor and birth. It will bring a sense of calm in stressful situations, and the yoga movement can bring you back in touch with your body and baby's needs. There are a many types of yoga: Raja Yoga, Hatha Yoga, Kudalini Yoga, Ashtanga Yoga, Lengar Yoga, Bhrama Yoga, Tantric Yoga, Laya Yoga, Sivinanda Yoga, and many others.

I like to do a combination of these and other types of meditations. They all utilize the "breath of life" or Pranayama breathing. This involves breathing in slowly, fully and deeply, then exhaling slowly with an open relaxed jaw. No hyperventilating just relaxed, primal breathing, slow and deep while making an ocean sound in the back of the throat. It takes practice but after doing it for a while you will feel the difference in the depth of your breathing. Doing ten pranayama breaths the firth thing every morning, concentrating, each time, on making the sound deeper and fuller, and then, to finish, breathe in once deeply, and let it quickly out.

Yoga breathing is one of the best ways to rid us of fear, guilt, confusion, stress and negative thoughts. Our breath is with us always until we are ready to leave this earth, so use it well. Moving with the breath is the yoking part of yoga; you are bringing the two elements together in rhythmic harmony. Asanas, or poses, are different for each type of yoga, but they all have the same philosophy of movement and breath being synchronized with each other. Seeking a yoga teacher is the best way to learn these exercises; it is hard to explain on paper and much easier to learn when guided.

Zack in the stream NY 1992

Water

Water has been used for its healing properties for centuries. Imprints of the womb are activated through warm submergence in water. It can give you a sense of weightlessness - helping to heal inner worries. Water is also a major portion of the planet's surface; it is also most of our body's volume as the cells in our bodies are made of water, salt and minerals much like the ocean.

It is just logical then to use water to support the birthing process. A laboring mom is supported by water's buoyancy. She usually has less fear and can relax so the muscles open; she can move more freely, and this helps baby emerge slowly and gently.

Swimming is very useful during your prenatal time as it promotes good circulation, calms the nervous system, gives the baby gentle exercise, and it's fun!

Water births are personally my favorite type of birth. I love to see babies, held by their mothers hands, slowly coming into the larger space of water and realizing that they have more room to move, its amazing! Looking up through the water, the babies stretch and kick, ready to face the atmosphere and take in their first breath of oxygen. As the baby's face emerges, her body is kept under the water to keep her warm. She does not feel stress nor does she cry in pain because the water is still supporting her delicate brain and nervous system. This promotes brain cell activity, as there is less stress from gravity and the cooler atmosphere.

There is no worry about baby inhaling water because the baby has not yet faced the cooler air that stimulates the respiration reflex. However, within the first 30 seconds of birth, we do bring the baby's face out of the water. Until then, the umbilical cord is supplying the baby with oxygen as it has been doing all along in the watery environment of the mother's womb.

Drinking water

Water is an essential part of our body's energetic systems and supports all of life. We need water to replenish our cells and drinking at least two quarts a day will prevent dehydration, headaches, mood swings, digestion problems, and aging. While pregnant it does all the same things for mom, but it is especially important for the baby as it supplies nutrients via the placenta, and it refreshes the amniotic fluid every 24-48 hours. If a pregnant mom is not drinking enough water for herself, her baby will also become dehydrated and possibly have other problems associated with not getting enough vital nutrients/fluids to support the baby's growing organs and nervous system. Water is an amazing element on our planet and needs to be respected and used properly.

Preparation for water birth

First find a good pool, either buy one, make one or rent one from a birth pool company **(see in back for resources)**. It is easy enough to make one, and then have extra income from it later by renting it out. A stock tank can be used and later will be available for watering animals or collecting grey water for your garden, or you can find a kiddy pool that has enough depth and strength to lean on. After setting the pool up, check your water heater for cleanliness. You can use your tap water from the kitchen sink (you may have to buy an attachment) and a regular garden hose to fill it.

Clean out your hose by putting half a cup of hydrogen peroxide in it and curling it into a U shape. Then attach it to the faucet and fill the hose with very hot water. While keeping the U shape, swoosh the water around by moving the hose back and forth for about five minutes, then let hot water flow through the hose for up to ten minutes. Put the hose into a clean garbage bag and store it until the labor begins.

For cleaning your pool, use vinegar or biodegradable soap and make sure to really rinse it well afterwards. Cover it to keep it clean, or buy specially made plastic disposable sheets from a birth pool company. Have a thermometer that floats or has a weight on the bottom, which will sit at the bottom of the pool for making sure the temperature is even.

Get a little fish net to take out debris as it appears, there is no worry about urinating in the pool, urine is fine, fecal matter depends on how much, but scoop out as much as you can. Usually it falls to the bottom and as the baby will be coming up and will not inhale it anyway, don't worry. The temperature should stay within 95-99degrees with 98 as the ideal. This is because your Amniotic fluid is that temperature, and the baby will not inhale if he comes into the same temperature as the mother's womb.

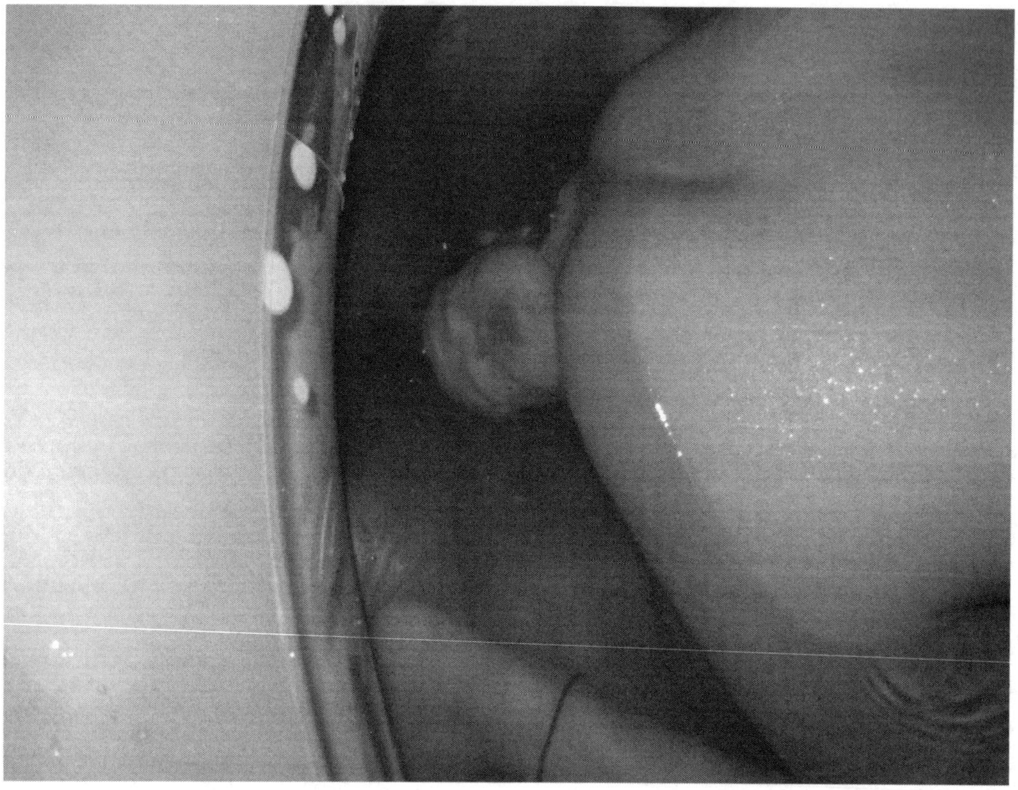

Rebecca giving birth in water 2006

Benefits of Water Birth:

It is like a huge warm compress all over your body. It helps promote stretching of the yoni tissues, the sensations feel less intense for most women, and it acts as a natural aesthetic. It facilitates a graceful labor, it is relaxing and gives you more freedom of movement within the pool. It is easier to create a safe sacred space in water where no one can enter unless you allow them to.

Risks of Water Birth:

Problems during a water birth are rare, but if you know what they are you can prevent them:

Getting an infection from dirty water.

Being exhausted from being in the pool too long or

Getting in too early in labor, which slows the labor down.

Drowning from passing out in the water.

Over exhaustion from lack of nutrition.

Dehydration during labor.

The baby inhaling water or the baby drowning.

These things rarely happen when the pool is used properly and is managed with clear guidelines. Learn all you can during your pregnancy about water birth, and you will be fine.

Michal Odent MD., one of our pioneers of gentle birth, states in many of his films on water birth that in over 2500 water births, he has never seen an infection in either mother or baby, or has never seen anyone die or pass out from exhaustion. This is because they are using clean water, not staying in too long without coming out for breaks, the moms are getting enough to drink and eat, and these women are encouraged to listen to their instincts.

I have attended approximately forty water births, and I also have never seen any ill effects from this method of birthing. I have only seen calm, happy mothers and babies.

Aroma Therapy

Smells, they are everywhere! They can make us smile, cry, gag, feel good, feel better, induce vomiting, lesson labor sensations, or increase labor sensations. Aroma Therapy is yoga for the nose. Everywhere nowadays there are people who study this modality, and it is useful in everyday life to remedy a headache, heal a cold sore, get the brain going, slow labor, start labor or support labor in some way. There are many uses for Aroma Therapy, it calms the mind, relieves menstrual symptoms, helps bring on a cycle if stagnant, and cures the ailments specific to female and male. Some brands are less potent than others are, so it is good to find someone who is an Aroma expert to show you how they are used and which ones to buy. I use oils almost every day of my life, in my bath, in my hair, during cycles, at births, with moms and babies.

Some basic tools for aromatherapy are a vaporizer, oil infuser, water, candle, some knowledge of oils and a place to relax. In pregnancy and birth, I have only used a few types of oils. Some are contraindicated for pregnancy, which means they should not be used. Sometimes it is not wise to use certain oils in the beginning of pregnancy, and then at the end of pregnancy these same oils may be used for a number of situations. Consulting with your nose and intuition is the best way to figure out how to use Aroma Therapy.

For headaches and relaxation, Lavender is calming and soothing. For restlessness, Rosemary oil is comforting. Geranium helps lift your spirits, and is good for depression and the oil itself helps heal wounds. I have used the oil straight off the leaves by rubbing them with my fingers and inhaling the cheery smell, plus geraniums are easy to grow. In Labor, I have used Rose and Rosemary, this seems to be good for keeping calm, increasing labor slowly, and relaxing mom and all who are involved. Just putting a few drops of the oil in a bowl of warm water in the room is sufficient. Some of these oils come in hydrosol spray bottles, and are helpful for rejuvenation when spritzed on faces and in the air, my favorite is Rose water.

Some good oils for labor and birth:

Clary Sage, Mandarin, Jasmine, Lavender, Chamomile, Ylang-ylang.

Young Living Oils has been my favorite brand over the years. This company's oils are very pure, and many of them can be taken orally. Oils are good for many reasons and can be used in your own cosmetics and lotions for their aroma. Use your instincts, sniff them out and choose the ones that are helpful to you.

Meditation

In most cultures, meditation is a time-honored tradition. Meditation is a healthy way to prevent physical and emotional complications due to the environment or our inner fear.

There are different ways people meditate. One is totally relaxing in the mind, body and breathing in deeply. Exhale fully with the intention to let go of the stresses of your day or some fear you are dealing with.

Sitting upright with your legs crossed is optimal as it allows the energy of your body to move freely and not become stagnant. It is also a way to remain awake during the meditation. Some people meditate through prayer. Follow your own tradition (if you have one) or learn to meditate in order to thank your Creator for this life and to relax and relieve stress.

In some cultures meditation is an everyday event, and people stop whatever it is they are doing too focus on that moment through their specific practice. In some religious meditation practices, mantras (prayers) are said while in meditation. This heightens the sense of freeing one's self through prayer, and also brings us closer to our oneness with our Creator.

A basic mantra is "Om Mani Padme Hum," meaning 'Salutations to the Jewel of Consciousness (the mind) which has reached the heart's lotus." A very powerful but simplistic mantra can create a harmony in one's mind during each day. Chanting this mantra three times is helpful to bring us into balance.

Whatever your meditation might be, it is a way to become calm, to empty any negativity and too allow positive influences into your life. Physically, it can bring great joy and balance into your world and create a way of healing ailments in your body. It does this by ridding negative thoughts or feelings that may cause suffering.

Like all of these alternative modalities, there are places and people who can help you learn and get on the road to fulfillment in your life.

Chakra Meditation: In Sanskrit, Chakra means "Wheel" and refers to spinning wheels of light associated with certain centers in our bodies. Using the seven points of light in our bodies called Chakras, we can clear anxieties, mental and physical ailments and open our energetic pathways for a more flowing life experience.

Dance

Dancing has been a way of expressing one's self in all cultures around the world since the beginning of time. It is amazing to see all the similarities in the way people move. Although unrelated in race or religion, they somehow have the connectedness of dance. For centuries it has been used in ritual, celebrations, marriage ceremonies, and funerals. Movement can provide more oxygen and give more emotional release to one's body than jogging miles a day. Dancing is a bodily expression of emotions that can help create a flowing labor and birth; it is a way to become closer to your divine inner self.

Belly dancing, for instance has been around for thousands of years, this is a way that women in labor would move through their fears, anxieties, joys and hopes for their baby's birth, allowing emotions, muscles and baby to be released through the movement of the body.

Moving the hips creates an opening for the birth too take place, wriggling the baby down with swift flowing waves of the hips. Labor is movement, it does not sit for long, it sways and rocks, it does not lie down. The sensuality that comes from dancing is pulling all living beings together in its movement. If you only feel comfortable dancing alone, dance in your room with the blinds shut. Just dance! Get used to moving and flowing with your body. Put on some good music that moves you. Be the Goddess of birth that you are created to be!

Martial Arts are also a form of dance, a more precise way of movement, but all the same, it is a flow of movement that can help keep any stagnation from building up. Tai Chi, Aikido, Chi Gong, Jujitsu, Judo, Kung Fu, Karate, Taiwanese Kick Boxing (and I am sure there are others I do not know about) are some Martial Arts' you might be interested in if you feel drawn to this form of exercise. There techniques can be of great importance for building up stamina, learning balance, building confidence, moving energies and knowing how to defend yourself naturally without a external weapon (these may be useful for a hospital birth).

Song

Song, during pregnancy labor and birth, is another one of those things we have been missing in our culture. Most cultures use song to express gratitude to their Creator, Gods and Goddesses as well as to put forth to the Universe their desires and needs. Singing opens up energy flow throughout the mind and body, promoting relaxation of the whole being and expressing our needs for communication and unity. We sing in church to praise the Lord, and in all cultures singing signifies the union with the earth and all its' creatures. All animals on earth and in the ocean sing, they all have a way to communicate to each other about predators that are in the area; they have mating songs, happy songs, sad songs, or songs to call the newly passed. Every emotion or feeling can be expressed through song. Be free to be, open your voice, let sound enter your being and share your songs with others.

Michal Odent M.D. offers parent-singing groups for his prenatal clientele. They gather for singing sessions each month, and use this as a prenatal breathing exercise. Even more importantly Dr. Odent states, "Singing is more of a priority than the physical exams given prenatally." He is an advocate for reviving the lost arts of lullabies in our culture today.

Singing to babies actually promotes inner-ear development as well as stimulates the brain receptors. The brain is forever re-routing its patterns and forming new pathways to store information. Song is a way to give our babies a pattern of peacefulness and inner calm (if it is not heavy metal).

Trust, relaxation, physical growth and intuition are all developed through sound. Even a hearing-impaired baby can hear or feel vibrations through his skull bones, which act as conductors, and is stimulated through the vibrations of his mother, father and environment. Thus, many hearing impaired children can and will learn and grow even more quickly than hearing children because their keen sensory receptors have been stimulated to work in a slightly different, and more sensitive way. Our unique body chemistry works to make sure that our five senses are all compensating for each other. If one or two do not work to their fullest, the others will work overtime to create a more stabilizing way for the body and mind to function. Singing, or using sound, was the telecommunication process for all of our ancestors, and if it is used properly, can be of great importance once again in our communities and in the lives of our children.

O Sing Unto the Lord, Sing Unto the Lord, All the Earth . . .

~Psalm :96

Birth Song

by: Alycia Chambers, 2005

From the beginning of time

With the first living seed

Life sprang from the earth

[CHORUS]

Trust in the dance- time trance of birth

Grandmother of time- Ancestral earth

Blessed baby is born- singing along

With the rhythm of the wombs- eternal birth song

From water to land – life evolved to explore

With hands and feet- growing from the core

Giving music a beat- and movement galore

With fire for heat- we could dance and more

[CHORUS]

The strong survive with the blood in our veins

Our mother is giving us life- as the wisdom remains

Fertile womb- with father's seed

Sown and grown- created are we

[CHORUS]

Trust and let go- dancing with the ebb and flow

Here we're giving birth- were the sons and our daughters

We inherent the earth

[CHORUS]

We do not need drugs to take the surge away

Or a monitor to tell us baby is on the way

If we listen to our instincts and do what we feel

Baby can be born and the future be healed

[CHORUS]

Kelly Courage with Osha 2000

Using Sound

All over the world people have used sounds–bells, horns, song, or vibrations of the earth–to call in the spirits. Nature's sounds were their inspiration; birds, animals mating calls, all the mysterious sounds of the planet call out to welcome, to warn, to mate, to run, to gather, or pray. We all need to make sound to be able to communicate with each other well.

We all make sounds, doing it from the time we arrive into the world with cries of hunger, happiness or discomfort; we vocalize our needs from the beginning. During birth, most importantly, we need to re-gain our strength to communicate our needs. Primally, we need to make sounds to flow through labor, if we do not, all our energy gets caught up inside and things then slow and manifest in outward manifestations of pain, fear and suffering. It all comes from not expressing our needs, when they need to be expressed.

If we listen to our bodies, we can send out the signal that our time is near to the birth, we can call out with sounds that radiate through the cosmos. Primal birthing sounds create a birth in which there is less pain, fear, and emotional stagnation. Some women do not make much sound and are fine, they close their eyes and moan a little just before the baby is born. Some women need to "howl at the moon" to let out that energy! It is all good, and we are all different, but holding in that energy just closes us up, it does not let things flow properly, and labor can be longer than if we just let it out.

Practice a few howls, growls and hoots. See how it feels. I do it when I go up the mountain, I get to the ridge, huffing and puffing up the hill, and then let it out Woooo! That's hard to do on paper, but try it for yourself. Howling makes all the stuffed up energies move … that is what birth is, a lot of energy moving. Therefore, you must make sound with it and move physically with it. As you near your time to give birth you will feel its strength and determination, it will give you a break and then you will begin to feel it coming on again, so when this happens just give a huge SYE-AHHH, then move into what natural sounds arise. EE, OO, YA, SA, whatever they may be for you–just listen to your inner sounds and let it OUT! It makes all the difference in the world; believe me!

OM, an ancient, universal sound can bring light and openness when chanted repeatedly. Just using the Om sound alone can do wonders for moving a baby down through the birth opening, just try it and see. It is a gentle and easy way to get the baby out without holding the breath, or pushing forcefully, it actually creates its own pushing feeling with the sound that carries with it.

I have often also used Tibetan singing bowls at births, this is a good sound that will balance any imbalanced energy surrounding the birthing area, it is a humming vibration that may be very soothing to the laboring mother. Chant some mantras, sing, dance, and love your birth experience. It will not ever happen again with that baby, it is the first and the only birth that baby and you will experience together. Let it be an enjoyable one!

"Read, every day, something no one else is reading. Think, every day, something no one else is thinking. Do, every day, something no one else would be silly enough to do. It is bad for the mind to continually be part of unanimity."

~Christopher Morley

Ritual

In the name of Isis of the thousand breasts, May your conception be blessed.

In the name of Isis of a thousand breasts, may your pregnancy be blessed

In the name of Isis of ten thousand breasts, May the birth be easy

and the life you bring forth be blessed!

"The Holy Book of Women's Mysteries" ~Zsuzsanna Budapest

Prayer of many kinds, if positive, can bring a sense of well-being into our lives. Prayer can manifest great feelings of goodness and gratitude, which in turn, become healthy mental states of being, body and spirit. They are blessings and thanks for all who have birthed before us, and all who will birth with us and after us, for compassion to all living beings and understanding of ourselves. Prayer is just a way of bringing all elements of spirit into one's life, as well as bringing harmony and balance into everyday consciousness. It's easy to do, and you do not have to subscribe to any specific religion to do it. I was raised in a non-specific religious family, gaining a sense of well-being from awareness that all living beings are a part of us, and that as women (I was raised by great women) we are powerful creators and can do anything.

My childhood was filled with spirit guides who helped me understand the great power of prayer. Doing rituals in nature gave me a feeling of oneness and connection. I would go off into the woods when I was young and bring fruit and flowers to offer to the trees, and thank them for this life. Even though my family did not subscribe to a specific religion, I somehow found it within myself to pray and bring offerings into nature. I also feel that having a Great Grandmother, Grandmother and Mother who were very strong women and knew themselves well, that I was able to get a sense of myself through them. They taught me how to believe in myself and to also respect my elders, as well as the earth.

Getting back in tune with nature is the most inspiring gift I have received from my family. If I had not realized this concept of prayer at a young age, I would have not been able to survive in this world. Being adopted imprinted on me a sense of separation from the beginning; I needed to re-connect myself to something we all have in common in order to fulfill my purpose in this life. Prayer is a powerful way of bringing all the elements of this world, and ourselves, together into a balanced state of being.

Today, too often, prayer has been neglected in our lives for one reason or another. For many, it has become just an empty ritual rather than a symbol of how we live and treat each other and view birth and death as a part of our belief systems.

Until recent times, ritual has always been a part of birth. The Navajo Indians have a ceremony of prayer and protection for the pregnant mother, father, birth and baby. Women gathered before a conception for the conception ritual as well as before a birth to sing, dance and pray for the spirits to come and gather and protect the mother, child and family in birth. Many rituals such as these are performed for birth all over the world. All cultures have some type of birthing prayer.

American culture has been so far removed from such rituals, that today, we separate ourselves too often from the natural events of life. Through prayer and rituals of some kind or another, we can re-connect ourselves with the Creator and our purpose on earth.

There are many different ways to prepare ourselves for the initiations of life. Simply, we all can become aware of these connections by being a part of nature and not separate from it. I find this at births; if a couple is using ritual in whatever form, the labor and birth are a lot more flowing and are very spiritually satisfying when using such rituals. Some of the couples I have worked with over the years have a great sense of well-being when using prayer, song and dance. I notice the difference between them and the ones that do not have a sense of ritual. It is clear that in the past, birth was considered a sacred event, and still in the present day, when prayers are used, they bring all the elements of nature into balance.

Modern Blessing Ways

It is easy for friends and relatives to create a ceremony for the mother to be. First, find where you would like to have the ceremony, and then call all the women you would like to invite. Traditionally, men are usually not at this ceremony. They have their own initiation, but you can invite men if you want. Give everyone a task to gather materials for the blessing and bring pillows, food, drink–all the basic stuff. It is important that everyone involved bring something to put her energies into for the blessing and birth. Find songs to sing and make copies for each person, and bring musical instruments to share.

The blessing ways I have been to are all very different. You can create an elaborate scene or a simple scene, but either way it will be a lot more meaningful than a typical American baby shower. Outside in nature, in a protected grove, or field where a small fire can be built safely, is the best place to do this type of ritual, weather permitting, of course.

Items to Gather for the ritual:

(All optional. Many things you can gather out of your kitchen or at a health food store)

1) Blue Corn Meal: for washing the mother's feet, cleansing her spirit and protecting her from ailments in the last month of pregnancy. Use blue corn kernels to string into necklaces for everyone to wear until after the birth. Blue corn Goddess will protect everyone in the group, and even create more fertility for everyone, so be careful!

2) Flowers: Lavender, rose petals, rosemary, chamomile flowers. Also bring sea salt, a large bowl, and a towel; this is for the foot washing ceremony during which everyone takes a turn washing the mothers' feet and telling her their prayer or hopes for the safe journey of her birth. It is a calming and emotional ceremony for everyone involved.

3) A ball of yarn: for the weaving ceremony, this is a special way to weave everyone's prayers and energies together by stringing the yarn around everyone's torsos in the circle and singing the weaving song at the same time. Using the piece of yarn around your waste to wear as a bracelet until after the birth, so every ones prayers are connected.

4) White Candles: everyone brings a white candle to light on the birth alter while saying their prayer for the protection of the family during the birth.

Sing while weaving Yarn

As Women have always woven, so we weave this yarn into the circle of our lives.

As women have always woven time and fate, so let us weave this yarn into the circle of our lives.

As women have always woven baskets and tools, so let us weave this yarn into the circle of our lives.

As women have always woven threads into clothing and shelter, so let us weave this yarn into the circle of our lives.

As women have always woven words into poetry, so let us weave this yarn into the circle of our lives.

As women have always woven, so we weave this yarn with the Goddess, who is with us,

The Goddess is always with us - may we feel her presence in our daily lives …

After this is sung and yarn is woven (clockwise) around everyone's waist, we will usually take a moment to say our prayers around the circle. One by one, each person gives their hope for the mother's birth, and cuts the yarn from her waist. Then they tie that piece to their wrist until after the birth of the baby. Each piece of yarn will represent the prayer of that person and connect her to the mother and child until after the birth.

Light a white candle, and say:

I call you in, all my ancestors,

To be present here for this Birth!

I call you in, all my Relations who have birthed before me

Since the beginning of time!

I call you in, my inner wisdom, to guide my heart, my hands, my voice,

To be conscious and full of life!

I ask for patience, for nourishment at this time …

Give this birth a moment in space, to be in timelessness …

All who enter here are humbled and not in fear,

I ask only those who will respect my sacred space to be allowed in this place.

I will open my heart,

I will enjoy my transformation into motherhood.

Thank you ancestors for being here,

I honor your wisdom and will follow my heart,

Wherever we are for this birth.

Blessings Be!

The Birth Alter

I have seen many different Birth Altars, but the one thing they all have in common is that they symbolize whatever the mother wishes for. You can make your own according to your own traditions or whatever seems pleasing. Having our own Birth Alter is specific to one's own desires.

Usually the Altar consists of a symbol of the womb, either a Gourd, which is a universal symbol of the womb, or a statue of a Goddess of Birth. You can sculpt a clay statue of a Birthing Goddess which symbolizes mother and child or a birthing woman.

Other items consist of a bowl for offering fruit or flowers. This is to ask for protection from the Birthing Goddess, giving her an offering of thanks. Candles, incense, and decorations of crystals, flowers, herbs of fertility, feathers symbolizing the spirit, and other decorative symbolic things can be used. This Altar can be used for any ritual of life, life 'initiations' if you will, and is very potent in ceremonies around the world.

Using white candles (white symbolizes purity, newness, meditation) in ritual is fairly common. In churches, on holidays, it symbolizes a coming of spirit and protection for the people. A candle is lit to bring hope, spirit and harmony into the hearts of all we love. Lighting this candle while saying a prayer can bring about many magical things.

The first thing I do, when I get a call from a mom in labor, is say a prayer, calling in all the great spirits of birthing, then I light a candle that I have set aside for that mother and family.

On my way to a birth, I call in all the Great Grandmothers, Shamans, Midwives, Great Grand Fathers and Wise Men and Women who have all given birth (or protected those giving birth) before us. I ask them to guide my hands and my heart to what I need to do for this birth and ask for protection and love to be present. On my way home after a birth, I thank all the Great Ones for their guidance and support of the family and myself. Then I bid them farewell until I call them in again. They feel like family to me now. This is a tradition with most midwives around the world. It works!

Unfortunately, American industrialized birth practices have become more and more removed from the ritual and connectedness of nature. The purpose seems to be to separate us from nature by controlling birth, and thus we become desensitized from our inner wisdom and power and others take control over our lives. This is a tactic in most cultures, wherein rulers control their people by keeping their own intuition and wisdom from them. Over time it has been successful, but it is not in harmony or balance with natural events. We can re-learn the power of prayer to bring back balance into everyday life and bring connectedness to natural things, such as birth. It is time to reflect; a sacred journey is at hand for Mother and Father, Child and Community. Now is the time to go inward to find our strengths and wisdom for the birth.

Call in all your Great Grand Mothers, all your Ancestral Elders, and ask them for guidance, thank them for the wisdom they have, and ask them to share it with you.

Prayer to Our Creator

We give thanks to our Creator for giving us this life.

We honor and respect this life that grows inside our bellies.

We will have trust and faith that our Creator

Is fulfilling a divine plan and will see us through.

We give thanks and gratitude for this new being coming into our family.

We believe in the great powers of Creator

As a part of our faith, and we give thanks.

We have faith that Creator will guide us

To be connected to nature and all its gifts.

We will continue to gain faith and wisdom through being in balance with nature and all its wonder in this world.

We will have faith in ourselves as Creator gave us power to see truth in all natural things.

We are grateful for this experience and miracle of life.

We will live in balance to the best of our ability and not forget where we came from.

We give thanks to You, Our Creator, for this abundant life

And for the new birth of our family.

We thank You, our Creator, for the many Blessings we have in this life

And for our families health and well being.

We thank You, our Creator, for You are a part of everything in this world

And we appreciate its bounties.

We thank You, our Creator, for all the pleasures of this world.

We thank You, our Creator for this time to reflect our desires for more connectedness

And balance of ourselves within nature.

Blessings Be,

We give Thanks !

Ubagami: Protector of the realms of

Birth and the Unborn

In Japan there is a birth, protector Goddess called Ubagami. I was drawn to her through reading and hearing from others about how the women of Japan climb hills to her altar in the woods. Soon-to-be mothers place little dolls and baby ornaments at her alter to represent their unborn children, or sick children who need protection in their time of illness. She then protects the unborn or dying babies to be safe in the realms of their alternate existence.

In China they have a sister Goddess, The Mother of Compassion, the protector of children. She is Kuan Yin. She is one I also give thanks to for protecting the unborn and birthing mothers. Her mantra is: "Namo Kuan Shi Yin Pu Sa."

Ubagami is a protector (like a nanny), for the realms of birth and death of babies. I believe as midwives, and assistants of birth, that is what we do. We support women in birth on all levels of consciousness. There has been more than once a feeling of connectedness to both of these realms when working with birth.

I feel the babies call for support from the spirit realm. Sometimes I have dreams of them asking me to tell their mother something. Sometimes they want to ask her to rest more or eat better, or sometimes that I should be prepared to be there at their births. Sometimes they tell me I am not needed, and that everything will go well and not to worry.

I just read a story of a mother who birthed her stillborn baby at home in water. She had the feeling all along that something was not right and went to her midwife to confirm that the baby was ok. However, a day before her due date, she got an ultrasound that confirmed the baby had died and was in a breech position. The child had not grown right and was very small compared to her other kids. She had faith, and knew there was a reason for this and went ahead and had her birth the way she wanted to at home in water.

In hindsight, she says she did what felt right, and that it was all in balance in its own way. These parents spent time with their baby and said their prayers for her soul, and their goodbyes shortly thereafter. This mom is pregnant again and is still planning a homebirth on her own.

It is wisdom that leads us into this life, and all we can hope for is that things go the way they should, even if it is not the way we would like.

Symbols like the Goddess Ubagami are everywhere around the world. We have them in every religion and culture; if we search in our own heritage we will find Goddesses of birth everywhere. Give them thanks and ask for protection. Feel connected with nature and its mysteries. It is feeling disconnected that creates more pain and suffering. Being conscious and aware of our fears allows us bring them into ritual and prayer, and this gives us the strength to alter our perceptions and accept whatever may come to be.

In our modern culture there is less acceptance of death, and in essence, a feeling, that to die is somehow to fail. When someone is nearing death because of illness or elderliness, we put him or her away in hospitals and nursing homes hoping not to see death approaching each day. We are ignoring reality by doing this and not giving our Elders the respect they deserve. When we are faced with it "head on," we do not know how to deal with death in a healthy way. I have had a lot of people close to me die; family, young friends, pets, neighbors, and my husband, it's everywhere. It is a part of life. A new life emerges on the other side of this one.

I have experienced a lot of loss, and so have most people in their lifetimes. Therefore, we, as a race, can learn how to respect death more and embrace it when it is foreseen. By helping those in transition move forward into another realm with support and kindness, acceptance and grieving, we no longer need to fear this natural everyday event. Since death is inevitable for all of us at some point, we need to discuss it and release fears associated with it before the birth of our baby.

The "what ifs" and "how to choose" are up to you. In certain circumstances, it is seriously difficult to know how to handle it. Wherever we choose to have our baby, who we choose for our care giver, or if we choose to go it alone, we all need to at least ponder the thought for a few moments. How will I deal with such an event if it should arise? In my childbirth classes, we discuss this once and then refrain from the notion for the rest of the pregnancy. This is because it is just a slight possibility, and we do not want to dwell on the thought and create a fearful situation. We do, however, need to be responsible for our choices and make a plan to either deal with death ourselves, if it does happen, or call in professionals to handle it with us, or for us. In some places, home burials and cremations are legal, and in some they are not. To find out, call your local coroner and ask. Most hospitals will tell you "Absolutely in no way, can you deal with it yourself," and they will manipulate you into going to have an autopsy and hand-over your child. In some cases, I feel it is good for parents to have autopsies, if it is not apparent why the baby might have died, and it helps the family "get clear" with the death. However, in other cases when it causes undue interventions with exams and questioning, it may be best to stay home and grieve in your own way. A couple that feels they do not want that type of interference in their private situation, then it may be best to either wait awhile and make peace with the baby's spirit, or have someone come to you so the interrogation does not make matters worse. Shame and guilt are a part of the healing process when something like this happens, it is normal to feel whatever feeling comes up. Over time though–wisdom and faith in all natural things such as death–can be a healing and growing experience.

So, after making your choices, listen to your inner wisdom and ask yourself how you would handle death and how it has been handled in your past.

What can you do to feel ok with your decisions?

Do you have a faith that can guide you?

What are your fears surrounding death, if any?

Write down what this topic brought up in your mind:

Visualizing Negative Thoughts to Disappear

This is not necessarily a modality, but a visual practice that can create a positive state of mind. Through affirmations (which I discuss in other parts of this guide), we can create stable reinforcement in our lives. Through this visualization, any thought that is disconnected or fearful can be diluted.

I believe most common hysteria comes from fear of the unknown. When we clear our minds and are able to tune into our divine plan, most fears dissolve on their own. This is not to say that if you feel there is something wrong with yourself or the baby, that you shouldn't seek help. You should do whatever you need to feel secure in your situation. This is just another way of helping clear our minds.

With this quick meditation, you can redirect any negative thought within a moment, just **XXX** (cross out) the negative thoughts once they creep in, before they consume your mind. The easiest way to explain how to do this is to close your eyes, see a huge ***black X***, push it away with your minds eye, when another one comes up, push that one away, then another, always thinking about what it is you are canceling out of your thoughts. Physical ailments are one way this can work in everyday life. If you have a bothersome headache for example, visualize **XXX**'s over your mind while telling the headache to go away. Do this three times; taking in deep slow breaths each time said. Tap your forehead when doing this while visualizing the **XXX**. Any ill thought of someone else also needs to be **XXX**'d out, it is not good to think badly of anyone when you also want others not to think badly of you. At least I do not want someone giving me the evil eye, but if it happens, I just smile at him or her and **XXX** him or her out of my energetic field.

This whole visualization takes two seconds, and it can do wonders in childbirth. In my prenatal classes I ask couples to write down any fears or negative thoughts, then if something comes up in the pregnancy, labor or birth, I remind them to visualize the feeling and "**XXX**" it out. It works!

Acupuncture/Acupressure

All of us have pressure points located along energetic pathways throughout our bodies called Meridians. These dictate the flow of energy or "Chi" to organs and brain function. Sometimes the energy becomes stagnant and needs release. Over time, if they are not released they can cause many complications emotionally and physically.

Cancers have been known to heal from the release of energy through acupuncture, and many emotional pains can also be remedied through this type of treatment. It is wise to seek someone who has knowledge about these healing modalities, and read books to teach yourself what each can bring into your life.

Acupressure accesses the pressure points through touch; pressure is placed on the point and held for a short time, when released, the point is then activated and energy freed.

Acupuncture uses needles to activate the pressure points. There is rarely any pain, and sometimes there is a great sensation all over one's body as the stagnated energy is released.

It is easy to do some points on your own. Get educated on these modalities and try them out, they can be very healing.

Self-Hypnosis

When I was in labor, I can remember being in a hypnotic state; focusing inward, I had no pain, and labored and birthed easily. During my training as a teacher and assistant to birth, I researched more on the subject. Practicing the tools I had learned and am still learning, I found that with the homework I gave my clients; (doing affirmations, visualizations, drawing, etc.) they had more concentration and could relax through labor with grace. I am sold on hypnosis as a self-induced process. Hypnosis does not necessarily take all the feeling away or put you in a trance, however it may help you relax and birth freely and without a struggle.

Self-hypnosis has probably been used for thousands of years by people who had no other means to sustain them through injuries or traumas, but had to rely, instead, on their ability to go into a trance like state often attained through prayer or meditation.

Hypnosis does not mean that someone will be swinging a watch in front of your face or anyone, for that matter, need not be involved. Self-hypnosis is a self-induced way of relaxing and letting one's body totally flow with labor and birth as it unfolds. There is a process that seems to aid in this trance like state of being. The best-known way to get ready for a birth is to begin using the technique with other challenging events while you are pregnant. Taking a few minutes to cut off any distractions, turn off your phone ringer, shut the shades to make it dark, or find a space that is dim–anyplace that you can relax in. It is ideal to practice this at night if you have children, so you can get space, peace and quiet. Later, it won't be necessary to have any concern for others around you. You will learn how to self-hypnotize and nothing will disturb your state of being.

Lie in a cozy position with pillows, blanket or whatever you need to feel relaxed. Close your eyes and take in 10 deep slow breaths, let them out the same way, slowly and deeply. With each breath in, contract the muscle you are focusing on, then, let it go with the exhale breath. Start with your toes, contracting them and letting them go. Move up to your next set of muscles: the calves tighten, then let go; the thighs squeeze, then let go; the Kegal (PC, pubic coccygial) muscle squeezes, then lets go; the belly tightens, then lets go; the arms flex, then lets go; the hands make a fist, then lets go; the mouth opens and stretches, then lets go; the nose schrunches; then lets go; the eyes shut tight, then relax and let go; the entire body tenses, relaxes, and lets go …

As you do this time and time again, you will notice how you let go fully more and more. It's a body awareness exercise that may help guide you into a self-hypnotic state, so when in labor and giving birth you can fully surrender and let your body do what it needs to do, and not feel the need to control the situation.

Energy Healing

I call the light

I open to the light

I receive the light

I am the light

~Reiki

Energy healing is a very profound and unique "hands off" technique used to help others and ourselves overcome emotional, spiritual and physical ailments. In my early years of study, I took Reiki initiations, which means, "Universal Life Force Energy."

"Ki" pronounced "Key," known as "Chi" in Chinese, or "Prana" in Sanskrit, and "Mana" in Hawaiian, is the "non-physical" life force energy that sustains us in mind, body, and spirit.

"Rei" pronounced "Ray" represents the intelligence, which is focused on the spiritual and physical planes of consciousness.

Dr. Mikao Usui, the founder of Reiki, dedicated his life to finding the proper ways in which we may live in order to enhance our own lives and benefit the planet by using this "Universal Life Force Energy."

This is a subtle energy force we all have as a birth right, and can utilize if we are open and focused enough at any given time or place to help support and heal ourselves and one another. This form of healing has been around for thousands upon thousands of years. Varying from culture to culture, it embodies ancient, wisdom healing techniques, which have become the foundation of today's healers and wise Elders practices. We have forgotten about this form of energetic healing in our modern culture of medicine, but it has not ever left us. Because we are already born with this type of energetic healing potential, we are capable of re-remembering its importance and practicing its magic.

The five Principles of Reiki
(Sound familiar?)

Just for today, do not worry

Just for today, do not anger

Honor your parents, teachers and Elders

Earn your living honestly

Show gratitude to everything . . .

These principles of Reiki are the universal principles of all cultures and are simplistic, yet powerful, tools for self-transformation. To gather more healing wisdom sign up for the next Reiki class in your area, and you will benefit from re-remembering its healing powers within you! Laying on of hands, focusing in our minds, changing our perceptions, educating ourselves through birth, and being kind to ourselves and the earth, these practices are the foundation of a healthy life style and something for all of us to learn and to live by. We are the creators of our planet, our world and our existence. Learning what we already have within ourselves is a huge beginning to a better life now, and a more fulfilling life later for our children and their children.

All is within you; you are surrounded in light, love, and wisdom.

You are the one who can make great progress in making this world a better place for our children and all who come after us.

Reflexology

Reflexology works by stimulating the points of the face, hands, and feet that are connected to all other pathways of organs in our body. The points which conjunct with the internal organs to heal digestive discomforts and facilitate labor, and the reproductive points in the ankles, are most commonly used in late pregnancy.

Understanding the bodily map work is key to also understanding how all of our systems are related and function with each other. No organ or system is alone. They are all working together, so if one is not functioning well the others may suffer. That is what reflexology is good for. It is much more time-consuming to treat each individual body part than to work on one hand, for instance, to heal four body parts. This also corresponds to the idea that we are a complete system without segregation. The whole body can be worked on through simple massage of hands and feet, consolidating the wholeness of the body, therefore healing wholly.

Reflexology has been one of my favorite things to have done on myself and do with others. It is simple and fun, uses less time, and covers a broader range of inner bodywork than just focusing on the topical body part. Utilizing the pressure points in the feet and hands, which relate to specific internal body organs can help reduce tension, digestive problems, constipation, headache, stagnant labor, birth adjustment, baby tension, and many other things. Most alternative health-care providers will know how to use this type of modality, or send you to the right person who can help. It is also easy to learn and can be a part of a daily ritual for couples, helping each other stay healthy.

NOTES:

YOUR Birth Story Here:

Various Birth Stories

Mati's Birth Story of her Children Taru and Holly
Psalm and Zoya's Unassisted Twin Birth Story
Donna Colelli's Birth Story of Ciro
Unassisted Birth of Zoyya Xuxa
Valerie Nordstrom, "Beautiful Baby Boy"
Births I Have Been Blessed to be at
Three Births of Breech Babies Born at Home
Two Scenarios of Bleeding in the Forth Month of Pregnancy
A Long Awaited Birth Six Weeks after Original Due Date
Tubal Ligation of Rh- Mom and her Un-Assisted Water Birth
Faith and Heart Abnormalities
"Wicanpi Cikala 'Little Star,'" Sara Brave Heart's Son Cedar Everett
My Mother's Biological Child's Birth on Mother's Day
My Adoption Story and My Brothers Adoption Story
Christina El-Abid's Unassisted Breech Birth of Sami
Mohammad El-Abid's Story of his Little Brother
Alaina Smith's Parent Assisted Birth of Brittany

Brianne Rice, My Teacher

Friends, Family, and those whom I have had the pleasure of working with over the years, donated all of these Birth Stories. I feel that everyone has a unique way of expressing themselves, and have not edited these stories, in respect to all their unique creative expressions.

I have added my own versions to some that I wanted to share in hopes they would be helpful in decision making regarding various situations in birth.

Have fun and enjoy these real life birth stories, and always remember your story is unique and cannot be compared to anyone else's.

Mati's Birth Stories

By: Mati Fuller

My first birth experience was very traumatic. I was in the hospital, nothing was opening up, it was very scary and heavy, I felt a strong fear of death for both my baby and me.

When I got pregnant the second time, I was still afraid of giving birth, since my body did not "seem" to have a clue what to do the first time. Part of me wanted to go to the hospital, since they are prepared for possible difficulties, and part of me felt that going to the hospital was traumatic in itself and maybe even the cause of some of my difficulties.

I had a very hard time making up my mind, and kept postponing the decision as long as I could. The last month of pregnancy I was doing tincture of Black and Blue Cohosh in addition to my Nettle and Red Raspberry tea, and I felt that my body was better prepared this time.

I had contractions throughout my pregnancy and they were getting stronger towards the end, so when my due date was getting close I was already almost 3 centimeters open.

On my due date I was so tired of being pregnant I decided to climb a mountain, thinking that either I'll make muscles, or I will go into labor. When I came back the contractions definitely felt a bit stronger than before. I went to bed that night hoping to get some sleep, and I woke up about 1 am with some pretty heavy sensations. I woke up my husband, and filled the bath with warm water. We tried to time the contractions but they were nothing like the textbooks. They were short, strong, and not regular in any way, so I could not really tell how close I was to giving birth. According to the books, the contractions were too short and too far apart, but I guess they did what they were supposed to do. About 3 am I was feeling miserable, and needed some advice, so I called Zuki, and she came right over. She immediately made me feel safe and well taken care of, and since there was no way back we just went for it at home.

My husband was holding my hand and was able to communicate with me in that half-absurd space you go to when you are in labor, and our conversation was quite funny at times, since none of what I said made any sense. I felt the baby go through my cervix, which was such an amazing feeling that I announced to everybody "the baby is coming!" A few seconds later, they could see the head. We took it slow for a few breaths so I could stretch as much as possible, and then I pushed the baby out. I jumped around to see my baby, and found out that it was indeed a little girl, just as I had thought she would be.

Psalm and Zoya's Unassisted twin birth

By Mindy Goorchenko (Their mom)

When my husband and I learned we were expecting our third child, we scheduled our prenatal appointment with the same midwives we had worked with for our second son's birth two years earlier. I truly believe that if women knew how midwifery care differs from the standard obstetrical experience, they would flock to their local midwives in droves. We once again savored the first five months of visits to their lovely Pasadena location. Each visit lasted at least two hours, during which time we would check the basics, like blood pressure, fundal height, etc. The rest of our visit we devoted to exploring our thoughts, feelings, and concerns about our pregnancy and birth and truly forming a partnership with our chosen birth attendants.

All this sounds too easy in retrospect! About halfway through our pregnancy, my uterus began measuring bigger and bigger than it should have for just one baby. We suspected twins, scheduled an ultrasound, and sure enough, immediately saw two heads on the screen and the rest of their adorable little bodies--a boy and a girl. It was a relief to see the evidence and know we were growing two babies, not one, since we had already grown so attached to the idea! However, our midwives were no longer willing to attend our birth in a professional context, due to their licensing restrictions. They referred us to a few obstetricians, but both my husband and I felt extremely opposed to having our babies in the hospital. What little information I could find about twin pregnancies led us to question the excessive use of interventions in a multiple gestation, the cesarean rate alone for twins terrifying us. Since we had conceived our babies naturally, we had no reason to think we couldn't give birth to them naturally as well. We started looking for a midwife.

This was easier said than done. We interviewed several yet none quite meshed with how we wanted this experience to be. Rather than trusting in the process, most of the midwives had fear about the birth of the second twin and I did not feel comfortable having that attitude around me during birth. We decided to simply go it alone. I had always wanted an unassisted home birth...I just didn't think it would be with twins! My husband trusted me to make that decision and felt comfortable being the only "attendant" at the birth. I knew in my heart, soul, and bones that these babies needed to be born at home into the safest environment possible and that the birth would go well.

At about this time, we were referred to a midwife about 2 and a half hours away who was willing to work with us. We paid her a visit and she truly embodied the spirit of acceptance we were looking for in a birth professional, although our involvement before the birth was minimal due to the distance factor and also because I was quite far along at this point, at least 34 weeks. Also, the chance was definitely there that she would not arrive in time because my last two labors were pretty quick and easy. I did appreciate her experience and wisdom and enjoyed listening to all the stories she shared with me about the births she had attended.

Looking back at the birth of our twins, it was extraordinary yet so perfectly normal at the same time. I realized how much of a big deal birth is turned into, when in actuality, it is such a straightforward and ordinary event. In my 40th week of gestation, I spent a few hours at home having strong contractions in the late evening. I went to bed and woke up on January 25th feeling disappointed that I was not in active labor. Within an hour, however, the contractions started again, at around 7 in the morning, and I called our midwife to have her come down. I also called my friend Kari, whom we had invited to be with us at our birth.

The contractions were strong and demanded my calmness, strength, and surrender almost immediately. I draped myself over my birth ball, which I placed on the bed, and rocked through each one, sometimes moaning to myself. My husband, in the meantime, filled up our birth tub and also tended to our two year old. After an hour and a half, I headed into the bathroom, took my clothes off, and sat down on the toilet. The grunting in my voice told me the births were imminent, and I occasionally reached inside myself to see where the first baby was. The sac bulged out and broke. I felt his head descend quickly, got down on all fours, and let my uterus push him out into my hands. This was our first arrival; a little boy named Psalm Victor who cried just enough to let us know he was okay but otherwise settled into a deep calm, not even opening his eyes but one time in the first hour when we placed him next to his sister.

When I started having contractions again after fifteen minutes or so, I clamped his cord with our only two cord clamps and gave him to my husband to bundle up in blankets. My friend Kari thankfully arrived at this point to help Alex, who was now watching our two year old, holding Psalm, and filming the birth, all at the same time! I reached inside me once again to check on my progress, and felt momentarily confused as to what body part was presenting itself. It felt like a hand, possibly, tucked up near the head, but then I realized it was our daughter's foot. I calmly stated my only profanity of the morning--"Oh f*ck, it's a footling breech," although I wasn't afraid, just surprised. My husband asked what he could do and I responded, "Nothing. Just film." A foot and leg quickly came out, followed by a second foot and leg (I could feel her literally pushing her knee out of me). Next came her body, hands, and arms, as I supported her with my hands reaching under me. Her head popped out and our daughter Zoya Olga was born, with spurts of blood coming with her and a train roaring by outside. It took less than 30 seconds from the time her first foot emerged. She yelled lustily to announce her presence and immediately stared at her family with wide, alert eyes. After ten or fifteen minutes, I clamped the cord with shoelaces, gave her to my husband, and birthed the placenta into a big glass bowl. Their two placentas had fused into one big butterfly with two cords emerging from it.

Though I didn't use the tub during the labor, it was absolute heaven to get into it after our babies were born. My body felt strange and imbalanced after carrying so much weight in front, so I welcomed the water and didn't get out for at least an hour, taking turns bathing each baby before our midwife (who arrived about 45 minutes after the birth) did the assessments, measuring, etc. And to simply get into bed afterward without having to deal with the hospital, separation from our babies, etc.--heaven!

As a vegan, I must admit how gratifying it was to share their birth weights with our parents, who always questioned my protein intake and how I was possibly getting enough calcium, iron, etc. Our son weighed 7 pounds, 10 ounces. Our daughter weighed 8 pounds, 11 ounces. All in all, I gained 80 pounds during this pregnancy and it was by far my easiest and most favorite of the three. I felt so healthy the entire time, and I feel my diet had a lot to do with it. In the early part of our pregnancy, I kept a food diary for a few days and discussed it in depth with our midwives. I found a few areas I needed to improve and we brain stormed some easy ways to bolster my diet. For instance, dried apricots (unsulphered) provided a tasty source of iron and vitamin A. I also learned a lot more about good fats and was very conscientious to eat lots of avocados, flax oil, etc. Again, it's painful to think of how obstetricians weigh their patients each month without ever asking the simple questions, "What did you eat last week?"

In addition to paying close attention to my diet, I received chiropractic adjustments two to three times a week from Dr. Dominique Scott at Life Chiropractic in Manhattan Beach; homeopathy from Dr. Robert Gramlich in Los Angeles, and a four-day mind-altering experience with Anthony Robbins during this pregnancy. I prayed and journaled almost constantly. I attended La Leche League meetings regularly with our two-year-old and enjoyed the close friendships I had formed and the loving relationship with my husband. All in all, this pregnancy epitomized the joy and miracle of life, with all its unfolding exploration and discovery. A wonderful gift.

My Midwife Birthing Experience

November 6, 1985

By: Donna T Colelli

I was living in NYC when I became pregnant with my only son, Ciro, and knew that I wanted to have my child outside of a hospital setting, yet was not confident to have a home birth. My circumstance was only mildly complicated by my partner Maltbie, who at that time was in the city for work however his home was Hawaii, and he could not guarantee that he would be in town for the birth.

I had friends who were also expecting their first child and they told me of a wonderful place they were going to have their child at called "The Maternity Center." It was a midwife-based practice that only took in "Low Risk" pregnancies. I was 25 that year, a personal trainer and competitive bodybuilder and in the prime of my life. My partner was 32, a recreational athlete who had competed in triathlons back home. Our son would have some of the best potential to be a healthy active child, and I went into the pregnancy knowing that he would be breast-fed once born.

When I had my initial appointment, my best friend Gail volunteered to go with me. She was a massage therapist by trade, and great emotional support. After the medical intake of all practical needs, the midwife looked at me, then my friend and asked rather bluntly, "Is there a man involved in this pregnancy?" We had to laugh out loud. Gail promptly responded, "Well, how do you think she GOT this way?" Apparently, we were mistaken for an "alternative couple" with my long hair and her contrasting short bob cut. Since I was not married to my partner, I was classified as a single parent and referred to their in house social worker for an evaluation. Once I passed that exam, I was accepted into their program.

The months flew by as my belly grew bigger, and I went to all of my exams there at the Maternity Center on 92nd Street, between Park and Madison Avenues. The Building was donated to the center and had been someone's three-story home at one time. It was a beautiful place to have a child. Someone I worked with at the Health Club suggested I read up on the circumcision "controversy" and provided me with literature. I had not considered the alternative up to that point; however, an ultrasound in my 5th month confirmed a male child. My partner did not have an opinion on that subject at the time, so after reading information on both sides of the issue, I decided that my son would not be subjected to what I considered at the time to be a cruel practice.

My Due Date was October 19th, coincidently the same birth date as my partner. I did not go into labor until two weeks later, and had it been a day later would have been referred to a local hospital. I guess the baby knew, and I began going into labor on the 5th of November, I had two friends with cars that were on call for "the time." Holley got me up to the Center, and they sent me home because I hadn't dilated much at that point. My parents and sister were called to head down to the city - Maltbie was out of town.

Gail was by my side, and within twelve hours I was in full-fledged labor, and this time my friend Laura was the driver.

I was in the "Family" room initially, and I had it all planned out. I brought my cassette tape player, some Prince music, and a small bottle of champagne. We ended up being an all woman crew for this birth and my son was the only male present! My midwife, Ann Linden, was checking my progress every 30 minutes or so, and knew I was getting fatigued after 11 hours of heavy contractions.

While I was on the exam table she explained what was going on, and asked me how I was holding up. It was the most intense feeling in the world, I felt my body's responses were beyond my control and was at the mercy of this birth. Gail, now my birth coach, once again reminded me to breathe and massaged my legs and lower back. All of a sudden, my water broke while I was on the table. Ann did a quick jump out of the way just in time.

After that, I was walked to the birthing room. Actually, I waddled, and had to stop every few steps because the contractions got stronger and harder. Midwife on one side and birth coach on the other, I got onto the bed and was lying on my side at first, one leg held up by Gail. By this time, the room had filled with my mother, sister and both Holley and Laura; midwife Ann, along with her very pregnant assistant. Prince was our accompanying music during the entire ordeal.

When the baby's head crowned, they asked me if I wanted to see him and held up a mirror. I remember shouting "NO! I want to see ALL of him!" and they went back to the moment. His shoulders became stuck and he was kicking furiously while they pulled out one arm, then the other. He was a big baby and his chest and head were the same size- 35 mm, no wonder he couldn't get out without their help! They gently pulled him out the rest of the way and laid him on my chest. He was clean as a whistle and had a good hearty cry. My mother got to cut his umbilical cord, and then commented on the size of the placenta as it was dispelled from my body, "It looks like a Liver, so big!" We collectively sized up the new little boy, Ciro William Colelli, a 22 inch, 8 lb. 11 oz. Wonder. He was perfect, his head a bit conical from the passage, and I commented that he looked like a little Aztec baby. He had a Mongolian Spot on his lower back, inherited from his father's Polynesian genetics, lots of hair and all digits perfectly formed. The midwives made a print of his foot, (it measured 2.5 inches), and we waited for the doctor to authenticate the birth, and then I got to go home.

A midwife was dispatched to my home the following day, and she went over nursing techniques with me and did the routine check up. I was fortunate enough that an episiotomy was not needed during the birth, so I recovered quickly. I actively began my workouts again in two weeks, and Ciro thrived on my milk. I nursed him for 9 months total and he was always in the highest percentile for his age and weight.

In retrospect, I am grateful that I had such a problem free birth with my first baby. I am eternally indebted to the Maternity Center for existing as it was a truly special place, the only one of its' kind in Manhattan at that time. When I experienced subsequent post-partum depression, it was Miriam, the Social Worker from the Maternity Center that helped me get through the changes new motherhood would bring. Since that time I have endorsed Midwifery as an alternative to medical birthing where appropriate.

Ciro is now almost 20 years old and lives in Knoxville, TN. I live in Nashville. Maltbie in Oahu, HI.

Parent Assisted Birth

The Birth Of Zoyya Xuxa

By: Laurie Darveau-Willms

I knew I was nearing the last days of my third pregnancy, but felt as though I had a few days left and I was really enjoying what time was left. I wasn't quite ready for the birth and hadn't thought much about how I hoped it would go. A few things were certain though, it would be an unassisted birth, and I would deliver her myself. I had my second son unassisted 19 months earlier and had labored alone and caught him myself while my husband and older child watched. I loved the experience and hoped for something similar.

On the evening of April 21st I started feeling some stronger contractions. They seemed to be fairly rhythmic and I started wondering if perhaps this was the beginning of labor. It was around 10pm and I let Jon know that things might be progressing. I relaxed for a while and worked on some last minute projects to keep myself distracted. I was still hesitant to declare myself in labor, but I was quickly becoming convinced.

Around 11pm the boys started stirring a little in the bedroom. I went in to lay down with them and just enjoyed being snuggled between them. I knew our family was changing and just wanted to enjoy a little time with them. After some pretty strong contractions lying down, I figured it was time just to take a nice relaxing bath and prepare myself for what was to come.

Somewhere between midnight and 1am I decided this was definitely labor and I warned Jon to get some sleep because he would be on full-time Daddy/errand boy duty the next day as I was sure we were going to have a baby by then. He figured that sounded like a good idea and headed off with the assurance that I would wake him if I needed anything.

Happy to have some peace and quiet to deal with the contractions, I busied myself preparing some labor-ade, picking out music and lighting candles. It was getting harder to distract myself and walking was getting harder. It was definitely time to get in the tub for a while. I got in and out of the water and paced around for a while then got back in. The water was nice and it helped some, but the pain was becoming harder to gain control of. I kept reminding myself that I *COULD* do this and I *HAD* done it before. I really enjoyed the quiet of night and was so thankful for another night labor. I loved being alone and hoped no one would wake up just yet.

Around 4:15 am or so I started laboring on the toilet. My poor stomach felt horrible and the contractions were becoming too much. I wasn't sure if I should wake Jon and the boys in case they wanted to watch or if I should wait a while longer. After several contractions I figured I would drain the tub and fill it with fresh water then wake them. I could hear that my younger boy was awake anyway and wanted to be sure he was okay. Sure enough they were all awake and I told Jon it wouldn't be long. They made their way to the living room and I went back to the toilet to deal with another contraction figuring I would fill the tub after that.

Immediately after that contraction was another, then my water burst. I practically leapt off the toilet and into a squat on the bathroom floor. I looked down just in time to see a head full of hair coming out. Before I even had time to think, her slippery little body was in my hands. In shock I yelled out, "She's born!" and Jon and the boys made their way down the hall. Jon immediately began covering the baby with towels and blankets and then got me comfortable to wait for the placenta. I delivered it in a few minutes. The boys just marvelled excitedly at their new sister. After the placenta was delivered Jon held our new daughter while I cleaned myself up a little then we made our way out to the living room, where Jon had set up the futon and prepared a nice little bed for us to get to know our newest member.

After about 30 minutes or so I realized that I was becoming alarmingly dizzy. I was losing gushes of blood every time I moved and was having trouble focusing. I made my way to the bathroom and took some cayenne capsules and cursed the fact that I hadn't picked up any Sheppard's Purse. I nearly passed out and spent what seemed like forever on my hands and knees on the bathroom floor. I had to crawl back to the living room as I couldn't stand. I had Jon bring me some RRL tea and encouraged my toddler to nurse to help the uterus contract. I warned Jon that I thought I was losing too much blood and told him to make sure I didn't pass out.

After a few more minutes it became clear that I had lost far too much blood. I was having a really hard time keeping conscious and so I got Jon to cut off a small piece of the placenta for me to eat. It seemed like almost instantly after I swallowed it I started to feel better. I was very weak, but at least the bleeding was under control. Nature really is amazing to provide such a perfect remedy! After some chlorophyll, lots of fluids, a big meal, and some sleep I am feeling much better.

All in all it was an amazing experience! What a wonderful way for our girl to enter the world. We are thrilled that she was born on Earth Day, seems so fitting for a child of ours.

The official stats are:
Name: Zoyya Xuxa
Born at 4:45am, weight is approx. 9 lbs, beautiful healthy girl

Beautiful Baby Boy

By Valerie Nordstrom

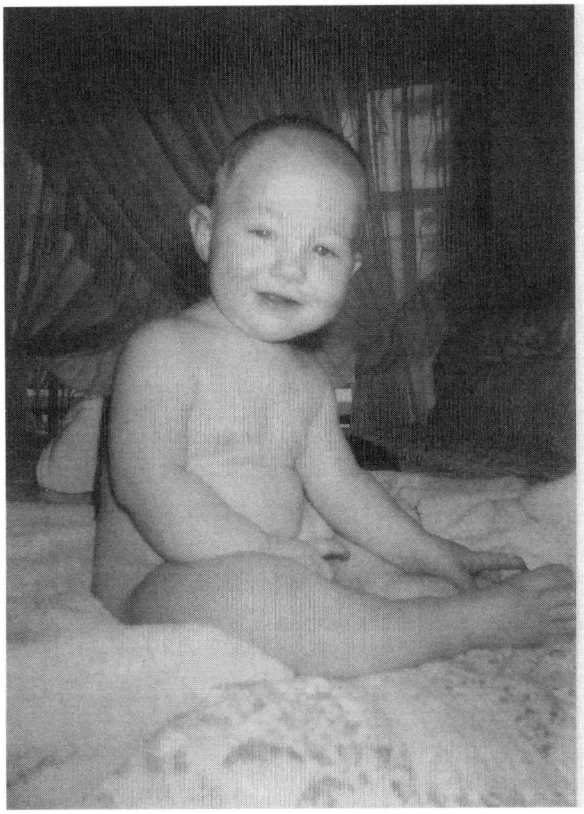

The most beautiful baby in the world was born one night last summer. I am so honored to be his mom. His name is Timothy Dennis, and he makes my heart sing.

Tim was in a hurry to be here, in a rush to be conceived. I didn't understand that and didn't really like it. I was trying to finish my degree and had a baby already and didn't appreciate feeling crowded by some hovering, impatient spirit. While I was still pregnant with Kari, I had dreams about him, and when she was still really little, one Sunday morning in church, I heard, so clearly I wondered if anyone else had heard it, "I'm coming sooner than you think." I thought, "Like heck you are," and shortly felt so claustrophobic I had to get out of the room. There were dreams of a red haired boy born easily and quickly, of a child swirling around my head pestering me. And then it was quiet. I didn't hear a thing as I continued steady progress toward graduation… and then at Christmas time, five months before graduation, I realized I was pregnant. Indeed, sooner than I thought. I had been thinking about babies in terms of "if" not "when." I was ambivalent, but let it be, let it go, and even though I knew it was the red haired boy, I told myself it might be a girl or a different baby. Sure, Val.

As my graduation approached, it looked more and more like I had a basketball under my shirt, but I didn't say anything about it to anyone, and nobody seemed to notice. Until the Monday, my mom called me up and said, "Honey? Can I ask you a personal question?" Ask if you dare, Mom! How many grandchildren do you have now? My mom is good to me. She said that she knew we had so many kids and that she should be worried about my health and be sensible and practical, but really, she could not wait to hug that baby. Every time she has been near him ever since the night of his birth, she has wrapped her arms around him in the biggest bear hug. Tim brings that out in everyone. He's an amazing person, honestly.

The pregnancy was uncomfortable and wonderful at the same time, as if that makes any sense. When my belly finally appeared, it was tight and hard. It felt like the child swelled right under the skin. Right away, I could feel lumps of him, the shape of him turning, and I loved that. The other kids loved it. We played with Tim every day, the older kids poking at the spots wondering if it were a butt or a knee, and when he'd leap they'd say, "He knows we're here!" Often Tim would wake up just by hearing Kari's chirpy voice. I had Charlie horse pains in the curve of the belly every day and every night, and his dad would rub those for me when he was home. He has the warmest hands. Tim seemed to like that too.

I know that women are supposed to eat well while they're pregnant and I did try. Sort of. I was plagued by disgusting, horrible heartburn and also by a fear of how big my baby might grow. One of his brothers weighed ten pounds, and I was nervous about how big Tim might get if he came late, since a couple others had been weeks overdue. All were healthy and fine, but this was on my mind. So between the heartburn and the fear, I tried to not gain too much weight. I am not sure how much I did gain, but it was less than 20 pounds. As my legs and arms got progressively skinnier and skinnier, the belly got rounder and tighter, if that were possible. In the end, I lost ten pounds, and he weighed ten five.

Along about seven months, at the end of June, I decided we should paint the living room and while I was doing that, I injured myself. I stood on a kitchen chair, squatted down on it, reached with my brush to the paint pan on the floor, and then stood up again to paint near the ceiling, over and over. That night when I woke up to and tried to get up and go to the bathroom, I could hardly get out of bed because of the pain in my pubic bone. This is what caused me trouble, between that and the heartburn, for another two months.

We went to the lake in the middle of July until early August and I was so tired, partly because my legs kicked so much at night. I was so tired I actually cried when they brought a kiddy CD along to listen to in the car, stupid Disney music, I was so mad at them; I didn't even make sense to myself. The older girls propped me up the whole vacation, loading and unloading the car, chasing after two year old, rebellious Kari, and helping me with a million little things. In spite of all this though, the most beautiful belly kept on growing. It felt like I could feel the sweetness of Tim radiating right out through my skin. I didn't cover that belly, turned it out to the sun until it was toasted brown. I loved the shape and feel of it, the weight. My grown kids were even drawn to it too; big grown boys would reach out and put a palm against it, asking how the baby was in there. What could I say? The baby is good. He's really good. That belly was so divine I actually had professional black and white photos taken of it. I am a pretty woman, but with Tim living in me, I was so beautiful it wasn't even like being me.

The photographer wrapped me in tulle and a sheet, and in the filtered sunlight of a hot August afternoon, with the sound of kids playing the yard next door to her house, I turned this way and that as she directed me. I could feel Tim's feet sliding around under my hand, and the weight of his head down in the bones of my pelvis. In the photos I look like an angel, not like my normal earthly self at all.

Two weeks before Tim was due, I felt like he was falling out. It felt like he was resting, brow against my sore pubic bone, as low as a baby could go. My skinny brown legs were numb off and on, and yet his feet kicked so hard against my guts that one day I ridiculously wondered if his feet could kick right through the fundus. (I believe this is impossible.) And he still moved lower. For a couple days I wondered if I were trying to go into labor. It felt like it, but it seemed too soon. It felt worse than due. It felt vastly overdue. My creaky pubic bone hurt every step. I felt choked up over Hallmark commercials on TV. I could not do anything with my two year old unless she let me, and the agile little elf was taking major advantage of that fact. If she ran away when it was time to change a diaper, I just left her go until I could catch her when she came close later.

I took my second daughter for her driver's permit test and the parking lot seemed miles away from the testing center. We walked so slowly together, and while I waited (she did pass) I had contractions so sharp I thought they might break that water on the bench as I sat there. On Thursday, I baked and froze birthday cakes for Dan and Heidi, just in case I had the baby before their birthdays in a week. That night I was awakened by contractions every half hour. Thirty minutes on the dot and hard. They'd build until it felt like things were breaking inside, pulling the bones and then a feeling like shattered glass. And then I'd fall back to sleep again until thirty minutes later when the next one would wake me up, dizzy and confused for a minute, and then I'd lie there and try not to move or resist them, breathing slowly or not at all, thinking that if it was going to be like this, I did not want to be pregnant for the rest of the weeks the calendar said it might be.

In the morning, Jay knew I'd been awake more or less most of the night, and he made me promise to call if anything happened. It did not. In fact, as the hazy dawn of the summer morning turned to bright sun, the contractions spaced out again and became less regular. I did things around the house like it was a normal day until around lunchtime when I kept having to stop for contractions that kept coming back. About 1 pm, I went into the bedroom to lie down on the bed. I thought if I could rest—I felt so tired. I turned on the TV, but as the contractions came, the chatter and singing about mops and laundry soap irritated me, so I put the closed captioning on and muted the volume. Then I could just open or close my eyes if I felt like it and not have to hear the noise. The kids came and went from the room, but I was boring, just lying there. About 3 pm, I fetched a Popsicle from the freezer and sat up to eat it, and the contractions were icky. They hurt. Some of them made me dizzy and my mouth water in a really nauseous way. When Tim would give a good lurch with his head down and feet up, the bounce against the cervix would trigger a series of strong contractions. I started thinking maybe I would have my baby born by morning. By 4 pm I was trying not to move a whisker, trying to not trigger any contractions I could avoid.

The older boys were home from work by then and stood around in the bedroom, trying to make small talk, and each of the kids must have offered me food at least once. I had someone hand me the phone and called Jay and said come home now. Please, whatever, just get home. I really wanted all the kids to go so I could have the space to myself and Jay 3. To be holding my baby. Jay came home about 5, and as soon as he showed up, the older kids took the younger ones and they all went over to my parents' for the evening, maybe overnight. Along about 4, I'd told the girls to pack pajamas for the little kids, and they came and kissed me and wished me good luck. I was so touched by that—wishes of luck and the offers of food, them mothering me.

As soon as they left, and Jay went to take a shower, I started walking around the house, thinking, "Okay. Bring it on. I want my baby." I knelt on the couch for some of them, face on the arm of the couch, breathing. Come on out baby; just let's do this. I walked up and down the length of our long living room and dining room and thought I wish I could just push him out now. We boiled the scissors and cord ties, watched the news, and about 6:00, my water broke when I was sitting on the bed watching the news. Since my jeans were now all wet, I thought I'd go hop in the tub for a minute and then get into a nightgown. Jay came in there in a little while, and sat on the lid of the toilet and ate a ham sandwich. He talked to me and kept me company as the contractions rolled by over and over, and wished I could just push the baby out now. I thought to myself, after a really intense one that had that rough feeling like a skinned knee feels, only inside, that if I had 20 more contractions, I would undoubtedly be closer to the birth. I could do this. The water was nice, since I could more all around in it, this way and that, sitting, leaning back, leaning forward, however I felt like moving.

Shortly Jay started muttering to me about getting out. "Do you want to go to the bed?" "Do you think you should get out now?" etc. etc. I said no, thinking I was going to miserable wherever I was at that point, what really would be the difference? He said things looked "really puffed," that's why he was concerned. I put a hand over my vulva and thought it didn't seem any more puffed than it had for the last month, so what was he talking about? On the 5th contraction of the 20 I was counting, I realized Tim was coming out. He was sliding right on down and oh my, my body was pushing.

Jay leaped up and said, "You're not having that baby right here in the bathtub, are you?" I answered, "Yes I am," and had another surge of pushing energy coming at me. I stood up so my baby wouldn't fall in the water and was looking at where I could move to on the floor, in case Jay had to go for a shoulder. I pushed again and Jay was kneeling in front of the tub, trying to peer between my legs, saying he could see the head, and I could certainly feel the baby's hair as I put my hand across there. As I pushed again, I asked if the head were out and he said it was, and he tried to feel for a cord. It was looped across Tim's back. I opened my eyes and could see his wrinkled wet head, hair all swirled, and his wet, lavender shoulder. Feeling the cord with my fingers, I tried to slip it toward Tim's head. Jay said it was loose and he could just come through it, so I pushed again and our four hands caught this sprawling, long armed boy!! As we caught him, a big splash of bloody water fell into the bath. Slippery baby felt everywhere, his arms and legs flew out straight, reminding me of a starfish as he spun above the water. That pure sense of giddy exhilarated joy washed over me as we caught him. I had seen his tiny penis as he tumbled out into our hands. We turned him over, anxious to see his sweet, beautiful face. "Awww, Darling. It's you, Timothy." My tears went onto his head.

I knelt back down on my knees in the water with Tim cradled in my hands on my lap, and we rubbed him and told him how much we loved him, waiting for him to say something. He was gasping and gulping and seemed a little startled, but soon he found his voice and gave a squawk. The pinkness bloomed from his chest and was already spreading across his face. I could not stop saying, "Oh my God, Timothy, oh my God…" over and over like a prayer. Jay's arm was around me and he wondered how we would get from the bathroom to the bed. We were both dripping wet and naked. Should he carry us? I told him I thought if we went now, we could walk. If we sat there too long, I'd become a sandbag and not be able to move, but I could go now. I slid Tim up higher and we headed down the hall to the bed and waited while Jay threw down some towels for the bleeding and then still connected, Tim and I flopped onto the pillows. Jay covered us up and Tim was bawling loudly and I was still gasping, "Oh, Oh, I can't believe this," and all those months of waiting and limping around and loving that brown belly… here he was in my arms, yelling.

We called the kids at my parents house and put the phone up to Tim's yelling out to all of us. They were excited and Kari said, "Tim-fee, in a baff-tup?" The older kids told me my dad was verklempt on hearing we'd named the Tim's middle name Dennis, after him. We'd talked about it, and it wasn't a secret, but I guess my dad hadn't been in on any of those conversations? James was delighted to have a brother with a name that matched his: "Jimmy and Timmy!" he chortled. The news told to the ones who needed to hear it, I lay back on the pillows with my boy in my arms and just breathed, trying not to cry along with Tim. Jay flopped onto the bed next to me, talking to Tim, telling him how glad we were he was born and that he was our Tim, calling him 'Big Guy' and making consoling noises. I tried to comfort him, but Tim was upset. I hugged him close and patted his hip, wishing I could do more to reassure him that this was all good here.

In a little while I helped him get started nursing and that made him feel better. We were warm under the covers and Jay brought me something to drink and we hugged our baby. The afterpains hurt so much. They radiated from my uterus to my pubic bone and down both legs to the knees. But we had Percodan tablets left over from the some dental problem, so that helped in a little while. Eventually, shortly before my parents and the kids came back, the placenta came out and we cut Tim's cord. We caught the placenta in the same special bowl we've used before, the pink one from the 50s, shaped like a leaf with sparkly gold trim, and we tied his cord with colorful embroidery floss.

The kids and their grandparents, my parents, came pouring into our room until it was full of people who love Tim. We trimmed his cord and everyone held him. The smiles were a mile wide on every face. There was the most boundless joy in that room as all those other beloved babies welcomed this one. Dan balanced the scale, we got Tim's weight, and then the girls handed me things while I dressed him. My mom sat on the foot of the bed, holding Kari, my "old" baby, and it was just the most perfect evening, possibly the most wonderful evening of a lifetime. I'd imagined I'd have my baby by morning, never even considered by 7:00! Eventually we'd taken all the pictures we could and everyone had kissed Tim at least ten times, and my parents took the kids back to their house for a sleepover, so Jay, Tim and I could sleep late in the morning. The oldest boys went to their apartment in the city and a wonderful birthday party was over for the night. Jay went with me to the bathroom so I could check on the bleeding and put on a pad. He knelt in the doorway and talked to Tim while I took care of this. After one other birth I fainted, so I wanted him close by the first time I got up on my feet. Then he put us both of us back to bed and went to a 24-hour place and got food. We ate a little celebratory feast in bed and then went to sleep. I put Tim on my pillow, nose to nose with me, so I wouldn't have to look far for him whenever I wanted to see him. All I had to do was open my eyes.

In the days and weeks that followed I was so tired that I felt disoriented and emotional most of the time. I don't know why, but the postpartum was not any easier than the pregnancy. I was short of breath, and weepy, and my pubic bone ached like a big bruise would. My legs often kicked involuntarily at night, keeping me awake far more than Tim did. But Tim was so beautiful, red fuzzy hair, milky skin, burly shoulders, and so incredibly sweet in my arms. He smiled at four days. He drank milk and then would throw his head back, full, and it felt like abundance defined. He's three months old and I still can't put him down. I don't want to put him down. I hold him all night long because he's completely delicious and I can't waste a moment of this on something as mundane as sleeping.

The other kids adjusted quickly to him, only seeming stressed once in a while, nothing troublesome at all. As two months arrived, I felt my old brain returning, and though I'm glad to have it back, I would gladly live this whole summer over again, just to sun that gorgeous belly one more time, to feel those long arms moving around under my skin, to push that sprawling boy baby out, standing in my bathtub, to hold him, bawling in my arms…to see the huge grins on the faces of the others as they filled our bedroom that night, welcoming their new brother… I've been to the top of the mountain. I've touched the sun. I've kissed the cheeks of Timothy. I'm laughing, but it's true. Nothing could ever lift me higher, there is no finer view than the view I've seen from this peak.

First Child, Born at Home, In Water, into Mother and Father's own Hands

by: Elizabeth and Barry Dehaan

Anna was born in our living room on January 11, 2005. She was delivered out of the womb into warm water and her father's open arms. She cried just enough to clear her lungs then opened her bright eyes to gaze at her parents. A perfect little girl and a blessing from God. Her father and I had decided she would be born this way months before. We chose to have an unassisted home birth because we believe that is what God would want from us; to put our complete trust in the One who had created the miracle of this child in the first place.

One thing I had told myself during pregnancy was that I could not allow fear to be present during labor and delivery. I often prayed that God would remove all fear and help me to put my complete trust in him. Still I am surprised at how calm I was through it all. My water broke at about 5:30 AM after sleeping all night through light contractions. I rested and didn't wake my husband until later when I felt like we ought to call my brother-in-law and his wife. They were going to drive 3 hours to come and help out with the birth.

That morning, when the contractions were light and sporadic, I cleaned the house and prepared both mentally and physically for the baby's arrival. I even thought of making some bread to have while family was here. I had prepared myself mentally for a long labor, but around 10 AM the force and length of the contractions increased and I realized that making fresh bread would be out of the question.

Family arrived around noon. They helped out that afternoon by making sure I ate and drank, checking the water temperature in the tank, and keeping the atmosphere calm and relaxing. We had a fire in the fireplace and Enya playing softly in the background. Soon after they arrived I felt like getting into the birthing tank to see if it would ease the pain of the contractions. The warm water was so relaxing that it seemed the contractions actually went away for a while, but they eventually came back in full force and I was feeling the urge to push.

The position that was most comfortable for me was on my knees with my head in my arms, leaning on the side of the tank. My husband was in the tank with me. He was rubbing my back, encouraging me, and checking the position of the baby. I pushed with my entire body, including my lungs. At the time I did not realize that I was making much noise, but watching the video afterwards I am embarrassed at how loud I truly was. I was groaning with every push. At one point my bag of waters was bulging. I instructed my husband to break it and as soon as he did there was the crown of Anna's head and visible hair. My husband would go under the water wearing goggles to check her progress. It seemed like no time at all and Anna was out and we were holding her.

She was born a little before 3 PM. We were surprised that she was a girl, for some reason we had thought we were going to have a boy. It was a good surprise. She was pink, alert and healthy. I felt no pain immediately afterwards despite the fact that I bled quite heavily and had several small tears. We kept the placenta attached to Anna for a few hours and then dad tied and cut the cord. I remember how Anna would just stare up at us, too distracted to nurse right away. She was and still is a very wide eyed little girl.

I look back on the delivery and I am shocked at how long it lasted. To me it seemed like only a few hours. I don't even remember the pain, as if I was disconnected from my body for a short period of time and I immediately returned as soon as Anna was born. I feel so blessed that we were able to have Anna at home and in water. I can not imagine trying to concentrate on delivering a baby and then having to deal with strangers poking, prodding, and asking questions all the time. Not to mention the cold, harsh environment that Anna would have had to enter. We were able to hold and comfort her immediately. I like to think that is partly why she is such a peaceful happy baby and a blessing to our family.

A few examples of pregnancy, labors and births, I was invited, and honored, to attend. Patience and faith is, and always will be, the key to successful birth outcomes throughout time.

A Scary Start

One of my dearest friends, Catherine, had a heavy bleed in her fourth month of pregnancy. She sent a neighbor over to get me. I got a note that was left at my door an hour or so later. The note said "come quick!" Cat was bleeding. She was four months pregnant at the time, and living in an RV while building her home.

The midwife she had at the time could not make it for some reason or another. I grabbed my little herb bag and doppler and drove full-speed to her home. Meeting her partner on the road, he not knowing what was going on yet, I flagged him down to tell him briefly that I got this note; we all fled up the mountain to their little trailer, where Cat was waiting … I found her in a shambles: bleeding and crying, we got her down and pillows under her legs in the shock position, head low and legs higher. Her partner told her he was sorry that this was happening and stood aside while she and I talked about the events that took place before the bleeding began.

She was afraid, of course, that she would lose the baby. We spoke quietly about how she really did not want the baby in the beginning because of the relationship not being so good, we then discussed what she wanted now, what was her wish for this baby? Her true feelings came out; she wanted the baby but felt bad that she was not happy in her present situation.

I checked the baby's heart tones and they were fine, we made a batch of tea with some wild yam and false unicorn, I suggested she take some herbal iron and vitamin C&E for a few days.

The emotional healing that needed to take place, we believe, came out in this bleeding episode. I suggested getting an ultrasound, if that was what they wanted to do, to determine the cause of the bleeding. She tried, but because she was planning a home birth, the doctor wouldn't give her one. Her faith grew, and she left it up to the universe to decide what would happen. During the rest of her pregnancy, she and I worked together every few weeks with massage and affirmations, dietary changes and good humor.

She never had any more bleeding, gave birth to her daughter full term, and had a quick and easy birth, which I almost missed because it happened so fast. Her partner caught the baby girl, born early on a cold January morning weighing the same as her big brother, 6lbs 8oz.

We never found out what caused the bleeding, but that same year, another community member bled in her fourth month also, and we did the same thing as with my friend to try and figure out the bleeding dilemma, but soon her bleeding stopped as well, and she too had a healthy baby at term, also a girl.

So to conclude this particular scenario, it's difficult to say what may happen. Mother Nature has her own reasons, and sometimes it's up to us to have trust and faith in whatever happens. Sometimes there are no physical reasons, maybe they are spiritual or mental. Both moms had emotional issues with their partners, both were stressed out and both had bleeding around the same time and same month as one another, I really can't say what that's about, but sometimes I see similarity in peoples' situations around the same time with pregnancy and birth.

Maybe it's the planets way of reaching us and opening our eyes a bit more to what it is we really need to be focusing on within our lives.

Cat with Cedarrose, and Khensu a day after her birth

Breech Birth Stories

One year, within six months, I had the honor to witness three breech births. It was definitely a pop quiz to how much I really had been listening to my teachers over the years. Only 3-4% of all full-term babies are breech. All three of these moms had their babies within two days of their estimated due date, and one on his due date. I felt blessed to be invited and share in these breech experiences with the parents.

Seventh Baby, third Breech Natural Birth

(It was too dark to see in the water pool, but we think she was a footling breech)

This breech was obvious to me, the baby had settled into the breech position about a couple of months before her arrival. Not really abnormal, since most babies remain breech until a few weeks before birth. So I thought nothing of it at first. By 36 weeks, the baby was still breech. It is possible a breech baby will turn within the last few weeks--or even up until the day of labor--but because of this moms previous history with breeches I felt this needed attention. The mother is tall and thin, so it was apparent through her belly with a huge hard mass at the top of her uterus. She had already given birth to 6 children, the first two being breech and born naturally. So I had no doubt she could do it. The mother was also RH-, therefore we did not want to try and manually turn the baby, this is in case of placental separation (Rh- contraindication) and did not feel it was worth the risk. I feel babies know the way they need to be born, there is always a reason we may not understand but should trust. She tried to do "tilts" twice a day for fifteen minutes each time. At one point, we thought the baby had turned head down, but I realized that she was still breech. The parents however did not believe me (they were a little bit in denial at that point).

The mom phoned me in the early evening in September to let me know her labor had started, and it was only a few days away from her "Due Date," I went over and checked on things, made teas, herbal packs for her perineum, and folded some clothes. Soon enough, a bunch of her friends showed up and filled the house, not only with all the parent's kids but other peoples' kids as well, and a lot of women were running around helping to prepare for the birth. I think that was the only birth I have ever attended that had so many onlookers--30 people or more! Everyone cooperated and joined in the bedroom to support her. The birth pool was set up and all was ready to go. Her labor got intense right away and she moved into the birth pool, expressing herself freely. At one point she asked me if making love would help, I thought it wouldn't be a problem (Amniotic sac intact) and so we all went out to give them some privacy.

I held guard at their door while others tried to enter the sacred domain, I held them back, no one else really knew what was going on except that we had all left the room. The eldest son, who was also born breech 15 years prior, was making his mom and dad tea, everyone present was working in harmony!

After about fifteen minutes, mom called us back into the room and asked us to all gather around for support. One loud sound came from her, and I looked down and saw a torso and legs floating in the water, another midwife from Cambodia was there, and she was freaking out, yelling "that's not right!" It was her first birth in the States and her first water birth, and as she was a hospital midwife this was very different for her. I tried to keep calm and centered, which was not easy with everyone crowding me and a midwife yelling at me in a different language, but I managed to keep my calm while the father helped support the baby's body, we moved to a standing squat since the baby was still not out, and I had to do a maneuver to get to the arms. Then once arms were out, her head followed immediately. Mom sucked her nose and mouth out with her own mouth, the baby took a few shallow breaths, but was still a little limp. We gave her a small breath just once over her mouth and nose, and she cried to let us know she was alright. She just stared around while mom and baby relaxed on their bed and nursed. We let the cord stay attached, as I encourage with all babies, and detached it the next day.

All was well and no problems postpartum. Seventh baby, third natural breech, baby girl: 7lbs 14oz.

Great Job Guys !

A first-time mom gives birth to her 9lb breech baby at home

This second breech was more of a surprise. This was the first child of a young active couple in their mid-thirties. They had sought me out after meeting another one of my clients that had given birth in water a few months before. She phoned me, and we connected well. We started working together soon after that. Her prenatal course was straightforward. She was healthy, willing to educate herself and do homework, very active, had a good attitude towards birth and was fun loving.

She was eating well, sticking to her vegetarian diet and adding some fish now and then. When she phoned me to come over a day before her "Due Date" to see if she was really in labor, I went over and sure enough things were happening. It was slow and relaxing the first day, their friends showed up and video taped us hanging out and eating. The mom and dad also tried to get some rest, relaxing and cuddling a lot. Since this was their first baby, I encouraged a lot of that. My assistant and I left for a while but stayed in contact, I felt it would be best to give them some privacy with their friends. Later that afternoon we were called back and hung out, things were still moving along, but slowly. All night we rested and kept an ear and eye open for sounds of progress, but mom was pretty quiet and relaxed, cuddling with her husband the whole evening until dawn.

We awoke, or half of us were already awake, before the sun came up. Mom was in good active labor. We waited, and by early afternoon we all went and took a nap. It seemed like we all drifted off together to another time in space. I heard Mom say, after about a half an hour, "My water broke!" and I sat up from a dead sleep, and we were all excited; she seemed fine and happy, the baby sounded good, the water was clear and all was well. We ate lunch, cleaned and went to town to do errands and to give them some space so that, once again, they could rest without us hanging over their heads.

When we returned, they wanted me to see what was happening in there so I looked. To my surprise, I saw a lot of black goop (meconium, the baby's first poop). I also saw a very well-fitted bottom behind the poop. So I stepped back for a moment and took some deep breaths before saying a word. Everyone was calm and collected as I presented the situation's new twist.

Everything was well--other than the baby was coming breech. She was fully dilated, and the bottom of the child fitted well with room to spare, so there was no immediate danger to either of them. Both parents were calm and did not seem to feel it was an emergency, and I was willing to support them as long as things kept going well. Therefore, we decided to rest some more until mom felt like pushing, but all that came was more poop! She lay against her husband for hours, flowing with her expansions and never obviously "losing it." One time, I just told her, if she really wanted to have the baby, to go sit on the toilet for a few expansions; she did for one and came back and expressed not feeling ready that it was too intense, so we all waited patiently for things to happen. Another few hours went by, after checking inside by opening her labia just a "smidge," we could see that the bottom was crowning from the slightest baring down effort from Mom.

She needed to become more emotionally ready, and we supported her in that. I also believe that the baby needed to poop more before he would be able to come through. Although all this time had passed, from the first realization of the breech presentation, never did the baby's heart rate sound in distress nor did either parent have any overwhelming sense of fear.

Both friends and father cheered mom on while she attempted some test pushes, we watched the bottom slide out and back in a few times, but still we needed to have patience for a bit longer so she could stretch little by little and get emotionally ready. At about twelve hours after full dilation, mom went to the toilet and finally felt the bottom coming down into her hands, the whole time she was calm and centered with little obvious pain, we helped her back to the bed where she would be more comfortable and supported by her dear husband. Within a minute, the bottom and legs came out; I supported the body with some towels and felt for arms. The cord was pulsing well and the baby's color was pretty good, so when the next expansion came, we cheered mom to push the rest of baby out; she expressed that she couldn't do it any longer, but we all cheered, "You can do It!" I had to find the arms and rotate the body a bit, then one arm came down, then the next.

About another minute passed, I could see the baby making a breathing motion and told mom to bare down while I did some fundal pressure to help, but still no head! Another few seconds had passed, and I got her to the edge of the bed to try and let the baby's head flex a bit before trying again. I finally decided, after the baby attempted breathing again, to do a small episiotomy, and as soon as I did that his little face appeared and out he came.

The cord pulsing great the whole time, but he was a bit limp for a minute. After massaging him, talking to him, and suctioning almost 9cc worth of fluid from his airway, he breathed on his own. At the point of doing the snip (first time ever doing one) I had my assistant call 911 for back-up (first time for that also) because my O2 tank was not working for some reason. By the time they showed up a few minutes after we called, he was fine. He was warm, breathing and wide-awake with great color and reflex--all within a few minutes of birth. The head EMT was a woman (thank you Goddess!), and she came in gently and just hung out and watched as I did baby and placenta exams. I had them take mom and baby to the hospital a few hours later for suturing (since I had not done a cut before, I felt she would benefit from having more experienced "suturers" do the job). Also with some breech babies there can be birth trauma, and I was exhausted. Because of the long and hard birth, I also felt that it would be best if the doctor they had been seeing during the pregnancy looked at him. So they went and everyone was fine. When they came back a couple hours later, they told me about the doctor yelling at them for doing the breech birth at home, but he also said they were fine and that they did a good job. Wow! A compliment from doctor!

First baby boy born breech at home 9lbs (could have been 10 before all that pooping!).

We were all born breech at home!

Another "kind of" surprise breech birth

This next one was another kind of surprise. I say 'kind of' because I had worked with this couple for another one of their births, and we felt comfortable with each other while knowing there was something a little different about this pregnancy. This mom was expressing to me during the last part of the pregnancy that it "felt" different then the other two kids she had. We discussed that the baby could very well be breech and that they usually will turn by 34-38 weeks or so. She felt confident in her abilities to birth, and I too felt confident that she would be able to birth her baby, whichever way the baby chose to be born. I palpated but could not absolutely determine the position. Some babies are tricky, but it was lying long and not sideways--that's the most important fact--as long as they're up and down and not twisted around they'll come through.

Well this moms' labor began also the day before her Due Date. She phoned, and I went over. Her last labor was on Thanksgiving, and we all ate and hung out with the family patiently awaiting the birth. This time, it was on the birthing Mother's, Mother's birthday (Grandma). So they anticipated a double celebration. But like the last labor, this one was slow going. Unlike the last, labor her water did not break early on. We had set up the pool weeks before so it was ready. Dad came home from work and mom was reading the kids to sleep while I quietly puttered around the house getting things organized. My partner was next door at the Grandmothers' house putting her kids to bed (a 2yr old and a 7yr old).

Time went by and labor progressed. At about 11pm, mom was feeling strong expansions that led her in and out of the birthing pool several times. I was listening while resting nearby; my partner came and took over so I could go in the bedroom and center myself for a while. Mom and dad got into the pool for some really intense expansions. At about 2 am mom wanted me to check her in the back room, and when I did her bag broke, then it came on full force with every expansion she felt more pressure. Mom expressed to me that it felt different, she couldn't explain it, it just did. Not a bad different, just strange. So when she said that, I remembered the breech conversation we had a month before. I was curious to see what was happening so in-between a pushy expansion, I looked, without having to really look too hard, and saw a bit of poop and knew the baby was going to be breech. I didn't say anything since all was moving so fast and so well. The next few expansions, with mom and dad in pool, I asked them to feel down there and tell me what it felt like. The dad said, "Well, it doesn't feel like a head, it's smooshy!" That was the only clue I could give them since mom was so deep in her birth dance I did not want to break it. The next expansion came quickly and mom wanted to stand up, so she got out of the pool and with one smooth push the baby came out, first the bottom, then legs, arms and head, all into my hands, all within a few seconds. Grandma watched with her eyes wide, and my partner and her 2 yr old daughter (who didn't go to sleep), also watched in amazement as we handed the baby up into mom's arms. I told her "he came out backwards, by the way," she was relieved and said, "That's why it felt so different! (giggling)" I apologized for not saying anything, and she thanked me because she was concentrating so hard and doing so well instinctually that she didn't need the distraction of knowing. All was well, and everyone was happy with the experience. Baby Boy born breech at home, 8lb 2oz.

A Long Awaited Birth

I had a couple move in with me after one year of living in my community. They had just married and the Mom already had two other children with her. They wanted me to be their birth assistant/educator and to live with me while they built their home. I thought it was fine and took them all on.

It was not easy living with clients. Although I had done this before, their circumstances were difficult for me to handle, and I was having difficulties of my own at the time. Their "Due Date" was for "Mother's Day" and they felt they were having a boy.

Now, "Due Dates" are something I do not hold onto, nor do I encourage my clients to hold onto them because they can be so off that people tend to get to anxious and worry when a date does not work out the way they had planned. So after seeing this mom's growth was not consistent with the due date, I expressed that it could be way off. They felt they were right on with that date, so I took a step back.

I was patient for them, but they were getting very impatient. Three weeks before the "Due Date," I realized that we needed to work on a lot more patience because the baby was not anywhere near being ready. We counseled and worked on affirmations that the baby was indeed not ready and to gather more patience. The "Due Date" came and went. Friends, who came for the birth, came and went.

Finally on the morning of "Fathers Day," I got a call. Mom was in labor, and I went to my home to check on her (I was living in a converted school bus out on some land I had bought for awhile to give them space). When I got there early that morning, mom was in the bathtub in good, active labor; the father was asleep upstairs and our other roommate, an English woman, was with her. I asked our house-mate to go get the dad and tell him this was finally it! Mom was in her labor dance and doing great! I waited outside the bathroom to give mom and dad some space. Mom came out a half an hour later and knelt down in front of me by the couch. As her baby crowned, I reached for the father's hands to bring them to his baby's head, but he didn't understand what I was trying to do, so he just looked at me funny and continued to focus on the mother's face. Soon the baby slid into my hands and out she came, mom turned to gather her baby into her arms and all was well. So much for a baby boy on Mother's Day--they got a beautiful baby girl on Fathers Day, not overdue at all. Just on time!

"An Unexpected Home Birth"

Mati's Birth story ~ (My version)

A friend of mine, Mati, was planning a hospital birth. Her last baby was born in the hospital, but Mati expressed really disliking what had happened there with her and the baby. She was 38 at that time with her first one, and they did all sorts of tests on her and induced her labor, it just was not fun sounding. The next pregnancy, a few years later, she was with a new man and had a different life. She felt better prepared than the last pregnancy, and gathered herbal tinctures and did affirmations, kept me 'up to date' when I would see her from time to time, about what was happening. I supported her in doing her birth her way, whatever that was. I even offered to go with her to the hospital if she wanted me to, even though I really dislike that scene.

One day she phoned and asked me if I thought her "symptoms" of labor were true labor. I told her sometimes labor comes on slow and moves over a few weeks or days, and that she was probably doing something in there.

That evening I went to bed with my phone because my intuition told me too. We had never "officially" talked about a home birth at all. The phone rang at 3 am in the morning and it was Mati, she had a sound in her voice that made me feel it was happening now! She asked me to come over to assess things and see if she was in real labor, so I did. When I arrived, she was in the bath with her husband by her side flowing fast with her expansions and doing well. After a few minutes I gathered my basic bags from the car and came back in, her husband knelt beside the tub and was totally calm and collected with her every move. I just asked her if she wanted to still go to the hospital because, if so, it was a forty-five minute drive and she seemed to be very close to giving birth. It was also very snowy out, and I really didn't feel she would even make it there, but I also felt it was up to them to make that decision, so Mati and her husband decided to do a dilation check and then figure it out.

After a few more really intense expansions, she got out of the bath for me to check her. I found her to be at about 8cm and fully effaced, I told her, and she and her husband decided they were not going anywhere.

Her husband expressed his feelings that he didn't really like the doctor anyway, and he was hoping for a home birth secretly. So here I am unplanned and "in the raw." But I felt because I knew Mati as my friend already, it would be fine. I felt that she would do great! It was a few minutes past since I had checked her, and we wanted to clean the bath properly for the birth, so she got out and went into the living room. I started to get the bath clean, and she called me in, the dad was also busy trying to get some towels together and didn't have enough time to gather everything in the room, since they were not planning a home birth everything was a bit scattered.

Her husband and myself supported her in "hands and knees position" and after another few minutes I could see the head starting to crown, then a hand popped up beside the baby's face. I helped the dad hold her head and I held the hand so it wouldn't pop out too fast. We then realized the cord was wrapped around her hand and face and shoulders, so dad and I caught her together and unraveled the cord quickly and calmly. Mom turned around quickly to take her baby up into her arms and held her cheek to cheek, caressing and kissing her. The parents felt so great after the birth, they decided to call the hospital to let them know they just had their baby! Mom called while dad and I dressed and warmed their new baby girl, and then they went off to get checked for any tearing we thought she might have from her previous episiotomy.

They called me the next day happy and satisfied with very little to repair on her perineum, and their baby needed a bit of warmth from being out in the cold, but other than that they felt great and had a growing experience, and were glad they went with the flow, following their intuition …

A Cyst, Tubal Ligation, RH- Mom and a great Parent Assisted Water Birth

When I first moved to my town, I received a couple wanting to do their own birth after finding out they had a miracle happen. I decided to serve them the best I could, the way they wanted.

Before this couple knew they were pregnant, the mom had excruciating pain in her pelvis. Going to the hospital they found a cyst on one of her fallopian tubes and a 9 week fetus in her womb. Being that the operation needed to take place immediately, they forewarned the mom and dad that she may lose the baby during the operation, and to make matters worse, mom was Rh- making the risk even greater for the baby because dad was Rh+. So during the operation to remove the cyst, they witnessed a miracle.

The baby's heart rate went down to less than 60 beats per minute for a long period of time, and he survived. Mom and dad decided that this little miracle would be born into their own hands.

I met with them every few weeks, and we studied everything they needed to know about pregnancy and birth so they could have the experience they wanted. Being their first baby, they had a lot of questions and wanted to know as much as possible about what to do if 'what ifs" came their way. I felt good about working with them because they had such a great faith in their Creator and told them I would be available if they should need me for anything. The day came when I got the call that they had a water birth, and their baby boy was healthy and fine. There were no complications, and mom felt great. I went to visit them that day and said "hello" to the little miracle baby born at home in water, into mother's own hands.

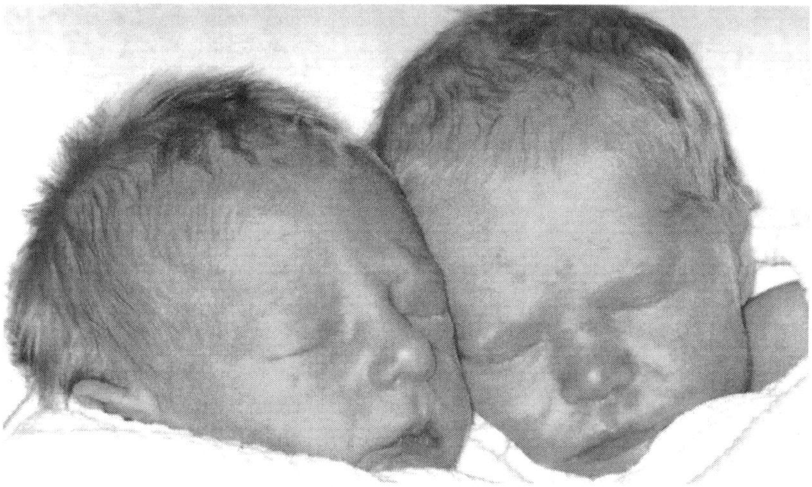

The births of baby Asher and Willow, fraternal twins.

A test of Faith, Trust and Time.....

I was honored to work with this couple on their first birth journey. We had no idea in the very beginning that there were two little blessings about to be born. We gathered every few weeks and watched as mama's belly grew fast. At 22 weeks or so I felt that there could be two in there and expressed my feelings to the mama and papa. They were shocked to find through an ultrasound that, indeed there were two instead of the one they thought. After discussing birth options and talked to the doctor they had gotten the ultrasound from, they knew they wanted their babies to be born at home without medical science interfering.

We worked on affirmations, visualizations, watched numerous films of birth, Psalm and Zoya's UC birth helped affirm this mother's capabilities to herself. This was their first birth, so there were many things to go over and questions to answer about twin variations of normal and also what "ifs."

I received the call on Monday morning of the 27th of March, at 7am. Mamas water broke. She is five weeks early. I went over to check on things, since sometimes twins especially early will come fairly fast. I got there and the mama was having sensations about ten minutes apart. She and I discussed the early concern, and they wanted to stay home and go with the flow.

Most babies at this stage will be able to breath on their own, though it varies, so we were diligent to make sure we had all of our O2 and resuscitation things ready in case. The house was warmed by a woodstove, about 90 degrees on an average, which also contributes to less stress on newborns, and keeps them from having respiratory difficulties.

About a few hours later she was already fully dilated and in very active labor. The birth "team" set up everything we needed and one of us went to town to get a few more things for her, that she had not gotten for the birth yet, thinking it would be another few weeks at least.

Later that evening she got to the feeling of pushing. Her tailbone hurt immensely and she wanted her friend who is a massage therapist to come and do some essential oils and counter pressure. Once her friend came she had some relief, but it took many turns and time to get the tailbone out of the way for the baby to come through. We kept this woman on "duty" for the rest of the birth.

She mentioned many times that she could not imagine doing this in a hospital setting, and that no one would "let" her labor as long as she did at home, gently with patience. Also to her amazement, she was extremely high on her endorphins and adrenalin. She enjoyed the sensations of her body's natural abilities to help her through the long labor(s) and births.

With lots of support, many resting periods, nourishment, hydration, encouragement, and many hours of reaffirming that her body was working and that she was progressing, she finally felt an urge to push her baby into the world. Exhausted, but still aware of her bodies cues to birth her baby. Once she knew what efforts she made, the intensity of them and consistency, she then had the right sounds and motions to get her baby out. This takes time for most first time moms to find within themselves the strength of the body and waves of movement.

This birth took in total about 21 hours from start to so-called finish. We were all exhausted by the wee hours of the morning, when finally at 2:50am on March 28th, little baby Asher, a boy, came into the world with his cord wrapped tightly a few times around his body, making him look like a mummy as he was being born. The papa held his son talking to him and welcoming him as he emerged into the world, slowly and gently we all helped untangle the cord as he slipped out of her body. Asher's eyes were opened and he breathed right away and actually had a 10 apgar. He was very small, no fat, skin almost transparent from being early. He weighed 4 lbs 12 oz.

We checked the second baby, Willow, and her heart rate seemed to be affected by the birth of her brother, possible shared placenta, so we decided to tie and cut Asher's cord, we were waiting to see if that needed to happen, and it did. They wanted a Lotus birth if possible, but knew that it was a possibility that we would have to detach the first baby if the second had any signs of distress. Asher did not flinch as we gently tied and cut his cord. He was alert and awake the whole time, calm and conscious. I think he just knew that his sibling needed the extras of his side of the placenta could give her while she was still inside. This made it a very smooth transition for him to be on his own.

Mama's labor seized. At 5am as the sun was just peering over the horizon, just enough for us to go out and take a break and pray that the second baby would come soon. We all needed to rest and recuperate catching a second wind before the next birth. Baby Willow's heart rate was always seemingly good, but no labor continued.

Mama, Papa and all of us decided to again, go with the flow, since rushing things may cause the second baby to become distressed, and also we didn't know yet if she was still breech or if they shared the same placentas, and a lot of other factors contributing to the labor stopping. As long as she sounded good, in there we would wait.

We waited all day into the evening. I had read in a few old obstetric books within my studies, that some twins will come hours or even days apart, so I was not too worried. I was exhausted but did not feel it was an immediate emergency. We did discuss the option of transporting, but at this time, things were not seemingly in a situation that would actually benefit anyone to go to the hospital, so we stayed with the natural flow and kept our faith intact.

Mama, Papa and new baby had time to adjust and get to know one another. They cuddled and nursed as best as they could, being still pregnant that was a bit difficult for them, but my helper had milk still, so she took over now and then to give the new one some nourishment. He needed something to keep him hydrated. He pooped a bunch of Mec, and was finally content.

After many hours of rest, nourishment and recuperating, by 5pm on the 28th, we all sat down and discussed the possibility of transporting, since her labor had not begun again. They really did not want too. I had mixed feelings, frustrated and trying to keep my faith in the mother's wisdom of her body. Everyone present decided to go for a walk, to give them some space to get geared up for the next birth. Emotional issues needed attention, especially since having two is always double the work.

We waited and waited. I was concerned about the labor stopping, but also knew that her body and baby knew that something needed to go slow for whatever reasons. Her FHT's were still fine, and she was slowly descending and getting into position. Her bag of waters was still intact. Therefore, we knew that she was cushioned and happy in there. I had a feeling that her hand was on her head, since during one internal I felt a hand reaching and grabbing for my fingers. It was a very bizarre feeling. It seemed like she was telling me to go away and not go in there anymore, so I did not. I did not want to break the bag unintentionally. There is always a reason for these things. Mother Nature knows her place and no one is above that.

All of us present, three of us, went outside and discussed the situation. We were all concerned and felt that if labor did not begin within a couple more hours that we would transport. Then as we said a prayer and gave it all up to the universe to show us what we needed to do, we went back in after an hour of pondering, and the mama said she felt like pushing! Yey! 19 hours after the first baby was born. It was a total of 22 hours once Willow was born, since her brother came into the world.

Now labor was full force once again. After about three hours of position changes, counter pressure on her back and lots of fluids of Vit C and green stuff, the mama pushed out her bag of waters for the second baby. She said she felt like it was the baby, but it was just the fluid filled sac. Baby's FHT's were still good, and the water was clear. We went ahead and dismissed the transport idea, as in this state of being how could we bring that up to them? It was just to close. So we went with the flow.

The baby girl, Willow came out as I thought, with her hand on top of her head, little fingers were the first thing we saw as she crowned and was born. Her cord was very long and pulsing well. She was not breathing right away like her brother, but she was pink and responsive to my touch and massage. I gave her a suck over her nose and mouth once or twice, then a few blows of air. Mama turned around and picked her baby girl up and sang to her, kissing her and asking her to come two. She finally took in some air and cried just enough for us to know she was fine. We gave her a little O2 and kept her with her mother and placenta attached. We did not detach them until late the next day. She was much more mellow then her brother, a very different personality for sure.

After 20 minutes or so the placenta began to detach. We were all very curious about what they had been living in, if they shared the same placenta or had their own, or two sacs or one, and many things. We took a look at the huge placenta that they shared. Two compartments of membranes were present. Asher's cord was normal and inserted into the center of his side of the placenta. Willows cord was only attached to vessels in the membranes. She had no insertion into the placenta, this is called a Velamentous insertion. This was another reason that the water bag for Willow had to remain intact, so it would not rupture her vessels that were attached to the membranes keeping her oxygenated and nourished. If that had happened to soon, she may not have made it.

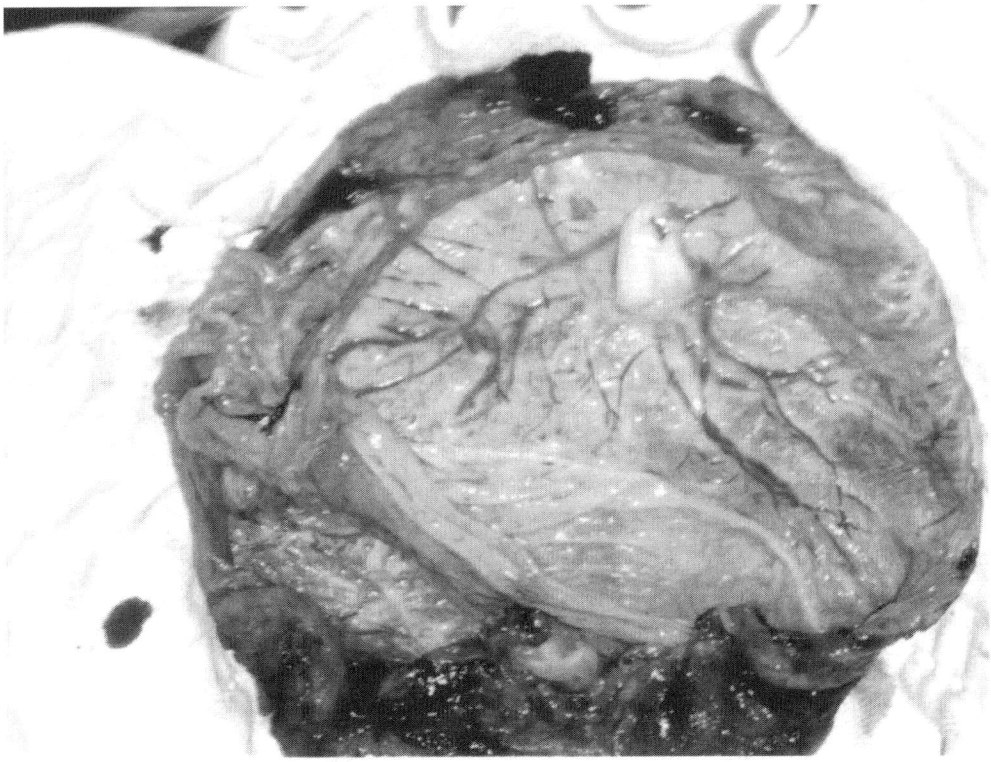

Now we all looked in amazement that the placenta and cords and mamas body knew exactly what to do to birth them safe. The first baby had his cord tightly around him during the birth, but he was a fast breather and had no sign of cord compression before he was born. She birthed in her own time and her own pace. Both babies were 4 lbs 12 oz and 17 ½ inches long and are still at home in the warmth and love of their parents. We are blessed to have been invited to witness this amazing miracle of birth, and support this faithful couple and their babies on their journey.

Thank you all who helped and supported us in times of doubt, and also who had faith in the mother for her own knowledge of her body and babies. We welcome little Asher and Willow into our community. They have taught us much about faith, trust and time being only something man made, not something Mother Nature has on a mantle, but an inner guide of wisdom that only comes from Great Spirit itself.

An update: One month later, little Asher and Willow are thriving at home with their parents. Keeping the house warm all this time by a wood fired stove, keeping them nourished and hydrated, which is hard for any new mom to get the hang of. Juggling the two little beings that came into the world early, small, and through their jaundice and hourly feedings. They are now 5lbs 6oz and content. Have grown one inch and have very alert and conscious attitudes. On their original due date May 5th, they were 6lbs 12oz and 6lbs 10oz and each are 20 in long! We are so proud of these parents and their diligence to birth in freedom and integrity! Here they are below a few months later at 15lbs!

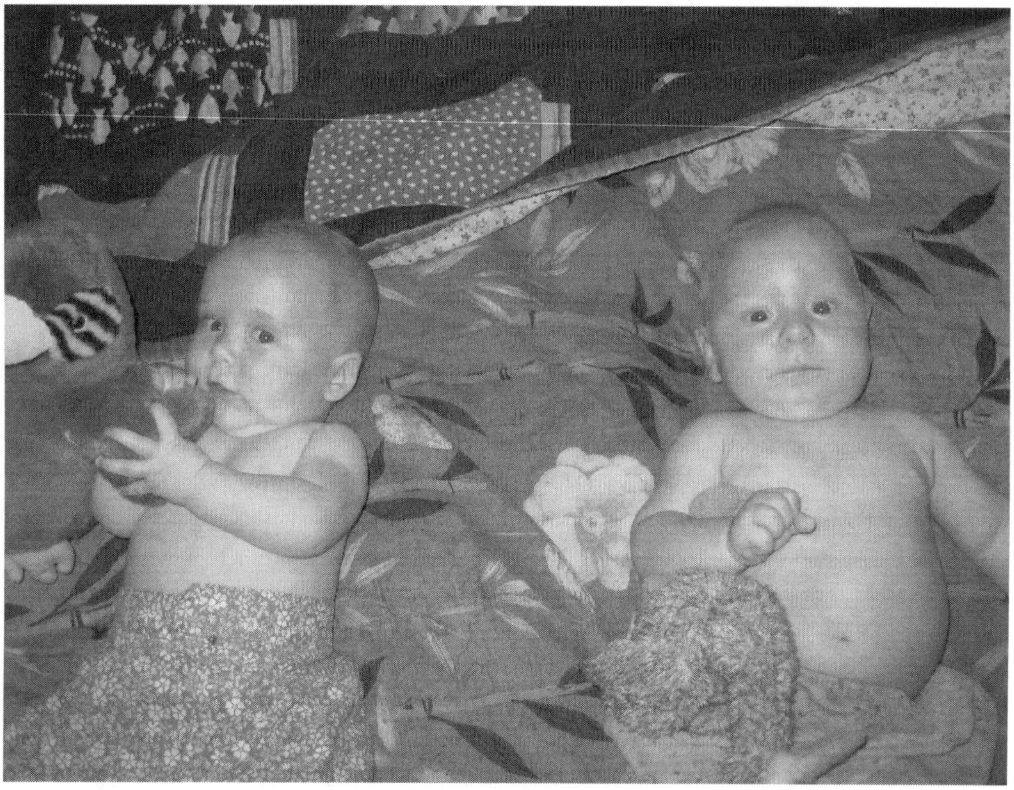

Leo boy born parent assisted at home in water, with a heart story to share.

I met this neat couple while the mother had been working in a nearby town practicing acupuncture. I believe she found my business card in a local health food store.

They wanted someone knowledgeable to support their desire to have an unobtrusive, parent assisted birth. They wanted me there with them, just not "over them." I agreed, and we met every few weeks. Their pregnancy was uncomplicated and normal. The baby was growing well, and mom felt good on her vegetarian diet. The whole family was involved in pre-natals and discussion. We planned to have a friend of theirs, who lived close by, to be on call with me since I live a couple of hours from them. The parents chose this lady to assist as she is an awesome homeopathic practitioner and also an RN, so I felt confident in being as far as I was.

During the last few weeks of the pregnancy, the mom had a bit of pain in her lower back and Urobilinogen in her urine (which can signal kidney congestion and also many possible other things). I thought maybe the mom was taking too many supplements and suggested she take a break from them, so she stopped the supplements until the next appointment a few days later. After a day or so, the pain stopped and the baby started showing signs of coming soon. He dropped very low into her pelvis, and she had some good expansions every day. I believe it was a day before her "Due Date" when we had a prenatal appointment again, and she wanted me to see what was happening inside. She told me that her expansions were more often but didn't feel that strong, she wanted me to do an exam, so we did, and she was indeed a few centimeters dilated, and her cervix was very thin. I felt that we had some time before the birth so I left to go to town and get a few things. I also had a friend with me who had a baby with her just a few months old, so I told her that if this mom goes into labor I'm getting her a hotel room in town. I phoned their home several times before leaving town to take my friend back home, which was two hours away from where we were. No one answered their phone, so I thought they maybe went out, and I trusted that she would call me when it was time for her labor to begin.

About a little more than half way home, my cell phone rang, and the mom said she's going to fill the birth pool up because her expansions were increasing in length and strength. I hurried home an hour away, dropped off my friend and her baby, went to my house to pick up last minute things then got another call from the mom. The mom told me she was definitely in labor and to come back right away! I hopped back into my car and headed off again. On the way, I had a sense of peace about not making it to the birth and accepted that thought, still driving quite speedily, but ok with not making it in time. I had to pee about 20 miles away from their house and pulled over. It was about midnight at that point, and I looked up at the summer starry sky. It was an amazing summer evening, and all at once I heard a voice saying, "He is born, he's fine and a boy!" Meanwhile I was watching shooting stars above my head. I got back into my car and headed over. At the house, I got out to head up to the door and heard a cry, it was the baby saying, "Hello, I'm here!" I walked in and the father greeted me at the door, eyes wide open a huge grin on his face. He gave me a great, big hug and laughed with me as I told him of my road-side experience. Yes, the baby had been born about the same time as I was peeing on the side of the road.

Mom and baby seemed fine, and the assistant was there the last few minutes of the birth, but she didn't need to do anything special. The placenta was already born when I arrived, and we left it attached for a few hours. The baby had a bit of fluid in his airway, so we gave him some homeopathy, and it cleared up. We checked his lungs and heart--everything seemed fine.

It wasn't until this incredible, little baby was about four months old that his parents noticed his color was getting darker. I think his grandfather was the first to see it. His lethargy also was a concern. Even though he was 9 lbs at birth, and during the first month and half, he grew fine; he quit growing. His parents took him to the doctor to get his oxygen levels checked out, and they were very, very low. They also found him to have a few heart anomalies that were causing his color to be off because he wasn't getting enough oxygen. This had probably been going on since the birth, and the more a baby grows the more the heart has to work to get oxygen to all parts of the baby's body. So this is a progressive deterioration, not seen a lot of times in the beginning, which is what happened here.

This baby was a miracle to these doctors; they couldn't understand how he had survived so long, but his body adapted to his heart condition enough to allow the flow of oxygen to his brain, so he was not brain damaged. The parents found out that his umbilical artery had not ever closed leaving a hole that siphoned air for him. He also had another hole between his Pulmonary Artery and Aorta. These holes suctioned off blood intended for the heart keeping it from developing normally.

This kid made it, and some of these doctors even told the parents that if he had been born in the hospital they would have done surgery too early, and he may have not survived. As it was, at four months old, he had difficulty with the open-heart surgeries they had to perform.

Because this baby had a fair chance at home, a gentle water birth, was breastfed and has conscious parents, he was able to make them aware of his difficulties when he really needed help. Being breast-fed and held through the whole ordeal by his parents helped in fighting off the infections that he contracted from being in the hospital, I believe that faith and love--not to mention great breast milk-- sustained him through this whole ordeal. Now, he is a healthy and spunky five year old Leo boy with the heart of the lion, sharing his love with all who enter his world!

The second home birth with the same parents three years later. . .on Valentines Day

I kept in fairly good contact with the couple (from the previous story) for a few years after the birth. We actually met a few times in-between the heart surgeries, and I was working with another one of their friends who planned a home birth. I got the call from this mom again saying she wanted to have another home birth, but that with the last birth ending up in an emotionally stressed situation, she wanted to get an ultrasound from the heart specialists that her son had seen. I totally supported her decision to have this baby checked out ahead of time for any heart problems, to ease any emotional worries, and also to be clear of any expected future preparations.

When she got the ultrasound and everything seemed fine, but the doctors told her that there was a one in a million chance of having another child with heart problems and to seek medical prenatal care. We discussed this choice, and both the parents felt secure with the ultrasound results and continued care with me for their water birth at home.

We met as much as we could, and the parents wanted to stick to the tentative plan of doing their own birth, like last time, with me there but not interfering. The father wanted to catch his baby like the last time. The pregnancy was again uncomplicated, free and healthy. The baby grew well, and the family was excited to welcome a new baby into their home. The little miracle child, with the mending heart, was so excited to become a big brother that every time I visited with them, he was in awe to hear the babies heart on the monitor. It was always a joy to go visit and have that time before the birth to connect with the whole family once again for a different, new spirit coming in. We discussed any cares or concerns with the whole family about the birth, and what we could do to make the transition smoother for all involved. This time, we planned on having the same Homeopathic Practitioner--RN, and another friend to come help with things.

It was February, and a couple of weeks before her "Due Date," when we got together for one of our last prenatals before the birth. We met in a town close to where I live at one of my friend's houses. The mom felt the baby was very low in her pelvis and was curious as to how far she was dilated and in what position the baby was. I checked her, and she was indeed dilated, and the baby was extremely low in her pelvis. She was dilated almost five centimeters, the baby's head was through her Ishial spines, in a +1 station. We discussed the possibility of the birth going very fast with these findings, and that I may not make it there, just like last time. We decided that whatever happened was fine and meant to be the way it was going to be, with or without me there.

A snow storm came in about a week later, and in the middle of that dark early evening, the mom gave me a call to tell me that she was feeling some consistent sensations, not painful but regular. She wanted me to come over. I jumped in my car and drove the normally two hour drive, which in this case, during the blizzard, took me almost five hours. I have done this before in a snow storm on the way to births, and it is not fun. When I arrived at the home, and actually am able to be there and help out, it is well worth the experience. I got to their home later that evening, and her sensations had stopped. We went to sleep and awoke with no noticeable labor happening the next morning. I went to town and did some food shopping, visited a friend and headed back over. It was February 12th, and the snow was piling on once again. That whole day, the mom had very few contractions, and I felt that maybe I should run home and gather a few more clothes and supplies while the weather was nice, in case it would be awhile for the baby to get there. It was still about ten days from her estimated "Due Date," so I felt ok with leaving and coming right back. It was a beautiful day, and the ride home went well. I meditated on this birth while I drove across the desert and felt it would be good if I went right back since we already knew a week before that the baby was really ready to come quickly once labor actually started.

I got home and received a call almost immediately that her labor had started again. It really felt like deject vu, but this time I had the feeling that I would actually be there when the baby came. I headed right back down and arrived a couple of hours later to find the mom out of labor once again. I discussed with her that I felt it was important to give them space to relax, and that I didn't want to be a distraction, which I felt may have been why the labor kept staling. We agreed that I would go visit some friends nearby and come back later. I left to stay at another person's house a few miles down the road. I phoned the family to make sure all was well before heading off to sleep, and we discussed any emotional issues of fears or any feelings that needed to be cleared to help facilitate her labor more.

After a few hours at my friends house I felt like I needed to get back and the mom assured me that, "You being here is not a distraction." So, I went back over to get some rest on their Futon in the living room. The next day it snowed like crazy. I got my car stuck in their driveway, and then felt insecure that if we needed to get out for some reason in an emergency it would be almost impossible with the snow and steep entrance to their home. I got my car towed out of the snow and decided to just stay put until it was all clear. We ate, talked, and relaxed all day. It was now Valentine's Day, and the third day since the first call. The mom and I talked about homeopathy being an option for getting things going since everyone seemed somewhat concerned about the baby's position. At one point, we checked heart tones, and it sounded like his cord was being squeezed between his shoulders and her pelvic bones. He had already been so low in the pelvis for so long that this was a concern. We had to fully discuss this since they wanted the birth to be un-interfered with, and it was important to discuss a few options.

I suggested that we just wait, or do some mild homeopathy to facilitate more action, but of course left the choice up to the parents to decide.

It was still early in the morning on Valentine's Day when the parents decided to try some homeopathy. The mom was going to school at the time to study homeopathy and felt that with it's mild actions that it would be the best choice to get labor on the move, so she started taking a diluted form of the pellets. The day went on with little action. We ate, played with the kids, cleaned and set up the birthing pool, which took several times to get right since their water heater was full of what looked like calcium deposits. We took the pool apart once, and then put it back together and decided to use water from the tap and some boiled water also to get the pool filled. That took a few hours of getting ready, but we needed something to do anyway while we waited for labor to get started. It was later that evening when the mom's sensations finally began and stayed, but she didn't tell anyone until she was sure that things would keep on progressing. We had the pool set up (finally!) and warm and the house cleaned. The mom was upstairs reading a book to the kids and putting them to bed when I heard her say, "My water just broke!" The dad asked me to go up and check on her, so I did.

When I went up, I saw her trying to get out of the bed where she had just put their little ones to sleep. I saw that indeed she was in labor, and her water looked clear; I helped her up out of the bed and down the stairs as she was supporting her belly with her hands. We got the pool uncovered and exchanged some of the water which was too hot and put some colder water in its place.

When the mom entered the pool, she said that it felt like the baby was already coming. She felt the urge to bear down, and asked me if she should; I said, of course, if she felt that way to move with it. I think she felt like it might have been too soon, but I reminded her that she had been open, and the baby low, for the last couple of weeks, so it must be time to let him out. Both mom and dad were in the pool getting ready to birth just twenty minutes or so after her water had broken. The baby moved through his mother's pelvis with ease, and his head crowned into his father's hands. I watched from the sidelines as mother and father slowly birthed their new baby into their arms.

The baby gave a little cry just for a moment to open his lungs then relaxed into his mother's bosom. We checked his heart, and it sounded just fine, then his lungs, all was good. The one friend who was asked to come help arrived during the last half a minute of the birth and got to witness the baby being born. The same assistant we used for the last home birth came in shortly after that. We all helped mom and baby out of the pool onto the futon next to it, and dried them off. We all gave her attention, handed her some fluid to drink and then did a little exam on both mom and baby. All was well and faith once again gave another family one of the most precious gifts there is: a gentle birth and a healthy baby.

Their third little miracle baby boy was born on "Heart Day," in tribute to his big brother with the huge heart, who was born in the same birthing pool a few years before.

I was honored and blessed to have experienced this family's strengths, challenges, hopes, and faith, along with their journeys of self-transformations in their births.

BraveHeart Family

Wicanpi Cikala

"Little Star"

Cedar Everett Brave Heart, Born Still, April 24,2002

By: Sara Brave Heart

(I wrote this letter when my third son Cedar would have been 12 days old)

Cedar Everett was my third son. My first two boys were born at home with midwives and family and friends present. Although I had miscarriages in the first trimester before Cedar's death, I was in no way prepared for dealing with the pain, sadness, grief, blame from others and anger that came in the days, weeks and years to come, after having a still-born son. Our family went on to have a fourth child, a daughter, born again at home. We were blessed to have a wonderful midwife help us work through our emotional issues we faced during pregnancy and birth. When my husband and I lifted our daughter's body from the water of the birthing tub together, and she looked at everyone, breathed and was alive and beautiful it was a very healing experience I am very proud to have had.

My Dear Cedar,

The night before you were born a strange wind blew. It was a warm wind and the temperature went up throughout the evening. It was one of many strange things that did not quite work right. Sweet grass would not stay lit, we could not find your heart beat or movements, things were just not where they belonged. Jane's water Fetascope, no Oxygen in her new tank, Mel cancelled class and finding that she was not scheduled to teach it, water leaking through our ceiling, and more. In the end, the thing that didn't work was your coming into this life.

My water broke a tiny bit, Wednesday, April 24 about 7am. Daddy was going to go to work to take care of a few things and then come home, but when we couldn't find your heart beat he decided to stay home.

As we were about to go to the hospital, Jane arrived and found your heart beat and movements right away. In retrospect, had we not been so continually distracted by your brothers and life, we would have checked for a heart beat sooner, and perhaps gone to the hospital and things may not have been so different. But we didn't check for such a long time, trusting things were OK.

The pregnancy had been so easy. Jane was stuck in traffic and construction, but arrived. We called Ceci to come, she and Ksapa played together. Dave took care of Cyrus, and they all set up the birthing tub. Jane checked and found your heart beat again about noon, but your Dad and I wonder about it and if your movement was just a limb sliding when Jane pushed on it. You turned towards my back and perhaps you were trying to unwind the cord that was wrapped around you, or perhaps you were so weak, that when Jane pushed on you, you just turned backwards. Perhaps you were in some suspended animation. I hope you were not in pain. Your Dad thinks you already died by then. I wonder also.

That afternoon Daddy worked around the house, laced a drum. I labored and even took a nap. Jane came back close to 7pm. We nervously awaited her and the arrival of the Doppler. I had not felt you move all day. The last time I felt you move was early that morning, before my water broke.

Before Jane left, Ksapa said there would be no heart beat because your heart was broken. Jane then tried to find your heat beat with the Doppler, when she could not find it we called the hospital. I packed a bag, we called my mom to come help. We left for the hospital. Daddy drove, Jane rode with us, we took the blue Geo. I knew we would not be going back home to birth you. I had cried that morning too, before Jane got there-so worried.

At the hospital they checked you with a Doppler and called for a C-section, so they could try to revive you. We resisted, not knowing how long you had been gone and still not wanting to believe you had died. They did an Ultrasound and confirmed your heart was not beating. I asked them to get Dave, he had been taken to the front desk to register me. We wept. A nightmare began, a dream of a new baby to love, ended.

At first I could not bare the thought of laboring on, and delivering you, but I thought of your brothers still at home needing a mom and how hard it is to recover from a C-section. I asked for medicine to help with the pain and the Dr. broke the bag of waters, then gave me a Pitocin drip in my I.V. We visited ,cried, talked. Talked about potty training with our Dr. And Nurse. Suddenly I had to push. Your head was out in a couple of pushes. They told me to wait and fumbled for instruments. Knowing your body was lifeless made this a very hard time. The Dr. had a very hard time cutting the cord that was wrapped not once, but twice, as well as your hand being along side your face. Then came your body in a couple more pushes. The cord wrapped around it again. Then we saw the knot in the cord. Then they wrapped you in a pink and blue blanket and laid you on my chest. I know I was wailing, I believe it was after they told me you were a boy that I wailed again and again, that my boy was gone from me. I knew that our time together was done. That I would never feel you move again, as I had while I was pregnant.

We held you and cried. Even now it seems that tears will never end. We called home to see if Ksapa was still up so that he could see you. Grandma came up, Dad told your Grandpa Basil and we called your Great-Grandma Nickum who told your Grandpa and he came. Lake and Karen came, Mel came. We all got to hold you. You were so beautiful. Your black wavy hair, high cheek bones, mouth like your brothers. Chin and nose like your Dad's. Big feet. Dark skin. Long fingernails. We touched you, kissed you, admired every inch of your body. They said you had only been dead a matter of hours.

We let them clean you. They took your foot and hand prints, and a lock of hair. A new born picture. Daddy and I spent some time alone with you. We were in shock. Amazed at what had just happened. We left, had decided to send your body to the Mortuary. We were not to see your body again until Friday afternoon. We took your placenta with us. It was hard to leave your body.

Daddy and I drove home. Jane drove with Mel. We met her at our house where she packed her stuff and shared with us that the cord's knot had probably cut off Oxygen for some time. We have learned more since. And know that your dying was a cord accident, and rare to occur. That cord haunts me my boy to this day. I pray that you were not in pain or suffering, and I am sorry you were not getting enough food or Oxygen and that I didn't know something so terrible was going on. I pray that you were cozy and warm, hearing our voices, feeling my touch, and that you knew you were loved. Although the though of a new baby was sometimes overwhelming, I loved you and wanted to take care of you. We all did.

Thursday- people came all day. Ceci had stayed overnight. It was good to have help with your brothers. We ate food from a neighbor, Julie Grade, had made the day before. We visited the funeral home. Jane, Lake and Karen came in the evening.

Friday- we made remembrance cards. Cut Dad's hair. Grandma Nick and Mary and Yoshi came and took Ksapa to story time and helped clean. At 3pm your body came home. I was excited to have you home, to see you, but collapsed when you arrived, overwhelmed by grief. Grandma Patterson held me. We all cried. The funeral home had brushed your hair and it looked straighter. Your brother's, Ksapa (4 years old) and

Cyrus(1 year old) touched you. The wake began. Many people came. Sweet grass and your turtle to hold your umbilical cord with Daddy's braid went into your casket. A yellow bundle of medicine also went in.

Saturday- up early and got ready to go to Pine Ridge. I had done most of the packing the day before. We took photos and video. The night before we had closed the coffin and covered it with red felt. We caravanned to Pine Ridge with Maggie, Stacey and kids in the blue car and Grandpa and Jan in Jan's car. It was the only time we ever got to ride together with you as a family. Your brothers and daddy and me. We cried a lot. We drove through rain clouds, mist and snow.

There was a big tipi set up. People were waiting for us. Your body was carried inside. Bob and the boys sang. Your coffin was opened. Grandpa Basil put Eagle Feather from the family Staff in with you. It was returned to Staff by Daddy at the end of the funeral. When Grandpa is gone Daddy will carry the Staff.

Auntie Babe's husband sang. Mary and Kevin told about losing their baby. Basil and Uncle Bob spoke. We cried, Grandpa and Jan were there.

We ate some food. Bob's boys stayed with you until about 2am.

Sunday-the wake.

We chose the grave site. Lake, Kevin and Bill made a pine box. The grave was very hard to dig. 15-20 men worked on it until dark. The wake was held up because the boys and Bob were still digging. We tried to get a back hoe. It was a beautiful day. Auntie Babe's husband sang to help pass the time for the starting of the wake. Schope spoke. Uncle Bill spoke. Grandpa Basil spoke. Spoke of family, growing up, ancestors, and the land you are buried in.

Finally we began the wake. Grandpa Basil and Father Tom blessed you with holy water. Bob and the boys sang. It is hard for me to remember what all happened, it was so hard. Ksapa was crying, Jane held him, Cyrus was sleeping, then up and I nursed him. I imagine nursing you on the other side, when I was nursing Cyrus. I think of your milk he is drinking. In my dreams I nurse you. Back to the wake....Agnes Tyon- your Grandma an Episcopalian Deacon, said good things. Father Tom said good things.

We ate. Daddy and I slept in preparation of the Ceremony that night.

Uncle Bernard told us that during this year we need to say good things, right things. Then by the end of the year it will be habit.

Ed Eagle Elk and his partner came. Around the fire Ed said he and his wife had lost three babies like this in the 60's.

We got up, put kids to bed in the Tipi and visited, sat, prayed and awaited the Ceremony. Red Clouds sang Peepte songs. Bob and boys sang some songs also.

[Aside- the night/early Am of May 6th, Ksapa dreamt you were born alive and you grew into a man and became a Warrior dressed in long time ago clothes. One week before you were born it was very hot and Ksapa slept in our room. In the morning he asked if we had seen the Bear and seven spirits in our room during the night. Daddy and I thought of Pleiades and the Bear bringing your spirit to us-now we know they were taking you home. . . .]

We stood around a fire outside. Then it was time to begin. The Buffalo robe was on the floor in the middle of the room, your coffin was on it. Daddy and I went and got the pouch with Wasna and Ni-Ni Milk in it. Spirit food we put in your little hand. Uncle Bernard prayed and sang and we spoke to you. Daddy first, then I spoke to you. Then each person sang four songs. It was a long Ceremony and your brothers woke up. Jan brought them to us. I held Ksapa, Grandpa held Cyrus. I spoke to you throughout the singing. . . We went to bed at 4:30 and slept a couple of hours.

Monday- Funeral, Burial, Gifts, Speaking. . . .

The boys got us up-well Cyrus got us all up. We visited and ate at Grandpa Basil's. Ksapa couldn't sleep. I was worried he would cry through the funeral as he had through the wake and the feeding the spirit Ceremony. But it ended up he was Ok. He was strong and really helped bury you by putting dirt in the grave with his hands.

The funeral began. Grandma Patterson sat by me, Daddy on my left and Ksapa on his other side. Father Tom blessed you with Holy water again. And we sang. There was a final viewing. People hugged us. We cried. Dave tied the Eagle Feather back on the Staff.

It was very hard to close your coffin for the last time. We put your hat on you, covered your body with a blanket, arranged the things in your coffin. We cried and cried. . . .

Burial

They loaded you in the back of a pick up. Your teenage cousins-Bj, Brandon and Amery, Bob's boys and Jared were the poll-Bearers. We all drove out to your grave. You could see the Black Hills in the distance. Jerry was talking pictures. I could see why it had been so hard to dig the grave. It was windy.

They balanced your little coffin across the grave. Sang songs. Lowered you into the ground. Father Tom sprinkled rest of holy water.

I threw the first handful of dirt. Then Daddy. Ksapa threw many. People worked around him. Auntie Connie took up a shovel in the first round. People shared in the work.

Jane brought moss roses and they got planted, she was the last to leave. We were second to last.

there was much food. Some flowers had been left behind at the tipi and we put a bouquet in Basil's and one in Bob's and gave one to Grandma Corrine and one to Auntie Babe.

People spoke. We gave away blankets.

Ed said many good things. It was good he was there.

Red Clouds helped a lot.

So then it was done. The next night there was a sweat Daddy and others went to. We drove out in rain and snow. We left unable to tie flags or spread our dog Mo's ashes at your grave because it was very snowy that Wednesday. We hoped to stay another day, but everyone else left, so we did also. . . .

We drove to Mitchell and stayed over night. We were all so tired. Even today, twelve days later we are still very tired. Your brothers talk about you. We cry and are still in disbelief. We miss you so much.

We feed your spirit everyday. This Friday we'll have everyone over who was here when you were born and give gifts.

Jane- a star quilt, picture and rug

Mel-Blanket, maple sugar candy

Ceci- Star quilt, picture, maple syrup

Grandma-Lavender stuff

Grandpa-Sweet grass and Sage

Lake and Karen-Purple rose in glass

We love you so much. I am wishing I had meditated, connected with you more while you were here. Your stay was way to short.

We have learned much compassion, humbleness and lessons from your death. Because of this experience I have decided to learn now to take care of people's bodies when they die and to learn how to assist mother's giving birth.

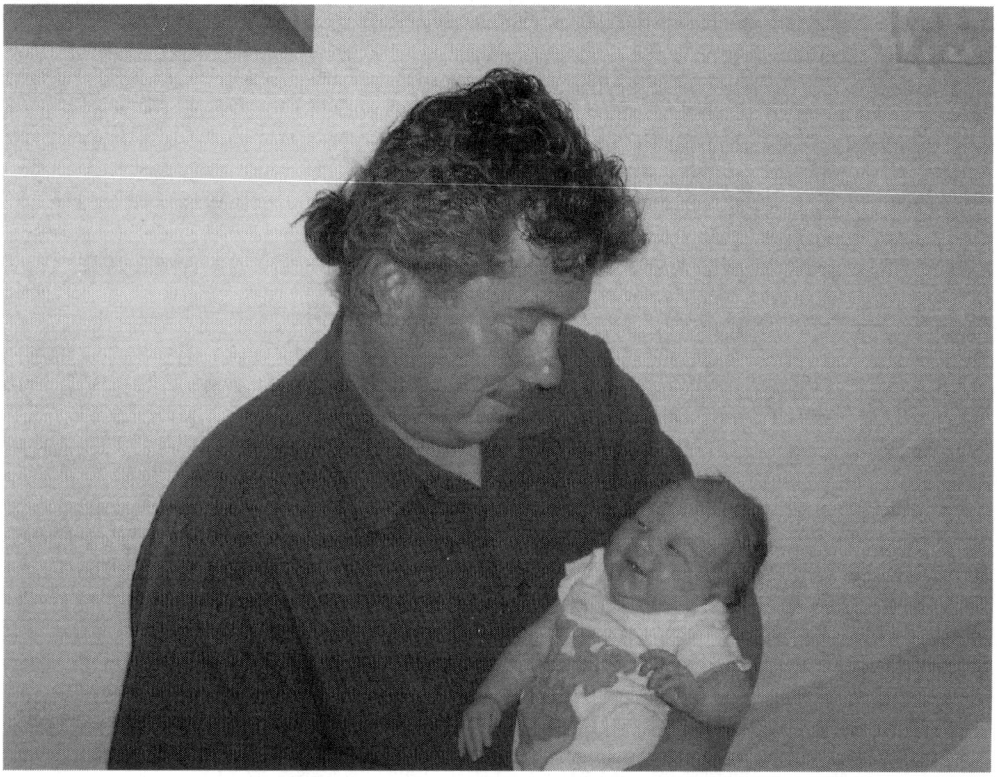

Dave BraveHeart with Ambry, Cedar's little sister born at home in water…

My Kids

by: Jean Abbott

Eric, Michael and Zuki

It was May 10, 1970 (Mother's Day). I was in the hospital waiting for my son to be born. The plan was to have one biological child and later adopt our second child.

While in labor, I went to the bathroom to relieve myself. A nurse came into the room and ordered me back to bed saying that the baby's umbilical cord could wrap around his neck and kill him. Terrorized by that thought, I immediately went back to bed. Twelve hours later it was decided that I needed a caesarian section and was given general anesthesia.

Then, the heartbreak, Eric was born with every defect possible and we were told that he must be hospitalized in a nursing home and would never develop past the three month stage. Eric was also blind and deaf. We were also told, that if he were to be taken home, he would die and charges would be brought against us. As his mother, I wanted nature to take its course, but was not allowed that option.

He was born on Mother's Day. . . Heartbroken, we left the hospital without our baby.

Plan B. We spoke to several agencies in the U.S. about the possibility of adopting a baby and was told that we needed time to "get over" the birth of our son. Thirty-five years later, I am not "over" the birth of my son. . . Next, since my Mom had been to Lebanon several times and had friends there, and the laws (at least at the time) were very lax, we decided to try adoption there.

My Mom had heard of a baby girl that had been born in July (three months after my sons' traumatic birth) and was available for adoption. My mother and I arrived in Beirut, Lebanon in late September of 1970, we immediately went to the hospital where our "soon to be baby daughter" was, awaiting us in her plastic box in the nursery. The nurse unwrapped her and changed her, while my mom and I watched. She was so tiny and beautiful. Just about 8 weeks old. I fell in love with her. When we returned to the doctor who owned the hospital, he simply asked if I wanted to adopt her. I said yes!

The adoption process began. . . Forty-eight days later, now going into November, we boarded a plane for the U.S. by way of Italy. We knew that we had a problem because we did not have a Visa for the baby and asked my dad to work out a solution for us so we could enter the country without a problem.

During the sixteen hour flight, we had no idea what would happen once we exited the plane. Just after the plane landed, a stewardess called out my name and I answered. She had a plane ticket for myself and the baby, who now was named Zuki. My dad was our hero! At that time the law was that you could stay in the U.S. for up to ten days without a Visa, as long as you had a ticket to go to another country. Although the U.S. Embassy would not issue a Visa for a tiny Lebanese baby, Canada did, without any problem at all. The tickets were for Bermuda! So we spent some time there scuba diving until we could get back into the U.S. without immigration problems.

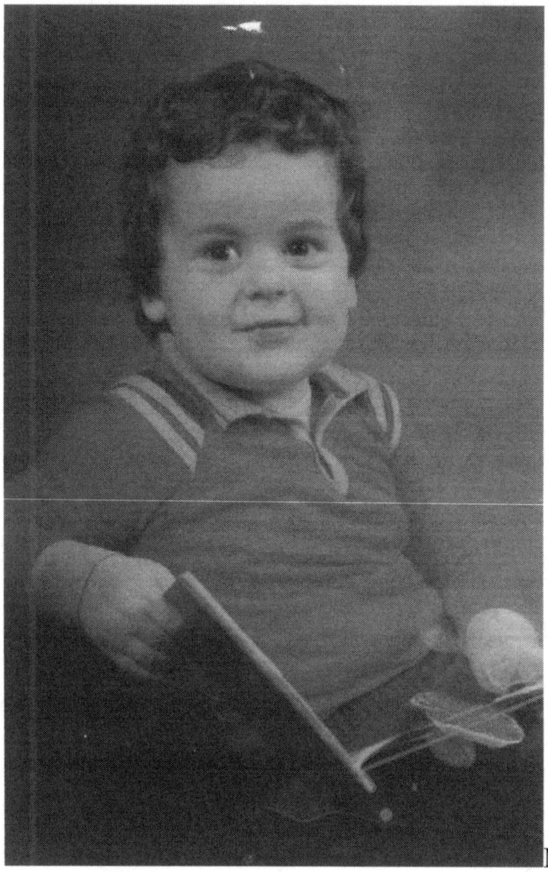
Michael Abbott 1983

Mike's Adoption Story

Mike was 3 1/2 years old and cuter than you can even imagine when I first met him. He was at an amusement park and was "tagged" as a child up for adoption. We spoke to his adoption worker and told her we were interested in adopting him. My first memories of Mike was that he couldn't take his eyes off of me and while on the Merry-Go-Round, his eyes would meet mine each time he went around and around. When resting, he constantly ate potato chips, happily for him!

The term they used was, "Legal risk" which meant that the court would decide if he would become adoptable, or if he would return to the parents. His biological parents beat him and his siblings until his sister became brain damaged and had to be institutionalized for life! Social workers had been "watching" the family for years and this was actually allowed to happen to this sweet child. How sad. . .

One and half years later, the night before we were to legally adopt Mike, I received a call from the Social Worker. She told me that although we were adopting Mike, he would continue to visit his biological parents on a regular basis. I became extremely angry and refused to subject our now 5 year old child to such confusion. How was he to know the difference? How could he understand that he was now an important member of our family? Who was this to serve and why? I told her that the adoption would not take place with her demands. In a second call, sometime later, she agreed that the visits would not take place. Each visit he had with them left him unhappy and confused and it had to stop. And they did.

His adoption day was one that was not short of FANTASTIC! The judge held him on his lap and treated him as his own. I have never regretted for a moment adding Mike to our family.

My 'babies' are of my heart, although not of my body.

Parent Assisted Breech Birth

Sami's Entrance

By: Christina El-Abid

There are several reasons why I have chosen to have an Unassisted Childbirth (UC). When my husband, Bassam, and I decided to have another child, I wanted to have a better birth than what I had with my first son, Mohammad. I had a short labor with this first son, less than 3 hours. However, I had to argue with the nurses several times.

There were two nurses who came to administer the IV. The nurses, one on each side, started getting upset with each other and ripping out the IV because the other one did not do it right. I was poked nine times, and it hurt! I had a bruise up and down my arm. The nurses would come and check in on me letting me know when I was having a contraction and when I was not, as if I did not know what I was feeling.

Finally I told the nurse that I felt the urge to push. She explained to me how she just checked me and I was only dilated to a three. She went on to explain how I would not have my son for another ten to twelve hours. Finally after five minutes of arguing, she checked me and I was dilated at a ten. The nurse then instructed me not to push and she held my son in with her hand pushing on his face. I had to wait for the doctor to arrive, she said.

Throughout the entire experience, the nurse was telling me how to breathe or when I should push. I was a solider taking orders.

Earlier, I asked to be drugged for the birth. But since he was earlier than the nurse had expected, it was too late for medication. I was told that the medication wouldn't kick-in till after I had my son, so there was no point to take it.

Now looking back, I am thankful that I did not have any medication. After I had my son, he was taken by the nurse to get cleaned up. After a few minutes, the nurses put Mohammad in my arms. They gave me two or three minutes with him and then took him out for more tests. I wasn't even able to breast-feed my son until he was several hours old. The nurses were not kind to bring him to my room so I could see or feed my newborn son. Might I add, my son was completely healthy at birth. There was no need to keep him away.

When Bassam and I decided to have another child, we looked into having a midwife. Still, there was no difference to me between a midwife and a doctor except that one is in the hospital while the other is at home. The midwife would tell me what I was feeling and experiencing, which is not what I wanted.

One afternoon, I was complaining to my friend about my first birth and how I felt a midwife would be no different than a doctor. She told me how she had a UC with her last child. She had a beautiful birth and it was similar to what I was looking for. I realized that a UC was what I was searching for and what I really needed. My friend gave me websites and Yahoo, and groups that support and encourage UC. I believed that I could do the UC because I knew everything I was feeling during my first son's birth, and without medication.

I went back home and explained the UC to Bassam. I think he probably thought I was crazy at first. I used every angle I could to make him think about it. I probably didn't have to try so hard, but I didn't want to risk any chance of him saying no. Bassam was willing to look into having a UC. We went to the library and checked out some books on the practice of midwifery. We started reading stories online about people who had UC and going through emails on "yahoo groups." The more we read the more we felt UC was what we wanted. Soon I was pregnant and we were determined to have the UC.

Although we had decided that we were going to have a UC, Bassam still wanted me to go to a doctor or a midwife to get regular pre-partum and post-partum care. Fortunately, my health care/insurance provider offers Nurse Midwives as a substitute for OB/GYN doctors. I found a midwife who I liked. She was relaxed with the fact that I was refusing almost all the tests and not coming in regularly for check ups. I started visiting her every six to eight weeks from my second trimester to my thirty-sixth week of pregnancy.

June 3rd, I felt my baby Sami move for the first time. It was such a great feeling. Throughout the pregnancy, I would feel him moving and kicking around. A month or so later, I felt as if my son was going to pop his foot out of me. I started telling my friends, "I swear, one of these days that foot is just going to pop out!" It really felt that way whenever he kicked. I couldn't imagine that it would be any other feeling than the feeling of his foot kicking down. Little did I know I was going to be right!

I felt great during my pregnancy, and I was excited about having a UC. I worked on my house and did some activities that I loved doing. I would go roller-blading, rock climbing and biking. A few times I would take pictures and send it to my friends just because they thought I was nuts. The night before I had my son I took my older son for a bike ride. I did have some problems with my diet. I could not have soda, sweets and other types of food. I would get bad heartburn. My diet became very mild. I think I would have been diagnosed with gestational diabetes if I had taken the test. Both my mother and my sister have it during their pregnancies. I figured I would just moderate my diet on my own.

I went in for the regular check-up at thirty two weeks of pregnancy. I told the midwife that I still felt as if Sami was going to pop his foot out. She did an ultrasound to see where he was and said that he was breech. She let me know that if Sami did not turn before labor, he would be delivered with a c-section. She told us she was not good with ultrasounds, but it was clear to us that his head was on top. We had initially thought he was a butt breech baby. The midwife gave us a few exercises to try and had me come back at thirty six weeks to see if he had turned his head.

I went in at thirty six weeks. I knew Sami had not turned yet, I could still feel him attempting to get his foot through. The midwife did another ultrasound and sure enough his head was still up! So the midwife informed us she could no longer see us and that we had to go to a doctor now. Breech babies cannot be delivered by midwives. That's the procedure of our health provider. She also gave us a slip to go and get a "tummy twist procedure." My husband and I told her, on the previous visit and this visit, repeatedly that we were not interested, but she would not drop it. We went to the doctor who was going to perform the tummy twist procedure. The nurses asked me to strip and prepare for the procedure. No one had yet even explained to me what the tummy twist involved. Of course, my husband and I knew already because we researched it on our own. We told the nurse we were not going to do the procedure until someone told us what it involves. The doctor finally came to talk to us. He looked very tired. He needed lots of sleep. He said that he was dealing with a tough delivery. If he was a friend visiting my home, I would not have allowed him to drive home in fear that he would fall asleep at the wheel. Needless to say we really didn't like the doctor. He still managed to explain to us the tummy twist procedure. It is very risky. The placenta could separate. The water bag could break. And above all, there would be stress to the baby. In fact they are prepared to do a c-section right there in case anything goes wrong. We thanked the doctor for explaining it to us and were ready to leave. He asked us how we plan to have the baby and we answered, "Naturally, breech or not." And Guess what! He is the only doctor among our health providers who would deliver a breech baby with the condition that the baby is coming out butt first. Unfortunately, he doesn't like to deliver breech babies anymore because of the liability. And he might still do it, only if he was working at the hospital when it is time for my baby to come out.

That doctor would not come in just to deliver a baby breech. The doctor present in the hospital at that moment would have to deal with me and then it will be a c-section. None of this matters to us. We were still determined to have our UC home birth. We were just trying to show the health provider that we were doing almost what they want.

At thirty eight weeks, I went to the OB/GYN doctor who was referred to me by my midwife. Surprisingly, she was not only a OB/GYN doctor but also the health provider's Chief OB/GYN of the entire San Francisco Bay Area. Previously, I told the midwife I was planning to have Sami vaginally, whether he is breech or not. As a result, this chief doctor set aside an entire hour to discuss our options because a breech baby is a huge problem for my pregnancy. She wanted us to have a planned c-section right away, backing her recommendation with lots of serious risks associated with breech deliveries. I asked her to explain the difference between a planned c-section and an unplanned one, which is a c-section during natural labor at the end of the pregnancy term. She said they would be prepared with the best of their resources for the c-section with the best relaxation and concentration from the doctor and the patient. That way, they would reduce the risk to a minimum. On the other hand, an unplanned c-section would end up being operated at the end of the term, during labor, at an unknown time, and maybe with an unprepared staff and a doctor who has to rush in from home in the middle of the night. To us, it seemed that it's basically a convenience and liability issue for the health provider. The doctor agreed and added that they don't have full staff during the night. She also explained how dangerous a breech delivery is. She used as many scare tactics as possible. She stated that her doctors don't want to deliver a baby breech because of the high risk, and that no doctor wants a baby to die in their hands. I asked her if her doctors are incompetent. She didn't answer that question. Instead, she went on to explain to me how Sami could get his head stuck by his ears! S he gave my family a visual to show us how he could come out, how the ears could not be able to pop out and how that could get him stuck in me. At the end of her lecture, she said that the hospital would have to deliver me vaginally if I continuously requested it. However, she emphasized that I should not do this to the doctors because they are not that much experienced in vaginal breech deliveries.

I asked the doctor if she was going to do an ultrasound because we enjoyed having ultrasounds to see Sami. She thought that I wasn't going to let her do that since I refused the tummy twist procedure. She wasn't even going to offer it. Eventually, she did the ultrasound. And guess what we saw? We saw a foot pushing on the cervix from the inside towards the birthing canal. At that moment, the doctor said that, "This changes everything!" There was no way we could deliver naturally. She explained that there were more risks and complications in a footling breech than in a butt breech.

Knowing all of this, we said that we want to wait until the last possible moment before choosing between a c-section and a vaginal delivery. That way, we were giving Sami time to turn out of his breech position if he wanted to. Of course, all of this didn't matter. We were just buying time and keeping the doctor away from realizing that our real plan was to have an unassisted childbirth for our son at home.

My family and I left the room laughing and shaking our heads. It was just unbelievable that a baby would hang by his ears during delivery.

Still, I was nervous about having a breech delivery. After I found out that my baby was breech at thirty two weeks of pregnancy, I logged on to the "UC Yahoo Group" and asked the other members of the group about their thoughts. I also did a lot of research on having a breech delivery. The more I read and heard about UC the more I realized that if I didn't have a reason to have a UC before, I surely do have a lot of reasons now. There was no way I was going to let the doctors cut me open! The "Yahoo group" was very supportive, and the stories I read raised my confidence level. I knew we could do this. It was Bassam's job to learn the complications of breech presentation and how to handle them. He felt confident that he could deliver a breech baby and believed that it is no different than a vertex baby.

Bassam and I felt that Sami was breech for an undetermined reason. We thought that even if we managed to flip him by conducting some exercises or the tummy twist procedure, he would go back to his comfortable breech position. Moreover, the exercises and the tummy twist procedure might prove to be harmful to his health during and after pregnancy.

I went back to the OB/GYN doctor at thirty nine weeks of pregnancy. I knew Sami had not turned; I was still feeling his foot pushing down at the bottom of my belly trying to come out. The doctor did an ultrasound and confirmed that Sami's feet were still at the bottom. Positively though, the doctor pointed out that Sami's lungs were contracting in an attempt to breath. She said that was better than seeing the heartbeat in the ultrasound. It's a very healthy sign. Sami was practicing breathing outside my body once he's delivered. We were able to get a glance of my file as she was updating it. She managed to write over a page about our previous visit. The doctor was nice to us this time and did not give us any problems or lectures. She thought we were going to give her what she wanted. Obviously, she doesn't know us well.

My next appointment with the OB/GYN doctor was November 28th 2003, the day after Thanksgiving. When the doctor's office called to confirm the appointment, I cancelled it. I wanted to go out and do some shopping the day after Thanksgiving sale. I also didn't want to go back to the doctor anymore. I really didn't see a need for it. I knew Sami was going to be stubborn and not flip before his birth.

I really hoped for Sami to be born on Thanksgiving day. I thought it would be great to have a turkey baby, and it would coincide with Eid El Fitr, which is an Islamic holiday that comes immediately after Ramadan, the month of fasting. Sami's due date was November 26th. Because Bassam's employer had planned to relocate to Reno, we were scheduled to be in Reno the 26th through the weekend to close on escrow there. Thank God that the employer decided to stay in San Francisco. We could have ended up having Sami in a Reno hotel.

Thanksgiving day, I went and got the newspaper and plotted my shopping route for the next day. In the evening, I called my good friend Connie and complained that Sami wasn't coming anytime soon. Knowing my luck, I remember telling her that he would come the next day and spoil my shopping spree. Of course, I was just kidding about being upset of him spoiling my shopping plans. Later that night, I was chatting online to my father-in-law (FIL). He is abroad. At 9:50 p.m., I told him that it didn't seem that Sami wanted to be among us for EID:

FIL (9:51:03 PM): hi christina

Me (9:51:14 PM): hi baba

Me (9:51:17 PM): no sami yet

FIL (9:52:00 PM): Will come soon

Me (9:52:07 PM): inshallah (God Willing)

Me (9:52:14 PM): I was hoping he come today for EID

Bassam had finished making dinner and we sat down to watch a movie together. At 10:10 p.m., I felt something in my lower abdomen. I asked Bassam what time it was and told him about the pain. It didn't really feel like a contraction. I felt the same thing twice again 10 and 20 minutes later. I thought this might finally be it. We turned off the movie and got our birthing bag out. In the bag we had a shower curtain, some old clean towels, dental floss, a sterilized scissors, and rubbing alcohol. I thought it might be labor since there were 3 pains 10 minutes apart, but the pain was not bad nor did it feel like labor. Bassam and I figured we needed to decide where to have Sami and to make sure that we had everything. We hadn't done this before and figured we should practice before I do go into the real labor.

At 10:30 p.m., we went upstairs to our room and prepared everything. We decided to have Sami near the bathroom. So we went for the vanity area. We laid down the shower curtain. I got the birthing chair and tried it in different locations on the shower curtain. We took everything out of the birthing bag and placed it on the counter. I decided to take a shower and see if the pain would become more or less. The shower felt good. Sometimes I would ask how long had it been since the last pain and other times I would say, "I think that was a contraction!"

We wanted to keep my FIL, who's on the other side of the globe, up-to-date with what was happening in our adventure. We assigned few tasks to Mohammad to make him feel as an active participant in the birth of him brother. His tasks were to keep his grandpa informed of what was happening, to call our friends and inform them of my labor and Sami's birth, and to record the time labor and birth. Mohammad was happy to do these tasks for me. And he did an excellent job. The following is copied from Mohammad's chat session with his grandpa:

Mohammad (11:12:01 PM): hi!!!!!!!!!

FIL (11:13:24 PM): how are you

Mohammad (11:13:38 PM): good

Mohammad (11:13:49 PM): It Is Mohammad

FIL (11:14:32 PM): how's your mom

Mohammad (11:15:01 PM): Good----Ummm In Pain

FIL (11:15:49 PM): What kind of pain

Mohammad (11:16:15 PM): We Think Labor

FIL (11:17:00 PM): Good ------bassam there

Mohammad (11:17:21 PM): Yup. it is 11:17

Mohammad (11:17:37 PM): Another Contraction

FIL (11:19:13 PM): So your ready to help your mom

Mohammad (11:24:24 PM): Yeah, just did

An hour ad eighteen minutes after the first pain, I sent out an email to my friends telling them that we still weren't sure if this was it: "We are waiting to be sure before calling; you can reach us on the cell!"

After I had sent the email, we went for a walk outside. I felt few more contractions. Some really hurt like contractions. Others I couldn't decide if it was contractions or not. I had read a lot on the pain of childbirth and learned that most of the pain is caused by fear. And I believed it when I read it. I was also able to look back at my first childbirth and see exactly how fear had controlled my pain. I tried not to be scared when delivering Sami. At some moments, I was fine and just beyond excited about having him alone at home, and other moments I was getting scared about him being feet first. On every very painful contraction, I was thinking about the risks of having him breech.

FIL (11:43:08 PM): Where are u

me (11:52:00 PM): we went walking

me (11:52:08 PM): christina here

me (11:52:13 PM): I thought it would help

me (11:52:14 PM): it didn't

FIL (11:54:02 PM): So will see sami today inshallah (God Willing)

FIL (11:56:25 PM): I will be back

We came back in the house and I thought I would take a bath. I had wanted a water birth in the beginning of my pregnancy. I later changed my mind when I read few birth stories. I saw that some women were so set on having their babies in that they jeopardized the health of their babies to have the birth they wanted. So I decided that I would be open minded and not allow myself to get disappointment if I did not get the exact birth I wanted. After all, my body will let me know what to do when it's time for it. The most important thing to me was to have a healthy baby.

While I was in the bath, I had few more contractions. Again some of them were strong, and some I wasn't sure about. I figured it wasn't labor since the pain was not much. However, while I was in the bath, my tail bone started killing me. I thought that this had to be real labor. It's no longer feeling like false labor. I felt bad sitting in the tub, so I got out. By that time, I was having bad pains at my tail bone that made me really hope that this is real labor and that delivery is very soon. I couldn't take it for a long time.

I went back to my bathroom, and all the sudden I felt something funny. I yelled for Bassam to come in and check me. I should have realized what it was. It felt like there was a water balloon squeezing out. As soon as Bassam showed up, my water bag broke. I laughed. I turned to Bassam and said, "This is it! I'm in labor!"

Fortunately, I was standing over the shower curtain. I called Mohammad up so he could record the time. We were all amazed with how much water was coming out of me. It was like a faucet turned on high. Mohammad asked if I was peeing, and I explained that it was just the water bag emptying. I told Mohammad to record the time and to tell my FIL about the good news.

Moments later, I told Mohammad and Bassam I had the urge to push. I got scared for a second. It was too soon. If my body was telling me to start pushing seconds after the water bag had broken, I thought it meant I would be pushing for a long time before Sami was all out. Mohammad was born forty five minutes after my water bag broke. So I thought it would be another thirty minutes or more before Sami was in my arms. When I felt the urge to push, I dropped on all fours over the shower curtain and was in the water from my water bag. I don't know why I got in that position. I had thought I would use the birthing chair or squat to open up as much as I could for an easy delivery. When the time came for Sami to come out, my body was urging me to be close to the ground and on all fours.

I didn't know where Bassam and Mohammad were when I went down on all fours. I knew they were in the room, but I had no idea whether there was anyone behind me to catch Sami or not. I gave a push and felt Sami's feet popping out. It was an incredible feeling. I gave another push and Sami's body came out up to his shoulders. It felt good to get him out, but there was one part still inside: his head. I got scared again for a moment. I didn't understand why he was not all out yet. During Mohammad's birth, he only needed one push. So I expected Sami to require the same amount of pushes. I told Bassam that I had to get him out now. I thought that I should change my position and stand. Bassam suggested the same. So I stood up, leaned over the sink and gave the biggest push I could have ever given. Sami's head popped out.

When I was leaning over the sink, I saw Mohammad in the door way. I did not know where he was until then. I wanted Mohammad to be there for the birth. It made me so happy to see him standing there so proud and full of emotions. His eyes were full of water. His smile was as big as the Grand Canyon. And his body was trembling with excitement. I watched him looking at Sami's head coming out. It was very calming to see Mohammad watching the birth. He was confirming my feeling that Sami was coming out fine.

Sami started spitting immediately when he came out. Bassam held him facing downwards and got all the mucus out of his nose and mouth. Sami cried a little. Then he was happy. He opened his eyes and watched us admiring him.

Mohammad informed his grandpa that Sami was finally here. He called our friends to let them know that Sami was here and that we were all doing well. I think he was quick on the phone because he didn't want to miss a moment with Sami.

FIL (12:31:56 AM): ya Mohammed where are u

Mohammad (12:37:57 AM): mama just broke water bag

FIL (12:40:38 AM): U must take her to hospital

Mohammad (12:40:42 AM): 12:40 Sami comes

Mohammad (12:40:45 AM): he is here!!!!!

The time between the first small pain and the birth of Sami was less than two and a half hours. I would say I didn't really believe that it was labor until the last ten or fifteen minutes before the birth. Maybe I was in denial. I don't know. It wasn't that painful the first two hours. I have had cramps worse than my labor pains. There was only three minutes between the water bag braking and Sami coming into the world.

Throughout the birth, the only time Bassam spoke to me was when he suggested that I should stand. This was along the path of everything we read about the best breech delivery. I, on the other hand, talked a lot. I was vocalizing everything I did. I think it helped me to stay focused, and I wanted Bassam to be ready to catch Sami if he flew out in one push just like Mohammad.

The labor itself was not painful until the last five minutes before the water bag broke. Pushing his feet and shoulders out did not hurt either. It started to hurt after his shoulders were out and his head was still inside. When I stood up to deliver his head, I gave a grunt and pushed hard. I tore when his head came out. The same happened with Mohammad's birth ten years earlier. Overall it was not that painful.

Bassam handed me Sami and I sat down on the birthing chair with him. Bassam got the dental floss and scissors to cut the umbilical cord. He made sure I kept Sami warm while I tried to breast-feed him. However, Sami did not want to eat yet. Then we remembered that we had set up the camcorder to record the birth. Even though it's too late to shoot the birth, we turned it on to record Sami and the scene. Bassam cleaned up while we waited for the placenta to come out. Mohammad and I talked about the birth. I was so proud of him for being there.

We waited thirty minutes before deciding that it's time to cut the cord. Bassam took the dental floss and tied it in two spots on the umbilical cord. I held Sami and watched Bassam cut the cord. Now looking back, I wish we had thought about this more. It would have been really neat to have Mohammad be the person who cut the cord. Bassam cut the cord and some blood splattered over Sami and I. We laughed. We were not expecting the blood to splatter on us. Bassam took Sami into the bedroom, cleaned and wrapped him up while I continued to wait for the placenta. Mohammad stayed with me, and we just talked about Sami's birth.

Waiting for the placenta drove me nuts. I was having what I would usually consider as contractions. Sitting in the birthing chair was not helping. After the cord was cut and Sami was taken to the bedroom, I was able to stand. I paced back and forth waiting for the placenta to come out. Mohammad kept me company while Bassam was with Sami. He laughed at me and said I had a tail between my legs. The cord reached to the ground as I stood up. It took almost an hour for the placenta to come out. This was the longest part of the birth. It was such a relief when it came out.

Now it was shower time. And it felt great. While I was in the shower, Mohammad watched Sami. Bassam started cleaning up. Afterwards, I took Sami downstairs. My friend next door came over to see our new family member. Sami was just two hours old. Our friend went home after an hour of visiting. And the boys were all tired. They all went to bed and crashed when Sami was five hours old. It was 5:30 in the morning. Since it is the day after Thanksgiving, I tried to talk Bassam into doing some shopping for the sales day between 5:30 and 6 in the morning. Unfortunately, he was too tired. But still, I couldn't sleep. My adrenaline was too high. I think I was still in shock and disbelief. It was almost too easy that it seemed unreal. So while the boys slept, I started cleaning the house and doing the dishes. I knew I would have more visitors later on, and I didn't want anyone to see our dirty dishes. I didn't get any sleep the night Sami was born. That wasn't because Sami kept me up all night long, but because I was just too excited. I tried to lie down next to Sami, but then I just wanted to hold him and talk to him. So I got back up and cleaned some more.

More friends came to visit by noon that day. Sami was "a happy camper" being held and loved by all. He opened his eyes all the time and was lifting his head up for brief moments. I felt great. I was still having small contractions whenever I breast-fed Sami. But it wasn't enough to hold me back. When Sami was fourteen hours old and after my friends left, we went to Applebee's for lunch. It is right next to a shopping center. We were all starving. I took a picture of us in the restaurant to send to my friend just because she thought I was crazy for going out so early.

On the way to Applebee's, I called the health provider's office to make an appointment for Sami. I would have rather waited a week before taking Sami in if it wasn't for my dear husband and friends who would not let it rest until I did. The pediatrics clinic insisted that I take him to the hospital for both of us to receive a full postnatal care. I told them there was no need for that since it's been hours after the birth and we're both fine. I just wanted a regular health check appointment. So the lady on the phone said they weren't able to schedule an appointment till Monday, which was three days away. That was fine with me. I wanted to wait as long as I could.

After we had lunch, we went to "Babies R Us" to pick up few items. We stopped at few other stores in the center and just walked around. I missed most of the "Day after Thanksgiving" sale. So we went to "Target" for few more items.

While we were at Babies R Us, the clinic called again and said they could give us an appointment later that evening. We had to agree to take the appointment. I was somewhat disappointed since I really wanted to go as long as I could before going in. I also wasn't able to hit all the stores that were on my list.

Sami was about seventeen hours old when we arrived at the pediatric clinic, which turned out to also be the pediatric urgent care center. The problem with this is that you have healthy kids in the waiting room mixed with very ill kids. I did not like this at all. Everyone there seem to know who we were. We were clearly labeled as "difficult" for the hard time we gave them on the telephone. They insisted on administrating all kinds of shots and the eye drops onto Sami. I refused the eye drops and they insisted on it saying that it was the law. Bassam let them do it as well as a blood test, which was attempted twice. And both times were not done right. So we delayed it for another day. Sami was finally weighed and measured. He was almost eight pounds at birth and twenty inches and three quarters of an inch long. We left with an appointment to come in the next day.

We came in the next day to have Sami be seen by a new doctor. Again it was clear to us that we were well known within the department. The nurse told me how she had heard of us not in a nice way at all. So I asked, "Exactly what does that mean?" She told me how she knew it was very difficult to get me in the clinic and that I was refusing to have my son be seen by a doctor. I explained to her that I never refused him to be seen, I just refused to go to the hospital. The doctor came in with an attitude as well. I refused earlier to let them take Sami's temperature through the rectum. So the doctor said that he would not see Sami until I let them take his temperature through the rectum. Again Bassam gave them the permission to do so.

During both visits, all the nurses and the doctors wanted to know who cut the cord. They even quizzed Bassam on how he knew what to do. And they asked him if he was trained on cutting the cord. To them, cutting the cord was rocket science. To us, it was as simple as cutting a string. It amazed us that they were more interested in who cut the cord then how we caught Sami and made sure he got out safely.

The doctor gave us the lecture on how risky it was to have Sami at home and how "lucky" we were that Sami was safe and healthy. When he heard that Mohammad had witnessed the birth, he was in shock and said, "No child should have to see that, how traumatic!" I bit my tongue so hard and I didn't fight back. The doctor gave

Sami a clean bill of health. However, he scheduled an appointment for Sami to have an ultrasound done on his hips when he's four months old. Apparently there are some complications that can hit breech babies in their hips.

Our next pediatrician appointment was two weeks later. This time I decided we would go to a different location with a different doctor. I was hoping to get someone who had not judged us already. And I was lucky. This doctor was funny. I don't think he believed our birth story though. He asked us where Sami was born. We told him at home. He asked if the paramedics were there to help us. We said no. He then asked if we called 911 to know what to do. We said, again, no. He asked Bassam if he was in the medical profession. Of course, we said no. So he asked if I hard training in Lebanon for this. We said no. He finally said that we were back to the Stone Age when people deliver their own babies in their own homes. Today, nobody delivers at home. We let him believe whatever he wanted to believe as long as it made him happy with us.

Sami received a ton of medical attention, but not me. It had been three weeks since his birth, and it seemed that my OB/GYN doctor had forgotten about me. I was happy about that. Unfortunately, I received a phone call from my doctor. At first I didn't know who it was because I totally forgot about her. But then I quickly remembered her. She told me that my midwife was asking about me. That made her realize that she hadn't seen me in some time. S o she pulled up my chart, which did not show, three weeks after my due date, that I delivered yet. There were so many things I wanted to tell her at that time. But it wasn't appropriate. I wanted to tell her that, with all of the schooling she went through, she wasn't able to deliver my baby naturally while my untrained husband was able to do the job perfectly. I also wanted to tell her that my baby didn't get hung up on his ears. But I didn't say anything at all. I just told her it was all over before it started and we just never made it to the hospital. She let me know that, if I wanted, I could come in for a six week check-up appointment with my midwife. It was funny that she let me know I "could" because everything up till that phone call was I "had" to do. I think she realized I was going to do what I want and not what they want.

Six weeks after Sami's birth, I went to the midwife, not mainly for her to check me, but mostly to tell her the story of our birth. I thought she would be happy for us. And I was right. I was amazed on how excited she was to hear about our birth. She told me how proud she was of us trusting in ourselves to have Sami at home alone. We told her about the details of the birth but never admitted that we had planned this from the start. She told us that we did the right thing by doing nothing at all while Sami was being born. We found out in this visit that she does home births outside of our health provider group. I did get a physical check and everything was fine as I suspected. When it was time to go she gave us a big hug and again told us how proud she was of us.

When I first looked back on the birth, I couldn't imagine changing anything. Now weeks later, the only thing I wish I had done differently is have Mohammad cut the cord. Other than that, it was the perfect birth.

After going through this amazingly blessed experience, I can't imagine ever going back to a hospital to give birth to another baby. The differences between the births of my two children are like the night and day. After having Mohammad, I never wanted another child because of the pain I went through during his birth. Now I truly believe I can handle a dozen more births like Sami's. And I don't care if they were all breech. Reminiscing about Sami's birth makes me so happy. I like to remember how great and easy it was. I wish I had that with Mohammad's birth. I can't wait to do it all over again!

My Little Brother

By: Mohammad El-Abid

I have always wanted a brother or a sister since I was six years old. My mom tried to get pregnant when I was. My mom tried a lot of ways to get pregnant. We also went to the doctor a lot!! My mom took pills to help her get pregnant. We watched her spit and take her temperature to see if she could get pregnant. The day came when my mom showed me a pregnancy test, I was already feeling that this day was weird. Then I found out my mom was having a baby. I was the first my mom told about her being pregnant.

I was happy but felt my mom might be tricking me. She likes to play tricks on me all the time, and I thought this might be one of them. I thought she wasn't really pregnant. But then I started to believe that she is really pregnant after she showed me the pregnancy test information on the box. I thought my life was going to change a lot. I was also previously watching a show on TV about animal birth. It made me think about Sami coming out of mom. That seemed to be very gross. I didn't want to watch something like that.

Mom's pregnancy felt like a short time. I went to every doctor's visit with my mom and dad. I got to hear the heartbeat. I also got to see that it was a boy in the first ultrasound. Several months later, my mom had to have several ultrasounds. We thought my brother was butt first. I got to feel him kicking my mom. I took a class on babysitting to get ready for him. I couldn't wait for him to come!!!! I was so excited.

We prepared for Sami. We went and got a stroller. I got to pick out 3 things for him. We got his room ready. We sanded and painted it. We put his socks, outfits, hats, and diapers where it belongs. We had 2 baby showers. We must have received a lot of things for Sami!!! There was so much stuff that our car was full on the way back home from the bay showers. Every week for the last month of my mom's pregnancy, I wrote email updates about my brother showing how I felt about the pregnancy, how long until his due date, how many stuff he received in the baby shower, and other cute things. People would ask me if I was ready or happy to be a big brother.

The day Sami was born, I had a friend over. We watched the "Terminator 3" movie. Then my friend left. We went ahead and started to watch "Bowling for Columbine." Twenty minutes through the movie, my mom said she had a pain. So we went for a small walk. Then we went back in. My mom and dad thought it was false labor. So they did a drill for the real thing. I was downstairs watching TV. I had the Walkie Talkie. My mom said something. But I didn't understand. So I went upstairs and saw water coming out of her. It looked like pee. I saw my mom's umbilical cord. It looked like a tail when it was still in her after it was cut from Sami. I called our neighbor. She came hopping. I told her that the placenta was not out yet. When Sami was out, he cried a little, not a lot. And then I went to feel him. The whole time I was crying and smiling at the same time. I also told my grandpa on "Yahoo! Instant Messaging" when the water bag broke and when Sami was born.

I called a number of people. I only reached two of them. On of the two was the same neighbor who came over hopping. She came back again. But this time, she wasn't hopping. I told my dad that she was downstairs. He brought Sami down. She stayed for awhile. After she left, we got to play with Sami.

Brittany's Parent Assisted Birth Story

By: Alaina Smith

I had been having early labor signs on and off for four weeks before my due date (July 1). Because of that I was sure she would be born early. As my due date came closer I started to lose hope that she would be. Once my due date came and went I accepted the fact that I would not have things my way. I hoped she would be born on the 4th of July for fun but was willing to patiently wait.

At 2:30 am on July 7th I woke up to use the bathroom and everything seemed normal. I dozed off and on for the next two hours. I woke up from one dozing session around 4:30. I vaguely wondered why I was awake until I realized I was having a contraction that hurt. I figured it was just Brittany's position that was making it hurt so I tried to go back to sleep. 10 minutes later I had another contraction that hurt. I changed positions and tried to go back to sleep. When the next painful contraction came 10 minutes later I began to wonder if I was in labor.

After the next contraction I got up to go to the bathroom. There was a bit of blood and a lot of mucus. I knew then that I was most probably in labor. I went back to bed and attempted to sleep. After another half hour I was having a hard time dealing with the contractions laying down. I knew from past experience that it wouldn't hurt as much if I sat up so I went downstairs and played on the computer for an hour or so. During this time the contractions were barely noticeable. I was still getting a little blood so I knew it was definitely labor.

When Randy came downstairs at 7:00 I was sitting on the couch trying to get some rest. I asked him if he felt like taking time off work. He asked if the baby was coming and I told him yes. He said, "Okay!" and e-mailed work to let them know I was in labor and he would be taking time off.

The contractions stayed irregular and barely noticeable throughout most of the morning. I distracted myself by playing on the computer. I wasn't too hungry but made myself eat a bagel for breakfast. I also gave Randy the chore of making sure I got enough water.

Around 11:00 the contractions became regular at about 5 minutes apart. They were still easily manageable, though. Around 12:00 they became more intense and started to get just a little closer together. I ate a light lunch with my family and continued trying to distract myself with computer things. Around 12:40 it became unbearable to do so, so I took up residence on the couch.

I had Randy get my birth kit out so I could get things arranged as to when I would need them and tell Randy what was where. He cleaned up toys in the living room, pulled the area rug back and cleaned under it. I also had him start a labor record. He recorded at 12:49 possible transition starting. I wasn't quite sure it was transition yet. 10 minutes later I was positive.

At about 1:15 I got up to use the bathroom and started having pushy feelings and saw the bleeding had increased a lot. When I got out I told Randy to put the pillows on the floor and cover them with chux pads. As he was doing so I got an intense urge to push. I told him to hurry, which was kind of dumb since he already was going about as fast as he could. I was pushing through a contraction at that point.

As he went to put another pad onto the pillows I saw blood start dripping onto the floor so I told him to put that pad under me. No sooner had he done that than I could no longer hold back and I instinctively squatted all the way down and started pushing. Two pushes later I felt Brittany's head descending and with the next push I reached down to support her head as she came out.

My legs got tired at that point so I knelt onto the pillows. I had intended to kneel all the way onto them and use the couch as support but ended up using the pillows as support instead. My kneeling position was very low so that my perenium was only a couple of inches off the floor.

With the next push, Brittany's head came halfway out. I took over my body at that point and pushed to get her out, not listening to my body as much. I finished pushing her head out, guiding it backwards onto the floor. I then took a 5-10 second break and pushed her shoulders out, continuing to guide her. My other babies had slipped out at that point but Brittany didn't. I gave it one last push for her hips and as she came out, I placed her gently on the floor.

Randy looked right then and said, "It's a girl!" I was in shock at that statement. We thought for sure she'd be a boy! I had to turn around and look for myself. I took a quick peak and decided it wasn't important. I picked Brittany up and placed her on the pillows where I could cuddle and comfort her while waiting for the placenta. She coughed and spit up the fluid in her lungs so I didn't have to suction her. I also made note of her APGAR scores (1 min was 8, 5 min. was 9, 10 min. was 10). Randy gave me a little thyme and shepherd's purse tinctures at this time and told me she had been born at 1:27 pm. We also wrapped her in towels to help keep her warm.

The placenta came about 7 or 8 minutes after Brittany was born. It came out completely but I could tell something was still attached. I sat down and felt to see if I could gently pull the rest out. As I gave a slight tug I felt it was attached real good so I quit tugging. I waited a couple of minutes to see if it would detach on it's own. When it didn't I asked Randy to call Zuki, who had been present at my last two births. She had me see if it was just the amniotic sac or part of the placenta that was attached and gave me some suggestions, including nursing, which I followed as Randy and I called our families to tell them the news.

As I was talking with my mom we cut Brittany's cord and weighed and measured her. I watched as Randy moved past 8 lbs and onto 9. Then was even more surprised as he kept moving the ounces farther and farther up the scale. The final reading was 9 lbs. 11 ° oz., only 3 ° oz. more than I had guessed her to be only the day before. We measured her length at 20 inches, head circumference at 14 inches and chest circumference at 16 inches.

An hour and a half after Brittany was born, the sac still had not detached so I called Zuki back. I wasn't quite sure how to handle the situation since I had never heard of it happening before. As I talked with her I noticed that I had NOT hemorrhaged like I had with all of my previous babies. I also cut the sac so I could move and take a bath. The bath was nice, but did nothing to help detach the sac. We had a friend pick up some herbs that Zuki felt may help. So far (25 hours after Brittany's birth), nothing has worked but since there have been no signs of anything serious I'm taking the wait and see approach.

The unassisted experience was certainly interesting. I loved not having anyone but family there. It was nice to not have to guess at who would do what. It made for a much more relaxing birth. I could tell, once Brittany calmed down from her initial crying, that she was happy to have been born at home and happy to be surrounded by the familiar sounds.

The Birth Story of Tristan Darby Rice: My Child,

My Teacher

By: Brianne Rice

It has been 5 weeks exactly, since I had Tristan. I have really been hard on myself about transferring to the hospital when just 2 hours after arriving I had a perfect little baby. I think about it everyday, and I always try and talk to Eric about it, hoping to get all my feelings out, so that I won't feel like such a failure. He just blows it off, like it was no big deal. Maybe it wasn't to him. Maybe he feels that I am fine with the outcome, or better yet, maybe I have led him to believe this. I have really great self-esteem, but I don't feel very good about this still. Here is Tristan's birth story.

I am going to back up just a bit here, and talk a little about the long road I had, before finally deciding on a UC. When I first found out I was pregnant, I was not nearly as open-minded about birth as I am now. I started seeing the OB who delivered me (I am 24). I saw him a few times, but I left his practice when I got scolded for refusing a second ultrasound, and I was told I would have to lie on my back during labor, and I would not be able to get up at all. With a posterior baby, I now know this would have been impossible. Heck, I can't even lie in bed with menstrual cramps. I left at 20 weeks.

I then decided I wanted a midwife. I found a group of hospital midwives, and saw one a couple of times. I quickly "fired" this woman too, when she told me that I would have to either take the RhoGam at 28 weeks (I am RH-), or I would have to be delivered by an OB. I left at 28 weeks! I received no prenatal care after this. I am paying these people to provide care to my baby and I, and they are telling me what I will have to do. Hospital policy or not, this is my birth.

So finally, I talk Eric into having an Unassisted Childbirth, and he is sold after a few late night discussions. We do all the research, buy some birth supplies, and really become comfortable with our decision as the days go by. Then I hit 40 weeks, and then 41, and then 42, and finally on day 15 I have my first contraction at about 2AM on 8/15. I was dreaming that I was having contractions, and then I wake up and realize it is not a dream. I was so happy, and there was no way I could go back to sleep. Considering it was 2AM on a Monday, I did not want to wake Eric, as he had to be at work at 6AM, and I knew it could be along labor since this was our first.

I go in the living room to watch some TV. At this point, contractions are coming every 10 minutes, and they are not all that strong. I watch the news until 5:30, and then I hear the alarm go off in our bedroom. I rush in the room and tell Eric that I am in labor. Of course he is happy about this, since it seems like we waited FOREVER for it to happen. He calls his boss to let him know, and his boss insists that he stay home, despite this being our first baby. I tell Eric I want him to go to work, so I don't feel like a "watched pot," but his boss will not have it. I tell Eric that I am hungry, and so he goes to get me an omelet from my favorite breakfast joint. Meanwhile, I clean the kitchen, take out the trash, and clean the bathroom. My phone rings, and it is my Mom. She can hear the excitement in my voice, even though I am trying to act casual. First lesson as a new Mom…"A Mother can read her child like a book." I tell her that I am having contractions, but it is nothing to get excited about, since it could be a long labor. She asks me if I want her to come over, and I tell her "no." This must have been so hard for her to hear. I feel ashamed as soon as I say this, but I am convinced that it will only inhibit my labor. I think now that if I did, maybe she would have helped me through enough so I wouldn't have had to transfer. She seems to think she could have helped me, but I still have my doubts. Now that I have a daughter, it would be torture for me to see her in so much pain, and I would feel helpless. Maybe Mom would have? Maybe I made a mistake.

When Eric returns, we watch "American Pie" and eat our breakfast together. As I watch the movie, I realize that my time as a child is ending, and a new chapter is beginning. As the "kids" in the movie are talking about sex, parties, and alcohol, I am saying good-bye to all of those things, and embracing motherhood. I am elated.

At about 9AM, contractions are about 5-6 minutes apart, and getting more uncomfortable. I am still telling myself that I will have a fast, easy labor, since contractions seem to be changing in intensity so fast. I start to vocalize a little more, but labor is still manageable.

Somewhere around 12PM, contractions jump to 2 minutes apart. Eric fills the bathtub for me, thinking this will help. I lay a towel down and get in, but the water is not hot enough for me and I feel too cramped. A contraction gets me while I am trying to change positions, so when it is over I quickly get out. Once I am out, I start shivering from being wet, and I feel even worse. I grab a blanket and tell Eric to sit on the couch, and I kneel on the floor and lay my head in his lap. Each time I have a contraction, I grab onto his shorts and vocalize into his lap. This goes on until about 2PM. Eric asks if he can turn on the TV, and I get angry with him and tell him "NO!" I remembered that during the movie I could hear people laughing and having fun, and it was really annoying, and just added to my pain. As I lay my head in his lap, he is rubbing my back. I feel him falling asleep, and I shake him to wake him up, getting angry again. I think to myself, "it must be nice to be able to sleep."

At around 3PM, Eric lights one of my soy candles, but the flowery smell bothers me, and I tell him to blow it out. He calls my Mom again to give her an update.

4PM, and contractions have hit one minute apart. There is a knock at the door, and it is the neighbor lady wanting to visit with me. Eric tells her that I am asleep, just as I am having a contraction. I bury my face in the pillow I am now using to kneel on, so she can't hear me. The phone rings, and it is my Mom, wanting another update. Eric goes outside to talk to her, and she tells him that this is the last time she will call, but to please keep her posted.

5PM, and boy am I hurting. Contractions are very painful, and I am very restless, unable to escape the pain. I go from room to room, squatting, kneeling, breathing, sitting on the toilet, squatting again, kneeling with my back arched, leaning against the wall...anything to help me through the pain and bring the baby down. At this point, I am VERY loud. I decide that sitting on the toilet backwards with my back arched is the best position for me. Eric sits on the floor behind me, massaging my lower back. Every time a contraction hits, I tell him to not touch me. We stay this way until about 8PM. I now become very frustrated with the pain, and decide to check my cervix. I do a quick check, and still feel more of it than I would like to. It is soft, but not all the way thinned out. I throw up, and I think to myself that this is transition. Pain is no longer tolerable.

6PM and there is no change.

7PM and still no change.

8PM I am now praying with all my might that the baby comes down, so I can get her out.

9PM Contractions are under a minute apart, and I feel my body starting to tire. I try to push a little, but I don't feel that it is time yet. I still must have a ways to go still.

10PM, I throw up again. Contractions are about 45 seconds apart, and I am now wondering why the heck baby is not coming down. Eric takes a break to get on the phone to my Mom, and I do another check. What is this I feel??? A soft, mushy mass. Must be the bag of water!! Here is where I wonder if I made a mistake or not. I nick the bag with my fingernail to break the water, and a huge gush of clear, sweet smelling fluid flows onto the chux pads on the living room floor. I yell to Eric that I just broke my water, and he quickly hangs up the phone. I think to myself that the baby must come within the next hour or so, since my water bag has been broken and now there is more room for her to come down. I was so desperate!!! I tell Eric that I can't take this anymore, and he tells me I am strong and I can do this. He told me afterwards that he decided if I had not had the baby by midnight and still no change, he would take me to the hospital if I wanted.

11PM, still the same. Cervix doesn't feel much different. I am becoming a wild animal from the pain. I am growling, praying, moaning, and crying out for the baby to come. The pain is unbearable.

12PM, I am begging for the pain to stop, and now I am in a heap on the floor, not caring what position I am in for each contraction. Nothing I do helps me through them. Eric asks if he should put the washcloths for my perineum on the stove to boil, and I give him a nod. I think now that he could hear the change in my moans. It is obvious I was pushing a little now, but I know that it can spell disaster if I push too soon. I just ride the contractions like waves, wondering what my body will tell me to do next.

12:30, and I finally tell him I cannot do this anymore. I know I am close because I am grunting after each contraction, but I am in so much pain I don't care. He asks me what I want to do, and I tell him I want to go to the ER, since nothing is happening. He says that he will take me if I really want to go, and I say yes. He asks me if I am sure, because he knows that I will just be sorry later on, but I am so tired I don't ask myself if I really want to go. I wonder now why here I didn't pray. Why didn't I ask God for guidance? Why did I give up so fast, when all through my pregnancy He showed me the way? This is the part that I replay in my head, over and over again. If I could just go back in time, I would have stayed. He finds some pants for me to wear, and he races out the door to open the truck door for me. I start to walk out the door, and realize the stove is still on, so I turn it off. Why I even looked at the stove, I have no idea, but I am so glad I did. Eric races around like a madman, trying to get us to the hospital. He even runs a red light. He told me afterwards he was certain the baby was a breech. I could have told him otherwise. I am now prepared for a bad time at the hospital, but little did I know it would be so horrible!!!

We get to the hospital, and I do a half walk, half waddle into the ER. As I walk in the door, I remember thinking that I have made a terrible mistake, and it is here I become afraid for the first time since my labor began. I start to shake as my beautiful labor is stolen from me, and handed to the strangers at the hospital. A contraction hits, and the security guy looks at me in horror as I scream through it. My husband yells at him to get me a wheel chair, and he scrambles to find one. A male nurse comes out from behind his desk, and asks what the problem is. The lady behind the counter asks who my doctor is, and I tell her I don't have one. She says that we are going to have to fill out some paperwork, so Eric stays and I go up to maternity. I feel alone.

We get up there, and the nurse asks me if this is my first baby. I say yes. She wheels me into a room, and tells me to put this ridiculous gown on. I have never been in the hospital before, so everything is foreign to me. She tells me I can go in the bathroom to change, but as she turns around I am already naked, trying to put the gown on. I am in no mood to be modest. She asks me a million questions, and I ignore her as I try and get through my contractions, which are now right on top of one another. While all of this is going on, my grunting at the end of each contraction is getting louder and louder. She tells me not to push. In my head, I curse her for saying this. Obviously she has never had children. Another nurse comes in and starts an IV for hydration. She asks me when my water broke, and I tell her about 40 minutes ago. She asks when my due date was, and I quickly blurt out "yesterday." I knew that if I told her the truth, they would do a section. I also tell her that my labor started as soon as my water broke. I knew that they would not be happy if they knew I started labor 23 hours ago. She takes a separate IV bag, and starts to hook it up. Eric asks her what it is, and she says it is antibiotics for Group B Strep. He tells her that I don't have it, and she says it is for precautionary reasons. He tells her that there is no way on earth I am taking any antibiotics for something I MAY have. He also tells her that while we are on the subject, there will be no vaccines, eye crap, Vit K, no RhoGam, or anything else. She says that we will have to sign waivers, and we say fine.

So the nurse checks my cervix, and tells me I am 8 centimeters. I am surprised that I am not 10 by then, but I try and act surprised and proud of myself. All of the nurses are in awe, thinking I just went into labor 40 minutes ago with my first baby, and now I am at 8 centimeters. All of the sudden I feel excruciating pain in my back. I hear the word "posterior," and I start to realize the baby turned "sunny side up" during labor. But baby was ROA the whole pregnancy! It now hits me like a ton of bricks…this is why labor was taking so long. What have I done? This has all been a mistake, and now I am going home to have my baby. Too late.

About 30 minutes after I arrived, the nurse says it is time to start pushing. I push and push and push, for 45 minutes actually. This feels so unnatural. The baby's head starts to crown, and it is a beautiful feeling. I reach down and feel my sweet baby's head. Surprisingly, I feel no pain. The nurse tells me that when the contraction ends, to keep pushing a bit to keep the head there. Then the nurse calls another nurse over, and points to my area, and I hear "meconium." I remember saying "oh great" out loud, because I knew what a big deal they were going to make out of this. They call pediatrics to wait on the side for the baby. There goes my delayed cord clamping. My water had already broke with clear fluid (I told them this) but they were more worried about her swallowing some, saying it gives them the runs. I want to scream at them that meconium is natural, and to leave my baby alone, but I am in so much pain that I don't feel like fighting with them.

Just when I finally get the head fully crowned, she tells me to stop pushing. I start screaming that I need to get it out NOW, and she says no, because the doctor is not there. I keep pushing anyway, and then the doctor comes in. I am happy to see it is a woman doctor, but as you will read, this makes no difference. The doctor yells at me to stop pushing, until she gets her gown on. I keep pushing anyway. The doctor starts pulling on my vaginal opening and perineum to accommodate the head, as if to punish me for not complying with her demands. This is truly the worst pain I have ever felt in my life. When she wasn't pulling on me, the head did not hurt me coming out, but when she would pull again, I would scream with all my might. It felt like she was cutting me with scissors all around my vagina. She coldly tells me "it is either this, or I give you an episiotomy, so keep pushing." As if I am not in enough pain, she then starts pressing on my stomach with both hands to get the baby out faster. I was later told that there were 9 babies born that night, so this explains her lack of patience. I start screaming again while trying to jump off the bed, and now Eric is really pissed. He yells at her to quit that, and she does it a couple more time, then stops. I attribute my baby's hip injury to this stupid procedure, since she would be pressing on the right side while baby was turning. OB grabs baby's head with her fingers, trying to pull her out. She leaves three bloody holes in my baby's head. Baby slides out, and immediately starts screaming. Pediatrics team grabs her and starts suctioning her stomach. Nothing comes out, so they keep trying. Still nothing. They take out the tube. OB yanks out my placenta, and starts stitching up a couple of small tears in the hood area. Eric makes sure he watches everything Peds does to make sure nothing else is done to her. I ask "what is it," but nobody hears me. I ask again, and Eric tells me we have our little girl. I cry softly to myself. The doctor leaves without saying a word to me, and I never see her again. I feel like I have just been raped.

So, after all is said and done, I think about Tristan's actual birth and I am horrified. My sweet baby deserved the most gentle birth I could give her. I think of my long labor, and despite the pain, I know in my heart that I could have done it by myself. The labor was beautiful, and my husband was such an inspiration to me. I think now about the pain I felt at home, and then the pain I felt in the hospital. In the scheme of things I felt less pain at home, and it makes me so depressed that I left the comfort of home to go somewhere foreign to give birth to our child, with strangers watching me. I have to get over this, and focus on my beautiful new little baby. There will be one more child in about 2 years, so maybe I have learned a few things from Tristan. I will tell her this story when she is older, and let her know that she helped play the part as a teacher, and nobody can ever take away her beautiful labor. At least I did that on my own. I will tell her that she is powerful too, and that she can have her babies just by listening to her inner self, and letting all of the well intended "advice" about birth slide right off her back. She has everything she will ever need to give birth nicely tucked away inside her.

I feel like I am a complete woman now. I have gone from a girlish size 6 to a size womanly 10. I have hips, and stretch marks, and full breasts, and I feel ready to take on the world, and put this minor setback behind me. I am a woman who knows that I can give birth without anybody's help, and that is a powerful thing in itself. I will have my UC!!!!!

This story is dedicated to all of the strong women of the world. I sympathize with those women who view birth as a mechanical process, rather than the beautiful, sacred, and awesome miracle that it is. They will never know what it feels like to awaken that part of their soul. I guess I still don't either.

Brieanne- who is a little wiser now

Giving Thanks to:

My Love and Blessings go out to:

All the Wise Women from all corners of the world, who taught, loved and supported women throughout time.

For all the women, who were murdered for their wisdom of healing, birthing, and for burying the dead.

For all the Wise Men, who stood up for their women and were killed at the hands of church and state.

All the Birthing Goddesses who have taught me to be patient and compassionate with myself and others on this journey.

My Love and my prayers go out to my Birth Mother "Souad," who died in an Israeli invasion sometime in 1986, She was approximately 32 years of age and was never allowed to hold me for very long, but who gave me this body and this life to explore … I love you wherever you are.

Zack 2006

I give all my thanks for my present life to my son Zackery Tyler Lavin; if it were not for you, I would not be here now. You are my true guide/teacher. I hold you with great respect; you are the light in my world, and have given me a purpose to be here now.

Michael Lavin holding Zack 1989

In addition, my love and prayers to my late husband, Michael John Peter Lavin (1968-1992), for giving me the gift of life before you left this world.

My heart and soul are grateful to my Mother, Jean Abbott, for traveling across the planet to find me, and taking me into your heart and home. Thank you for all the swimming, skiing, and adventures shared through this life I hold so dear.

My Great Grandmother, Anna Abbott (1889-1983), (who passed on my thirteenth birthday), thank you for speaking in our native tongue when I was young, for teaching me how to crochet, for singing to me songs of prayer. I am blessed to have known you while you were here.

Anna Abbott playing her drum 1975

My Grandmother Helen Abbott (1915-1999) for being supportive when I was down, for lifting my spirits off the ground, and encouraging me to be the best I could be through all the hard times that have fallen upon me. Also for letting me hold your hand while you passed on from this world into another; it was an honor.

Helen Abbott 1960

For my Grandfather Fred Berk (1912-1996) who was the only father I knew. I thank you for being a gentle man, for teaching me yoga and nutrition, for taking me to the plays, playing tennis, going to ballets and the opera. I do so appreciate those days.

Fred Berk 1946

I give thanks for all who have entered into my world, or who have stumbled upon it. All have inspired me in their own unique way to become more conscious of what could be, should be and is.

"The Gathering"
Photo by: Amanda Wright 2006

This book is dedicated to the little ones who invited me to their births and came into the world without violence, thank you for sharing your birth stories with me, and others here in this book....

Donna Colelli, my dear friend for donating your story and beautiful picture, and keeping in touch over the long years apart.

Mati Fuller and Family, for your friendship, understanding, and contribution to this book.

Mary Winn Anderson for permission to use your story and your mother's stories from her book, "Come gently Sweet Lucina."

Laura Shanley and David Shanley, for sharing your lives with me and encouraging me through this process, as well as giving me permission to use stories and pictures from your website.

Suzanne Arms, I thank you for being real, for your dedication and inspiration to so many of us working for better birthing experiences.

Jeanine Pavarti Baker, I thank you for all of your support on my path as a midwife and free birth activist. You are an inspiration! All the long phone calls and support really helped me to remain on this path. Thank you!

For Galadrial for being my partner for as long as you could. Giving support and working long and hard hours for this cause.

I want to also thank Alycia for her part in our community birth awareness, you will be a wonderful midwife!

Barbara Harper, for water birth knowledge, wisdom, and consort when I've needed it.

Samite, Tobias & Ari for your beautiful birth photos, friendship, and the support you have given me in this work.

Delfin, Spyce & Kerri for being in my life, you are my family and blessed to be here & share life with you!

Jody Maclaughlin, for all the long talks and advice that has been so appreciated, and also for the permission to use Compleat Mother Articles and incredible artwork, and for being supportive of this path.

To Patti & Brian Nagel who recently gave birth at home in water, holding faith and working through obstacles for what you knew was truth. Thank you for contributing your intimate photos and sharing your story.

Dearest thanks to Kindle, Travis & Tristen, for inviting me to share in your family birth experience and for donating your beautiful pictures for this book.

Nina, Jacob and the twins, Asher & Willow. You all are an inspiration for me to keep going. Holding the light of faith. Thank you for sharing your story with this book and all who will benefit.

Beldon Johnson, for your wisdom as a father and sharing your poem with us.

The Keck Family, for sharing your birth experiences with me and your pictures for this book ... love to your children who are a light in this world: Bryant, Kaycee and Royce.

The Jackson family, for your support and encouragement for me to continue on this journey, and for sharing your two water births with me ... working with you has been a joy! Love to Bret, Kayla, Jason, Nathan, and little Alec & another on the way!

The Smith family, for being open to this change and seeking truth within yourselves, to continue on this path of self-realization, and for raising your children at home, home schooling and birthing; love and light to Rebecca, Crystal, Kyle, Brenna, and yet but not least little Brittnay who was born unassisted into her mother's own hands.

DeAnna Elliot, for her knowledge and wisdom about cellular memory, re-birthing, and the importance of infant massage, thank you for being in my life!

For all the ladies at C-Birth, you know who you are, and I give thanks for you being there for each other!

All who have contributed to this project I hold dear to my heart and wish you all many blessings for your families and your children's future prosperity!

References & Resources

Judith Goldsmith *"Childbirth Wisdom, from the World's Oldest Societies." Congdon & Weed, Inc. New York* (1984)

Leonard Orr *"The Secrets of Youthing" Inspiration University*, Chico California (1994)

Leonard Orr and Sondra Ray *"Rebirthing in the New Age." Celestial Arts* (1983)

DeAnna Elliot *"Cellular Echos." Cellular Imprinting Documentary, Crestone, Colorado* (2004)

Sherman J. Silber MD *"How to Get Pregnant." The Warner Books Edition* (1980)

Merryl Winstein *"Your Fertility Signals", Smooth Stone Press* (1999)

Rima Beth Star *"The Healing Power Of Birth" Celestial Arts* (1985)

Sheila Kitzinger, *"The Complete Book of Pregnancy and Childbirth"*, 11th ed. *New York,* (1986)

Sheila Kitzinger, *"Homebirth, The Essential Guide to Giving Birth Outside of the Hospital," Dorling Kinderfley Limited, London* (1991)

Sheila Kitzinger *"The Complete Book of Pregnancy and Childbirth." Alfred A.Knopf. New York* (1999)

Barbara Harper, R.N *"Gentle Birth Choices." Healing Arts Press* (1994)

Joan Gomez, M.D *"Anemia in Women." Hunter House Inc, Publishers* (2002)

Daphne Singingtree *"Midwifery Workbook" 3rd ed. Eagle Tree Press* (2000)

Henci Goer Article *"Gestational Diabetes" "Parenting Village.com" (2001)*

Thimerosal Litigation online at *"thimerosallitegatoin.com"* (2005)

Anne Frye *"Holistic Midwifery Vol: One." Labrys Press* (1998)

Anne Frye *"Understanding Diagnostic Tests in the Childbearing year." 6th ed. Labrys Press* (1997)

Mango Mama's website at "*mangomama.com*" (1999)

Thimerosal News online at "*thimrosalnews.com*" (2004)

Hygeia Halfmoon Ph.D "Primal Mothering in A Modern World." (1998)

The Boston Women's Health Book Collective *"Our Bodies Our Selves." Simon and Schuster* (1973)

The Boston Women's Health Book Collective "*Our Bodies Our Selves, For the New Century." Simon and Schuster* (1998)

Hygeia Halfmoon Ph.D *"Primal Mothering in a Modern World." Maul Brothers Publishing, san Diego Ca.* (1998)

Gayle Peterson Ph.D. *"An Easier Childbirth." Shadow & Light Publications* (1993)

The Dalai Lama *"Healing Anger." "Snow Lion Publications," (1997)*

Anne Kent Rush *"Getting Clear." The Book Works* (1977)

Michal Odent "*The Farmer and The Obstetrician" Free Association Books Limited* (2002)

David Hoffman "New Holistic Herbal" (1991)

Jeanne Rose "*Modern Herbal." The Putnam Publishing Group* (1987)

Susan Weed "*Childbearing Year." Ash Tree Publishing* 1986

Michio and Aveline Kushi *"Macrobiotic Pregnancy and Care of the New Born."* (1985)

Viktoras H. Kulvinskas, M.S., *"Survival into The Twenty first Century." 21st Century Publications* (1975)

Murray Enkin, Marc J.N.C. Keirse, Mary Renfrew, and James Neilson "*A Guide to Effective Care In pregnancy and Childbirth." Oxford University Press,* 2nd ed. (1996)

Anne Hubbell Maiden and Edie Farwell *"The Tibetan Art of Parenting, From before conception through early*

childhood." Wisdom Publications (1997)

Michal Odent M.D "Birth reborn." *Birth Works Press, Medford, New Jersey* 2nd ed. (1994)

Lynn M. Griesmer "*Unassisted Homebirth, an Act of Love." Terra Publishing* (1998)

Judith Walzer Leavitt *"Brought to Bed, childbearing in America 1750-1950." Oxford University Press* (1986)

Heinrich Kramer and James Spenger *"The Malleus Maleficarum." Dover Publications, INC.* republished in (1971)

Barbara Ehrenreich and Deirdre English " *Witches, Midwives and Nurses A history of Women Healers" Feminist Press* (1973)

Stella Chess M.D and Alexander Thomas M.D *"Know your Child." Basic Books, Inc.* (1987)

Pediatric Round Table "New Perspectives in Early Emotional Development" (1998)

Thomas Szasz *"The Manufacture of Madness" Syracuse University Press* (1970)

Richard W. Wertz and Dorothy C. Wertz *"Lying - In", Yale University Press* (1989)

Jamie Murphy "*What Parent Should Know About Childhood Immunization." Earth Healing Products* (1993)

Sondra Ray *"Celebration of Breath." Celestial Arts* (1986)

Grantly Dick Read Article *"Childbirth Without fear" Ladies Home Journal Magazine June* (1957)

Dawson Church *"Communicating with the spirit of your Unborn Child." Aslan Publishing* (1988)

Ina May Gaskin *"Spiritual Midwifery" 3rd Ed. The Book Publishing* (1990)

Rahima Baldwin and Terra Palmarini Richardon *"Pregnant Feelings, Developing trust in Birth." Celestial Arts* (1986)

Laura Shanley *"Unassisted Childbirth." Bergin &Garvey* (1994)

Sarah Ban Breathnach *"The Simple Abundance Compaion." Warner Books* (2000)

"The Bible," New Testament.

"The Book of Mormon" *Published by the Church of Jesus Christ of Latter-Day Saints* (1981)

"Course of Miracles" *One-Volume ed. Study & Teachers Manual, The Guernsey Press Co. Ltd.* (1975)

"The Real Eve" *Film documentary by Discovery Channel*

Lennart Nilsson *"A Child is Born." A DTP/Seymour Lawrence Book* (1993)

Diana Korte and Roberta M. Scaer *"A Good Birth A safe Birth" 3rd ed. The Harvard Common Press* (1992)

Robbie E. Davis Floyd *"Birth as an American Rite of Passage." 2nd ed. University of California Press* (1992)

Alice B. Stockham *"Tokology." Chicago (*1899)

Richard W. Wertz and Dorothy C. Wertz *" Lying -In" expanded ed. Yale University Press (*1989)

Susan McCutcheon- Rosegg with Peter Rosegg *"Natural Childbirth the Bradley Way"* (1984)

Mary Renfrew, Chloe Fisher, and Suzanne Arms "Bestfeeding, Getting Breastfeeding Right For you." (1990)

Diana Korte and Roberta M. Scaer "A Good Birth A Safe Birth" 3rd edition (1992)

Michelle Leclaire O'Neill, Ph.D, R.N. *"Creative Childbirth." A Papyrus Book (*2003)

Sanaya Roman *"Personal Power through Awareness. HJ Kramer Inc. Publishers"* (1986)

Colleen K. Dodt *" Natural Baby Care." A Storey Publishing Book (*1997)

Susanna Napierala *"Water Birth, a Midwife's Perspective." Bergin & Garvey (*1994)

Robin Lim *"After the Baby's Birth, A Woman's Way to Wellness, A Complete Guide for Postpartum Women." Celestial Arts (*1991)

Elizabeth Davis and Carol Leonard *"The Circle of Life." Celestial Arts* (2002)

Jeanne Rose *"The Aromatherapy Book." North Atlantic Books* (1992)

Paul Beyerl *"The Master Book of Herbalism." Phoenix Publishing Co. (*1984)

Zsuzsanna Budapest *"The Holy Book of Women's Mysteries." Wingbow Press* (1989)

Diane Stein *"Casting the Circle, A Women's Book of Ritual." The Crossing Press* 1990

Dr. David Frawley, O.M.D *"Ayurvedic Healing." Passage Press* 1989

Dr. Bhagwan Dash "Ayurvedic Remedies, Ayurvedic cures for common diseases." (1996)

Laura Scheerer Whitney *"Blessing the Way" Sage Mountain Films* (1998)

Barbara Ann Brennan *"Hands of Light, A Guide to healing through the human energy field." Bantum Books* (1987)

Laura Shanley, *"Is Unassisted Childbirth safe?" UnassistedChildbirth.Com (*2005)

Robert S. Mendelsohn,M.D. "*How to raise a Healthy Child in Spite of your Doctor.*" *The Random House Publishing Group* (1984)

Susan McCutcheon- Rosegg with Peter Rosegg "*Natural Childbirth the Bradley Way.*" *E.P. Dutton* (1984)

Nancy Wainer Cohen and Lois J. Estner "*Silent Knife,*" *Cesarean Prevention and Vaginal Birth After Cesarean.*" *Bergin&Garvey* (1983)

Mary Renfrew, Chloe Fisher and Suzanne Arms "*Bestfeeding, Getting Breastfeeding Right For you.*" *Celestial Arts* (1990)

Debra Stewart Peterson "*Breastfeeding the Adopted Baby.*" *Corona Publishing Company* (1994)

Nicky Wesson "*Natural Mothering.*" *Healing Arts Press* (1997)

Thomas J. Ritter, M.D,. and George C. Denniston, M.D. "*Doctors Re-examine Circumcision*" *Third Millennium Publishing Co.* (2002)

Fiona Giles "*Fresh Milk*" *Simon & Schuster, Inc.* (2003)

Resources, Services, Books, Videos . . .

As far as I know these resources are all current.

ALACE: Association of Labor Assistants and Childbirth Educators

(888) 222-5223 or (617) 441-2500 online: alace.org

NAPSAC: International Association of Parents and Professionals for Safe Alternatives in Childbirth

(314)238-2010 online: napsacinternational.com

NOCIRC: National Organization of Circumcision Information resource Center. (415)488-9883 or online: nocirc.com

CAPPA: Birthing Companion Resources for the Nation

online: cappa.net

Le Leche League International

(800) 525-3243 or online: lelecheleagueinternational.com

24 hr Breastfeeding Support hotline (800) 835-5965

ITA: International Twins Association:

Po Box 77386, station C, Atlanta GA 30357

ICAN: International Cesarean Awareness Network

(717)585-4226 or online : ican.com

NSSA: National Swim School Association

(813)896-7946

Australian Swim School

1202 Banbury Cross

Santa Ana, Ca . 92705 (714)731-6666

Compleat Mother Magezine USA (701) 852-2822

or online : compleatmother.com

Spirit Led Childbirth: Support for Parent Assisted Childbirth and more

(888) 683-2678

Suzanne Arms, founder of Birthing the Future, and author of *"Immaculate Deception."* Co-author of many books about birth and breastfeeding. An amazing photographer of many birth related books, and films.

For more information call 877-BIRTHING or online: birthingthefuture.com

Water Birth International, Global Maternal Child Health Organization

(800) 641-2229 Water Birth Videos, Birth Pool Rentals, and Conference information and Dates.

Babyworks (800)422-2910 natural baby products and supplies

Baby Trekker (800) 665-3957

Frontier Co-op Herbs (800) 669-3275

Herbs Etc. (888)433-1212

The Relaxation Company (800)788-6670

Simple Alternatives (800)735-2082

Mountain Ark trading Company (800) 643-8909

Active Parenting (800) 825-0060

Healthy Mothers healthy Baby Coalition (800) 673-8444

Midwifery Today (800) 743-0974

Herbs for Health and Herb Company (800) 645-3675

Mothering Magazine (800) 984-8116

Biotic Foods (800)331-5888

Blessed Herbs (800) 489-HERB

Nature's Herbs (800) HERBALS

Rainbow Light Nutritional Systems (800) 635-1233

Nature's Way (800) Nature

Essential Oil Company (800) 729-5912

Aroma Vera (800)669-9514

Aroma Land (800) 933-5367

Aura Cacia (800) 437-3301

Nelson Bach USA Ltd (800)314-2224

Boiron-Borneman,Inc. (800)Boiron-1 Homeopathy

Homeopathy Books, (800) 663-8272

Lotus Light (800) 548-4824 Books, resources

The Herbal Information Source (800) 373-7105

The BhaktiVedanta Book Trust (800)927-4152 Free books

Cascade Midwifery Supplies (800)443-9942

Mountain Rose Herbs (800)879-3337

The Wellness Store (800) 598-6944

Herbs and Homeopathy (800) 547-4891

The March of Dimes (get your CPR Class) (800) 321-0186

The Alliance of Genetic Support (800) 336-gene

The School of Natural Healing (800) 372-8255

ONLINE RESOURCES:

Breast feeding:

breastfeedingonline.com

moms4milk.org

allianceforbreastfeeding.com

hmhbwa.org

bfmoms.com

Lotus Birth:

natureschild.com

labouroflove.org

birthpsychology.com

sarahjbuckley.com

Natural Childbirth, Homeopathy, &

Birth Supplies:

bornfree.com

motherfriendly.org

thelaboroflove.com

unassistedchildbirth.com

empoweredchildbirth.com

empoweredplanet.com

gentlebeginnings.org

homeopathy.biz

homeopathy.com

birthsupplies.com

birthwithlove.com

Diaperfreebaby.org

Athomemothers.com

Bygpub.com

Nw-ap.org

Mothernature.com

Bellysling.com

Babyandmefitness.com

Nurturedcub.ca

Cesarean Support

inhishands.com

1cascade.com

motherstuff.com

waterbirth.org

preciousarrows.com

auquadoula.com

junebugbaby.com

mothernurture.info

Cesareanbirth.com

Motherfriendly.org

Pregnancytoday.com

ICAN.com

Circumcision

azurewraps.ca

unique4baby.com

blueribbonbaby.org

raisingintactsons.com

intactgroup.com

bornfree.com
mothersagainstcircumcision

nocirc.com

wholebaby.com

intact.com

noharmm.org

Post Partum Depression Hotlines

PPD Alliance hotline 1-847-205-4455

Evanston Northwestern Health Care 1-866-364-6667

NC Family Health 1-800367-2229

National Hopeline Network 1-800-784-2433

PPD Helpline 1-888-773-7090

Canada kids help line 1-800-668-6868

Websites to research

Pacific Post Partum Support Society - postpartum.org

Post Partum Stress Center- postpartumstress.com

Post Partum International- postpartum.net

Books and Videos

Global Maternal Health Organization- Great Films on Birth !

(800) 641-2229

Unassistedchildbirth .com

Amizon .com

Laura Shanley's "Unassisted Childbirth" Book

Films of Unassisted Childbirth and great Books...

Online: unassistedchildbirth.com

Farm Videos online: inamay.com

many farm births, breeches, twins, spiritual midwifery. . .

homebirthvideos.com

birthintobeing.com

My favorite teaching Videos:

*You can find these films at **1cascade.com**, **waterbirth.org** &*

unassistedchildbirth.com

Birth into Being

The Experience of Water Birth

Birth Day

Water Babies

Gentle Birth Choices

Unassisted Twin Birth of *"Psalm and Zoya" at " earthbirthproductions.com"*

Clear Road to Birth

Birth in the Squating Position

Index

NOTES: